MATH

EDUCATION

Level 5

Angela O'Dell
& Kyrsten Carlson

Author: Angela O'Dell
Kyrsten Carlson

Master Books Creative Team:

Editor: Craig Froman

Design: Terry White

Cover Design: Diana Bogardus

Copy Editors:
Judy Lewis
Willow Meek

Curriculum Review:
Kristen Pratt
Laura Welch
Diana Bogardus

First printing: March 2016
Seventh printing: July 2022

Master Books, P.O. Box 726, Green Forest, AR 72638

Master Books® is a division of the New Leaf Publishing Group, Inc.

ISBN: 978-0-89051-927-1
ISBN: 978-1-61458-515-2 (digital)

Images are from shutterstock.

Unless otherwise noted, Scripture quotations are from the New King James Version of the Bible.

Printed in the United States of America

Please visit our website for other great titles:
www.masterbooks.com

Dedication

To my favorite students, who were also my teachers.
I love you!.

Author Bio:

As a homeschooling mom and author, **Angela O'Dell** embraces many aspects of the Charlotte Mason method yet knows that modern children need an education that fits the needs of this generation. Based upon her foundational belief in a living God for a living education, she has worked to bring a curriculum that will reach deep into the heart of home-educated children and their families. She has written over 20 books, including her history series and her math series. Angela's goal is to bring materials that teach and train hearts and minds to find the answers for our generation in the never-changing truth of God and His Word.

Scope and Sequence

Using This Course

Features: The suggested weekly schedule enclosed has easy-to-manage lessons that guide the reading, worksheets, and all assessments. The pages of this course are perforated and three-hole punched so materials are easy to tear out, hand out, grade, and store. Teachers are encouraged to adjust the schedule and materials needed in order to best work within their unique educational program.

Lesson Scheduling: Students are instructed to read the pages in their book and then complete the corresponding section provided by the teacher. Assessments that may include worksheets, activities, quizzes, and tests are given at regular intervals with space to record each grade. Space is provided on the weekly schedule for assignment dates, and flexibility in scheduling is encouraged. Teachers may adapt the scheduled days per each unique student situation. As the student completes each assignment, this can be marked with an "X" in the box.

Approximately 30 minutes per lesson, five days a week, for 36 weeks

Solution Manual for worksheets is available in the back of this book

Review sections can be used as quizzes

Worksheets are included for each section

Designed for grade 5 in a one-year course

Course Description

Welcome to the fifth book in the *Math Lessons for a Living Education* series! You will find that *Math Lessons for a Living Education* is a unique approach to learning math. A blend of stories, copy work, oral narration, and hands-on experience brings the concepts to life and invites the child to explore the world around them. The tone of this math book is meant to speak personally to each child, and the method is easily adapted to any teaching style.

The first 30 lessons have a story about the twins, taught through hands-on learning and provide review time. After the story, there are exercises for students to practice the lesson they learned and to review what they have learned earlier. The last 6 lessons are focused reviews, covering topics learned throughout the first 30 lessons.

Note: You can supplement the worksheets in the *Math for a Living Education* series with additional worksheets, activities, and quizzes in *Practice Makes Perfect*, also available from Master Books®.

Course Objectives:

Students completing this course will

- Review basic operations
- Learn how to find greatest common factor and least common multiple
- Explore new concepts like fractions, mixed numbers, decimals, and percents
- Add, subtract, multiply, and divide decimals.

Teaching mathematics as a living subject

As a teacher and a mother, I have discovered that true education is based on relationships: the relationship the child makes with the amazing concepts in the world around them; the relationship the teacher and the child make with each other; and most importantly and ultimately, the relationship the child makes with their Creator. It is built on discovering the God of the Universe — the One who holds the universe in His hands, but at the same time, lovingly dwells in the heart of children. The story in Book 5 is meant to reach into a child's world, grab their attention and invite them into the learning process. The concepts are not taught through drill only, but also through encouraging the student to hone their critical thinking skills and think outside of the box. This curriculum teaches the student math, but it is not result-oriented, focusing only on grades; instead it is skill and process-oriented. I have discovered that it is in the everyday that we grow and become who we are meant to be. It is in the little discoveries all along the path of life that we grow, learn, develop, and discover who God is and, in turn, see ourselves the way He sees us.

Math concepts are learned well, as it is learned in the context of living, in the midst of discovery, and through the worldview glasses that focus on the bigger picture.

About manipulatives

In the back of the book, you will find a manipulatives section. It is recommended that you prepare these before you start the book. You will need these resources:

- ☐ contact paper and construction paper
- ☐ large index cards
- ☐ brass fasteners
- ☐ crayons, markers, and colored pencils
- ☐ glue or paste
- ☐ hole punch and hole reinforcers
- ☐ rings to keep flashcards together
- ☐ a plastic shoe box with lid in which to store manipulatives
- ☐ stickers to use for flashcards (optional but helpful)
- ☐ pictures from old magazines
- ☐ poster board (several large pieces)
- ☐ foot ruler (with inches marked)
- ☐ simple indoor/outdoor thermometer (non-digital)
- ☐ rice or beans (for use in measuring)
- ☐ measuring devices
  - cup set: 1 cup, $\frac{1}{2}$ cup, $\frac{1}{4}$ cup, $\frac{1}{3}$ cup
  - spoon set: 1 tbs, $\frac{1}{2}$ tbs, 1 tsp, $\frac{1}{2}$ tsp, $\frac{1}{4}$ tsp
  - large plastic bowls (mixing bowls, ice cream buckets, or similar)

Grading subjective assignments

Most often with math the grading is very objective. For example, 2 + 2 = 4, and no amount of individual expression changes this answer. However, there are times in this course when the answer may depend on a student's reflections of what he or she has learned on a particular day or in a week of assignments. In these subjective cases, the teacher can base a grade for these responses on several more objective measures. Does the student seem to understand the question and answer it as clearly as possible? Does the answer seem complete or does it fail to answer all aspects of the question? So a student may receive full credit if they seemed to meet all the assignment requirements, may get a passing grade if they meet some of the requirements, or may need to repeat the assignment if they didn't meet any of the requirements.

A – Student showed complete mastery of concepts with no errors.

B – Student showed mastery of concepts with minimal errors.

C – Student showed partial mastery of concepts. Review of some concepts is needed.

D – Student showed minimal understanding of concepts. Review is needed.

F – Student did not show understanding of concepts. Review is needed.

Extra Resources

Welcome to *Math Lessons for a Living Education Book 5*. If this is your first year using this math curriculum, please take the time before you start, in order to familiarize yourself with the layout of the course. *Math Lessons for a Living Education* uses a unique approach to teaching and learning math concepts. Unlike many math curriculums, *Math Lessons For a Living Education* does not focus on memorization of computation to the exclusion of conceptual and critical understanding. In this course, you will find plenty of practice and reinforcement of concepts and computation. This is not a course that will allow students to quickly shove facts into their short term memories for the sole purpose of passing a quiz and getting a good grade. Grades are not the focus of this course; long term understanding and developed critical thinking skills are the desired outcome and will form a firm foundation on which higher math can be built.

Before you begin this book, please make sure you have prepared the charts from the manipulatives section. You may laminate a copy of each chart for each student, or if you prefer, make copies to store in a file and distributed as needed throughout the year.

Here is a list of topics that are used as crosscurricular focuses throughout the year. You may wish to have library books about topics of interest.

- the country of Peru
- a good Bible story book
- recipe books (or boxes)
- the history of the Volkswagen "Bug"
- Dewey Decimal System
- recycling
- Mexico
- Creation Science vs. Evolution
- Ancient Mayans
- auto mechanics shop
- the art of quilting
- Christmas traditions
- banks and personal financing
- geometry-focused books
- wilderness survival

First Semester Suggested Daily Schedule

Date	Day	Assignment	Due Date	✓	Grade
		First Semester-First Quarter			
Week 1	Day 1	Read Lesson 1 • Page 15 Complete Lesson 1 Exercise 1 **Review Week** • Page 16	08/12		
	Day 2	Complete Lesson 1 Exercise 2 • Page 17	08/13		
	Day 3	Complete Lesson 1 Exercise 3 • Page 18	08/14		
	Day 4	Complete Lesson 1 Exercise 4 • Page 19	08/15		
	Day 5	Complete Lesson 1 Exercise 5 • Page 20	08/16		
Week 2	Day 6	Read Lesson 2 • Page 21 Complete Lesson 2 Exercise 1 **Review Week** • Page 22	08/19		
	Day 7	Complete Lesson 2 Exercise 2 • Page 23	08/20		
	Day 8	Complete Lesson 2 Exercise 3 • Page 24	08/21		
	Day 9	Complete Lesson 2 Exercise 4 • Page 25	08/22		
	Day 10	Complete Lesson 2 Exercise 5 • Page 26	08/23		
Week 3	Day 11	Read Lesson 3 • Pages 27-28 Complete Lesson 3 Exercise 1 **Review Week** • Pages 29-30	08/26		
	Day 12	Complete Lesson 3 Exercise 2 • Page 31	08/27		
	Day 13	Complete Lesson 3 Exercise 3 • Page 32	08/28		
	Day 14	Complete Lesson 3 Exercise 4 • Page 33	08/29		
	Day 15	Complete Lesson 3 Exercise 5 • Page 34	08/30		
Week 4	Day 16	Read Lesson 4 • Page 35 Complete Lesson 4 Exercise 1 **Review Week** • Page 36			
	Day 17	Complete Lesson 4 Exercise 2 • Page 37			
	Day 18	Complete Lesson 4 Exercise 3 • Page 38			
	Day 19	Complete Lesson 4 Exercise 4 • Page 39			
	Day 20	Complete Lesson 4 Exercise 5 • Page 40			
Week 5	Day 21	Read Lesson 5 • Pages 41-42 Complete Lesson 5 Exercise 1 **Review Week** • Page 43			
	Day 22	Complete Lesson 5 Exercise 2 • Page 44			
	Day 23	Complete Lesson 5 Exercise 3 • Page 45			
	Day 24	Begin Lesson 5 Exercise 4-5 • Page 46			
	Day 25	Finish Lesson 5 Exercise 4-5 • Page 46			
Week 6	Day 26	Read Lesson 6 • Page 47 Complete Lesson 6 Exercise 1 **Review Week** • Page 48			
	Day 27	Complete Lesson 6 Exercise 2 • Page 49			
	Day 28	Complete Lesson 6 Exercise 3 • Page 50			
	Day 29	Complete Lesson 6 Exercise 4 • Page 51			
	Day 30	Complete Lesson 6 Exercise 5 • Page 52			

Date	Day	Assignment	Due Date	✓	Grade
Week 7	Day 31	Read Lesson 7 • Pages 53-54 Complete Lesson 7 Exercise 1 • Page 55			
	Day 32	Complete Lesson 7 Exercise 2 • Pages 56-57			
	Day 33	Complete Lesson 7 Exercise 3 • Pages 58-59			
	Day 34	Complete Lesson 7 Exercise 4 • Page 60			
	Day 35	Complete Lesson 7 Exercise 5 • Pages 61-62			
Week 8	Day 36	Read Lesson 8 • Pages 63-64 Complete Lesson 8 Exercise 1 • Pages 65-66			
	Day 37	Complete Lesson 8 Exercise 2 • Pages 67-68			
	Day 38	Complete Lesson 8 Exercise 3 • Pages 69-70			
	Day 39	Begin Lesson 8 Exercise 4 • Pages 71			
	Day 40	Finish Lesson 8 Exercise 5 • Pages 72			
Week 9	Day 41	Read Lesson 9 • Pages 73-74 Complete Lesson 9 Exercise 1 • Pages 75-76			
	Day 42	Complete Lesson 9 Exercise 2 • Page 77			
	Day 43	Complete Lesson 9 Exercise 3 • Pages 78-79			
	Day 44	Begin Lesson 9 Exercise 4-5 **Review Time** • Page 80			
	Day 45	Finish Lesson 9 Exercise 4-5 **Review Time** • Page 80			
		First Semester-Second Quarter			
Week 1	Day 46	Read Lesson 10 • Pages 81-82 Complete Lesson 10 Exercise 1 • Pages 83-84			
	Day 47	Complete Lesson 10 Exercise 2 • Page 85			
	Day 48	Complete Lesson 10 Exercise 3 • Pages 86-87			
	Day 49	Complete Lesson 10 Exercise 4 • Pages 88-89			
	Day 50	Complete Lesson 10 Exercise 5 • Page 90			
Week 2	Day 51	Read Lesson 11 • Page 91 Complete Lesson 11 Exercise 1 **Review Week** • Pages 92-93			
	Day 52	Complete Lesson 11 Exercise 2 • Page 94			
	Day 53	Complete Lesson 11 Exercise 3 • Page 95			
	Day 54	Complete Lesson 11 Exercise 4 • Pages 96-97			
	Day 55	Complete Lesson 11 Exercise 5 • Page 98			
Week 3	Day 56	Read Lesson 12 • Pages 99-100 Complete Lesson 12 Exercise 1 • Pages 101-102			
	Day 57	Complete Lesson 12 Exercise 2 • Page 103			
	Day 58	Complete Lesson 12 Exercise 3 • Page 104			
	Day 59	Complete Lesson 12 Exercise 4 • Page 105			
	Day 60	Complete Lesson 12 Exercise 5 **Review Time** • Page 106			
Week 4	Day 61	Read Lesson 13 • Page 107 Complete Lesson 13 Exercise 1 • Pages 108-109			
	Day 62	Complete Lesson 13 Exercise 2 • Page 110			
	Day 63	Complete Lesson 13 Exercise 3 • Page 111			
	Day 64	Complete Lesson 13 Exercise 4 • Page 112			
	Day 65	Complete Lesson 13 Exercise 5 **Review Time** • Pages 113-114			

Date	Day	Assignment	Due Date	✓	Grade
Week 5	Day 66	Read Lesson 14 • Pages 115-116 Complete Lesson 14 Exercise 1 • Pages 117-118			
	Day 67	Complete Lesson 14 Exercise 2 • Page 119			
	Day 68	Complete Lesson 14 Exercise 3 • Page 120			
	Day 69	Complete Lesson 14 Exercise 4 • Page 121			
	Day 70	Complete Lesson 14 Exercise 5 • Page 122			
Week 6	Day 71	Read Lesson 15 • Page 123 Complete Lesson 15 Exercise 1 • Page 124			
	Day 72	Complete Lesson 15 Exercise 2 • Page 125			
	Day 73	Complete Lesson 15 Exercise 3 • Page 126			
	Day 74	Complete Lesson 15 Exercise 4 • Page 127			
	Day 75	Complete Lesson 15 Exercise 5 • Page 128			
Week 7	Day 76	Read Lesson 16 • Pages 129-130 Complete Lesson 16 Exercise 1 • Page 131			
	Day 77	Complete Lesson 16 Exercise 2 • Page 132			
	Day 78	Complete Lesson 16 Exercise 3 • Pages 133-134			
	Day 79	Complete Lesson 16 Exercise 4 • Page 135			
	Day 80	Complete Lesson 16 Exercise 5 **Review Time** • Page 136			
Week 8	Day 81	Read Lesson 17 • Pages 137-138 Complete Lesson 17 Exercise 1 • Page 139			
	Day 82	Complete Lesson 17 Exercise 2 • Pages 140-141			
	Day 83	Complete Lesson 17 Exercise 3 • Page 142			
	Day 84	Complete Lesson 17 Exercise 4 • Page 143			
	Day 85	Complete Lesson 17 Exercise 5 **Review Time** • Page 144			
Week 9	Day 86	Read Lesson 18 • Pages 145-146 Complete Lesson 18 Exercise 1 • Pages 147-148			
	Day 87	Complete Lesson 18 Exercise 2 • Pages 149-150			
	Day 88	Complete Lesson 18 Exercise 3 • Page 151			
	Day 89	Complete Lesson 18 Exercise 4 • Pages 152			
	Day 90	Complete Lesson 18 Exercise 5 **Review Time** • Pages 153-154			
		Mid-Term Grade			

Second Semester Suggested Daily Schedule

Date	Day	Assignment	Due Date	✓	Grade
Second Semester-Third Quarter					
Week 1	Day 91	Read Lesson 19 • Page 155 Complete Lesson 19 Exercise 1 • Page 156			
	Day 92	Complete Lesson 19 Exercise 2 • Page 157			
	Day 93	Complete Lesson 19 Exercise 3 • Page 158			
	Day 94	Complete Lesson 19 Exercise 4 • Page 159			
	Day 95	Complete Lesson 19 Exercise 5 • Page 160			
Week 2	Day 96	Read Lesson 20 • Pages 161-162 Complete Lesson 20 Exercise 1 • Page 163			
	Day 97	Complete Lesson 20 Exercise 2 • Page 164			
	Day 98	Complete Lesson 20 Exercise 3 • Pages 165-166			
	Day 99	Complete Lesson 20 Exercise 4 • Page 167			
	Day 100	Complete Lesson 20 Exercise 5 **Review Time** • Page 168			
Week 3	Day 101	Read Lesson 21 • Pages 169-170 Complete Lesson 21 Exercise 1 • Page 171			
	Day 102	Complete Lesson 21 Exercise 2 • Page 172			
	Day 103	Complete Lesson 21 Exercise 3 • Page 173			
	Day 104	Complete Lesson 21 Exercise 4 • Page 174			
	Day 105	Complete Lesson 21 Exercise 5 • Pages 175-176			
Week 4	Day 106	Read Lesson 22 • Pages 177-178 Complete Lesson 22 Exercise 1 • Page 179			
	Day 107	Complete Lesson 22 Exercise 2 • Page 180			
	Day 108	Complete Lesson 22 Exercise 3 • Page 181			
	Day 109	Complete Lesson 22 Exercise 4 • Pages 182-183			
	Day 110	Complete Lesson 22 Exercise 5 **Review Time** • Page 184			
Week 5	Day 111	Read Lesson 23 • Pages 185-186 Complete Lesson 23 Exercise 1 • Pages 187-188			
	Day 112	Complete Lesson 23 Exercise 2 • Page 189			
	Day 113	Complete Lesson 23 Exercise 3 • Page 190			
	Day 114	Begin Lesson 23 Exercise 4-5 • Pages 191-192			
	Day 115	Finish Lesson 23 Exercise 4-5 • Pages 191-192			
Week 6	Day 116	Read Lesson 24 • Pages 193-194 Complete Lesson 24 Exercise 1 • Pages 195-196			
	Day 117	Complete Lesson 24 Exercise 2 • Page 197			
	Day 118	Complete Lesson 24 Exercise 3 • Page 198			
	Day 119	Complete Lesson 24 Exercise 4 • Page 199			
	Day 120	Complete Lesson 24 Exercise 5 • Page 200			

Date	Day	Assignment	Due Date	✓	Grade
Week 7	Day 121	Read Lesson 25 • Page 201 Complete Lesson 25 Exercise 1 **Review Week** • Page 202			
	Day 122	Complete Lesson 25 Exercise 2 • Page 203			
	Day 123	Complete Lesson 25 Exercise 3 • Page 204			
	Day 124	Complete Lesson 25 Exercise 4 • Page 205			
	Day 125	Complete Lesson 25 Exercise 5 • Page 206			
Week 8	Day 126	Read Lesson 26 • Pages 207-208 Complete Lesson 26 Exercise 1 • Pages 209-210			
	Day 127	Complete Lesson 26 Exercise 2 • Page 211			
	Day 128	Complete Lesson 26 Exercise 3 • Pages 212-213			
	Day 129	Complete Lesson 26 Exercise 4 • Page 214			
	Day 130	Complete Lesson 26 Exercise 5 • Pages 215-216			
Week 9	Day 131	Read Lesson 27 • Page 217 Begin Lesson 27 Exercise 1 • Page 218			
	Day 132	Finish Lesson 27 Exercise 2 • Page 219			
	Day 133	Begin Lesson 27 Exercise 3 • Page 220			
	Day 134	Finish Lesson 27 Exercise 4 • Page 221			
	Day 135	Complete Lesson 27 Exercise 5 • Page 222			
		Second Semester-Fourth Quarter			
Week 1	Day 136	Read Lesson 28 • Page 223 Complete Lesson 28 Exercise 1 • Page 224			
	Day 137	Complete Lesson 28 Exercise 2 • Page 225			
	Day 138	Complete Lesson 28 Exercise 3 • Page 226			
	Day 139	Complete Lesson 28 Exercise 4 • Page 227			
	Day 140	Complete Lesson 28 Exercise 5 • Page 228			
Week 2	Day 141	Read Lesson 29 • Page 229 Complete Lesson 29 Exercise 1 • Page 230			
	Day 142	Complete Lesson 29 Exercise 2 • Page 231			
	Day 143	Complete Lesson 29 Exercise 3 • Page 232			
	Day 144	Complete Lesson 29 Exercise 4 • Page 233			
	Day 145	Complete Lesson 29 Exercise 5 • Page 234			
Week 3	Day 146	Read Lesson 30 • Page 235 Complete Lesson 30 Exercise 1 • Page 236			
	Day 147	Complete Lesson 30 Exercise 2 • Page 237			
	Day 148	Complete Lesson 30 Exercise 3 • Page 238			
	Day 149	Complete Lesson 30 Exercise 4 • Page 239			
	Day 150	Complete Lesson 30 Exercise 5 **Review Time** • Page 240			

Date	Day	Assignment	Due Date	✓	Grade
Week 4	Day 151	Read Lesson 31 • Page 241 Complete Lesson 31 Exercise 1 **Review Week** • Page 242			
	Day 152	Complete Lesson 31 Exercise 2 • Page 243			
	Day 153	Complete Lesson 31 Exercise 3 • Page 244			
	Day 154	Complete Lesson 31 Exercise 4 • Page 245			
	Day 155	Complete Lesson 31 Exercise 5 • Page 246			
Week 5	Day 156	Read Lesson 32 • Page 247 Complete Lesson 32 Exercise 1 **Review Week** • Page 248			
	Day 157	Complete Lesson 32 Exercise 2 • Page 249			
	Day 158	Complete Lesson 32 Exercise 3 • Page 250			
	Day 159	Complete Lesson 32 Exercise 4 • Page 251			
	Day 160	Complete Lesson 32 Exercise 5 • Page 252			
Week 6	Day 161	Read Lesson 33 • Page 253 Complete Lesson 33 Exercise 1 **Review Week** • Page 254			
	Day 162	Complete Lesson 33 Exercise 2 • Page 255			
	Day 163	Complete Lesson 33 Exercise 3 • Page 256			
	Day 164	Complete Lesson 33 Exercise 4 • Page 257			
	Day 165	Complete Lesson 33 Exercise 5 • Page 258			
Week 7	Day 166	Read Lesson 34 • Page 259 Complete Lesson 34 Exercise 1 **Review Week** • Page 260			
	Day 167	Complete Lesson 34 Exercise 2 • Page 261			
	Day 168	Complete Lesson 34 Exercise 3 • Page 262			
	Day 169	Complete Lesson 34 Exercise 4 • Page 263			
	Day 170	Complete Lesson 34 Exercise 5 • Page 264			
Week 8	Day 171	Read Lesson 35 • Page 265 Complete Lesson 35 Exercise 1 **Review Week** • Page 266			
	Day 172	Complete Lesson 35 Exercise 2 • Page 267			
	Day 173	Complete Lesson 35 Exercise 3 • Page 268			
	Day 174	Complete Lesson 35 Exercise 4 • Page 269			
	Day 175	Complete Lesson 35 Exercise 5 • Page 270			
Week 9	Day 176	Read Lesson 36 • Page 271 Complete Lesson 36 Exercise 1 **Review Week** • Page 272			
	Day 177	Complete Lesson 36 Exercise 2 • Page 273			
	Day 178	Complete Lesson 36 Exercise 3 • Page 274			
	Day 179	Complete Lesson 36 Exercise 4 • Page 275			
	Day 180	Complete Lesson 36 Exercise 5 • Page 276			
		Final Grade			

Review of All Addition and Subtraction

Lesson 1

There was much excitement in the Stevens household. The four older children had volunteered to help with the younger classes at their church's fall Vacation Bible School. Their church had been serving the community and surrounding areas with this outreach for twenty-five years, and this year's VBS was going to be a celebration! There was a record number of children signed up, and there was a lot to do to get ready. Each of the Stevens children were in charge of a craft, a song, and a game with the younger children.

Charlie was signed up to work with the six- and seven-year old boys. They were going to learn about and put on a skit depicting some of the miracles of Jesus. Hairo was going to work with the same boys learning some songs and building props for the skits. Charlotte was going to help take care of the kindergarten age children, and Natty was going to help lead the worship songs with all of the age groups. Natty was also going to do something else special. Mrs. Andrews, the VBS organizer, had asked Natty to share her story with all of the children during one of the morning sessions. Natty had agreed, but now she was so nervous! She had been working on what she was going to say to the group.

"Mom! I have gone through at least ten pieces of paper! I can't seem to get my thoughts down," Natty sighed in frustration.

"Do you want me to help, Natty?" Charlotte asked her sister.

"I don't know. In fact, I don't know WHY I said I would do this!" Natty scowled as she balled up yet another piece of paper and threw it, rather forcefully, into the wastebasket. "I just can't seem to be able to sort through my thoughts. They are all jumbled," Natty sighed again as she took a clean piece of paper and started over.

"I know! Maybe you could use math to tell your story!" Charlie suggested. Charlie thought the answer to all of life's problems was MATH. Charlie loved math. In fact, math was probably his most favorite thing in the world — math and cars.

"Oh Charlie!" Natty started to giggle. "How could math help me? My story has nothing to do with math!"

"Well, I don't know about that! All of us here could say that Jesus SUBTRACTED our sins away from us when He died for us on the cross, and then He ADDED us to His family. And because we love and obey Him, He MULTIPLIES our blessings! And of course, He said that when He comes again, He will DIVIDE the wheat — that's us — from the chaff — that's the ones who don't choose to follow Him! If that isn't math, I don't know what is!" Charlie finished with a flourish.

"Oh Charlie," Natty gasped between giggles, "you need to be a preacher! And you are right! Your math did help me! I know what I am going to write now!"

Name________________________________

Exercise 1 Day 1

Mental Math

20 + 8 + 6 + 11 + 3 + 5 =

110 + 120 + 350 =

1,090 + 10 + 100 =

650 + 40 + 8 + 2 =

200 + 60 + 9 + 10 =

4,001 + 9 + 80 =

Facts Review

Work quickly.

+	4	6	10	8	2	3	5	1	9	7	0
6											

+	6	4	8	0	1	2	9	3	5	7	10
9											

+	2	5	8	1	10	3	6	4	0	7	9
8											

+	8	2	9	6	0	7	1	4	3	10	5
7											

Name________________________________

Exercise 2 Day 2

Addition Review

```
  520        613        95,011      90,345
  294        356      + 15,219    + 43,821
+  24      + 713      --------    --------
-----      -----

   38         24          41
   25         31          86
   35         26          26
+  14      +  15      +   38
-----      -----      ------
```

Fill in the Blanks

Write the subtraction equation you used to solve the problem underneath it. The first one is done for you.

8 + 7 = 15
15 − 8 = 7

5 + _____ = 11

4 + _____ = 14

9 + _____ = 17

7 + _____ = 12

9 + _____ = 12

10 + _____ = 20

8 + _____ = 16

8 + _____ = 17

3 + _____ = 11

2 + _____ = 12

7 + _____ = 16

Name________________________________

Exercise 3 Day 3

Subtraction Review

9,000	3,055	20,020	52,031
− 6,826	− 2,245	− 12,172	− 10,729

Need more practice?

300	600	300
− 144	− 149	− 226

Fill in the Blanks

Write the addition equation you can use to check the problem underneath it. The first one is done for you.

17 − 8 = 9 8 + 9 = 17	12 − _____ = 6	16 − _____ = 7
16 − _____ = 8	20 − _____ = 10	15 − _____ = 9
14 − _____ = 9	13 − _____ = 8	5 − _____ = 5
21 − _____ = 11	19 − _____ = 11	18 − _____ = 15

Name______________________________

Word Problems

Teacher

Please take the time to make sure your student(s) completely understand the process of solving word problems.

1. When Grandpa Stevens took the children to the State Fair, they counted 24 big rides in one area of the midway, 19 smaller rides in the children's area, and 15 rides along the old-fashioned board walks in the "Ole' Western Days" area. How many rides did they count all together at the fair?

2. How many more rides did they count in the midway than the children's area?

3. At the fair, Charlie bought cotton candy for $1.75, Hairo bought an ice-cream cone for $2.25, and Charlotte and Natty combined their money to buy a funnel cake for $5.90. How much money did they all spend together?

4. How much more did the girls pay for the funnel cake than Charlie paid for his cotton candy?

5. What addition clue words do you look for in a word problem?

6. What subtraction clue words do you look for in a word problem?

Name________________________________

Exercise 5

Day 5

Word Problems

Write your own word problems and solve them. Narrate to your teacher the steps of solving an addition word problem and a subtraction word problem.

My addition word problems...

1.

2.

My subtraction word problems...

1.

2.

Review of All Multiplication and Division

Lesson 2

Hello, everyone. As you know, my name is Natty Stevens. Mrs. Andrews asked me to share what has happened in my life since my adoption two years ago. I think most of you know that my brother, Hairo, and I are from Peru. Our first mother and father died when I was very little. I do remember them, though. I know that I look like my mother, and I know that they loved us very much.

Mom and Dad Stevens came to Peru three years ago, when we had just moved to the children's home. It has been almost exactly two years since we came to live with them as our second family. I want to share with you the biggest thing that has happened and is really still happening in my life.

When my momma and papa died, I was so very afraid. I didn't want to talk to anyone. I didn't want to trust anyone. I didn't want to love anyone ever again. I was afraid that they would leave me, too, so I did not want to take that chance. When I met the Stevens, I did not want to love them. I was not nice to them. I would not speak to the lady who is now my mom. I thought I could make her leave me alone by being unkind to her. It didn't work. No matter how much I ignored her, she kept right on being kind to me.

I will never forget the day I decided to let her love me. She was reading to all of the children at the children's home. She was reading the story of a kind man, named Jesus. I had heard of this Jesus before. It seemed like the teachers were always telling us stories of Him. I had always thought they were nice stories, but they did not mean anything to me. On this day, the American lady was reading a story about how Jesus was crying because His friend, Lazarus, had died. In the story, Jesus called out to the dead man to come out of the grave, and Lazarus obeyed!

This really startled me! I sat up to listen more closely. As the American lady was reading the story, she looked at me, and I saw the same look that my momma used to have when she kissed me good night or washed my hair or kissed my cheek...

To be continued...

"Do you think this is ok so far, Mom?" Natty asked in a worried voice.

"Oh, Natty, it is more than ok; it is wonderful! It really is! I can't wait to read the rest," Mom answered with tears in her voice, pulling Natty to her in a hug.

"Ok, I will finish it later, after we are finished with school today, ok?" Natty smiled up at her mom.

"Sounds like a plan, little lady!" Mom chuckled and handed Natty her math book. Natty smiled back and taking her book, she pulled out a chair and sat next to her sister, Charlotte.

"I can't wait to read it, too, Natty!" Charlotte whispered in her sister's ear and gave her a squeeze. "I'm super-duper proud of you!"

Name______________________________

Exercise 1 Day 6

Multiplication Review

x	1	2	3	4	5	6	7	8	9	10
0										
1										
2										
3										
4										
5										
6										
7										
8										
9										
10										
11										
12										

Division Review

When we divide, we are taking a large group and breaking it into smaller groups. Write the multiplication equation you can use to check each problem. The first one is done for you.

21 ÷ 3 = 7
7 × 3 = 21

36 ÷ _____ = 9

42 ÷ _____ = 7

40 ÷ _____ = 8

12 ÷ _____ = 3

56 ÷ _____ = 8

Name ______________________________

Exercise 2

Day 7

Multiplication Review

Write the division equation you used to solve each problem. The first one is done for you.

$4 \times \underline{5} = 20$
$20 \div 4 = 5$

$7 \times$ ____ $= 21$

____ $\times 7 = 28$

$9 \times$ ____ $= 36$

____ $\times 3 = 27$

$10 \times$ ____ $= 80$

$5 \times$ ____ $= 45$

$4 \times$ ____ $= 24$

$4 \times$ ____ $= 16$

Fill in the blanks with < or >.

4×4 ____ 3×6

5×5 ____ 3×5

8×7 ____ 3×5

7×7 ____ 5×10

2×6 ____ 3×2

6×3 ____ 4×5

Word Problems

1. If a square has sides which are 7 feet long, what is the area of the square?

2. What do 3 dozen roses cost, if 1 dozen cost $16?

Teacher

Please quiz your student(s) on their multiplication and division facts. Note which facts need review and study.

Name________________________________ Exercise 3 Day 8

Multiplication review.

$$\begin{array}{r} 32 \\ \times\ 2 \\ \hline \end{array}$$

$$\begin{array}{r} 64 \\ \times\ 32 \\ \hline \end{array}$$

Division Review

Divide and then check using multiplication. Use your Long Division Practice Mat for additional practice.

7	4,	2	0	2		

9	4,	5	0	9

Name______________________________

Exercise 4 Day 9

Word Problems

1. Some friends drove 513 miles in one day. It took them 9 hours. How many miles per hour did they drive?

2. Mom and the girls were helping make cookies for VBS. They made 10 dozen cookies. How many individual cookies did they make all together?

3. There are 12 preschoolers at VBS. If each of the preschoolers eat 3 cookies, how many will they eat all together?

4. How many cookies did all the preschoolers eat in 4 days? Show this as a multiplication equation and as an addition equation.

5. What multiplication clue words do you look for in a word problem?

6. What division clue words do you look for in a word problem?

Name________________________________

Exercise 5 Day 10

Teacher

Guide your students in coming up with their own word problems.

Word Problems

Write your own multiplication and division word problems and solve them. Narrate to your teacher the steps of solving an multiplication word problem and a division word problem.

My multiplication word problems...

1.

2.

My division word problems...

1.

2.

Review of All Geometry

Lesson 3

Natty stood in front of the group and bravely continued...

As the story about Jesus raising His dead friend to life continued, I listened carefully. If this Jesus was really alive, like the home workers were always saying, and He knew how to make something dead alive again... Well, I wanted to know more about Him! This pretty, American woman seemed to believe this was true, and all of the sudden, I wanted to know why she was so nice to me even when I was sulky and silent.

When the Stevens brought us home to live with them, I started to learn about how much Jesus loves me, Natty Stevens. He isn't just a great big God out there somewhere; He knows each of us. I learned that He sees and cares about me personally. As I have gotten used to belonging to a new family, I have also learned that the love of Jesus can win the war against fear. I am not afraid anymore because I know that, even if things go wrong in my life, He will never leave me or forsake me. Jesus has made me alive again because He is my Savior and Friend.

I know now that the love of Jesus is stronger than anything. I am thankful for my second family and for their love for Hairo and me. My mom has taught us children that this kind of love - the love of Jesus - is a fruit of the Spirit. It is a different kind of love than we can have on our own. Our own kind of love is not strong enough to conquer all fear. It is because Jesus died for our sins and rose from the dead, that His love can conquer fear, even fear of death.

Thank you for letting me tell you about how Jesus' love has changed my life. I hope each of you know Jesus and have Him as your personal Savior and Friend.

"Natty, I am so proud of you!" Hairo gave his little sister a hug. "You have grown up and changed so much since we came to the United States."

"She certainly has," agreed Charlotte, with a big smile for her sister. "You did such a good job sharing at VBS, too! Mrs. Andrews had tears in her eyes, and little Julie Smith asked Jesus into her heart because of what you shared."

The children were gathered in the family room, waiting for Mom to come in for school. The first two days of VBS were over, and according to Mrs. Andrews, they had been a huge success.

At that very moment, Mom came into the family room with a big box in her arms. She had been out in the yard pulling weeds from the flower garden, when the postman had dropped off the package. The children gathered around to see what was in it. The return address indicated that it came from Grandpa and Grandma Stevens. As the tape came

off of the box and the flaps opened, the children could see that the package was full of new puzzles and games!

"Yeah! I love math games," Charlie hooted in delight. "Mom, could we play some new games for school today?" he asked.

"That is a very good idea, Charlie! But first, what was Charlotte saying about Julie Smith when I came in? Did I hear you say that little Julie asked Jesus to be her Savior, Charlotte?" Charlotte nodded with a smile. "Oh my goodness! That is wonderful! Thank You, Jesus! Ok, you two boys make sure all of the breakfast dishes are cleared and placed in the dishwasher, please. Charlotte, Natty, you two make sure Ella is ready to start preschool. I will unpack these games and puzzles. They will fit nicely into the top shelves in our new classroom...." Mom's voice trailed off as she carried the stack of new games down the hall.

The children smiled at each other. Mom was always talking to herself. This was going to be a fun day! They were going to play a new game, which would help them to review all they had learned about geometry.

Name______________________________

Geometry Review

Use your Geometry Chart in the Manipulative Section to do this project.

With an orange colored pencil, draw an acute angle on the protractor.

With a red colored pencil, draw an obtuse angle on the protractor.

With a green colored pencil, draw a right angle on the protractor.

Narrate to your teacher what each one is.

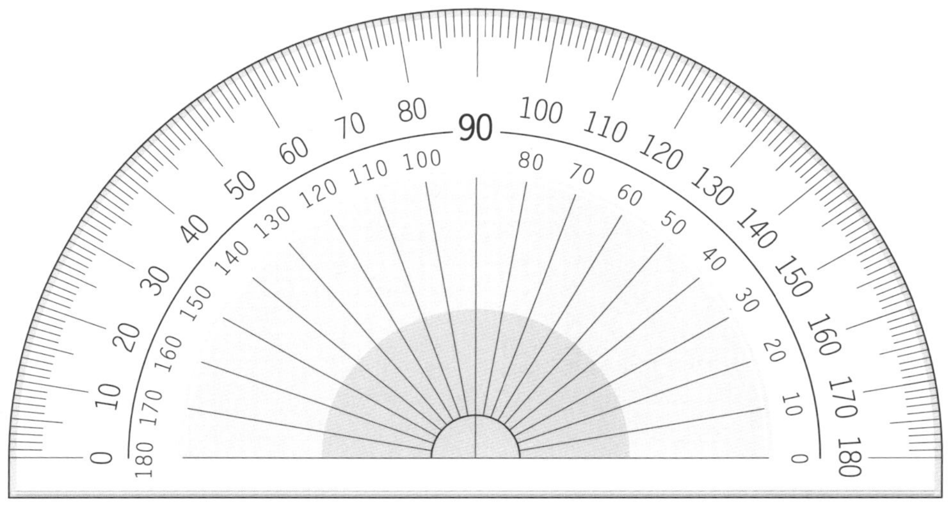

1. If a rectangle has a length of 22 cm. and a width 5 cm. what is the perimeter?

2. What is the area of the above rectangle?

3. What is the perimeter of a triangle with two 3 inch sides and one 1 inch side?

4. If a square has sides that are 9 yards long, what is the perimeter? What is the area?

5. How do you find the perimeter of a square?

6. How do you find the perimeter of a triangle?

7. How do you find the area of a square?

Name________________________________

Exercise 2

Day 12

Matching

Match the shapes with the names and descriptions. Use your Geometry Chart if you need help.

A heptagon has 7 sides.

A rectangle has 4 sides.

A pentagon has 5 sides.

A triangle has 3 sides.

A hexagon has 6 sides.

An octagon has 8 sides.

A nonagon has 9 sides.

A square has 4 equal sides.

Name________________________________

Copywork

A vertex is the point where two sides meet. For example, a triangle has three vertices.

____

____

____

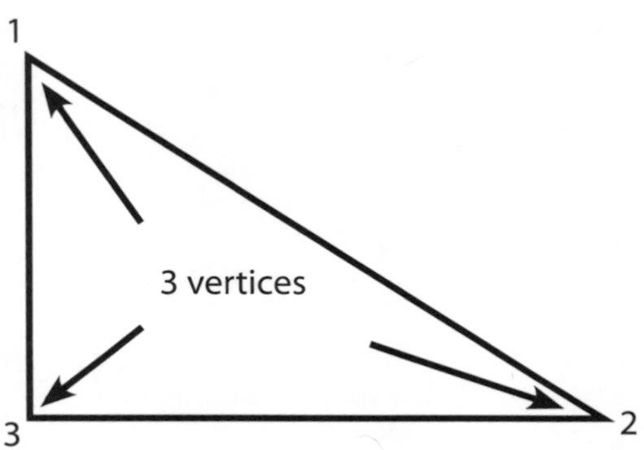

Write how many sides each shape has. Use your Geometry Chart if you need help!

hexagon	octagon	pentagon	nonagon	heptagon
______	______	______	______	______

Tell your teacher how many sides each shape has.

- ☐ triangle
- ☐ nonagon
- ☐ octagon
- ☐ heptagon
- ☐ rectangle
- ☐ pentagon
- ☐ hexagon

Name________________________________

Exercise 4 Day 14

Copywork

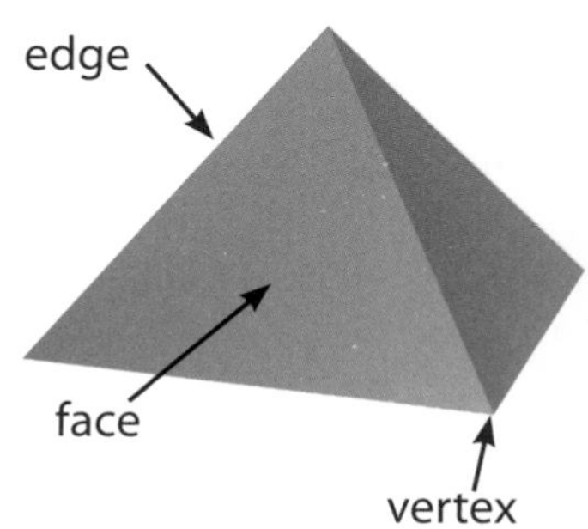

In a three-dimensional shape, a vertex is where three or more edges meet, an edge is where two sides meet, and a face is the shape formed by the edges.

Find real-life objects that have these three dimensional shapes in them. Sketch the objects and narrate to your teacher what you find.

Sphere:

Square pyramid:

Rectangular prism:

Cylinder:

Cone:

Name________________________________

Exercise 5 Day 15

Copywork and Show

If you need help, look at your Geometry Chart.

Lines that cross one another are called intersection lines.

____

____

Show an example:

Intersecting lines that form right angles are called perpendicular lines.

____

____

Show an example:

Lines that never intersect and are the same distance apart are called parallel lines.

____

____

____

Show an example:

Review of All Measurement

Lesson 4

"Natty, Charlotte! Could you two grab that end of the paper and hold it down for us?" Hairo called to his sisters. Charlie and Hairo were each holding one side of a giant paper roll and trying to unroll it evenly.

"Sure, Hairo," Charlotte and Natty said together as they each grabbed a corner of the paper and held on firmly. "How much paper are you going to unroll, Charlie?" Charlotte asked her twin brother.

"Mrs. Andrews said she needs about $36\frac{1}{2}$ feet," Charlie called back to his sister, as he and Hairo moved together away from the girls, the unrolling paper stretching out between them. "She wants to have plenty of room for the kids to draw scenes from their favorite 'Miracles of Jesus' story!"

"How do you know how much paper to unroll?" Natty yelled down to the boys. They seemed to be a very long way away, all the way down the hall of the church basement.

"Hairo and I measured it before we started! We put a piece of blue tape on the floor on both ends. Look down by your feet! Do you see the piece of tape?" Charlie shouted back to the girls.

Natty and Charlotte looked around by their feet. Neither of them could see any blue tape.

"We don't have any tape on this end, Charlie!" shouted Natty. Charlie looked down at his feet and sighed. He could see the edge of a piece of blue tape sticking to the underside of his shoe.

"That's because it's stuck to my shoe!" Charlie shouted in reply. The boys carefully placed the roll of paper on the floor and walked back to the girls' end. "We are going to have to remeasure, I think. Mrs. Andrews said it needs to be $36\frac{1}{2}$ feet long."

"I know! We can use the squares in the floor tile to measure it!" Charlotte exclaimed. Each one is one foot by one foot square. That means thirty-six squares plus $\frac{1}{2}$ of another square."

"Great idea!" Charlie smiled in approval.

"I can't wait to help with VBS!" Charlotte commented as she and Natty held firmly to their end of the paper. Charlie and Hairo were working on placing tape on the floor to show where the girls were to stand with the loose end of paper as the boys unrolled the right length from the other end.

"I know I can't either! I wonder what pictures the kids are going to draw on this paper," Natty said with excitement. "I know which picture I would draw! I love the story of how Jesus raised the little girl to life. That's what I would draw!"

Name________________________________

Exercise 1 Day 16

Measurements Review

Fill in the blanks. Refer to the Measurements Chart in the Manipulatives Section if you need help.

______	feet = 1 yard	______	feet = 1 mile
______	quarts = 1 gallon	______	days = 1 year
______	cups = 1 pint	______	hours = 1 day
______	items = 1 dozen	______	pecks = 1 bushel
______	seconds = 1 minute	______	pounds = 1 ton
______	ounces = 1 pound	______	quarts = 1 peck

New Measurement to Learn

1 kilogram (kg) = 1000 grams (g)

The gram is much smaller than an ounce.

(an average sized paper clip weighs about a gram)

The kilogram is larger than a pound.

Write M for each metric unit of measure. Write E for each English unit of measure.

______	liter	______	quart	______	inch
______	pound	______	centimeter	______	meter
______	ton	______	foot	______	kilogram
______	yard	______	gram	______	ounce

Name______________________________

Exercise 2 Day 17

Measurements Review

Fill in the blank.

1 foot = _______ inches	1 yard = _______ feet
1 dozen = _______ items	60 minutes = _______ hour
60 seconds = _______ minute	1 year = _______ months
1 ton = _______ pounds	1 pound = _______ ounces
_______ quarts = 1 peck	_______ pecks = 1 bushel

Number from smallest to greatest.

______ peck	______ year	______ ounce
______ gallon	______ day	______ ton
______ bushel	______ hour	______ pound
______ pint	______ minute	
______ quart	______ month	
	______ second	

Fill in the blank.

_______ pounds = 1 ton

_______ feet = 1 yard

_______ items = 1 dozen

_______ hours = 1 day

_______ pecks = 1 bushel

_______ days = 1 week

Name________________________________

Exercise 3

Day 18

Copywork:

I kilogram (kg) = 1000 grams (g)
A gram is much smaller than an ounce.
(An average sized paper clip weighs about a gram.)
A kilogram is larger than a pound.

Measure and Draw

Start on the ★.

5 cm ★

$4\frac{1}{4}$ inches ★

5 inches ★

Mixed Review

$$\begin{array}{r} 619 \\ 427 \\ +\ 132 \\ \hline \end{array}$$

$$\begin{array}{r} 15,021 \\ -\ 9,492 \\ \hline \end{array}$$

$$\begin{array}{r} 62 \\ \times\ 41 \\ \hline \end{array}$$

$$8 \overline{)\ 1,042}$$

Name________________________________

Word Problems

Write your own measurement word problems and solve them. Narrate to your teacher the steps of solving each word problem.

My English measurement word problems. (Use English units in your story problems.)

1.

2.

My metric measurement word problems. (Use Metric units in your story problem.)

1.

2.

Work quickly.

x	4	7	9	8	10	12
6						
7						
8						

Name________________________________

Exercise 5 Day 20

Hands On!

- ☐ Measure your bedroom. What is the perimeter?

  What is the area?

- ☐ Measure your front yard. What is the perimeter?

  What is the area?

- ☐ Measure the smallest room in your home. What is the perimeter?

  What is the area?

Teacher

Measurement is a great topic to take cross curricular! Have fun with it! Here are some examples for exploration:

- *Geography: state, country, or world! Oceans or lakes, depth or area of states or countries.*
- *Science: distances to each planet, comparing sizes and distances.*
- *Class projects showing research results.*
- *Ask your student(s)!*

Review of All Fractional Concepts

Lesson 5

The sun shone brightly through the kitchen window as Mom and the two older girls worked side-by-side. Mrs. Andrews had asked the Stevens family to supply the cookies and veggie trays for the big celebration at the end of VBS. The girls had been excited to help; they loved making cookies!

"Girls, we are going to need to open another bag of flour to have enough for this recipe," Mom told the girls while pushing her hair out of her face with her wrist. The girls stifled giggles, as a long, white streak of flour appeared on their mom's forehead. "Could you two lift that bag up onto the counter for me? My hands — and now my face — are covered in flour!" Mom grinned at the girls.

"Sure, Mom! We're strong, and if we work together, we can do it!" Charlotte replied as she and Natty hefted the 25 pound bag onto the counter next to their mother. "How much more do we need?" Natty inquired. "Should we open it and fill the flour bin?"

"Yes, please do, Natty. Of course the whole thing won't fit in the bin, but I think it will hold $\frac{1}{4}$ or $\frac{1}{3}$ of the bag. Be careful not to spill too much on the floor!" Mom instructed the girls as they carefully opened the bag and began scooping the contents into the flour bin. They were learning that baking cookies for such a large number of people was a lot harder than baking for their family! All of their cookie and bar recipes made enough for their family, and the girls were learning that, in order to make bigger batches, they had to double, triple, and sometimes, even quadruple the recipes! They were thankful that Mom had taught them how to work with fractions! Like Charlie said, math is almost always the answer!

"Do you know what these cookies remind me of, Mom?" Charlotte asked as she measured the raisins for the oatmeal cookies.

"No, what?" her mom answered between counting tablespoons of unsweetened orange juice concentrate they were using to sweeten the cookies.

"Aunt Kate and Uncle Justin. It was so much fun to have them here during the summer," Charlotte answered with a wishful smile. "I still miss them!"

"I know how you feel, Honey!" her mom answered. "I don't get to see my sister nearly as much as I would like!"

"Abby was so fun to play with!" Natty's eyes sparkled, as she remembered all of the fun times they had shared with their cousins from Florida. "And Sean was always very nice, too!"

"Mom, do you think Uncle Sean and Aunt Kate will come again soon? I wish they could come for Christmas! Abby has never had a white Christmas; can you just imagine? What is Christmas without snow?" Charlotte talked as fast as her hands moved.

Orange Zesty Oatmeal Raisin Cookies

$\frac{3}{4}$ cup raisins
$\frac{1}{2}$ cup fresh orange juice
4 tbsp orange juice concentrate
$\frac{1}{3}$ cup unsalted butter (softened) or $\frac{1}{4}$ cup vegetable oil
2 teaspoons vanilla
1 tablespoon orange zest
1 teaspoon lemon zest
3 tablespoons molasses
2 eggs
$1\frac{1}{2}$ cups quick-cooking oats (uncooked)
$1\frac{1}{2}$ cups all-purpose flour
2 teaspoons baking powder
$\frac{1}{4}$ teaspoon salt
$\frac{1}{4}$ teaspoon ground cinnamon
$\frac{1}{4}$ teaspoon ground ginger
$\frac{1}{2}$ cup chopped pecans (optional)

Directions:

1. In a small saucepan, bring orange juice to a boil.
2. Add the raisins, cover, and remove from the heat. Allow to sit for 15 minutes, drain juice off of raisins.
3. Cream together: butter (or oil), vanilla, and zests.
4. Add egg, juice concentrate, and molasses - beat until well blended
5. Sift together dry ingredients.
6. Stir oats and drained raisins into wet mixture and add dry ingredients mixture slowly, mixing well.
7. Stir in nuts (optional).
8. Refrigerate batter for at least 2 hours.
9. Drop tablespoons of dough onto parchment lined baking sheets and flatten slightly with a spoon.
10. Bake at 350° for 10–12 minutes.

NOTE: Teacher should oversee the cooking process.

Name ______________________________

Exercise 1 Day 21

Fraction Review

Adding and subtracting mixed numbers.

$$3\frac{1}{6} + 1\frac{3}{6} = \underline{\qquad}$$

$$6\frac{1}{3} + 4\frac{1}{3} = \underline{\qquad}$$

$$5\frac{1}{8} + 7\frac{1}{8} = \underline{\qquad}$$

$$9\frac{5}{7} - 2\frac{2}{7} = \underline{\qquad}$$

$$3\frac{3}{4} - 1\frac{2}{4} = \underline{\qquad}$$

$$7\frac{7}{11} - 3\frac{3}{11} = \underline{\qquad}$$

Check your answers on the following.

$\frac{1}{3}$ of 24 = _____

$\frac{1}{5}$ of 10 = _____

$\frac{1}{7}$ of 56 = _____

$\frac{1}{7}$ of 63 = _____

$\frac{1}{6}$ of 36 = _____

$\frac{1}{12}$ of 24 = _____

Name_______________________________

Exercise 2 Day 22

Fraction Review

Multiply each numerator and denominator by 4 to find equivalent fractions. The first one is done for you.

$\frac{1}{5} = \frac{4}{20}$ $\quad$ $\frac{2}{6} =$ _____ $\quad$ $\frac{4}{5} =$ _____

$\frac{1}{5} \times \frac{4}{4} = \frac{4}{20}$

$\frac{5}{8} =$ _____ $\quad$ $\frac{3}{9} =$ _____ $\quad$ $\frac{2}{7} =$ _____

Divide each numerator and denominator by 3 to find equivalent fractions. The first one is done for you. This is called reducing.

$\frac{3}{9} = \frac{1}{3}$ $\quad$ $\frac{6}{18} =$ _____ $\quad$ $\frac{3}{15} =$ _____

$\frac{3}{9} \div \frac{3}{3} = \frac{1}{3}$

$\frac{12}{36} =$ _____ $\quad$ $\frac{9}{27} =$ _____ $\quad$ $\frac{9}{18} =$ _____

Solve.

$\frac{2}{8} + \frac{3}{8} =$ _____ $\quad$ $\frac{1}{7} + \frac{4}{7} =$ _____ $\quad$ $\frac{4}{19} + \frac{15}{19} =$ _____

$\frac{10}{13} - \frac{7}{13} =$ _____ $\quad$ $\frac{4}{11} - \frac{3}{11} =$ _____ $\quad$ $\frac{18}{30} - \frac{9}{30} =$ _____

Name______________________________

Fraction Review

Read these mixed numbers to your teacher. Choose two to illustrate. The first one is done for you.

$5\frac{1}{4}$ $8\frac{1}{2}$ $7\frac{7}{8}$ $10\frac{2}{3}$

Example

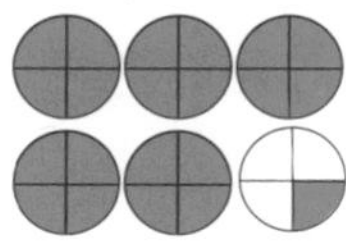

$2\frac{4}{5}$ $1\frac{8}{10}$ $3\frac{1}{6}$

Complete the problems.

$\frac{1}{4}$ of 32 = _____ $\frac{1}{2}$ of 22 = _____ $\frac{1}{8}$ of 64 = _____

$\frac{1}{3}$ of 63 = _____ $\frac{1}{9}$ of 36 = _____ $\frac{1}{2}$ of 120 = _____

$801\frac{4}{7} + 719\frac{2}{7}$

$915\frac{5}{12} + 647\frac{3}{12}$

$292\frac{6}{11} + 188\frac{3}{11}$

$442\frac{14}{15} - 378\frac{6}{15}$

$200\frac{9}{10} - 196\frac{1}{10}$

$763\frac{2}{10} - 196\frac{1}{10}$

Name________________________________

Exercise 4-5

Copywork

The top number in a fraction is the numerator. The bottom number is the denominator. The numerator tells us how many pieces of the whole we are talking about. The denominator tells us how many total pieces the whole was divided into.

____

____

____

____

____

____

____

____

Hands On!

With your parent's (or older sibling's) help, go through your family's recipes. Choose something you would like to make.

Write what you are going to make here: ______________________________

Are there fractions in your recipe? Write them here? ______________________________

What types of measurements did you use? Circle any that you used in your recipe.

tablespoon teaspoon cup ounce liter gallon quart

Teacher

Day 24 instructions: instruct your students to bring a recipe from home to be used on Day 25. Gather measuring devices listed above.

Day 25 instructions: as a class, go through the gathered recipes. Talk about, examine, and compare the measurement devices.

Review of All Decimal Concepts

Lesson 6

According to Mrs. Andrews, VBS had been a smashing success. The weather had been wonderful, and the children had been well-behaved. The Gospel had touched the hearts of twelve children, and they had accepted Jesus as their Lord and Savior. Yes, it had been a wonderful week!

The Stevens children had helped as planned, and all of them felt that they had learned as much as the children they had helped teach. Even though it had been hard work, they definitely wanted to help again next year!

"I would like to give a special thank you to Sean and Madelyn Stevens and their children for the refreshments tonight. Their children, Charlie, Charlotte, Hairo, and Natalia, have all worked tirelessly this week. I honestly don't know how I could have done it without them! Thank you, children, so very much! Let's give the Stevens family a hand," Mrs. Andrews announced from the front of the church dining room. Everyone stood to their feet, clapping and smiling at the Stevens family, who smiled back.

"Now, for some more serious business," Mrs. Andrews continued. "We are going to take a free-will offering tonight in order to start raising the funds for our Christmas outreach program. This program will consist of a two-day outreach to the community and the surrounding areas. We would like to raise enough money to 'adopt' five families in-need for Christmas. These families will be receiving a food basket full of items for Christmas dinner, gifts for each family member, and a $100 gift card to our local grocery store. We will also be serving Christmas dinner for those in need, right here at our church, and we will be making three dozen care packages for the residents at Memory-Care Residence. The whole program will come to a close on Christmas night, with a Christmas carol sing-along and a wonderful presentation by the Peace River Homeschool Co-op. Madelyn Stevens and Yolanda Rand will be leading the homeschool co-op presentation that evening, so if you would like more information about that, please talk to one of them. Thank you, everyone, for coming tonight and for helping support our outreach efforts. Let's close our evening in prayer..."

"Dad, do you know how much money we raised for the Christmas outreach program?" Charlie asked.

"I think it was $268.75, Charlie," his dad replied. "We need to raise about $2,000 more to be able to do all of the outreach projects we have planned."

"I know! Hairo, Natty, Charlotte, and I are going to have a lemonade stand after school hours, for the whole month of September! All of the money we make is going to go for the outreach project. Mom said that we can use those two big cans of lemonade mix we've had in our pantry since this spring. She said it needs to be used anyway before it expires. How much money do you think we can make on our lemonade stand, Dad?" Charlie asked excitedly.

"Well, I don't know, kiddo, but, you know, God honors a giving heart. We will make the lemonade, and then trust Him to make everybody thirsty, okay?" Dad responded with a twinkle in his eyes.

Name________________________________

Exercise 1 Day 26

Copywork

In decimal place value, the place to the right of the decimal is the tenths place.

The second place to the right of a decimal is the hundredths place. We write the worth of a quarter as \$.25 because it is $\frac{25}{100}$ of a dollar.

When we add or subtract decimals, we need to line up the decimal points.

0.3 is read three tenths

0.03 is read three hundredths

0.6 is read six tenths

0.06 is read six hundredths

Name______________________________

Exercise 2 Day 27

Solve

4.7 + 0.2 =

5.2 + 1.4 =

14.23 + 1.3 =

$$\begin{array}{r} \$30.91 \\ -\ 19.32 \\ \hline \end{array}$$

$$\begin{array}{r} \$260.95 \\ -\ 216.20 \\ \hline \end{array}$$

$$\begin{array}{r} \$460.00 \\ -\ 15.63 \\ \hline \end{array}$$

Write these as fractions and decimals.

- ☐ eight hundredths
- ☐ eighty-three hundredths
- ☐ twenty-one hundredths
- ☐ sixty hundredths
- ☐ fifty-three hundredths
- ☐ six hundredths

Name____________________________

Exercise 3

Day 28

Copywork

Fractions, decimals, and percents are three ways to name part of a whole. All three have numerators and denominators.

$\frac{50}{100}$ shows 50 parts of 100.
The decimal 0.50 is read 50 hundredths and shows 50 parts of 100.
Percent means hundredths, so 50% also means 50 parts of 100.

Solve

Use your Fraction/Decimal/Percent Chart to show these fractions as decimals and percents.

- ☐ $\frac{36}{100}$
- ☐ $\frac{12}{100}$
- ☐ $\frac{67}{100}$
- ☐ $\frac{86}{100}$
- ☐ $\frac{34}{100}$
- ☐ $\frac{87}{100}$
- ☐ $\frac{5}{100}$
- ☐ $\frac{52}{100}$

Name________________________________

Solve

Write each amount as a decimal, fraction, and percent. The first one is done for you.

$.50	________	________
$\frac{50}{100}$	________	________
50%	________	________

Copywork

I dollar (whole) has 100 cents (parts).
I whole dollar is $\frac{100}{100}$.
I whole dollar is 100%

____

____

____

Solve

On your Fraction/Decimal/Percent Chart use a washable marker to do the following exercise. Show these fractions as decimals and percents on your chart. The first is done for you.

- ☐ $\frac{50}{100}$
- ☐ 0.67
- ☐ 0.78
- ☐ 80%
- ☐ 0.20
- ☐ $\frac{75}{100}$
- ☐ 82%

What it looks like...	Fractional	Decimal	Percent
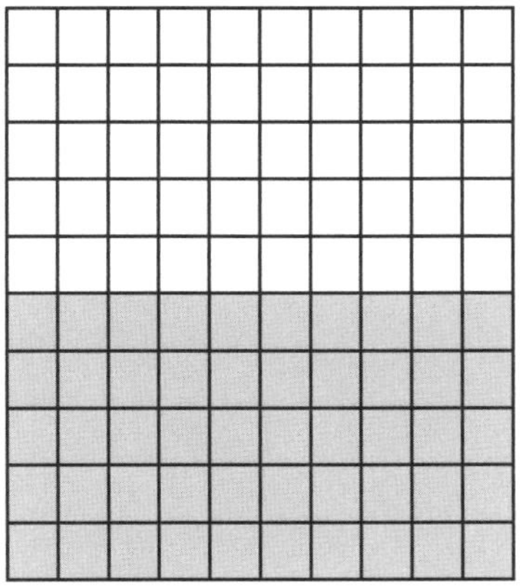	$\frac{50}{100}$	.50	50%

Name________________________________

☐ Narrate to your teacher everything you know about decimals.

☐ Optional: practice counting money.

☐ Write down combinations of coins you used to make this amount: $1.83.

Grocery Shopping

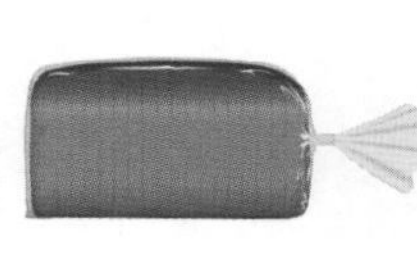
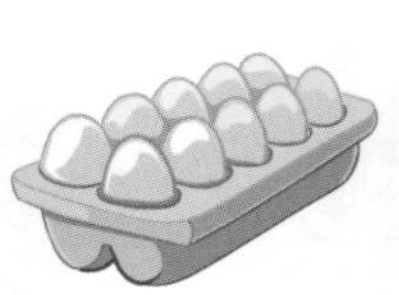

milk (gallon)	bread (loaf)	eggs (dozen)	syrup	butter	blueberries
$3.89	$2.76	$1.69	$.99	$2.99	$4.49

Make a shopping list for a meal you want to make for your family. You have $35.00 to spend. There are 8 people in your family. Make sure you buy enough!

Write your total amount spent: ____________.

What is your change?

10, 100, 1,000 (multiplying/dividing) Lesson 7

"Mom, I'm so tired! Can we just take it easy today?" Natty asked her mom, punctuating her question with a yawn. The children sat around the kitchen table, eating breakfast, and talking about VBS. It had been a wonderful experience for all of them, but they had to admit, they were exhausted from their week of hard work.

"Actually, Natty, we are going to take it kind of easy today and tomorrow," Maddie Stevens replied, smiling at her daughter. "I have a pretty laid-back school plan for you all. Today, we are going to do our Bible study, followed by one chapter from our read aloud book, one math lesson, and one language lesson. We are not going to start a new spelling list this week because we only have two days left. If you kids want to stay comfy in your jammies today, that's fine with me," she said. "In fact, I'll just read our Bible story here at the table while you children finish up your breakfast, okay?"

The children all nodded sleepily in response while Mom went to fetch her book basket.

"Today, our story is about how Jesus multiplied a small amount of food to make enough for 5,000 men, who also had their families with them. Here it is in the book of Matthew, in chapter 14, verses 13 through 21...

When Jesus heard of it, he departed thence by ship into a desert place apart: and when the people had heard thereof, they followed him on foot out of the cities.

And Jesus went forth, and saw a great multitude, and was moved with compassion toward them, and he healed their sick.

And when it was evening, his disciples came to him, saying, This is a desert place, and the time is now past; send the multitude away, that they may go into the villages, and buy themselves victuals.

But Jesus said unto them, They need not depart; give ye them to eat.

And they say unto him, We have here but five loaves, and two fishes.

He said, Bring them hither to me.

And he commanded the multitude to sit down on the grass, and took the five loaves, and the two fishes, and looking up to heaven, he blessed, and brake, and gave the loaves to his disciples, and the disciples to the multitude.

And they did all eat, and were filled: and they took up of the fragments that remained twelve baskets full.

And they that had eaten were about five thousand men, beside women and children. (KJV)

"See I TOLD you the answer to all of life's problems is MATH!" Charlie exclaimed as Mom finished reading the story. All of the children had become so interested in the Bible story that they were sitting up quite alert now.

Mom smiled at her son. "Yes, Charlie, I knew you would like this story. I actually chose this story about Jesus multiplying the food for the crowd, because it goes so well with what we are learning in our math lesson today. Multiplication is a very useful concept in life. Jesus used it in our story to feed thousands and thousands of people, who had come to hear Him speak and to have their sickness healed. Today, I'm going to show you a simple way to multiply any number by 10, 100, or even, 1,000."

The children went to get their school books for the day. Although the family had a new room for all of their school materials, the children preferred to sit together around the kitchen table. It was easier to do projects and play games together, and of course, the smells coming from the oven were always heartwarming!

Name________________________________

Exercise 1 Day 31

Let's Practice a New Concept!

We have learned the 10s multiplication table. You have probably noticed that each of the 10s facts ends in zero. When we multiply any number by 10, we simply add a zero. When we multiply any number by 100, we simply add two zeros. When we multiply any number by 1,000, we simply add three zeros.

Example:

2 × 10 = 20	6 × 10 = 60	9 × 10 = 90
2 × 100 = 200	6 × 100 = 600	9 × 100 = 900
2 × 1,000 = 2,000	6 × 1,000 = 6,000	9 × 1,000 = 9,000

Here is another way of showing this type of problem:

$$\begin{array}{r} 21 \\ \times\ 100 \\ \hline 2{,}100 \end{array}$$

This is called "letting the zeros hang."

$$\begin{array}{r} 126{,} \\ \times\ 1{,}000 \\ \hline 126{,}000 \end{array}$$

Now you try!

x	10	100	1,000	In this space, use the "hanging zero" method to show one of these.
4				
8				
22				
30				
126				

Math Review!

$$\begin{array}{r} 852 \\ 514 \\ +\ 699 \\ \hline \end{array} \qquad \begin{array}{r} 390 \\ 354 \\ +\ 42 \\ \hline \end{array} \qquad \begin{array}{r} 8{,}000 \\ -\ 3{,}816 \\ \hline \end{array} \qquad \begin{array}{r} 75 \\ 45 \\ 23 \\ +\ 41 \\ \hline \end{array}$$

Name______________________________

Exercise 2 Day 32

Review

We can multiply even larger numbers by simply following the same rule we learned in Exercise 1.
Look at these!

124,456 × 10 = 1,244,560
52,620 × 100 = 5,262,000

Reminder! When writing BIG numbers, we place commas every three digits starting at the right side.

Now you try!

×	10	100	1,000
5,123			
77,023			
99,000			
6,010			
153,724			

When multiplying any number starting with 1 and followed by ALL zeros, we simply count the zeros and add that many them to the number we are multiplying by.

Look at these!

45 × 10,000 = 450,000
45 × 100,000 = 4,500,000
45 × 1,000,000 = 45,000,000

Now you try!

×	10,000	100,000	1,000,000
239			
56			
22			
146			
600			

Name_______________________________

Exercise 2 Day 32

Mixed Review!

Charlotte wanted to know the average amount of raisins in each bar on the cookie sheet. There were 9 bars on the pan. She counted the following number of raisins: 10, 8, 12, 4, 7, 3, 9, 7, and 12. What was the average amount of raisins per bar?

Measurements for copywork:

1000 meters = 1 kilometer

____

1 kilogram = 1000 grams

____

100 centimeters = 1 meter

____

Name________________________________

Exercise 3

Day 33

Concept Practice

Let's build on this concept again...

What happens when we want to multiply a number by more than one group of 10?

Look at these and tell your teacher the pattern.

3 × 3 = 9	4 × 2 = 8
3 × 30 = 90	4 × 20 = 80
3 × 300 = 900	4 × 200 = 800
3 × 3,000 = 9,000	4 × 2,000 = 8,000

Now you try!

2 × 3 = 6	2 × 2 = 4	4 × 3 = 12
2 × 30 =	2 × 20 =	4 × 30 =
2 × 300 =	2 × 200 =	4 × 300 =
2 × 3,000 =	2 × 2,000 =	4 × 3,000 =

Now, let's reverse the multiplication problems above to make them division problems. Pay special attention to any patterns you see. Narrate to your teacher. Write them on the lines below.

6 ÷ 3 = 2	4 ÷ 2 = 2	12 ÷ 3 = 4
______________	______________	120 ÷ 30 = 4
______________	______________	______________
______________	______________	______________

Name________________________________

Exercise 3 Day 33

Review!

Since there are 2 cups in one pint, we divide by 2 to convert cups (the smaller measurement) into pints (the larger measurement).

Solve these.

20 cups = ______ pints (20 ÷ 2)

16 cups = ______ pints (16 ÷ 2)

12 cups = ______ pints (12 ÷ 2)

18 cups = ______ pints (18 ÷ 2)

10 cups = ______ pints (10 ÷ 2)

6 cups = ______ pints (6 ÷ 2)

Solve and match with the problems that show the inverse operation with division.

2 × 3 =	15 ÷ 3 =
4 × 10 =	6 ÷ 2 =
3 × 5 =	40 ÷ 4 =
6 × 3 =	18 ÷ 3 =
7 × 3 =	21 ÷ 7 =
4 × 3 =	12 ÷ 3 =
3 × 3 =	20 ÷ 2 =
9 × 3 =	27 ÷ 3 =
2 × 10 =	9 ÷ 3 =

Solve and check.

5 ⟌ 5,005

4 ⟌ 600

Name________________________________

Exercise 4 Day 34

Let's Practice!

2 × 8 = 16

2 × 80 =

2 × 800 =

2 × 8,000 =

5 × 3 = 15

5 × 30 =

5 × 300 =

5 × 3,000 =

Now write the division problems for each of the above problems in the space below.

16 ÷ 2 = 8

____

____

____

15 ÷ 5 = 3

____

____

____

Review!

8	2	4	0

5	3	5	7

4	8	1	3	6

Name________________________________

Exercise 5 Day 35

Copywork

1 kilogram (kg) = 1000 grams (g)
A gram is much smaller than an ounce.
(An average sized paper clip weighs about a gram.)
A kilogram is larger than a pound.

____

____

____

____

____

Measure and draw from the ★.

6 cm ★

$2\frac{1}{4}$ inches ★

$4\frac{3}{4}$ inches ★

$10\frac{1}{2}$ cm ★

Circle the bigger one in each group.

ton or ounce	inch or foot	yard or foot
foot or mile	quart or peck	week or day

Name____________________________

Exercise 5 Day 35

Puzzle Time.

Sudoku is a very popular type of math puzzle! It has varying designs but it is usually seen in a 9 x 9 grid.

The puzzle below features a 9 x 9 box (the first row of blocks = 9 and the first column of blocks = 9) divided into three 3 x 3 grids. The game requires the player to use the numbers 1–9 only one time per 3 x 3 square, on each column, and each row. So when you read the numbers by row or by column or within the 3 x 3 squares, the numbers 1–9 appear only once.

See if you can solve the 3 x 3 square in the center of the puzzle. (**Hint:** Look at the numbers that already exist in the rows that are missing a number. Write down the missing numbers for each row and column. Now, compare those numbers to the numbers that already are either in the 3 x 3 square, row, or column. Then see how you can place the missing numbers and not repeat numbers 1–9 in the 3 x 3 area, the column, or the row.) It's a little hard at first, but remember this is a fun way to learn! (If you're not sure what to do, ask your teacher for help.)

3 x 3 = 9 Rows

3 x 3 = 9 Columns

8	7	6	5	4	3	1	9	2
5	4	3	2	1	9	7	6	8
2	1	9	8	7	6	4	3	5
1	9	8				3	2	4
4	3	2	1		8	6	5	7
7	6	5				9	8	1
3	2	1	9	8	7	5	4	6
6	5	4	3	2	1	8	7	9
9	8	7	6	5	4	2	1	3

Introduction to 2-Digit Divisors

Lesson 8

"The boys' responsibilities would be to help out around the shop in any way I need, sort and organize new stock as it comes in on the truck each Thursday afternoon, and clean out an old garage behind the shop. I'm not sure exactly what is in that old garage, because it was full of junk when I bought the place fifteen years ago. I've been intending to deal with the mess for years, but I've always been too busy to get to it. I am willing to pay the boys $5 an hour to work at my shop and help me get some odd jobs done. Do you think they would be interested?" Mr. Smith asked. He had approached Dad after church to ask about offering Charlie and Hairo a short-term, after-school-hours job.

"I'm sure the boys would be very willing to help you out, Mr. Smith," Dad said and glanced at Mom, who was standing next to him. She nodded in agreement, and it was settled. The boys would start tomorrow.

Charlie and Hairo were so excited! When they arrived home after church, they sat down to figure out how much money they would be making. If they were going to make $5 an hour, three hours a day, five days a week, for ten weeks. The boys scribbled away with looks of concentration — $750 each!

"Wow! That's a lot of money!" Charlie whooped.

"That's more money than I have ever had," Hairo commented with big eyes.

"Well boys, it looks like we are going to have to do a crash course of personal finance!" Dad said looking at the boys' figures on the paper. "That's way too much money to just have laying around. You don't want to just spend it foolishly! You will be working hard for your money, and you want to be wise with it. Besides, I think it's about time for you young men to know what God says about money too. When you have money, there is responsibility that comes with it." The boys quieted down and looked up at Dad. They could tell he was being serious.

"Dad, do you think Hairo and I could open our own bank accounts?" Charlie stood tall to show that he was definitely grown up enough for this big step.

"I don't know, Charlie, that's something that Mom and I need to talk about first. We will talk about it tonight — I promise. Then I will let you two know what we decide, okay?" Dad smiled and put his hands on his sons' shoulders. The boys eyes were serious now, and they both nodded.

"Charlie, I feel really grown-up, don't you?" Hairo commented. "Having a job, and maybe even a bank account... Well, it's like we are becoming young men overnight!"

“Yeah, I know what you mean, Hairo,” Charlie’s usually teasing eyes were serious. “This is really a big step for us. Dad said that Mr. Smith chose us out of all of the boys at church, because he believes we have been taught to be responsible. Hairo, when we are working at the shop, we need to remember to be as responsible and mature as possible. Auto shops can be dangerous places, with lots of expensive tools and equipment. Remember last year, when we were playing ball near the car when Dad had it up on the jack?” Now both boys had serious expressions.

“Oh boy. Do I ever! You threw the ball too close to the car, and I jumped to catch it. But instead of catching the ball, I lost my balance and hit the car. It’s a good thing Dad was able to get out from under the car as it came crashing down off of the jack! That would have been horrible!” Hairo’s eyes looked a little watery. He had experienced nightmares for a month after that incident.

“Yup. We are going to have be super careful and responsible on our new job. Working in an auto shop is a man’s work, so we’re going to have to be men. No little boy stuff and foolin’ around, Hairo. If Mr. Smith is willing to trust us with such a potentially hazardous job, then we are going to be trustworthy. Period,” Charlie said.

“Ok boys, this is the row of bins for these boxes on this pallet. You’ll have to carefully match the serial numbers...here...to the numbers on the sides of the bins...there...,” Mr. Smith explained to the boys as they stood between two pallets of boxes, stacked higher than the boys’ heads. “Then this pallet, here, has all of the alternators and starters that came in this morning. These need to be taken out of the packing boxes, their serial numbers checked, and the alternators placed into this corner shelf, and the starters on this shelf over here. Now, it’s extremely important for you to check the numbers, put them in the right place, and then mark it off on this invoice. This is a big shipment - about 345 auto parts. Do you think you can handle it?” Mr. Smith asked with a concerned look. Messed up inventory was one thing he couldn’t have in his auto shop; it slowed down the operation and made his customers unhappy.

“You bet, Mr. Smith. You don’t have to worry about a thing,” Charlie stood tall. He and Hairo were ready for this challenge! They looked up at the stack of boxed auto parts and then at the row of bins and shelves. Charlie saw it as a hands-on division problem, and his eyes began to sparkle.

“You know, Charlie, you were right, this is a man-sized job!” Hairo’s dark eyes gleamed. “Ok, let’s do this thing!” The boys rolled up their sleeves and set to work.

Rounding

Round each of the following numbers. Explain the steps to your teacher.

To the nearest 10.

27	20 or 30
12	10 or 20
76	70 or 80

To the nearest 100.

268	200 or 300
482	400 or 500
822	800 or 900

To the nearest 1,000.

4,200	4,000 or 5,000
3,015	3,000 or 4,000

Now let's add the concept of estimation. Try rounding the next problem in your head using the same steps.

```
  421  rounds to ________                    25
+ 246  rounds to ________                  + 49
   estimated sum: ________    estimated sum: ________
```

Let's Practice a New Concept!

Remember, estimation is simply deciding approximately what the answer will be.

Study the example below and then try a few problems on your own. This example shows a multiplication problem with one large factor (303) and one smaller factor (4).

actual	estimate
303 × 4 = 1,212	300 × 4 = 1,200

Steps to think through:

1. Round the top (larger) factor.
2. Multiply

Name________________________________

Your Turn!

In the space below, estimate the following problem, then work the actual problem. Compare the answers.

actual

$$\begin{array}{r} 632 \\ \times\ 6 \\ \hline \end{array}$$

estimate

This example shows a division problem. We estimate the dividend and work the problem.

actual

	1	0	7
3	3	2	1
-	3	↓	
		2	
	-	0	
		2	1
	-	2	1
			0

→

estimate

	1	0	0
3	3	0	0

Steps to think through:

1. Round the dividend.
2. Divide!

actual

5	2	1	0

estimate

Name ________________________________

Exercise 2 Day 37

Let's Practice a New Concept!

When we divide, we are taking a large group and breaking it into smaller groups. Up until now we have divided with a single digit divisor.

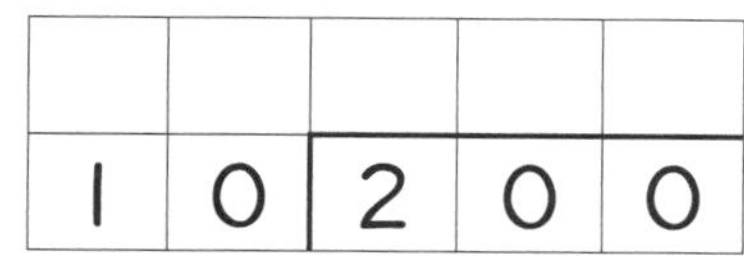

?

To divide with a two digit divisor, we have to use some mental math. For instance, in this problem, we look at the dividend (200), and we ask ourselves, can 10 (the divisor) divide into 2? No.

			2	
1	0	2	0	0

THINK: 10 x 2

We know that 20 ÷ 10 = 2, so we write the 2 above the ten's place in 200.

			2	0
1	0	2	0	0
	-	2	0	
		0	0	
		-	0	
			0	

Now we continue on with the rest of the problem, using the same steps of division we have learned.

Now you try!

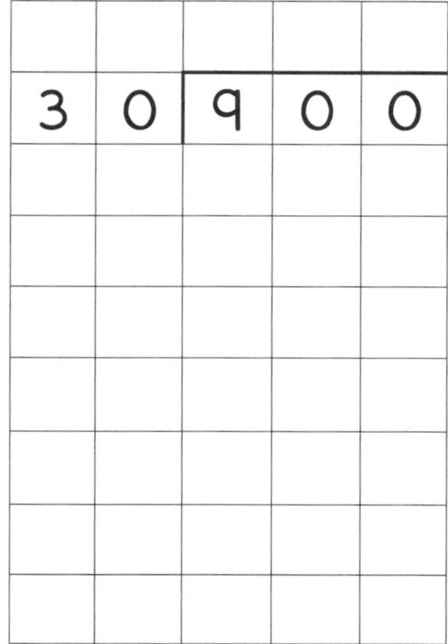

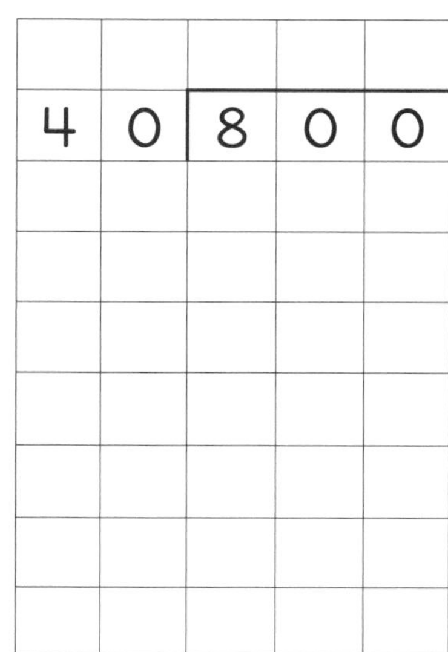

2	0	6	0	0

Name______________________________

Estimate

Look back to the example in Exercise 1 if you need help.

actual estimate

$$\begin{array}{r} 312 \\ \times\ 4 \\ \hline \end{array}$$

actual estimate

$$\begin{array}{r} 467 \\ \times\ 6 \\ \hline \end{array}$$

actual estimate

2	5	3	0

Name_______________________________

Let's Build on This Concept

We have learned that sometimes we have a remainder when we divide. We follow the same process when we have a two digit divisor.

Study this example. Notice that it follows the same process you learned in Exercise 2.

			3	0	R.4
1	0	3	0	4	
	-	3	0	↓	
			0	4	
			-	0	
				4	

check:

30	quotient
x 10	divisor
300	
+ 4	remainder
304	dividend

Remember, when you have a two digit divisor, you will always use at least the first two digits of the dividend.

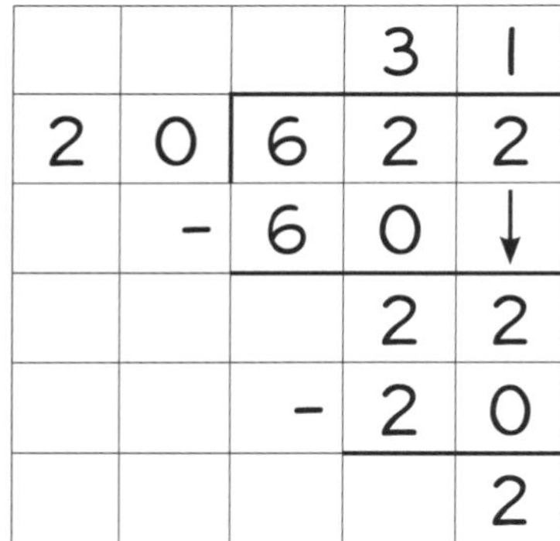

			3	1	R.2
2	0	6	2	2	
	-	6	0	↓	
			2	2	
		-	2	0	
				2	

In this problem, our first step is dividing 20 into 62. We round 62 to 60. Now comes the mental math exercise! We know there are 3 groups of 20 in 60 because 3 x 20 = 60 so, 60 ÷ 20 = 3. Next, we place the 3 in the ten's place of our dividend.

This shows an example of trial and error. The problem on the left shows how estimation can produce an incorrect answer.

			3	
2	0	5	7	2
	-	6	0	

INCORRECT

			2	8	R.12
2	0	5	7	2	
	-	4	0	↓	
		1	7	2	
	-	1	6	0	
			1	2	

CORRECT

Name________________________________

Now You Try

Solve and check each problem:

2	0	4	4	0

check:

3	0	6	7	2

check:

5	0	9	2	5

check:

4	0	7	8	0

check:

Name________________________________

Exercise 4

Solve

Solve and check each problem:

5	5	1	0

check:

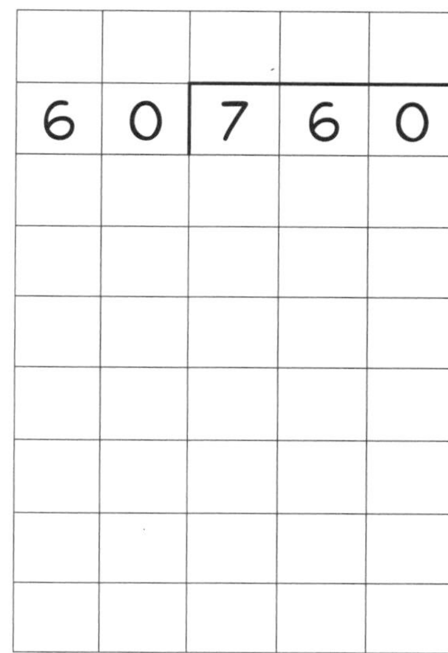

check:

9	2	7	0

check:

7	0	8	0	0

check:

actual

$$\begin{array}{r} 758 \\ \times\ 4 \\ \hline \end{array}$$

estimate

Narrate to your teacher what you have learned this week.

Name________________________________

Puzzle Time.

The **Sudoku** puzzle below features a 9 x 9 box (the first row of blocks = 9 and the first column of blocks = 9) divided into three 3 x 3 grids. The game requires the player to use the numbers 1–9 only one time per 3 x 3 square, on each column, and each row. So when you read the numbers by row or by column or within the 3 x 3 squares, the numbers 1–9 appear only once.

See if you can solve the 3 x 3 squares in the center of the puzzle. Steps: 1. Look at the numbers that already exist in the rows that are missing a number. 2. Write down the missing numbers for each row and column. 3. Compare those numbers to the numbers that already are either in the 3 x 3 square, row, or column. 4. See how you can place the missing numbers and not repeat numbers 1–9 in the 3 x 3 area, the column, or the row.) 5. If you're not sure what to do, ask your teacher for help.

2	1	9	5	4	3	6	7	8
5	4	3	8	7	6	9	1	2
8	7	6	2	1	9	3	4	5
4	3	2	7					1
7		5			8	2		4
1						5	6	7
3	2	1	6	5	4	7	8	9
6	5	4	9	8	7	1	2	3
9	8	7	3	2	1	4	5	6

More Work with Division

Lesson 9

The boys were getting used to their job. It had been quite a learning curve, but they had become familiar with the process of helping stock the inventory, and helping customers find items like tire patches, windshield wiper blades, and oil filters. Charlie and Hairo both felt like they had learned a lot and had become more mature.

Today, Mr. Smith was going to teach them how to change the oil in a car, and if there was time, a flat tire. The boys were excited to learn this new skill. After all, it was important for them to know how to care for their cars when they were older, and like Dad always said, "There's no time like the present to learn!"

"Boys, come over here and watch me," Mr. Smith instructed. He had grown quite fond of these two boys. They had proven to be wonderful helpers around the shop, and he knew that he would miss them when the ten weeks were over. The boys came to stand near the car that needed an oil change.

"Mr. Smith, can I take notes while you show us how to change the oil?" Hairo asked. "I remember things much better if I write them down." Mr. Smith nodded and smiled at Hairo.

"You go right ahead, son. Ok, the first step in changing the oil..."

"This is what I wrote down, Mom!" Hairo's eyes sparkled as he showed her his notes. He loved working at the auto shop! In fact, he had decided that, when he grew up, he wanted to own and run his own auto mechanics shop. He loved everything about it... the way the tools worked, the way the oil smelled, the way the engines ran... Everything was so interesting!

Charlie enjoyed the auto shop work, too, but not as much as Hairo. Charlie had dreams of becoming an architect when he grew up, or maybe an engineer. He knew he wanted to build stuff; he just wasn't sure if that was going to be buildings or amusement park rides.

"Charlie, did you take any notes?" Mom's voice brought Charlie back to the present.

"No, Mom, but I do remember what Mr. Smith said when he showed us how to change a tire," Charlie answered with a twinkle in his eye. "It's really not hard at all. The biggest thing is to remember to tighten the lug nuts, but not to put them on so hard that you can't get them off with the tire-iron if you have a flat while you are out driving. I've learned that most of the maintenance-type stuff you do on a car is just common sense."

Maddie Stevens looked at this son of hers and thought about how much he was like her husband — always wanting a challenge and always building something!

"Mom," Charlie added with a thoughtful expression in his blue eyes, "do you think Mr. Smith knows how to build an engine? I mean from scratch? Now, that's something that I would like to know!"

"I don't know, Charlie; why don't you ask him?" Mom answered and smiled. "You two need to go wash up for dinner. We can talk about this more later, okay?"

Both of the boys nodded and went to the bathroom to scrub the grease from under their finger nails. Neither of them said much — they were lost in their own world of thoughts.

"Boys, I'm thinking this evening would be a good time to start our personal finance course. I see you both brought home your first paycheck this afternoon. Mom and I have decided that you both may open your own savings account, so I think we need to learn a little about how to handle money. We will start right after dinner; the girls will help Mom with the supper clean-up so we can get right at it," Sean Stevens said as he looked across the table at the boys.

"Okay, Dad!" they answered together.

Teacher

This would be a great time to introduce money management to your student(s). You can find great teaching tools at crosswalk.com and daveramsey.com.

Name______________________________

Exercise 1 Day 41

Let's Practice a New Concept!

Sometimes we need to divide amounts of money. When dividing money by a whole number (one without a decimal), we follow the same division rules. However, before beginning to divide, we bring the $ and the decimal point straight up, as illustrated below.

	$	5.	1	5
5	$2	5.	7	5
-	2	5	↓	↓
		0	7	
		-	5	↓
			2	5
		-	2	5
				0

Now you try!

3	$6	0.	0	3

1	0	$8	0	6.	3	0

Name________________________________

Exercise 1

Day 41

Mixed Review!

x	10	100	1,000
42			
861			
7			

In this space, use the "hanging zero" method to show all the problems in the table above.

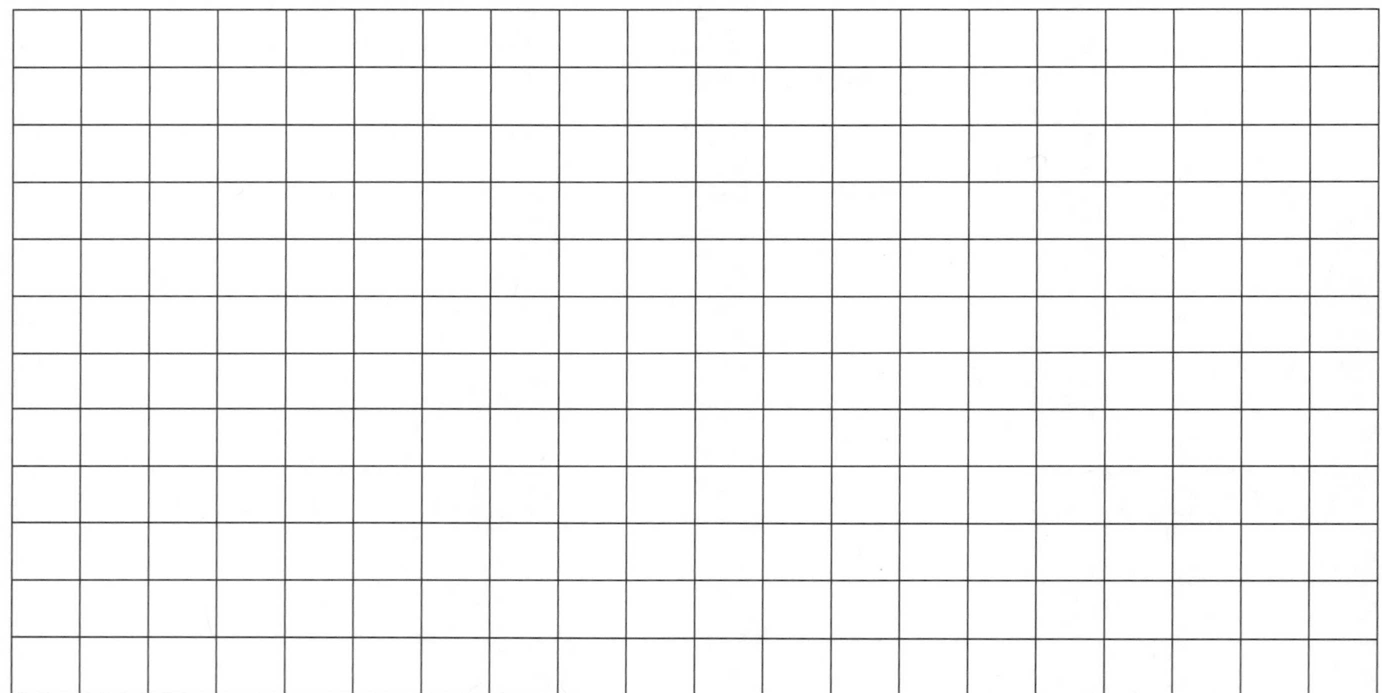

Round to the nearest 10.

25 20 or 30

16 10 or 20

34 30 or 40

Round to the nearest 100.

245 200 or 300

569 500 or 600

890 800 or 900

Round to the nearest 1,000.

4,367 4,000 or 5,000

3,789 3,000 or 4,000

Name______________________________

Exercise 2 Day 42

Copywork

When we divide, we are taking a large group and breaking it into smaller groups. To divide with a two digit divisor, we have to use some mental math. When you have a two digit divisor, you will always use at least the first two digits of the dividend.

____

____

____

____

____

____

____

Narrate to your teacher what you are doing, as you work through the problems.

2	1	8	5	0	

$$\begin{array}{r} 831 \\ 386 \\ +\ 702 \\ \hline \end{array} \qquad \begin{array}{r} 7{,}015 \\ -\ 2{,}649 \\ \hline \end{array} \qquad \begin{array}{r} 518 \\ \times\ 14 \\ \hline \end{array}$$

Name______________________________ **Exercise 3** Day 43

Copywork of a New Concept!

In a division problem, if both the divisor and the dividend end in a zero (or more than one zero), we can "cancel" the zero(s).

Study the examples below to understand this new concept. Then solve the rest of the problems.

1	Ø	1	0	Ø
	-	1		
		0	0	
	-	0	0	
			0	

		1	0	
8	Ø	8	0	Ø
	-	8		
		0	0	
	-	0	0	
			0	

			2	0		
1	Ø	Ø	2,	0	Ø	Ø
		-	2			
			0	0		
		-	0	0		
				0		

1	0	3	0	0

3	0	9	0	0

1	0	0	8,	0	0	0

Mixed Review

5	0	8	2	0

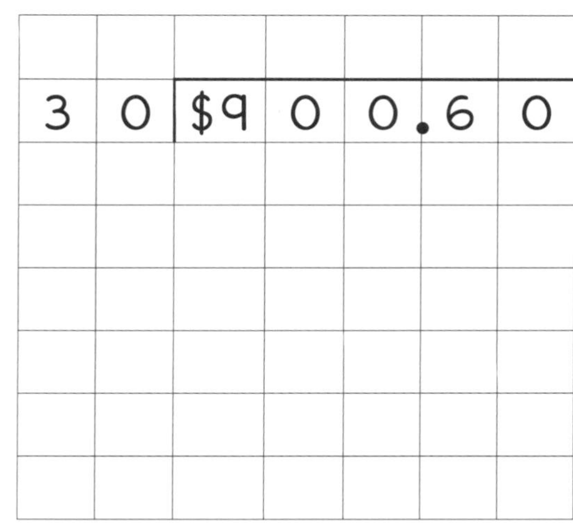

Read and Solve

Charlie and Hairo each received $125.00 in their paychecks. Dad and Mom told them that $12.50 (or 10% of $125.00 — you will learn more about this at a later time) should be set aside for a tithe to their church.

1. How much money did each boy have left?

2. Charlie decided to save $\frac{1}{2}$ of the remainder of his paycheck. How much did Charlie put in his checking account? How much does he have left?

3. Hairo decided to save $\frac{1}{3}$ of the remainder of his paycheck. How much did Hairo put in his checking account? How much does he have left?

4. Of their remaining amounts, Charlie and Hario wanted to save $25.00 each in an envelope towards buying a used go-cart. How much do they have left now?

5. How much money altogether do they have left for spending?

Name______________________________

Review Time!

Exercise 4

☐ Narrate how to multiply by 10s, 100s, and 1,000s

☐ Narrate how to round to the 1,000s place

☐ Estimate this problem and narrate to your teacher:
3,890 + 345 =

Exercise 5

☐ Solve and narrate to your teacher this problem:
887 ÷ 30 =

☐ Narrate the steps of dividing with money:
$36.12 ÷ 12 =

Three Ways of Division/ Remainders as Fractions

Lesson **10**

The garage doors creaked and sagged on their ancient hinges as Mr. Smith pulled them open for the boys. The inside of the old garage was dark and musty, with cobwebs hanging in thick strands from the ceiling. As their eyes adjusted to the dark interior of the building, the boys gasped in amazement! Every imaginable type of old lawn mower, obsolete farm tool, rotted wooden crate-type box, and ancient newspaper was piled to the ceiling, and all of it was covered in a layer of dust at least an inch thick.

"Whoa. I've never seen anything like this, Mr. Smith!" Charlie stood with his hands on his hips as he surveyed the contents of the building. "Is all of this stuff just junk, or is there anything valuable at all buried in here?" Both of the boys put their hands over their nose and mouth and started poking around in a box next to the door. Suddenly, Hairo sneezed several times in a row.

"I don't know, son," Mr. Smith answered. "I honestly don't know what's all in here. All I know is that it's all gotta come out. I got another notice from the city, last week, saying that I have until the end of October to clean up this back lot. They said it's been an eye-sore long enough! I'm not going to argue with them about it — I quite agree with them. Actually, Mrs. Smith has been after me for ten years to get it taken care of..." Mr. Smith's voice faded away, as he stood deep in thought, staring into the dark interior of the old garage. "I've ordered three dumpsters to haul away all of this junk — whatever it is! They should be delivered tomorrow morning. I've brought dust masks for you two to wear so you don't breathe the dust. Why don't you start in this corner and work from there? You can just start making separate piles of wood, plastic, and paper. Anything metal just put in these barrels over here. I can get some money for scrap metal, but all of the other junk can be put into the dumpsters when they come tomorrow."

The boys nodded and put on work gloves and the dust masks. Charlie started by pulling out a stack of wood crates full of old nuts, bolts, and screws, while Hairo attacked a tower of old newspapers taller than himself. The boys worked silently for a while, piling and sorting the junk, just as Mr. Smith had instructed.

Suddenly, Charlie stopped. "Hairo! Come look at this! What do you think this is?" Charlie yelled excitedly at his brother. Hairo came scampering over and bent down to see what Charlie was so excited about.

"I...I don't know! It kinda looks like a headlight of some kind," Hairo rubbed his hand across the round object. "Yes! That's what it is, Charlie!" he said. Now both boys started to pull junk away from the object, and little by little, they uncovered an old car! It had to be at least forty years old.

"Wow! This is so cool! Look, Hairo!" yelled Charlie as he shown a flashlight down into the interior of the old car. "It looks like it's in pretty good shape inside. Do you think we could get the door open? Come and help me try!"

Hairo came around the car next to Charlie, and together, they hauled on the door handle of the car. To their surprise the door opened! The inside of the car smelled like old leather, oil, and dust.

"What do you suppose Mr. Smith is going to do with this cool, old car?" Hairo's eyes shone with excitement. He ran his hand down the side of the car and over the rounded trunk. He had seen pictures of cars like this! This one was light blue and it had two doors. The headlights were round, and the bumper was chrome. Hairo was pretty sure that this was a Volkswagon Beetle.

"I don't know!" Charlie answered from the other side of the car. "You know, Hairo, this car isn't in that bad of shape. It has flat tires and it's really dirty, but other than that... It isn't even that rusty. We need to go tell Mr. Smith what we found!"

That evening at supper, the boys excitedly told the family the news. Mr. Smith had told them that they could have the old car if it was okay with their parents! Mom and Dad looked at each other, and both of them smiled a little and nodded. The children knew that their parents could communicate with their eyes, and the smile and nod meant that they agreed on something. The boys could keep the car.

"Wooooeeeeh!" Charlie and Hairo whooped together and high-fived each other. Their sisters looked at each other and giggled. Boys were so silly sometimes!

Name______________________________

Division Time!

There are three ways to show division. All of the following signs mean "divided by."

$\overline{)\quad}$ $\div$ $\frac{\quad}{\quad}$

All of the following are read: thirty divided by five.

$5\overline{)30}$ $30 \div 5$ $\frac{30}{5}$

Now you try!

Show the three ways of division in each of these problems.

1. nine divided by three

2. sixteen divided by two

3. eighty-eight divided by eleven

4. forty-five divided by nine

5. seventy-two divided by six

6. twenty-eight divided by seven

Name________________________________

Exercise 1 Day 46

Review!

x	1	2	3	4	5	6	7	8	9	10	11	12
1												
2												
3												
4												
5												
6												
7												
8												
9												
10												
11												
12												

Name______________________________

Exercise 2

Day 47

Quick Review!

Tell your teacher what a mixed number is.

Copywork

When reading mixed numbers, such as $2\frac{1}{2}$, we read the whole number first, then the word "and," lastly, the fraction.

New Concept

Writing remainders as fractions.

We can write the remainder of a division problem as a fraction. The remainder (in this problem, 1) becomes the numerator, and the divisor (in this problem, 8) becomes the denominator.

		5	$\frac{1}{8}$
8	4	1	
-	4	0	
		1	

Now you try!

$8\overline{)41}$ $3\overline{)91}$ $5\overline{)66}$

Mixed Review

Read these mixed numbers to your teacher.

$2\frac{1}{7}$ $4\frac{1}{3}$ $1\frac{1}{16}$ $7\frac{7}{8}$ $9\frac{4}{6}$

When we solve word problems, we notice the "clue word" that tell us what operation to use. Write add, subtract, multiply, or divide beside each of these "clue words."

in all ____________

have left ____________

times ____________

altogether ____________

share equally ____________

more than ____________

less ____________

both ____________

Name________________________________

More Practice

Write the remainders as fractions.

$3\overline{)49}$ $6\overline{)11}$ $9\overline{)20}$

Copywork!

There are three ways to show division.

Draw the three ways to show "divided by."

Solve.

$$610\frac{4}{9} + 518\frac{2}{9}$$

$$421\frac{9}{17} + 299\frac{6}{17}$$

$$57\frac{7}{12} - 43\frac{5}{12}$$

$$961\frac{8}{10} - 750\frac{6}{10}$$

Name______________________________

Copywork

A heptagon has 7 sides.

____

A rectangle has 4 sides.

____

A pentagon has 5 sides.

____

A triangle has 3 sides.

____

A hexagon has 6 sides.

____

An octagon has 8 sides.

____

A nonagon has 9 sides.

____

A square has 4 equal sides.

____

Name____________________________

Exercise 4

Day 49

Copywork

We can write the remainder of a division problem as a fraction. The remainder becomes the numerator, and the divisor becomes the denominator.

Mixed Review

Write the remainder as a fraction.

$$11\overline{)497}$$

Divide.

$$32\overline{)976}$$

Cancel your zeros and divide.

$$70\overline{)490}$$

Word Problems

1. Dad asked the boys how big Mr. Smith's garage was. The boys knew that it was 25 feet deep and 40 feet wide. They sat down to figure out the square footage of the garage. What should their answer be? Remember to label your answer in square feet. When you are finished completing the problem, read through the story problem again, circle the numbers you used, and underline the clue words and phrases.

2. What is the perimeter of the garage from story problem 1?

3. The boys came across 129 bent, rusty, old bike tire rims while cleaning out Mr. Smith's garage. Mr. Smith told them to divide them into piles of 12 each. How many piles of bent, rusty, old bike tire rims did they have? How many were left over? When you are finished completing the problem, read through the story problem again, circle the numbers you used, and underline the clue words and phrases.

Name________________________________

Exercise 5 Day 50

Mixed Review

Show the three ways of division in each of these problems.

six divided by two

thirty-six divided by six

two hundred twenty divided by ten

Solve

5 × 7 + 6 =

6 × 6 − 30 =

30 × 10 + 36 =

5 × 4 + 20 =

42 × 100 + 7 =

3 × 8 × 2 − 48 =

$$\begin{array}{r} 14 \\ \times\ 16 \\ \hline \end{array} \qquad \begin{array}{r} 42 \\ \times\ 8 \\ \hline \end{array} \qquad \begin{array}{r} 13 \\ \times\ 22 \\ \hline \end{array} \qquad 11\overline{)787}$$

Review!

Reminder:

A line goes on and on "forever" in both directions.

A segment is a section of a line.

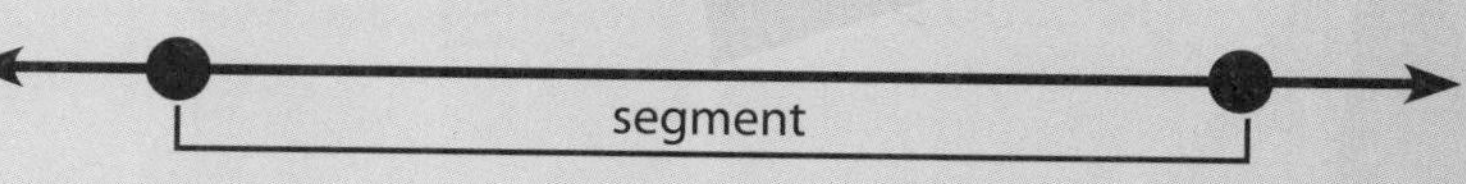

A ray has a starting point on one end and goes on "forever" on the other end.

Angles:

An obtuse angle is any angle which measures more than 90°.

An acute angle is any angle which measures less than 90°.

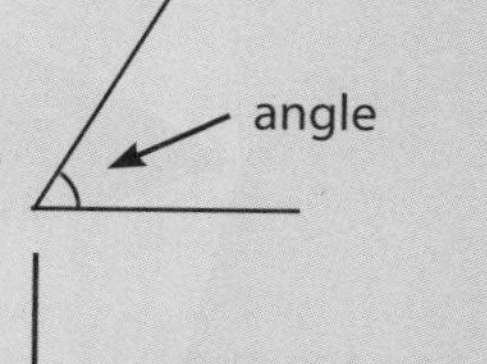

A right angle measures 90° and is shown by this symbol.

Area:

To find the area of a square:

side x side = square area

To find the area of a rectangle:
multiply the length by the width

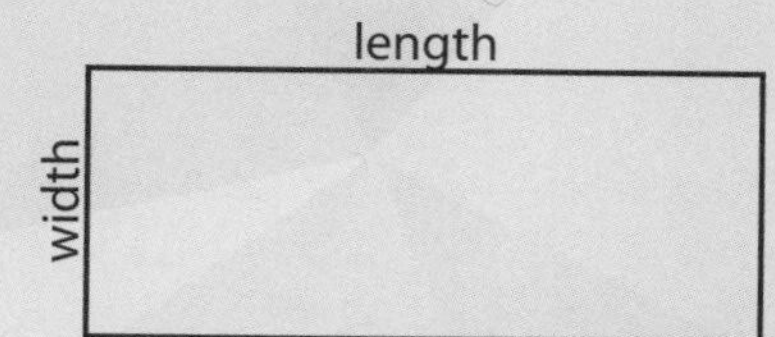

Perimeter:

Perimeter is the distance around a figure. A polygon is a figure made with straight sides. "Poly" is a prefix which means "many"; thus, a polygon is a shape with many straight sides. To figure out the perimeter, you just need to add up each side.

Name________________________________

Review Time

Copywork and show!

Lines that cross one another are called intersecting lines.

____

____

Show an example:

Intersecting lines that form right angles are called perpendicular lines.

____

____

Show an example:

Lines that never intersect and are the same distance apart are called parallel lines.

____

____

Show an example:

Name________________________________

Angle Review

With a blue colored pencil, draw a right angle on the protractor.

With a green colored pencil, draw an acute angle on the protractor.

With a yellow colored pencil, draw an obtuse angle on the protractor.

Narrate to your teacher what each one is.

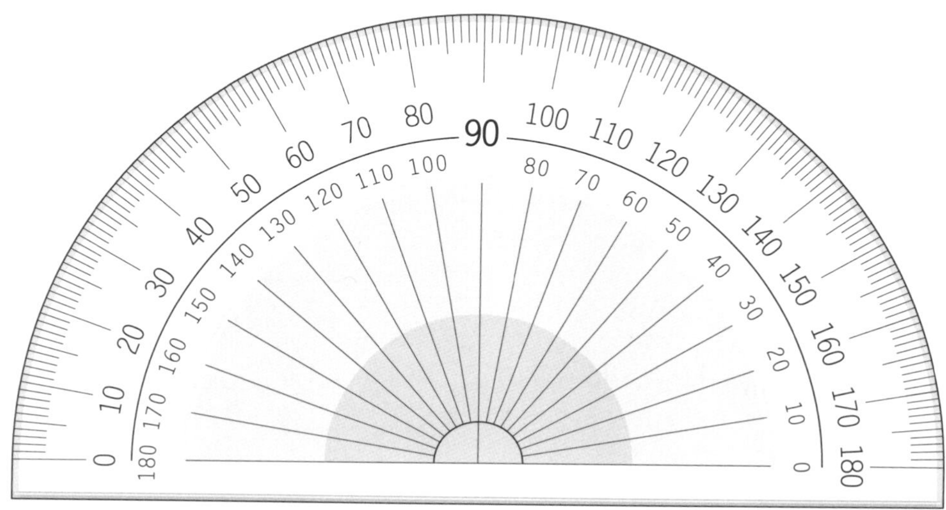

Mixed Division Review

Solve and check.

21 ⟌ 2,568

30 ⟌ 870

Name____________________________

Exercise 2 Day 52

Review Time

Circle the larger one in each group.

ton or ounce	inch or foot	yard or foot
foot or mile	quart or peck	week or day

Fill in the blanks.

________ feet = 1 mile

________ hours = 1 day

________ pounds = 1 ton

________ feet = 1 yard

________ cups = 1 pint

________ seconds = 1 minute

________ days = 1 year

________ pecks = 1 bushel

________ quarts = 1 peck

________ quarts = 1 gallon

________ items = 1 dozen

________ ounces = 1 pound

Write M for each metric unit of measurement and E for each English unit of measurement.

______ liter	______ pound	______ ton
______ yard	______ inch	______ meter
______ kilogram	______ ounce	______ quart
______ centimeter	______ foot	______ gram

Measure and draw starting at the ★.

$2\frac{1}{2}$ cm ★

$2\frac{1}{2}$ inches ★

Review.

68	721	89	923	463
x 22	x 34	x 11	x 45	x 23

Name______________________________

Exercise 3 Day 53

Review Time!

Copywork:

In decimal place value, the place to the right of the decimal is the tenths place.

The second place to the right of a decimal is the hundredths place.

When we add or subtract decimals, we need to line up the decimal points; this includes money problems. In division, we move the decimal point straight up into the answer.

0.3 is read three tenths, and 0.03 is read three hundredths.

Solve

$$\begin{array}{r} 52 \\ \times\ 48 \\ \hline \end{array} \qquad \begin{array}{r} 613 \\ \times\ 21 \\ \hline \end{array} \qquad \begin{array}{r} 82 \\ \times\ 10 \\ \hline \end{array} \qquad \begin{array}{r} 1{,}468 \\ \times\ 100 \\ \hline \end{array} \qquad \begin{array}{r} 32{,}052 \\ \times\ 1{,}000 \\ \hline \end{array}$$

Name______________________________

Exercise 4 Day 54

Review Time!

Copywork!

Fractions, decimals, and percents are three ways to name part of a whole.

1 dollar (whole) has 100 cents (parts).
1 whole dollar is $\frac{100}{100}$.
1 whole dollar is 100%

Let's Practice!

On your Fraction/Decimal/Percent Chart use a washable marker to do the following exercise. Show these fractions as decimals and percents on your chart. The first is done for you.

- ☑ $\frac{50}{100}$
- ☐ $\frac{20}{100}$
- ☐ $\frac{18}{100}$
- ☐ $\frac{5}{100}$
- ☐ $\frac{99}{100}$

What it looks like...	Fractional	Decimal	Percent
	$\frac{50}{100}$	.50	50%

Name________________________________

Exercise 4 Day 54

Review Time!

Write each amount as a decimal, fraction, and percent. The first one is done for you.

$.25

25%

____

____

____

____

____

____

Solve these.

$12\overline{)\$52.64}$

$$\begin{array}{r} 17 \\ \times\ 60 \\ \hline \end{array}$$

$$\begin{array}{r} 28 \\ \times\ 52 \\ \hline \end{array}$$

Name________________________________

Exercise 5 Day 55

Review Time!

Study the line graph below and answer the questions.

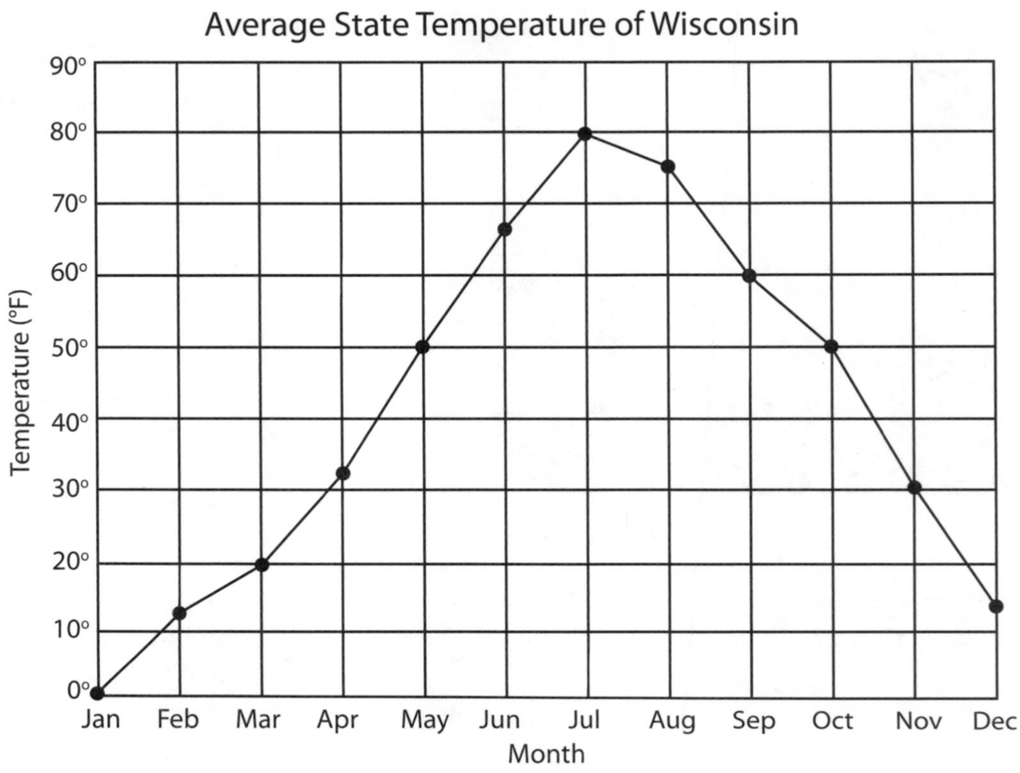

1. What is the title of this graph?
2. When was the average temperature the same?
3. What was the average temperature in March?
4. Which month had an average temperature of 65 degrees?
5. What was the difference in temperature between September and January?

Hands On!

On a separate sheet of paper, draw a right angle with two line segments measuring 4 inches and 3 inches, like this (not to scale) example:

This is a symbol for inches (″).

A
4″
B
3″
C

On your right angle, connect points A and C. Now measure the line segment that you just drew.

How long is it? _______

What is the perimeter of this triangle? ___________

Factoring

"Mom, do you think there is something that Natty and I could do like Charlie and Hairo?" Charlotte asked with her hands in the soapy dishwater. She had soap suds up to her elbows as she stood on the stool, scrubbing cookie sheets. She and Natty had made oatmeal raisin cookies for snack.

"I don't know Charlotte. Would you and Natty like to volunteer at the library? I heard Mrs. Drew saying that they are short on volunteers this fall. You wouldn't get paid for it, but it would be a nice opportunity for you!" Maddie Stevens answered thoughtfully.

"Oh yes! I know I would love to do that! I'll ask Natty, and if she wants to help, may we go today after school? Please?" Charlotte asked excitedly as she wiped her hands on the towel.

"Yes, that would be fine. Just make sure you both have finished your independent work first, okay?" her mom answered with a smile...

"We are going to head on down to the library now, Mom!" Charlotte called from the hallway. She and Natty had excitedly finished their school work, had their afternoon snack, and carefully brushed their hair. (Both of the girls were sporting a new hair-do, and they loved their trimmed bangs!)

"Ok, make sure you are home by 5:30 though!" their mother called back from the kitchen. "And both of you make sure you take a jacket!"

"We have them, Mom," they answered together. Linking arms, the girls skipped down the sidewalk and turned left down the street. Their house was only two blocks from the library, which meant they could go there by themselves.

"Mrs. Drew, we are here to sign up as library volunteers!" Natty said, smiling up at the tall lady behind the library desk. "Our mom says that we can volunteer after school, three days a week - just not Wednesdays because of Bible club that evening. Can you use our help?"

"Oh my, yes! You girls are an answer to my prayer! I've lost my helper, because Mrs. Snowden is finished working here with me - she's about to have her first baby, you know," Mrs. Drew whispered to the girls. Mrs. Drew always whispered - she had a lot of practice talking in her "library voice."

The girls nodded. They knew Mrs. Snowden was about to have her baby; Mom had just mentioned that this morning during prayer time.

"Mrs. Drew, can you show us how we can help?" Charlotte asked. Mrs. Drew tended to be a little absent minded, and sometimes had to be reminded what she was doing.

"Oh. Oh, yes, of course. Silly me," Mrs. Drew brought her attention back to the girls. "I was just thinking about my first baby..." The lady stood to her feet and came around the desk to the girls. "First," she instructed, "you two need to know about the Dewey Decimal System. Do either of you know anything about that? No? Well, ok, that is the best place to start..."

"Mrs. Drew told us about the Dewey Decimal System today, Mom!" Charlotte told her mom as she wiped off the kitchen table after supper. "She told us that it is like a big family tree, because it has branches like a tree." Charlotte giggled. Mrs. Drew was a very descriptive person and used rather flowery words. "Anyway, we learned about how each type of book in the library has its own numbers to tell us what branch it belongs to. It's still kinda confusing to me, but I know I'll get better as I practice. How 'bout you, Natty? Do you understand the Dewey Decimal System?" Charlotte asked her sister.

"Not really. But I'll get it," Natty answered. "Mom, what is the Dewey Decimal system for?" she asked her mother.

"Oh, I'm sure Mrs. Drew will tell you all about it!" their mom smiled. "But to put it simply, it's for organizing all of the books. In a way, it's similar to the charts you do in math. In fact, in some ways, it's similar to factoring, which is our next new concept in math. Do you think you girls are going to enjoy working at the library?" she asked them in a whisper.

"Yes!" they both whispered back.

Just for fun!

These are called "factor trees"! (This is one way to find factors. You will learn the other way in Exercise 1.)

```
   15            16               18              24
  /  \          /  \             /  \            /  \
 3 (x) 5       2 (x) 8          2 (x) 9         2 (x) 12
                    /  \             /  \            /  \
                   2 (x) 4          3 (x) 3         2 (x) 6
                        /  \                             /  \
                       2 (x) 2                          2 (x) 3
```

Name________________________________

Exercise 1 Day 56

New Concept!

Factors are all of the different numbers that divide evenly (without a remainder) into a number. Pairs of factors are two numbers that, when multiplied together, equal this number. Study these examples.

Example #1: Find the factors of 15.

Pairs of Factors	Factors
1 × 15	1, 3, 5, 15
3 × 5	
5 × 3	
15 × 1	

When we list the factors, we write each one only once, from least to greatest.

Example #2: Find the factors of 9.

Pairs of Factors	Factors
1 × 9	1, 3, 9
3 × 3	
9 × 1	

Now you try it!

Find the pairs of factors of each of these numbers and list them in order from least to greatest.

Pairs of Factors for 8	Factors
____________	
____________	____, ____, ____, ____
____________	
____________	

Pairs of Factors for 10	Factors
____________	
____________	____, ____, ____, ____
____________	
____________	

Name______________________________

Pairs of Factors for 7

____

____

Factors

_____, _____,

Pairs of Factors for 12

____

____

____

____

____

____

Factors

_____, _____, _____, _____, _____, _____

Review!

On Monday, Charlotte and Natty worked at their lemonade stand from 2:30 to 3:45 p.m. Then they worked at the library from 4:00 to 5:30 p.m. How long did they work on Monday?

Name________________________________

Practice the New Concept!

Complete the pairs of factors for these numbers.

18	20	35
1 × ____	1 × ____	1 × ____
2 × ____	2 × ____	5 × ____
3 × ____	4 × ____	7 × ____
6 × ____	5 × ____	35 × ____
9 × ____	10 × ____	
18 × ____	20 × ____	

Now list the factors for each of the numbers above.

18 ______________________________

20 ______________________________

35 ______________________________

Mixed Review!

Divide and write the remainders as fractions.

$21\overline{)840}$ $\qquad\qquad$ $15\overline{)313}$

Solve these mixed number problems.

$$\begin{array}{r} 203\frac{17}{19} \\ -\ 187\frac{9}{19} \\ \hline \end{array} \qquad\qquad \begin{array}{r} 87\frac{3}{8} \\ +\ 19\frac{2}{8} \\ \hline \end{array}$$

Name______________________________

Exercise 3 Day 58

Copywork of New Concept!

Factors are all of the different numbers that divide evenly (without a remainder) into a number. Pairs of factors are two numbers that, when multiplied together, equal this number.

____

____

____

____

____

More practice of the new concept!

Write the pairs of factors. **Note:** These numbers are called prime numbers. Their only factors are 1 and themselves.

5	3	7	11
________	________	________	________
________	________	________	________

Write any three factors for each of these numbers. **Optional:** write all of the factors for each of the following numbers.

24 ________________ 27 ________________

32 ________________ 64 ________________

Mixed Review!

____ ÷ 9 = 4 9 × ____ = 108 ____ + 7 = 16

43 + ____ = 60 500 − 17 = ____ 27 − ____ = 18

Name________________________________

Exercise 4 Day 59

Practice with Factoring!

Fill in this chart. The first one is done for you. Feel free to do as many as you can or do more tomorrow!

Number	Pairs of Factors	Factors
6	1 × 6 2 × 3 3 × 2 6 × 1	1, 2, 3, 6
12		
18		
25		
27		
49		
64		
72		
84		
96		
66		
50		
100		
42		
48		
11		

Name________________________________

Exercise 5

Day 60

Review Time!

☐ Take the time now to narrate to your teacher what you have learned about factoring.

Bonus Concept!

In Lesson 7, we discussed converting measurements. When we are going from larger units of measure to smaller units of measure, we multiply, as seen in the example:

3 yards = 9 feet

Since we know that 1 yard = 3 feet, we can multiply 3 x 3. So think: 3 groups of 1 yard (3 feet).

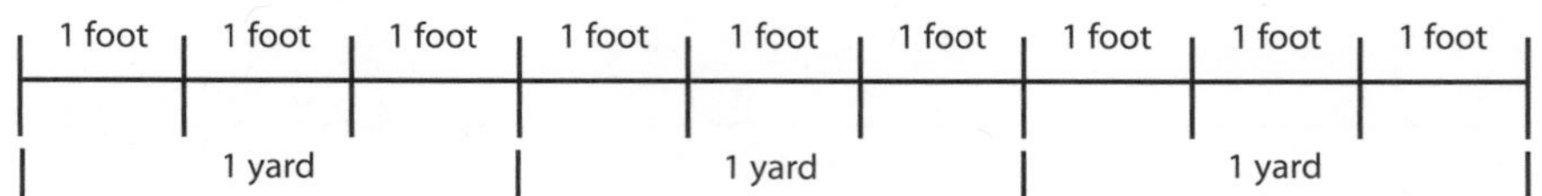

Now you try it!

There are 5,280 feet in 1 mile.
__________ feet = 2 miles

There are 12 items in 1 dozen.
__________ items = 3 dozen

There are 60 minutes in 1 hour.
__________ minutes = 24 hours

There are 1,760 yards in 1 mile.
__________ yards = 8 miles

There are 12 items in 1 dozen.
36 items = __________ dozen

There are 60 seconds in a minute.
3,600 seconds = __________ minutes

There are 2,000 pounds in 1 ton
10,000 pounds = __________ tons

There are 12 months in 1 year
132 months = __________ years

Common Factors, Greatest Common Factor, and Reducing Fractions

Lesson 13

"Ok, girls," Mrs. Drew whispered, "I made these cards for you. These are the categories in the Dewey Decimal System. Do you remember how I told you that the system is like a tree?" Both girls nodded in response. "Well, just think of these as the main branches, and all of them have hundreds of little branches and twigs coming off of them." Mrs. Drew giggled quietly — because she did everything quietly.

000 Generalities
100 Philosophy & Psychology
200 Religion
300 Social Sciences
400 Language
500 Natural Sciences & Mathematics
600 Technology (Applied Sciences)
700 The Arts
800 Literature & Rhetoric
900 Geography & History

"Thank you, Mrs. Drew," Natty answered politely. Mrs. Drew might be slightly odd, but the girls had decided she had a heart of gold.

"Yes, thank you, Mrs. Drew," Charlotte added with a wide smile. "We really appreciate you taking the time to make these for us. It can be a little confusing... Do you mind if we take a few minutes to walk around the library and locate the different areas of books?" she asked.

"By all means!" whispered Mrs. Drew. "That is an excellent idea, and when you two are finished looking around, come back here to my desk. I have a few projects I could really use help with."

"Yes, ma'am," the girls whispered back and smiled at the kind lady.

Name________________________________

Exercise 1 Day 61

Building on the Concept of Factoring!

A common factor is a factor that two or more numbers share. Complete the chart below. Circle the common factors in each pair of numbers. Study the example below before you begin.

Number	Pairs of Factors	Factors	Common Factors
6	1 × 6 2 × 3 6 × 1 3 × 2	(1), (2), (3), (6)	The common factors of 6 and 12 are: 1, 2, 3, 6
12	1 × 12 2 × 6 3 × 4 12 × 1 6 × 2 4 × 3	(1), (2), (3), 4, (6), 12	

Now you try!

Number	Pairs of Factors	Factors	Common Factors
8			
16			

Number	Pairs of Factors	Factors	Common Factors
15			
20			

Name______________________________

Exercise 1 Day 61

Divisibility Rules

In finding factors, divisibility rules are extremely useful! Therefore, in this week's exercises, we will be making flashcards for each of the divisibility rules. These will help you to know which factors are in larger numbers. Today's rule is about numbers that can be divided by 2, thus making 2 a factor.

Whenever you see this writing, you will be adding to your "Divisibility Rules" flashcards.

Thinking TOOLS!

Flashcard Copywork!

Can it be divided by 2?
A number is divisible by 2 if it is an even number.
(Remember! Even numbers end in 0, 2, 4, 6, or 8.)

Practice

Circle the numbers that are divisible by 2. Use the rule you copied.

29 42

179 360

1,420 1,893

26,732,546 3,333,338

Name________________________________

Exercise 2 Day 62

Hands On!

Get your Common Factors Chart/Greatest Common Factor Chart and the Reduce that Fraction! Chart that you laminated. You will be using the Common Factor side of the chart today. Using a washable marker, find the common factors for the following groups of numbers.

10 and 14	12, 18, and 24
36, 18, and 9	35, 20, and 15

Thinking TOOLS!

Flashcard Copywork!

Today, you will be making two flashcards.

Can it be divided by 5?
A number is divisible by 5 if the one's digit is 0 or 5.

Can it be divided by 10?
A number is divisible by 10 if the one's digit is 0.

Practice

Circle the numbers that are divisible by 5. Use the rule you copied.

16	150	25	2,000
254	75	3,210,062	4,001

Circle the numbers that are divisible by 10. Use the rule you copied.

210	16,210	10,004	107
2,000	1,400	550	16,222,005

Name_______________________________

Exercise 3 Day 63

New Concept!
The Greatest Common Factor (GCF) is the largest common factor any group of numbers have.

Hands On!

You will be using the Greatest Common Factor Chart side of the chart you made in Exercise 2. Using a washable marker, find the greatest common factor for the following groups of numbers. Study the example.

Number	Pairs of Factors	Factors	Common Factors	Greatest Common Factor
6	1 × 6 2 × 3 6 × 1 3 × 2	(1,) (2,) (3,) (6)	The common factors of 6 and 12 are: 1, 2, 3, 6	6
12	1 × 12 2 × 6 3 × 4 12 × 1 6 × 2 4 × 3	(1,) (2,) (3,) 4, (6,) 12		

10 and 14

12, 18, and 24

35, 20, and 15

Thinking TOOLS!

Today, you will be making two flashcards.

Can it be divided by 3?
A number is divisible by 3 if the sum of the digits is divisible by 3.
Example: the number 123 is divisible by 3
because 1 + 2 + 3 = 6, and 6 is divisible by 3.

Circle the numbers that are divisible by 3.

608   894   1,008   42   58

Can it be divided by 9?
A number is divisible by 9 if the sum of the digits is divisible by 9.
Example: the number 909 is divisible by 9
because 9 + 0 + 9 = 18, and 18 is divisible by 9.

Circle the numbers that are divisible by 9.

72   807   10,500   5,222   603

Name________________________________

Mystery Solved!

Have you been wondering WHY we have been spending so much time on factors, common factors, and greatest common factors? In this exercise, we will be showing you how to reduce fractions using the greatest common factor. Study the example on the back of your Reduce that Fraction! Chart which you prepared in Exercise 2. First, copy this important fact!

Copywork!

When you reduce a fraction, you aren't making it smaller. A fraction, which is reduced to its lowest terms, has the smallest numbers possible in the numerator and denominator. A reduced fraction is ALWAYS equivalent to the original, when divided by the Greatest Common Factor of both numbers.

____

____

____

____

____

____

____

Hands On!

Use your Reduce that Fraction! Chart to reduce these fractions.

$\frac{6}{12}$ $\frac{7}{21}$ $\frac{10}{45}$ $\frac{45}{50}$

$\frac{15}{18}$ $\frac{36}{40}$ $\frac{2}{10}$

Name________________________________

Exercise 5 Day 65

Thinking TOOLS!

Flashcard Copywork!

Can it be divided by 4?

A number is divisible by 4 if the last two digits are both zeros, or if they are divisible by 4.

Example: the number 400 is divisible by 4 because it ends in two zeros. The number 248 is also divisible by 4 because 48 (the last two digits) is divisible by 4.

Circle the numbers that are divisible by 4. Use the rule you copied.

800 242 680

375 1,424

Review Time!

Use your Reduce that Fraction! Chart to narrate to your teacher what you are doing as you reduce these fractions.

- ☐ $\frac{12}{14}$
- ☐ $\frac{42}{54}$
- ☐ $\frac{6}{12}$
- ☐ $\frac{18}{30}$
- ☐ $\frac{21}{24}$

Word Search

Find and circle the math words listed at the bottom.

T	W	E	N	T	Y	S	L	A	M	I	C	E	D
A	S	Q	U	A	R	E	Q	N	M	P	E	C	N
Y	O	U	A	C	U	T	E	G	U	R	L	K	U
F	R	A	C	T	I	O	N	L	L	Y	C	H	M
G	A	L	L	O	N	D	Y	E	T	H	R	E	E
E	K	S	O	L	V	E	O	R	I	V	I	V	R
O	B	T	U	S	E	M	I	L	P	M	C	N	A
M	I	L	E	B	N	H	X	B	L	N	E	O	T
E	A	D	D	I	T	I	O	N	Y	A	M	I	O
T	Z	P	R	O	T	R	A	C	T	O	R	S	R
R	J	R	E	D	N	I	A	M	E	R	B	I	H
Y	N	N	E	P	P	E	R	C	E	N	T	V	W
R	W	D	N	A	S	U	O	H	T	X	P	I	X
D	E	N	O	M	I	N	A	T	O	R	P	D	Z

ACUTE
ADDITION
ANGLE
CIRCLE
DECIMALS
DENOMINATOR
DIVISION
DOLLAR
EQUALS
FRACTION
GALLON
GEOMETRY
MILE
MULTIPLY
NUMERATOR
OBTUSE
PENNY
PERCENT
PROTRACTOR
REMAINDER
SOLVE
SQUARE
SUBTRACT
THIRTY
THOUSAND
THREE
TWENTY

Proper and Improper Fractions

Lesson **14**

"Charlotte, I don't know if we did this right. This looks kind of strange!" Natty's brow was furrowed with concern. "I've never seen a fraction like this — but I did exactly what Mom showed us to do when we add fractions."

"I know. This doesn't seem right. We better ask Mom about it before we start measuring the ingredients," Charlotte agreed. Both girls climbed down from their stools at the breakfast bar in the kitchen. They were working on doubling, tripling, and even quadrupling some of their favorite cookie and bar recipes for a big baking project.

"Mom!" both girls called. They could hear their mother's voice coming from somewhere in the house. Maybe she was in the bathroom with Ella. "Mom? Where are you?" they called together.

"I'm in here! Girls you have to come see!" Mom's laughing voice was coming from behind her closed bedroom door. When the girls opened the door and peeked in, they could see what she was giggling about; Ella was standing in front of the mirror, wearing a pair of Mom's high-heeled shoes. The little girl was posing and grinning, her lips crookedly smeared with her mother's dark pink lipstick.

"Oh Ella!" both of the older girls gasped and giggled together. Their little sister turned and curtsied, wobbling precariously in the shoes.

"I look like Momma!" Ella grinned and walked across the room to her sisters.

"Weeelll kind of!" Charlotte knelt to hug her little sister. It seemed to her that Ella was growing up entirely too quickly; it seemed like yesterday that she had first held her as a newborn. Mom snapped a picture of the tender moment between her daughters.

"Did you girls need something?" Maddie Stevens stood to her feet and turned to Natty and Charlotte.

"Oh yeah! We are working on choosing recipes for cookies and bars to make for the library reading program open house. We told Mrs. Drew that we would bring six dozen sugar cookies and four dozen chocolate chip bars. None of our recipes make that many cookies or bars, so we have to double and triple some of them. The problem is, when we try to do that, some of the fractions are strange," Charlotte said in a rush.

"What do you mean 'strange'?" her mother asked.

“Well, the top number — what is that called again?” Natty paused.

“The numerator,” Charlotte interjected.

“Yes. The numerator is bigger than the bottom number,” Natty continued.

“The denominator,” Charlotte interjected again.

“Yes, the denominator,” Natty agreed.

“Ok, so you’re saying that when you double some of the amounts for the ingredients, you get a fraction with a bigger numerator than denominator?” Mom verified.

“Yes, that’s exactly what happens! That means we are doing something wrong, right Mom?” Charlotte asked.

“Actually, no, Charlotte,” her mom said, “that just means you have an improper fraction.”

“An improper fraction? What is that?” Natty questioned. She had heard of improper behavior or improper dress, but improper fractions? What could that mean?

“Um, Mom, how can a fraction be improper? Doesn’t that mean inappropriate?” Charlotte was as puzzled as Natty.

Mom chuckled. “No, not always. Come on, you two, let’s go to the kitchen. I’ll show you what I mean. Come to think of it, this would be a good thing for you to learn...”

The girls followed their mother to the kitchen. They were going to learn about inappropriate...er... improper fractions.

Name__________________________

Exercise 1 Day 66

New Concept for Copywork!

An improper fraction is a fraction which has a larger number for the numerator than denominator. (Example: $\frac{7}{5}$) A proper fraction is a fraction which has a smaller number for the numerator than denominator. (Example: $\frac{2}{5}$)

____

____

____

____

Improper fraction

$\frac{7}{5}$

Proper fraction

$\frac{2}{5}$

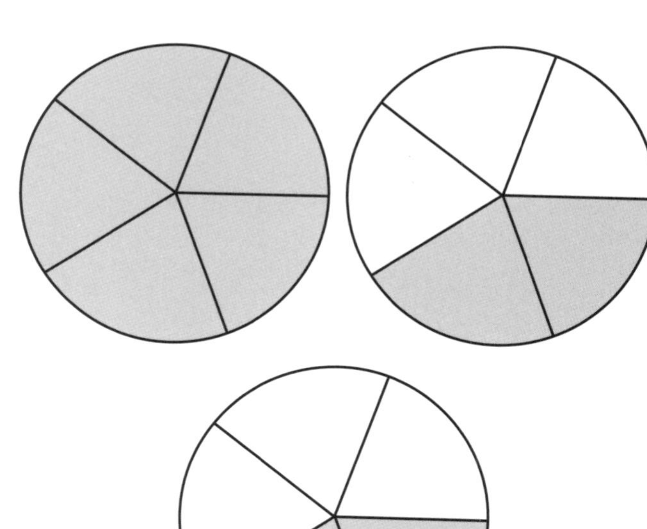

Name________________________________

Exercise 1 Day 66

Let's Practice!

Circle the improper fractions and draw them below. The first one is done for you.

$\frac{4}{9}$ $\frac{6}{5}$ $\frac{2}{3}$ $\frac{9}{3}$

$\frac{5}{2}$ $\frac{10}{5}$

My improper fractions:

$\frac{6}{5}$

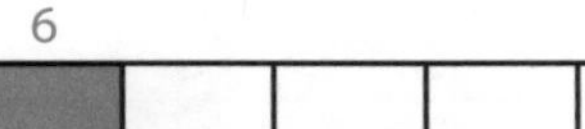

Name________________________________ Exercise 2 Day 67

Fraction Review

We have learned that the fraction bar is one of the division symbols. ⟶ $\frac{20}{4}$

In division, this problem is read: twenty divided by four.

As a fraction, it is read: twenty fourths

Read the following fractions as both a division problem and as an improper fraction.

$\frac{12}{4}$

$\frac{15}{5}$

$\frac{32}{4}$

$\frac{72}{6}$

$\frac{84}{7}$

Add and circle the answers that are improper fractions.

$$\begin{array}{r} \frac{9}{20} \\ + \frac{13}{20} \\ \hline \end{array} \qquad \begin{array}{r} \frac{7}{16} \\ + \frac{8}{16} \\ \hline \end{array} \qquad \begin{array}{r} \frac{4}{10} \\ + \frac{7}{10} \\ \hline \end{array}$$

$\frac{4}{5} + \frac{1}{5} =$

$\frac{3}{7} + \frac{9}{7} =$

Draw this improper fraction

$\frac{10}{5}$

Example $\frac{12}{4}$

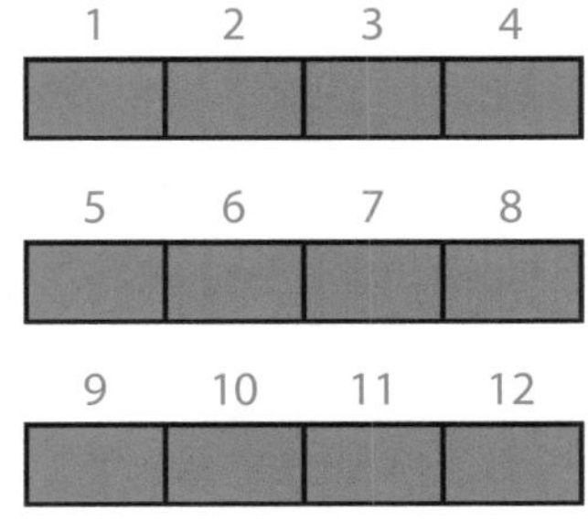

Name________________________________

Mixed Practice!

Divide and check.

$12\overline{)840}$

$9\overline{)700}$

Average:

402
396
+ 219

Add:

72,262
+ 49,888

1,978,423
+ 2,129,789

17
23
62
+ 58

Subtract:

40,010
- 39,879

2,972,345
- 1,893,456

5,000
- 698

Name______________________________

Exercise 4 Day 69

More mixed practice!

x	10	100	1000
23			
14			
602			
5			
12			

Use your Reduce the Fraction! Chart to reduce these fractions. Use your divisibility rules flashcards.

$\frac{3}{12}$ $\frac{4}{20}$ $\frac{15}{45}$

$\frac{30}{90}$ $\frac{11}{22}$ $\frac{8}{10}$

What are the three ways to show division?

1.

2.

3.

Natty and Charlotte are trying to make playdough for Ella. They measure $\frac{2}{3}$ cup of flour and $\frac{2}{3}$ cup of salt. How many cups of flour/salt mixture did they have?

Teacher

Gather measuring cups for Exercise 5, Day 70. You will need a larger measuring cup (such as a 2- or 4-cup Pyrex® glass cup) and some smaller measuring cups (such as $\frac{1}{4}$, $\frac{1}{3}$, $\frac{1}{2}$ cup). You will need water on hand.

Name________________________________

Exercise 5

Day 70

Hands On!

Today we will measure water from small measuring cups into a large (at least 4 cups) glass measuring cup.

Pour these amounts of water into the large measuring cup. Add them up and write as improper fraction. Read the amount as a mixed number on the large measuring cup. Write it down on the chart below.

Improper	Mixed Number
$\frac{1}{4}$ c. + $\frac{1}{4}$ c. + $\frac{1}{4}$ c. + $\frac{1}{4}$ c. + $\frac{1}{4}$ c. = $\frac{5}{4}$ cups	$1\frac{1}{4}$ cups
$\frac{1}{2}$ c. + $\frac{1}{2}$ c. + $\frac{1}{2}$ c. = ____ cups	______ cups
$\frac{1}{3}$ c. + $\frac{1}{3}$ c. + $\frac{1}{3}$ c. + $\frac{1}{3}$ c. = ____ cups	______ cups
$\frac{1}{4}$ c. + $\frac{1}{4}$ c. + $\frac{1}{4}$ c. + $\frac{1}{4}$ c. + $\frac{1}{4}$ c. + $\frac{1}{4}$ c. = ____ cups	______ cups
$\frac{1}{2}$ c. + $\frac{1}{2}$ c. + $\frac{1}{2}$ c. + $\frac{1}{2}$ c. = ____ cups	______ cups

Now you write more problems and solve them!

Improper	Mixed Number

Changing Improper Fractions

Lesson **15**

Charlotte and Natty came over to the kitchen counter where Mom was working. They were eager to learn about improper fractions. They had been working hard on doubling their favorite recipes and found that they ended up with improper fractions, which they didn't know how to measure. Mom was going to show them how to turn an improper fraction into a mixed number.

Mom grabbed a scrap of paper from the kitchen drawer and wrote one of the improper fractions that the girls had discovered in their recipes.

"You see, girls, we divide the numerator by the denominator, like this," Mom explained as she wrote. "When you have an improper fraction that divides evenly, like $\frac{12}{4}$, we have a whole number. But what if the improper fraction had been $\frac{13}{4}$? Let me show you what we would do..."

"So, $\frac{13}{4}$ cup of flour is the same as $3\frac{1}{4}$ cups of flour?" Natty asked.

"Yes, that's right," Mom nodded and pushed the bag of flour over to Natty. "You know, girls, this is really helpful and useful information. This is the kind of lesson that you will use in your everyday life as an adult."

The girls nodded solemnly. Baking and cooking was something they both took very seriously. They knew their mother did her best to make sure that they were learning everything that they needed to know to be successful in life. This working with improper fractions was real, grown-up business! They were growing up fast, and it was their responsibility to learn from their parents.

"So, girls, as we will be learning over the next couple of weeks, mixed numbers and improper fractions are related. Even though we usually use mixed numbers while we are baking, cooking, and measuring, we do need improper fractions, too, sometimes."

$\frac{13}{4}$ is the same as 13 ÷ 4.

When we divide 13 ÷ 4, and write the remainder as a fraction, this is the answer: $3\frac{1}{4}$

We could also write the process like this:

		3	$\frac{1}{4}$
4	1	3	
	− 1	2	
		1	

$\frac{12}{4}$

$\frac{12}{4}$ is the same as

12 ÷ 4, which we know is 3.

So $\frac{12}{4}$ cups = 3 whole cups

Remember?

The three ways to show division:

— (fraction line)

÷ (division symbol #1)

⟌ (division symbol #2)

REAL LIFE LINK!

Another mystery solved! This is one reason we learned to divide and write the remainder as a fraction!

Name ______________________________

Exercise 1 Day 71

Copywork

To change an improper fraction into a mixed number, divide the numerator by the denominator and write the remainder as a fraction.

This is what it would look like!

$\frac{11}{4} = $ ($\frac{1}{4}$ $\frac{1}{4}$ $\frac{1}{4}$ $\frac{1}{4}$) + ($\frac{1}{4}$ $\frac{1}{4}$ $\frac{1}{4}$ $\frac{1}{4}$) + ($\frac{1}{4}$ $\frac{1}{4}$ $\frac{1}{4}$)

$\frac{11}{4}$ ⟶

		2	
4	1	1	
	–	8	
		3	

⟶ $2\frac{3}{4}$

Let's Practice!

Change the improper fractions into mixed numbers and reduce them to the lowest terms. If you need help reducing, use your Reduce that Fraction! Chart. The first one is done for you.

Example:

$\frac{8}{6}$ $8 \div 6 = 1\frac{2}{6}$ reduced to lowest terms: $1\frac{1}{3}$

Now you do these:

$\frac{10}{2}$ $\frac{16}{5}$ $\frac{22}{7}$ $\frac{12}{10}$

$\frac{14}{4}$ $\frac{32}{8}$ $\frac{45}{8}$ $\frac{4}{3}$

Name________________________________

Exercise 2 Day 72

Review

Change these improper fractions to mixed or whole numbers and draw them as shown in Exercise 1.

$\frac{7}{4}$ $\frac{6}{3}$ $\frac{9}{5}$ $\frac{8}{4}$

$\frac{10}{6}$ $\frac{12}{4}$ $\frac{15}{5}$ $\frac{14}{8}$

Mixed Review!

Write two factors for each of the following numbers.

32 _____, _____ 16 _____, _____ 7 _____, _____

Use your Reduce that Fraction! Chart to reduce these fractions.

$\frac{3}{9}$ $\frac{11}{22}$ $\frac{8}{10}$ $\frac{4}{12}$

Do this multiplication work as quickly as you can!

x	1	2	3	4	5	6	7	8	9	10	11	12
11												
12												

Solve.

$$\begin{array}{r} 24,121 \\ +\ 16,268 \\ \hline \end{array} \qquad \begin{array}{r} 505 \\ \times\ 10 \\ \hline \end{array} \qquad \begin{array}{r} 60 \\ \times\ 12 \\ \hline \end{array} \qquad \begin{array}{r} 20,020 \\ +\ 12,172 \\ \hline \end{array}$$

Name_______________________________

Exercise 3 Day 73

Adding On to the Concept...

So far in this lesson, we have learned to take an improper fraction and change it into a mixed number. Most of the time, in real life, this is what we do, because it is easier to use mixed numbers. However, in multiplying and dividing fractions, which we will learn later in this book, we have to change the mixed number into an improper fraction. See the example below.

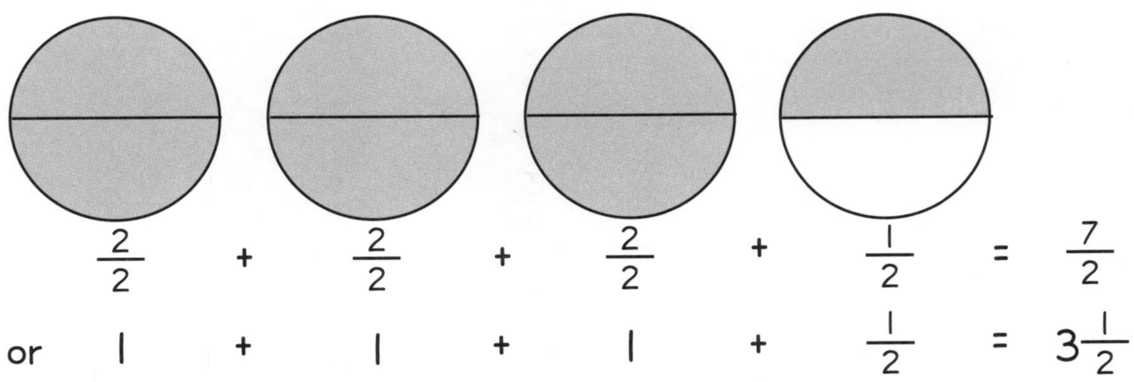

$$\frac{2}{2} + \frac{2}{2} + \frac{2}{2} + \frac{1}{2} = \frac{7}{2}$$

$$\text{or} \quad 1 + 1 + 1 + \frac{1}{2} = 3\frac{1}{2}$$

An easy way to turn a mixed number into an improper fraction is to multiply the whole number (3) by the denominator (2) and then add the numerator (1). Like this: $(3 \times 2) + 1 = 7$ We place the answer to our equation over the original denominator.

NOTE: Whenever you see an equation with parentheses, always do the work inside the parentheses first, then finish to find the answer.

Now you try it!
Change these mixed numbers into improper fractions.

$1\frac{1}{2}$ $\qquad$ $3\frac{2}{3}$ $\qquad$ $5\frac{1}{8}$

$1\frac{9}{10}$ $\qquad$ $1\frac{3}{11}$ $\qquad$ $2\frac{3}{4}$

Story Problem Workshop! In the following story problems, cross out the unnecessary information with a red pencil or crayon. Underline the clue words that will help you solve the problem with a blue pencil or crayon. Lastly, solve the problem!

1. The kids wanted a triple batch of lemonade for their lemonade stand. The directions called for $\frac{3}{4}$ cup of mix for one batch. One batch made two quarts of lemonade. How many cups of mix did they need for their triple batch of lemonade?

2. Write the answer to problem above as an improper fraction and as a mixed number.

Name______________________________

Exercise 4 Day 74

Fraction Circles

Today, you are going to make your own fraction circles. Use whatever size bowl, plate, or cup you want to make your circles. Make sure your circles are all the same size. Use a ruler to draw lines on your circles to make fractions. Make fraction circles to show these mixed numbers and improper fractions.

- ☐ $2\frac{1}{2}$
- ☐ $4\frac{2}{3}$
- ☐ $1\frac{3}{4}$
- ☐ $\frac{11}{5}$
- ☐ $\frac{16}{8}$
- ☐ $\frac{13}{6}$

Show and narrate to your family what you learned about improper fractions and mixed numbers.

Optional Review for Day 74 or Day 75.

Change these improper fractions into mixed numbers.

$\frac{11}{3}$ = _____ $\frac{12}{7}$ = _____

$\frac{19}{8}$ = _____ $\frac{22}{3}$ = _____

Change these mixed numbers into improper fractions.

$5\frac{1}{3}$ = _____ $7\frac{1}{8}$ = _____

$4\frac{3}{4}$ = _____ $9\frac{2}{5}$ = _____

Name______________________________

Exercise 5 Day 75

It's Time to Solve Another Sudoku!

You may have noticed the Sudoku puzzles becoming more of a challenge as you see examples with more of the numbers missing. While these are a bigger challenge, remember that the process to solve them remains simple.

Remember:

1. Look at the numbers already in the rows that are missing a number.
2. Write down the missing numbers for each row and column. (Hint: Writing on the edges of the puzzle in line with the columns or rows are a good way to keep these numbers in mind.
3. Compare those numbers to the numbers that already in the 3 x 3 square, row, or column.
4. See if you can place the missing numbers and not repeat numbers 1–9 in the 3 x 3 area, the column, or the row.
5. Confused or not sure what to do? Ask your teacher for help.

	7	6	5	4	3	1	9	
			2	1	9			
2	1	9	8	7	6	4	3	5
1	9	8		6		3	2	4
4	3	2	1		8	6	5	7
7	6	5		3		9	8	1
3		1	9	8	7	5		6
		4	3	2	1	8		
	8	7	6	5	4	2	1	

Sums Containing Improper Fractions

Lesson 16

Charlotte stood straight and tall, as she prepared for the Christmas presentation night and had been working on memorizing the entire poem that she was going to recite. She did a marvelous job as she smiled and recited,

"Stopping by Woods on a Snowy Evening"
By Robert Frost

Whose woods these are I think I know.
His house is in the village though;
He will not see me stopping here
To watch his woods fill up with snow.

My little horse must think it queer
To stop without a farmhouse near
Between the woods and frozen lake
The darkest evening of the year.

He gives his harness bells a shake
To ask if there is some mistake.
The only other sound's the sweep
Of easy wind and downy flake.

The woods are lovely, dark and deep.
But I have promises to keep,
And miles to go before I sleep,
And miles to go before I sleep.

Charlotte knew every word. She even knew how to stand still without shifting from foot to foot while she recited her poem.

"Good job, Charlotte!" the whole family said as they stood to their feet to clap for her. Charlotte smiled when her brothers gave her high-fives. Natty and Ella hugged their sister. They were so proud of her!

There was much excitement in the Stevens household! The church Christmas outreach program was right around the corner, and the children were busy planning and practicing for their part in the homeschool program. There was much discussion as they worked together to decide what each of their parts would be.

The boys were doing a presentation about the story of the old car Mr. Smith had given them. After some investigation, Charlie and Hairo had discovered the old VW Bug had belonged to a former mayor of their town! They had also done some research on when the VW Bug had been originally designed and made.

Their presentation was called "The People's Car," and it outlined the rather interesting history of this popular, little vehicle. The boys had used a huge, cardboard fold-out to artfully display their project, and each of them practiced taking turns to explain parts of their presentation. Charlie and Hairo had worked for weeks to research, write, draw, and design their project, and both of them felt that it had turned out splendidly!

The girls and mom decided to make Grandma Violet's Cranberry Christmas Punch Delight. Mom helped the girls adjust the recipe to serve the number of people expected at the party. The original recipe made ten $\frac{3}{4}$ cup servings.

Charlotte wrote:

$$\frac{3}{4} + \frac{3}{4} + \frac{3}{4} + \frac{3}{4} + \frac{3}{4} + \frac{3}{4} + \frac{3}{4} + \frac{3}{4} + \frac{3}{4} + \frac{3}{4} = \frac{30}{4} \text{ cups}$$

Mom wrote:

$$\begin{array}{r|l} & 7\frac{2}{4} \\ \hline 4 & 30 \\ & -28 \\ \hline & 2 \end{array}$$

and then she showed the girls what she did.

Grandma Violet's Cranberry Christmas Punch Delight

$\frac{1}{3}$ cup white pure cane sugar

2 cups cranberry juice

3 tbs. almond extract (vanilla may be substituted)

1 (2 liter) bottle of ginger ale

Mix first four ingredients and refrigerate for 24 hours.

Add ginger ale before serving.

Name________________________________

Exercise 1 Day 76

New Concept for Copywork!

When we add a group of fractions together, sometimes the sum is an improper fraction. When this happens, we change the sum into a mixed number and reduce if necessary.

___

___

___

___

This is how it looks:

$$\frac{3}{10} + \frac{4}{10} + \frac{5}{10} = \frac{12}{10} = 1\frac{2}{10} = 1\frac{1}{5}$$

Our answer is an improper fraction ($\frac{12}{10}$), so we change it to a mixed number ($1\frac{2}{10}$). Our mixed number needs to be reduced to lowest terms ($1\frac{1}{5}$).

Now you try it!

Add the fractions. If the sum is an improper fraction, change it to a mixed number, and reduce as necessary. If you need help reducing, use your Reduce that Fraction! Chart.

$\frac{7}{8} + \frac{7}{8}$

$\frac{4}{10} + \frac{7}{10}$

$\frac{4}{5} + \frac{3}{5}$

$\frac{6}{11} + \frac{5}{11} + \frac{3}{11}$

$\frac{2}{15} + \frac{7}{15} + \frac{11}{15}$

Name ______________________________

Exercise 2 Day 77

Building on the New Concept!

Study this example and read the notes.

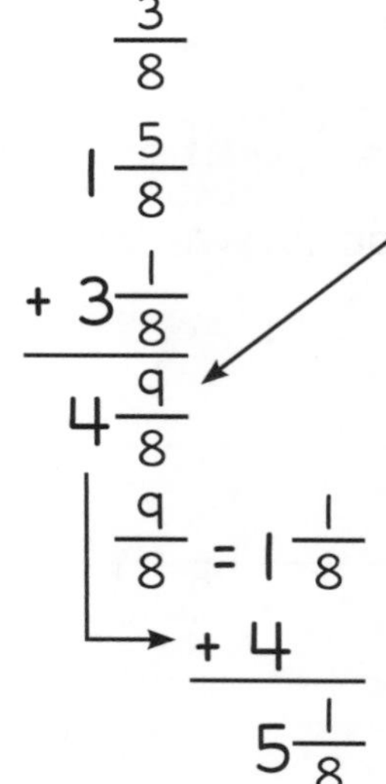

1. In this kind of problem, we have fractions and mixed numbers. The answer is a whole number (4) and an improper fraction ($\frac{9}{8}$). We cannot leave the answer this way!

2. After we solve the problem, we "set aside" the whole number part of the answer (4).

3. Next, we change the improper fraction part of the answer ($\frac{9}{8}$) to a mixed number ($1\frac{1}{8}$). Lastly, add the whole number (4) to the mixed number ($1\frac{1}{8}$), which equals $5\frac{1}{8}$.

Now you try it!
Add.

$6\frac{3}{4} + 4\frac{2}{4}$ $7\frac{2}{9} + 3\frac{8}{9}$ $3\frac{10}{11} + 8\frac{9}{11}$

Add and reduce. If you need help reducing, use your Reduce that Fraction! Chart.

$2\frac{7}{10} + 9\frac{5}{10}$ $11\frac{3}{12} + 17\frac{10}{12}$ $5\frac{6}{15} + 4\frac{12}{15}$

Roman Numeral Copywork:

I = one ______________________________

V = five ______________________________

X = ten ______________________________

L = fifty ______________________________

C = hundred ______________________________

D = five hundred ______________________________

M = thousand ______________________________

Name____________________________

Exercise 3 Day 78

Copywork

In some mixed number addition problems, the answer is a whole number and an improper fraction. Solve the problem, "set aside" the whole number part of the answer, change the improper fraction part of the answer to a mixed number, and add the whole number to the mixed number.

____

____

____

____

____

____

Solve

The first one is done for you.

$$1\frac{8}{9} + 1\frac{2}{9} = 2\frac{10}{9}$$

$$\frac{10}{9} = 1\frac{1}{9}, \quad 1\frac{1}{9} + 2 = 3\frac{1}{9}$$

$$3\frac{4}{7} + 4\frac{6}{7}$$

$$8\frac{1}{2} + 3\frac{1}{2}$$

$$13\frac{1}{10} + 17\frac{4}{10}$$

Fill in the Missing Roman Numerals.

I, II, _____, IV, _____, VI, _____, _____, IX, _____, XI, XII, _____, XIV, XV, _____, XVII, _____, XIX, XX

Name________________________________

Exercise 3 Day 78

Review

Solve, then do mixed review below.

x	1	2	3	4	5	6	7	8	9	10	11	12
0												
1												
2												
3												
4												
5												
6												
7												
8												
9												
10												
11												
12												

$10\overline{)\$215.60}$

$$\begin{array}{r} 58 \\ \times\ 29 \\ \hline \end{array}$$

$$\begin{array}{r} 322 \\ \times\ 48 \\ \hline \end{array}$$

Name______________________________

Exercise 4 Day 79

Fraction Review

Add. Reduce if necessary.

$$6\frac{1}{8} + 5\frac{7}{8} \qquad 6\frac{1}{5} + 5\frac{4}{5} \qquad 14\frac{2}{3} + 9\frac{2}{3} \qquad 6\frac{3}{4} + 8\frac{2}{4}$$

Subtract. Reduce if necessary.

$$55\frac{8}{9} - 46\frac{2}{9} \qquad 16\frac{7}{8} - 5\frac{3}{8} \qquad 23\frac{2}{5} - 16\frac{1}{5} \qquad \frac{17}{10} - \frac{7}{10}$$

Review.

In Lesson 12, Exercise 5, we learned how to convert measurements. Convert the following measurements. Use your Measurements Chart in the back of the book if necessary.

48 items = __________ dozen

6 minutes = __________ seconds

3600 seconds = __________ minutes

4 miles = __________ yards

5 years* = __________ days

108 months = __________ years

6 miles = __________ feet

12 yards = __________ feet

*With one leap year

Name______________________________

Exercise 5 Day 80

Review Time!

Solve.

55 × 10 = ________

183 × 1,000 = ________

72 × 100 = ________

45 × 10 = ________

Divide.

Check.

$20\overline{)600}$

List the three ways to show division. ________, ________, ________

Write 2 factors of each.

48 ____, ____ 21 ____, ____ 9 ____, ____

36 ____, ____ 10 ____, ____ 5 ____, ____

Which of the above is prime? Circle it.

Use your Reduce the Fraction! Chart to solve the following.

$\frac{10}{50}$ = ____ $\frac{16}{48}$ = ____ $\frac{8}{96}$ = ____

Change the improper fractions to mixed numbers. Reduce if necessary.

$\frac{22}{3}$ = ____ $\frac{19}{7}$ = ____ $\frac{15}{6}$ = ____

Change the mixed number to improper fractions.

$3\frac{1}{5}$ = ____ $2\frac{3}{8}$ = ____ $4\frac{1}{5}$ = ____

Least Common Multiples

Lesson 17

"Charlotte, if you put that square there, I'll put my matching piece here. There! Now it's symmetrical. Doesn't that look nice?" Natty asked Charlotte. The two girls were working on their project for the Christmas program. They had discussed what they should do for such a long time, they were now having to work very diligently in order to get it done in time for Christmas!

The girls had finally decided to make a memory quilt from some of their old sweatshirts and t-shirts and dresses. Their presentation would involve the quilt and taking turns telling the story behind each block. Charlotte and Natty each had seven stories to tell.

Their favorite piece in the quilt was the light green print that used to be one of their matching sundresses from the summer. These were the dresses they had worn when their cousins from Florida had come to visit during the summer. The girls had enjoyed playing with Sean and Abby! All of the cousins had spent hours in the clubhouse talking and playing. Natty had been made the president of the "Fearfully and Wonderfully Made Club"!

"I am so glad Mom agreed to let us use one of the dresses for pieces for the quilt! She said she would pack away the other dress for Ella to grow into," Charlotte agreed. "This is going to be such an interesting presentation! Do you have your stories memorized the way you want to say them, Natty?" Charlotte asked in a concerned voice. She knew how nervous Natty became when she had to speak in front of a large group.

Natty nodded but bit her lower lip. "I do. But I am still really nervous! I think it will help that there won't be a lot of light in the room. I like Mom's idea of using our kerosene lamps as the only light during our presentation. It not only sets the mood for our presentation, it will make it easier for me to pretend we are just at home practicing!" Natty giggled nervously.

The matching, antique kerosene lamps had been a present from Grandma Violet last Christmas. Grandma Violet told the girls that the lamps had been her grandmother's. These lamps had sat on the old kitchen table for more than thirty years, and they had been packed away in the attic of the old farmhouse for nearly eighty years. When Grandma Violet found them, she gave them to the girls in honor of their study about the American pioneers of the late nineteenth century. When the girls decided to do their memory quilt presentation, the lamps seemed to fit right in. In fact, they decided to include a little story about the lamps, too.

The girls worked quietly for a while, and then the silence was broken by a giggle escaping from Natty.

"What is it?" Charlotte asked.

"I was just thinking about the stories Grandma Violet told us about when her mom was a little girl. I am so glad we have grandparents who can tell us first hand about the times in history we have studied! Remember the story about Grandma Violet's mom when she was a little girl - the one when she was stuck out in the outhouse because of a skunk? Can you imagine, Charlotte? I wonder what would have happened if the farm dog hadn't come along and chased the skunk away!" Natty was laughing so hard that she gasped for breath. The thought of being stuck in an outhouse because a skunk was sitting in front of the door...

Charlotte giggled, too. "You know, Natty, Grandma Violet's mother may have grown up in a different time period, but we still have a lot in common with her," Charlotte commented after the giggling had died down. "Grandma Violet's mom was named 'Charlotte,' too, you know, and she was homeschooled, also! Grandma Violet told me the story of how her mother went to the country, one-room schoolhouse for only two school years, and then it burned down. The whole community was really sad, and eventually they did rebuild, but Grandma Violet's mom and her siblings were homeschooled until the rebuilding was finished, which took almost all of the rest of their schooling years."

"You know, Charlotte," Natty commented thoughtfully, "I am finding that families have a lot in common. I like belonging to this family, and I'm super glad you're my sister. Wow! Look at how much we have gotten done on this quilt today! We only have two more rows!" The girls stood back and looked at their handiwork. Both of them were thinking back to another little girl named "Charlotte" and the quilts she probably made with her sister... Yet another thing they had in common!

Discovery!

God is a God of impeccable order! He has created so many rhythms and cycles throughout His creation. We, as humans, are still discovering more every day! Charlotte and Natty were talking about how many characteristics the family had in common. Think about it! Aren't the ways God organizes the world, and all of creation, simply amazing? Take a moment to talk about how aspects of all creation (including how we count and communicate!) are organized into groups that have common characteristics.

Name________________________________

Exercise 1

Day 81

New Concept!

What is a multiple? Do you know how to skip count by 2s, by 3s, by 4s, etc? The numbers you say when you count by 2s, for example, are all the multiples of 2. Therefore, when we write the multiples of 2, we write them this way: 2, 4, 6, 8, 10. . . A number has endless multiples, which is why we wrote ". . ." which is called an ellipsis.

Now you try it!

List the next five multiples of each number. Remember, you are skip counting! The first one is done for you.

7: 7, 14, 21, 28, 35, . . .

5:

4:

8:

10:

12:

6:

Mixed Review:

Write the number one million:

Subtract six hundred from one thousand:

Write an equivalent fraction for $\frac{7}{8}$:

Change $\frac{21}{5}$ into a mixed number:

Average these three numbers: 38, 67, 99

Write 21 as a Roman numeral:

Add.

Reduce as necessary.

$$14\frac{16}{17} + 1\frac{2}{17}$$

$$13\frac{15}{16} + 14\frac{3}{16}$$

Name________________________________

Exercise 2 Day 82

Building on the Concept!

Copywork:

Common multiples are multiples shared by two or more numbers.

The least common multiple (LCM) is the smallest multiple shared by two or more numbers. We use the LCM to find common denominators between two or more fractions.

Fill in the following chart. The first one is done for you.

Number	Multiples	Common Multiples	Least Common Multiple
6	6, 12, 18, 24, 30, 36, ...	12, 24, 36, ...	12
12	12, 24, 36, 48, 60, 72, ...		
5			
8			
3			
4			

Name______________________________

Exercise 2 Day 82

Mixed Review!

Write each amount as a decimal, fraction, and percent.

______ ______ ______

______ ______ ______

______ ______ ______

Multiply.

$$\begin{array}{r} 1,482 \\ \times \quad 21 \\ \hline \end{array}$$

$$\begin{array}{r} 689 \\ \times \quad 72 \\ \hline \end{array}$$

Review your divisibility rule flashcards.

Name_______________________________

Exercise 3 Day 83

Hands On!

Get your Least Common Multiple Chart. Using your chart, find the least common multiple of these numbers.

4, 6 ________

8, 12 ________

5, 10 ________

9, 12 ________

2, 3, 4 ________

Mixed Review!

Solve and check these problems.

$32\overline{)913}$ $28\overline{)892}$

Story Problems

1. Charlotte and Natty used a recipe that they needed to double. The recipe called for $1\frac{3}{4}$ cups of sugar. How many cups of sugar do the girls need when they double the recipe? Reduce if necessary.

2. Mom gave the girls 2 packages of blanket trim that each contained $12\frac{1}{2}$ feet to use on their memory quilt. The quilt is 4 feet wide and 5 feet long. What is the perimeter of their quilt?

   How much blanket trim will they have left over?

Name________________________________

Exercise 4

Day 84

Practicing the Concept!

Circle the numbers that are multiples of the bolded numbers.

5: 2 40 10 5 12 62 70 15

11: 14 55 108 22 10 33 132 66

8: 36 64 66 72 46 54 96 84

9: 21 18 108 96 81 71 54 67

Use your Least Common Multiple Chart to find the least common multiple of these numbers.

8, 10

3, 7

4, 11

6, 9

5, 8, 4

Review Copywork!

In some mixed number addition problems, the answer is a whole number and an improper fraction. After we solve the problem, we "set aside" the whole number part of the answer. Next, we change the improper fraction part of the answer to a mixed number. Lastly, add the whole number to the mixed number.

___

___

___

___

___

___

___

Name________________________________

Review Time!

Use your Least Common Multiple Chart to find the least common multiple of the following numbers. Narrate to your teacher what you are doing.

- ☐ 3, 12
- ☐ 8, 16
- ☐ 3, 5
- ☐ 7, 8
- ☐ 9, 18
- ☐ 10, 50
- ☐ 3, 6, 30

Add.

Reduce as necessary.

$$22\frac{5}{8} + 3\frac{7}{8}$$

$$15\frac{4}{9} + 6\frac{7}{9}$$

$$17\frac{2}{3} + 8\frac{1}{3}$$

NOTE: Please make sure you have a measuring tape for a project in our next lesson.

Least Common Multiples/ Finding a Common Denominator Part 1

Lesson 18

Christmas Day arrived crisp and clear. The fields sparkled like an ocean of diamonds. There was enough new snow to cover up all of the dirty, old snow piled along the curb, and the weather forecast predicted a few more inches for later in the day. It was a perfect Christmas morning, complete with the family's traditional Christmas breakfast of orange French toast, fresh squeezed orange juice, and crisp bacon.

Mom snapped pictures as the kids opened their Christmas gifts, smiling at the squeals of delight.

"Oh Mom! Thank you so, so, so much!" Charlotte cried in wonder as the wrapping paper fell away from one particularly large box. Charlotte's eyes grew round as she saw her gift. It was a beautiful Singer™ sewing machine!

"It's not a super fancy or expensive one, Charlotte, but Dad and I thought it would be a great beginner machine for you and Natty to practice on," Mom answered with a smile. "You girls have done such a great job putting your presentation together for tonight. Well, we thought you should have your own machine. Natty has something for sewing, too."

"Natty, open this one! This one is from Mom and Dad! It's something for sewing!" Charlotte dragged a box over to Natty. Natty's hands ripped away the paper, and both girls laughed with joy. Natty's present was a big tub with material, patterns, and all sorts of sewing notions. Zippers of assorted lengths and colors, spools of thread, packages of needles and straight pins, scissors with bright orange handles, and even a rotary cutting blade and cutting mat for their next quilt!

"We thought you two girls could share all of the sewing items we bought. Also, your dad is going to put a sewing table in the corner of the learning room. That way, you can leave your machine set up with whatever project you are working on. How does that sound?" Mom asked. The girls nodded their heads together and smiled.

Ella sat quietly in the middle of the floor studying each present closely. Amongst the presents were three new puzzles. She made a cute picture sitting with all of her presents arranged around her. Mom snapped a picture — Ella wearing a new stocking hat and fuzzy blanket sleeper.

The boys, who had received new bob-sleds with metal runners, were already heading out the door to try them out on the hill behind the house when Dad called them back to the family room.

"Boys, don't go outside; we aren't finished yet. I have a gift for your mother, that I believe you will want to see, too," Dad instructed. Charlie and Hairo came back in and sat on the floor next to the tree. Everyone's attention was on Dad now. What could the present be? All he had in his hands was an envelope.

"Honey, this is my present to you this year," Sean Stevens smiled with anticipation as he sat next to his wife and handed her the innocent-looking envelope. She smiled and accepted it with a puzzled expression. She ripped open the envelope, pulled out a card, and read it silently.

"Sean! Thank you! Oh thank you!" Maddie Stevens was on her feet, jumping up and down, and squealing like a school girl.

"What is it? What is it, MOM!" the children crowded around her trying to see inside the card.

"This says that Aunt Kate and Uncle Justin and your cousins are coming! They're coming for a whole month! Actually, Aunt Kate and the cousins are staying for a whole month. Uncle Justin and your dad are going to be flying down to Peru to work at the children's home for two weeks. But I get to see my sister for a whole month!" Mom explained to the kids.

The whole room seemed to erupt into a jumble of squeals, laughing, and words all mixed together in a big, joyful, family celebration.

"Is Danielle coming, too?" Ella's little voice cut through the jumble of noise.

"Yes, Ella! Yes! Danielle is coming, too!" Mom scooped the little girl up and twirled her around and around.

"I hate to end this crazy celebration, but if we are going to be at the church in time to help set up for the outreach, we are going to have to get a move on here!" Dad's voice brought everyone to the present — Christmas Day!

> *"Oh Holy Night! The stars are brightly shining. It is the night of our dear Savior's birth. Long lay the world, in sin and error pining, till He appeared and the soul felt its worth. A thrill of hope the weary soul rejoices, for yonder breaks a new and glorious morn!"*

The words swelled throughout the church and every heart present. The words seem to fly up into the heavens, where the angel choirs joined in — a praise celebration of the King of Kings.

Natty reached for Charlotte's hand. This was her favorite time of year. The day they celebrated the birth of her dear Savior and Friend — Jesus! As Natty stood and sang the beloved words of her favorite Christmas hymn, she was no longer nervous about her part in the memory quilt presentation.

The church's entire dining room was filled to overflowing with people being served a delicious Christmas dinner. Outside, there was a gentle snow falling from the sky, and the temperatures had dropped, but inside the church was warm, the food smelled delicious, and hearts were light. The families, whom the church had adopted for Christmas, had opened their presents and in a few minutes, the homeschool co-op's Christmas presentation would begin. It had been a wonderful Christmas!

Name________________________________

Exercise 1 Day 86

New Concept!

Copywork:

Finding the least common multiple in two or more numbers is helpful in finding the least common denominator in two or more fractions. To find the least common denominator in a group of fractions, we find the least common multiple of the denominators of those fractions.

This is what it looks like...

Write the Fraction, Circle the Denominator	Multiples of Denominators (circle the common multiple)	Least Common Multiple	Least Common Denominator
$\frac{1}{④}$	4, 8, (12), 16, 20, (24), ...	12	12
$\frac{1}{⑥}$	6, (12), 18, (24), 30, 36, ...		

Story Problem

After the Christmas presentation and dinner, the ladies cleaning the kitchen packed up the leftover cookies and bars for the residents of the nursing home. There was $\frac{1}{3}$ pan of raisin-almond bars, $\frac{1}{4}$ pan of chocolate chip cookie bars, and $\frac{1}{6}$ pan of orange cranberry drops. Find the least common denominator for these three fractions.

Name________________________________

Exercise 1 Day 86

Fill in the Chart!

Use your Least Common Denominator Chart which is on the other side of your Least Common Multiple Chart to find the least common denominators of these fractions.

Write the Fraction, Circle the Denominator	Multiples of Denominators (circle the common multiple)	Least Common Multiple	Least Common Denominator
$\frac{1}{5}$			
$\frac{1}{10}$			
$\frac{1}{3}$			
$\frac{1}{6}$			
$\frac{1}{2}$			
$\frac{3}{12}$			
$\frac{1}{4}$			
$\frac{1}{5}$			
$\frac{1}{2}$			
$\frac{2}{3}$			
$\frac{6}{7}$			
$\frac{7}{8}$			

Name________________________

Exercise 2 Day 87

Let's Review!

Write the missing numbers to make equivalent fractions. Make sure to multiply both the numerator and the denominator by the same number. The first one is done for you.

$\frac{2}{3} \times \frac{3}{3} = \frac{6}{9}$ $\quad$ $\frac{5}{7} \times \frac{\_\_}{\_\_} = \frac{\square}{21}$ $\quad$ $\frac{4}{5} \times \frac{\_\_}{\_\_} = \frac{\square}{20}$

$\frac{3}{4} \times \frac{\_\_}{\_\_} = \frac{\square}{16}$ $\quad$ $\frac{4}{9} \times \frac{\_\_}{\_\_} = \frac{\square}{18}$ $\quad$ $\frac{6}{7} \times \frac{\_\_}{\_\_} = \frac{\square}{21}$

Let's Practice the Concept!

Use your Least Common Denominator Chart to find the least common denominators of these fractions. Narrate to your teacher what you are doing.

$\frac{3}{8}, \frac{1}{2}$

$\frac{4}{11}, \frac{5}{22}$

$\frac{3}{7}, \frac{3}{14}, \frac{1}{2}$

$\frac{1}{3}, \frac{2}{9}, \frac{5}{18}$

$\frac{3}{10}, \frac{7}{20}$

Solve These Word Problems

When mom and the girls made the cranberry Christmas punch, they did not want to add as much sugar as the recipe called for. They decided to use $\frac{1}{4}$ cup per recipe instead of $\frac{1}{3}$ cup.

If they made the recipe 10 times, how many cups of sugar did they use?

What is the least common denominator of $\frac{1}{4}$ and $\frac{1}{3}$ cup?

Name________________________________

Exercise 2

Day 87

Solve:

x	1	2	3	4	5	6	7	8	9	10	11	12
0												
1												
2												
3												
4												
5												
6												
7												
8												
9												
10												
11												
12												

Name________________________________

Exercise 3 Day 88

More Practice!

Use your Least Common Denominator Chart to find the least common denominators of these fractions.

$\frac{2}{10}, \frac{7}{20}$

$\frac{4}{5}, \frac{3}{7}$

$\frac{3}{5}, \frac{4}{5}, \frac{5}{6}$

$\frac{5}{12}, \frac{13}{108}$

$\frac{2}{11}, \frac{21}{121}$

Use your Least Common Multiple Chart to find the least common multiple of the following numbers.

- ☐ 5, 11
- ☐ 2, 7
- ☐ 6, 8
- ☐ 9, 12
- ☐ 3, 10
- ☐ 4, 10
- ☐ 4, 6, 9

Mixed Review!

Solve.

$$\begin{array}{r} 619 \\ 226 \\ +\ 214 \\ \hline \end{array} \qquad \begin{array}{r} 365 \\ \times\ 32 \\ \hline \end{array} \qquad \begin{array}{r} 22 \\ \times\ 69 \\ \hline \end{array} \qquad \begin{array}{r} 3{,}000 \\ +\ 1{,}846 \\ \hline \end{array}$$

Name________________________________

Exercise 4 Day 89

Solve These Story Problems

Cross out any information that is not necessary. Use a green pencil or crayon to underline any clue words.

1. Mom and the girls gathered up the leftover desserts after the Christmas outreach dinner to take to the nursing home the next day. They planned to serve tea with dessert for an elderly ladies' Christmas tea. They gathered $2\frac{3}{4}$ pans of brownies, $1\frac{1}{4}$ pans of butterscotch bars, and $3\frac{1}{4}$ pans of peppermint cocoa bars. How many pans of dessert were left over?

2. The girls used $\frac{2}{3}$ spool of white thread to hem stitch their quilt's edges and $1\frac{2}{3}$ spool of medium blue to sew quilting designs on the squares. Charlotte liked the dark blue better, but there wasn't enough of it to complete the job. How many spools did they use altogether?

Copywork

In decimal place value, the place to the right of the decimal is the tenths place.

____

____

The second place to the right of a decimal is the hundredths place.

____

____

Copywork

Name_______________________________

Exercise 5

Day 90

Fractions, decimals, and percents are three ways to name part of a whole.

____

____

____

____

Work with Your Fraction/Decimal/Percent Chart

Show these fractions as decimals and percents on your chart.

- ☐ $\frac{24}{100}$

- ☐ $\frac{12}{100}$

- ☐ $\frac{2}{100}$

- ☐ $\frac{56}{100}$

- ☐ $\frac{89}{100}$

Name______________________________ **Exercise 5** Day 90

Review Time!

Use your Least Common Denominator Chart to find the least common denominators of these fractions. Narrate to your teacher what you are doing. Narrate to your teacher the difference between the greatest common factor (GCF) and the least common multiple (LCM).

Write the Fraction, Circle the Denominator	Multiples of Denominators (circle the common multiple)	Least Common Multiple	Least Common Denominator
$\frac{2}{3}$			
$\frac{4}{5}$			
$\frac{1}{2}$			
$\frac{1}{3}$			
$\frac{1}{4}$			
$\frac{3}{5}$			
$\frac{1}{10}$			
$\frac{2}{15}$			
$\frac{3}{4}$			
$\frac{7}{20}$			

Hands On!

Do some research and find out the average height of a giraffe. Now use a measuring tape to measure that length on the floor or outside. Write it here: _____________ feet.

Now measure yourself and compare it to the average giraffe. How much taller is a giraffe?

_____________ feet taller.

Least Common Multiples/ Finding a Common Denominator Part 2

Lesson 19

"Mom, could we do something nice for our neighbors? I would like to make some fresh chicken, rice, and veggie soup, and maybe a loaf of fresh bread. Mr. Bennett has been in the hospital, and I think it would be super nice for them to come home to a nice meal," Charlotte and Natty asked Mom one morning while they were still on Christmas break.

"I think that is a very thoughtful idea, girls!" Mom replied. "I do believe that we have several chicken breasts in the freezer, and there are carrots, green beans, corn, and diced tomatoes that you could also use. Hmmm...let's see...yes! We do have another bag of wheat flour in here," Mom said while she looked around in the freezer and cupboard. "We have all of the ingredients except for chicken stock to flavor the soup. We can easily get that! You two can do this together, and if you would like, make a nice card with a thoughtful poem or Bible verse in it," she continued.

The girls nodded their heads together, and set to work. They loved to cook and bake, and they were becoming quite skilled at following recipes.

Would you like to make the soup that Natty and Charlotte are going to make? Here's the recipe!

Grandma Violet's Homestyle Chicken Rice or Noodle Soup

1. *Boil 4 or 5 bone-in, but skinless, chicken breasts in about 5 quarts of water. The water will boil down and the broth of the chicken will thicken it.*
2. *Boil chicken until it is falling off of the bone. Take chicken out of the broth and let the chicken cool.*
3. *Pick chicken off of bones and set aside.*
4. *Chop chicken as fine as you would like.*
5. *Chop and prepare any veggies that you want to put into your soup.*
6. *Add another quart of chicken broth (homemade or store bought).*
7. *Bring the pot of broth to a boil and add the veggies and chicken.*
8. *Season with salt, a little black pepper, a bay leaf (remove bay leaf before eating), and let soup simmer for awhile.*
9. *Add $1\frac{1}{2}$ cups of rice or 2 cups of egg noodles and cook for at least 30 minutes.*

This week you will be reviewing various concepts that you have learned recently. Each day you will be adding to your **Thinking Tools** flashcards by copying the concept onto the front of a new index card and illustrating it on the back of the card. Narrate what you have learned about each concept.

Review

Review your divisibility rule flash cards.

Copy the following concepts, each on a new index card.

Thinking TOOL #1 Factors are all of the different numbers that divide evenly (without a remainder) into a number. Pairs of factors are two numbers that, when multiplied together, equal this number.

Thinking TOOL #2 The Greatest Common Factor (GCF) is the largest common factor any group of numbers have.

Optional Review

5 × ________ = 500   6 × 60 = ________

100 × __________ = 10,000   55 × 1,000 = __________

$5\frac{2}{3} = \frac{\square}{3}$ $6\frac{7}{8} = \frac{\square}{8}$ $6\frac{2}{3} = \frac{\square}{3}$

$\frac{15}{2} = \square\frac{\square}{2}$ $\frac{17}{2} = 8\frac{\square}{2}$ $\frac{33}{5} = 6\frac{\square}{5}$

$30\overline{)600{,}323}$

$\begin{array}{r} 555 \\ \times\ 60 \\ \hline \end{array}$

Name________________________________

Exercise 2 Day 92

Fraction Review

Use your Reduce that Fraction! Chart to reduce these fractions:

$\frac{3}{12}$ = $\frac{4}{16}$ = $\frac{6}{24}$ = $\frac{9}{45}$ = $\frac{4}{18}$ =

Copy the following concepts, each on a new index card.

Thinking TOOL #3 An improper fraction is a fraction which has a larger numerator than denominator.

Thinking TOOL #4 To change an improper fraction into a mixed number, divide the numerator by the denominator and write the remainder as a fraction.

Optional Review

Write an equivalent fraction for each.

$\frac{7}{8}$ = $\frac{5}{9}$ = $\frac{1}{2}$ = $\frac{3}{4}$ =

Change the improper fractions into mixed numbers.

$\frac{109}{12}$ = $\frac{200}{4}$ = $\frac{39}{8}$ =

Change the mixed numbers into improper fractions.

$7\frac{2}{3}$ = $8\frac{7}{9}$ = $14\frac{2}{3}$ =

Name________________________________

Exercise 3 Day 93

Greatest Common Factor Practice

Use your Greatest Common Factor Chart to find the greatest common factor for these groups of numbers:

Number	Pairs of Factors	Factors	Common Factors	Greatest Common Factor
9				
36				
4				
18				
15				
18				
16				
24				

Copy the following concept on a new index card.

Thinking TOOL #5 In some mixed number addition problems, the answer is a whole number and an improper fraction. We cannot leave the answer this way! After we solve the problem, we "set aside" the whole number part of the answer. Next, we change the improper fraction part of the answer to a mixed number. Lastly, add the whole number to the mixed number.

Optional Review

Reduce if necessary.

$7\frac{7}{8} + 8\frac{3}{8}$

$14\frac{2}{3} + 2\frac{2}{3}$

$7\frac{6}{7} + 2\frac{2}{7}$

$6\frac{2}{9} + 2\frac{8}{9}$

Name________________________________

Exercise 4 Day 94

Least Common Multiple Practice

Use your Least Common Multiple Chart to find the Least Common Multiple for these groups of numbers:

Number	Multiples	Common Multiple	Least Common Multiple
5			
35			
6			
8			
10			
12			
3			
7			

Copy the following concepts, each on a new index card.

Thinking TOOL #6 Common multiples are multiples shared by two or more numbers.

Thinking TOOL #7 The least common multiple (LCM) is the smallest multiple shared by two or more numbers. We use the LCM to find common denominators between two or more fractions.

Optional Review

Circle the multiples for the following.

8: 35 16 49 24 40

12: 108 133 148 96 36

5: 78 100 35 76 40

4: 14 24 78 16 32

Name________________________________

Exercise 5 Day 95

Review

Copy the following concepts, each on a new index card.

Thinking TOOL #8 There are three ways to show division. All of the signs mean "divided by."

Thinking TOOL #9 We can write the remainder of a division problem as a fraction. The remainder becomes the numerator, and the divisor becomes the denominator.

Optional Review

Divide, write remainder as a fraction.

Check.

$5\overline{)1,478}$

Multiply

$$\begin{array}{r} 142 \\ \times\ 21 \\ \hline \end{array}$$

Add

$$\begin{array}{r} 1,472 \\ 6,342 \\ +\ 5,978 \\ \hline \end{array}$$

Average

$$\begin{array}{r} 5 \\ 4 \\ 6 \\ 3 \\ 2 \\ +\ 10 \\ \hline \end{array}$$

Adding Fractions and Mixed Numbers with Uncommon Denominators

Lesson 20

"Mom, what time does their plane land?" Charlie asked for what seemed to be the hundredth time in the last half hour.

"It's scheduled to land at 2:20, Charlie," Mom answered patiently. The time did seem to be dragging, as they waited for their family members from Florida to arrive.

"Mom! The monitor now says 'landed' next to flight #2431!" Charlotte and Natty stepped over to stare up at the huge screen mounted on the wall. "That means their plane is on the ground! May we move closer to the escalators?"

Mom nodded approval and helped Ella gather her coloring book and crayons from the little table at the coffee shop table they were sitting around. Maddie Stevens was thankful for the airport coffee shop! It was a great place to sit and let Ella color to her heart's content.

As the family moved toward the door near the escalators, Charlie let out a whoop!

"There they are! I see them!" he hollered and started to weave through the crowd as quickly as he could.

The family members from Florida came through the sliding glass doors at the bottom of the escalators, and suddenly there was hugging and kissing and crying all around.

"Oh my goodness, kids! You've grown at least two feet since the last time I saw you!" That was Aunt Kate staring at Charlie and Hairo with her mouth open in exaggerated surprise. She reached out and ruffled their hair.

"Momma, look how much Danielle has grown!" Ella stood in front of her little cousin, who was staring up at her with owl-eyes. The poor little girl looked so tired!

"Ok, guys, let's get our luggage and get out of here!" Uncle Justin said and grinned at his wife. Kate was hugging her sister like she would never let go, and both of them were talking a-mile-a-minute, stopping to laugh and cry every few seconds...

The next morning, the children gathered around the breakfast table to hear the morning Bible story. They were excited for the day! It had started to snow sometime during the night, and when they had awoken, there were already a few inches of fresh snow on the ground. The Florida cousins, as Sean, Abby, and Danielle were called, were excited to get out into the snow. Their moms had gathered enough winter clothing for all of them to get out and make a snowman, and, if there was enough snow, play a game of Fox & Geese.

After breakfast dishes had been cleared and all of the winter gear put on, the group of cousins rushed out into the winter day. The sky was gray and the world seemed to be wrapped in a blanket of silence.

"It looks like we live in a snow globe!" Ella exclaimed as she stood with her arms open and her face turned up to the sky. Huge snowflakes landed on her nose and eyelashes, making Danielle giggle with delight.

The older children started making the circle for their game of Fox & Geese, while the two younger girls watched in wonder.

"What are you doing, Abby?" Danielle asked with a perplexed look on her cute little face.

"We're making a big circle in the snow, Dani, so we can play our game!" Abby answered her little sister as she and Natty worked their way past Ella and Danielle.

"We want to play, too!" Ella called after the girls.

"Ok, but you have to wait until we are ready! And you have to wait for us to teach you the rules!" Natty called back over her shoulder.

"Okay, Natty!" Ella agreed.

Charlie and Charlotte gathered the other children around them to explain the rules of the game.

"Ok, here's how you play. See how we made a huge 'pie' in the snow?" Charlie asked. Everyone nodded. "We cut it into eighths. Ok, that's where we have to stay. No one can go off of the pathways or they are the 'fox.' So, first we have to decide who's the fox. That person is it and everyone else is the geese. The fox has to try to tag one of the geese by chasing them — but remember! Everyone has to stay in the pathways of the circle! That area we tromped down right in the center? Well, that's the safe place — the 'home circle.' Does everyone understand? So when the fox tags one of the geese, that person becomes the fox. Oh, and you can't stay in the home circle very long. You can go there to catch your breath or tie your boot or something, but you can't stay there!"

When the children were tired of playing outside, they went inside for hot chocolate and cookies. Their cheeks and noses glowed a rosy color as they sipped their drinks and told their mothers about their game.

"Mom, it's a huge circle cut into fractional parts!" Natty exclaimed. "I wonder what it would be like if we made TWO big pies like that and cut them into a different number of pieces. That reminds me, Charlie, you promised to show me how to add fractions that don't have the same bottom number...what is that called again?"

"The denominator," Charlie said around a mouthful of oatmeal cookie. "I can show you that — sure thing!" Charlie grinned. He was fast becoming the official math professor of the family. He grinned at his cousin, Sean. "You want to help me teach this youngin' about adding fractions with uncommon denominators, sir?"

"Sure thing, Professor Charlie," Sean grinned back.

Name____________________________

Exercise 1 Day 96

New Concept for Copywork!

When we add or subtract fractions, they must have a common denominator.

____

____

Let's Practice!

1. Find the least common denominator of 2 and 10, which is 10. (If you need help, use your LCD Chart)
2. Make equivalent fractions with 10 as the denominator.
3. Add (or subtract) the fractions with the common denominators.
4. Turn any improper fractions into mixed numbers. Reduce if necessary.

The first one is done for you.

$$\frac{1}{2} \times \frac{5}{5} = \frac{5}{10}$$
$$+\ \frac{3}{10} \times \frac{1}{1} = \frac{3}{10}$$
$$\frac{8}{10} = \frac{4}{5}$$

Finish this

$$\frac{1}{3} \times \frac{3}{3} = \frac{\underline{\quad}}{9}$$
$$+\ \frac{2}{9} \times \frac{1}{1} = \frac{2}{9}$$

Solve. Reduce as necessary.

$$\frac{1}{3} \times \frac{4}{4} = \frac{\underline{\quad}}{12}$$
$$+\ \frac{3}{4} \times \frac{3}{3} = \frac{\underline{\quad}}{12}$$

$$\frac{2}{5} \times \frac{\quad}{\quad} = \underline{\quad}$$
$$+\ \frac{3}{10} \times \frac{\quad}{\quad} = \underline{\quad}$$

$$\frac{4}{15} \times \frac{\quad}{\quad} = \underline{\quad}$$
$$+\ \frac{2}{5} \times \frac{\quad}{\quad} = \underline{\quad}$$

$$\frac{1}{9} \times \frac{\quad}{\quad} = \underline{\quad}$$
$$+\ \frac{3}{4} \times \frac{\quad}{\quad} = \underline{\quad}$$

Name________________________________

Exercise 2 Day 97

More Practice with the New Concept!

Reduce if necessary. Change any improper fractions into mixed numbers.

$$\frac{1}{4} \times \quad = \_\_ \qquad \frac{3}{7} \times \quad = \_\_ \qquad \frac{6}{18} \times \quad = \_\_ \qquad \frac{3}{4} \times \quad = \_\_$$

$$+\frac{3}{8} \times \quad = \_\_ \qquad +\frac{2}{14} \times \quad = \_\_ \qquad +\frac{1}{6} \times \quad = \_\_ \qquad +\frac{3}{10} \times \quad = \_\_$$

Mixed Review!

Reduce these fractions. Use your Reduce that Fraction! Chart if you need help.

$\frac{5}{30}$ $\frac{3}{33}$ $\frac{2}{22}$ $\frac{6}{18}$

Write the least common denominator of these fractions.

$\frac{3}{8}, \frac{1}{2}$ ______ $\frac{3}{11}, \frac{1}{22}$ ______ $\frac{1}{2}, \frac{1}{10}$ ______

Work quickly.

Solve.

x	1	2	3	4	5	6	7	8	9	10	11	12
7												
8												
9												
10												
11												
12												

Name ____________________

Review!

Reduce if necessary.

$$\begin{array}{r} \frac{1}{12} \\ \frac{7}{12} \\ +\ \frac{11}{12} \\ \hline \end{array} \qquad \begin{array}{r} 5\frac{3}{10} \\ +\ 2\frac{9}{10} \\ \hline \end{array} \qquad \begin{array}{r} 26 \\ \times\ 31 \\ \hline \end{array}$$

Copywork for review!

In some mixed number addition problems, the answer is a whole number and an improper fraction. After we solve the problem, we "set aside" the whole number part of the answer. Next, we change the improper fraction part of the answer to a mixed number. Lastly, add the whole number to the mixed number.

Adding onto this concept!

To add mixed numbers with uncommon denominators, we have to find common denominators first.

Now you try it! Reduce if necessary. The first one is done for you.

$$\begin{array}{r} 8\frac{3}{8} \\ +\ 4\frac{1}{4} \\ \hline \end{array} \quad \begin{array}{r} 8\frac{3}{8} \\ +\ 4\frac{2}{8} \\ \hline 12\frac{5}{8} \end{array} \qquad \begin{array}{r} 32\frac{4}{15} \\ +\ 19\frac{2}{5} \\ \hline \end{array} \qquad \begin{array}{r} 97\frac{3}{10} \\ +\ 28\frac{7}{20} \\ \hline \end{array}$$

Name______________________________

Fraction Review

Reduce these fractions.

$\frac{3}{9}$ $\frac{4}{28}$ $\frac{5}{15}$

$\frac{9}{81}$ $\frac{10}{90}$

Change these improper fractions into mixed numbers. Reduce if needed.

$\frac{18}{4}$ $\frac{42}{8}$ $\frac{21}{9}$

$\frac{12}{5}$ $\frac{109}{8}$

Change these mixed numbers into improper fractions.

$4\frac{2}{3}$ $7\frac{2}{5}$ $3\frac{9}{10}$

$5\frac{2}{7}$ $12\frac{2}{18}$

Name________________________________

Exercise 4 Day 99

More Practice

Reduce if necessary. Change any improper fractions into mixed numbers. Don't forget to add the whole number parts of your sum.

$$\begin{array}{r} 3\frac{1}{5} \\ +\ 2\frac{7}{20} \\ \hline \end{array} \qquad \begin{array}{r} 65\frac{6}{13} \\ +\ 27\frac{11}{26} \\ \hline \end{array} \qquad \begin{array}{r} 92\frac{9}{25} \\ +\ 11\frac{1}{5} \\ \hline \end{array}$$

$$\begin{array}{r} 32\frac{4}{15} \\ 50\frac{2}{5} \\ +\ 19\frac{7}{15} \\ \hline \end{array} \qquad \begin{array}{r} 16\frac{3}{10} \\ 26\frac{7}{20} \\ +\ 36\frac{1}{10} \\ \hline \end{array}$$

Complete this chart.

x	10	100	1,000
34			
123			
56			
83			
289			

Divide.

$52\overline{)3,575}$

Check.

Name ____________________

Review Time!

Narrate to your teacher what you have learned this week about adding fractions with uncommon denominators. Use this problem to show every step.

$$\begin{array}{r} 19\frac{3}{4} \\ +\ 84\frac{5}{12} \\ \hline \end{array}$$

Copy this concept and example onto a new index card.

1. Find the least common denominator of 2 and 10, which is 10. (If you need help, use your LCD Chart)
2. Make equivalent fractions with 10 as the denominator.
3. Add (or subtract) the fractions with the common denominators.
4. Turn any improper fractions into mixed numbers. Reduce if necessary.

$$\begin{array}{r} \frac{1 \times 5 =}{2 \times 5 =}\ \frac{5}{10} \\ +\ \frac{3 \times 1 =}{10 \times 1 =}\ \frac{3}{10} \\ \hline \frac{8}{10} = \frac{4}{5} \end{array}$$

Optional Review

50 × 10 = ________

60 × 3 = ________

4,000 × 100 = ________

50 × 4 = ________

5 × 5 ÷ 5 + 5 = ________

6 × 7 ÷ 2 + 4 = ________

14 − 7 + 6 + 7 − 10 = ________

5 + 4 − 6 + 3 − 6 = ________

Draw a line segment, a line, and a ray. Label each.

Subtracting Fractions and Mixed Numbers with Uncommon Denominators

Lesson 21

"Charlie, you, Hairo, Natty, and Charlotte need to make your lunches for tomorrow. We are going to be leaving for the science museum right after breakfast in the morning, so we need to make our lunches tonight. I made some egg salad — it's in that container right there. Make sure you place your sandwiches in sandwich containers and put the lid on tightly. We will pack all of our lunches in one cooler, so don't take out the lunch boxes, okay? Here is a check list of items you need to get ready..." Mom's voice trailed away as she disappeared into the pantry.

"Sure, Mom, we can do that!" Charlotte reassured her mother. "Do we have any yogurt and fruit to pack?"

The next morning Aunt Kate, Maddie, and their six older children piled into the family van. Danielle and Ella were going to stay with their daddies for the day, while the rest of the family drove into the city to visit the museum.

It was going to be an exciting day! There was a special exhibit at the museum about the Ancient Maya of Central America. On the way into the city, Aunt Kate told the children a little about the history of Central America. She also warned the children that although the science museum was a fascinating place, they would see and hear quite a bit about the theory of evolution. The Omni Theater movie, in particular, would have evolution being touted as truth.

"Mom, why do people believe that stuff?" Abby asked with her brow furrowed. "It just doesn't make sense! I mean, I'm eight, and I know better than that! It doesn't take rocket science to figure out that evolution is a bunch of bunk! I mean it's not even science because there is no true proof to support it!"

"Well, Abby, humans have tried to write God out of the story of life for a long time. Many people, who the world call intelligent, do not want to acknowledge that God is the Maker of their very souls. A lot of humans want to be their own god and decide what is truth for themselves. If they admitted that evolution was a faulty theory and threw it out, then where would they be? They would have to admit that there 'might' just be a God — and 'if' there's a God, they're not it! It's why the world is so full of relativism," Abby's mom explained.

"What's relativism?" Sean asked.

"It's when everything becomes relative to something else. It's when there is no baseline of truth. Nothing is either right or wrong. It's all based on what people want it to be. This kind of thinking has led the world down a very dangerous path of accepting things that God says are wrong!"

"Aunt Maddie, is that what your bumper sticker is about?" Abby asked her aunt. She had noticed the bumper sticker as she had gotten into the van this morning. It said: TRUTH is not relative. TRUTH is TRUTH. The first "T" in the word "TRUTH" was Jesus' cross.

"Yes, Abby, that is exactly what it means," Aunt Maddie replied smiling at Abby in the rearview mirror. "The only real truth is the Word of God. As Bible-believing, washed-by-the-blood-of-the-Lamb, Word-dependent Christ followers, we do not follow what the world says is truth. We only follow Jesus. We believe He is who He says He is, that He can do what He says He can do, and that we are who He says we are! That's our truth!"

"Wooooeee, Aunt Maddie! Preach it!" Sean whooped from the back seat. Everyone started laughing and clapping.

Name________________________________

Exercise 1 Day 101

New Concept.

Copywork:

Just as we learned in adding fractions, when we subtract fractions or mixed numbers with uncommon denominators, we need to find the least common denominator. Then we subtract as usual.

This is what it looks like.

1. Find the least common denominator of 2 and 10, which is 10. (If you need help, use your LCD Chart)
2. Make equivalent fractions with 10 as the denominator.
3. Subtract the fractions with the common denominators.
4. Turn any improper fractions into mixed numbers. Reduce if necessary.

$$\frac{1 \times 5}{2 \times 5} = \frac{5}{10}$$
$$- \frac{3 \times 1}{10 \times 1} = \frac{3}{10}$$
$$\frac{2}{10} = \frac{1}{5}$$

Now you try it! Reduce if necessary. The first one is done for you.

$\frac{11}{14} - \frac{2}{7}$ $\quad \frac{11}{14} - \frac{4}{14} = \frac{7}{14} = \frac{1}{2}$

$\frac{3}{4} - \frac{1}{3}$

$19\frac{11}{14} - 8\frac{2}{7}$

$96\frac{9}{11} - 89\frac{3}{22}$

$93\frac{4}{5} - 42\frac{3}{10}$

$509\frac{7}{10} - 69\frac{3}{10}$

Name________________________________

Exercise 2 Day 102

Let's Practice the Concept!

Reduce if necessary.

$$\begin{array}{r} \frac{11}{14} \\ -\ \frac{3}{7} \\ \hline \end{array} \qquad \begin{array}{r} 16\frac{3}{4} \\ -\ 9\frac{1}{2} \\ \hline \end{array} \qquad \begin{array}{r} 24\frac{1}{2} \\ -\ 16\frac{1}{5} \\ \hline \end{array}$$

Review Addition!

Solve and reduce if necessary.

$$\begin{array}{r} 61\frac{1}{6} \\ +\ 47\frac{1}{6} \\ \hline \end{array} \qquad \begin{array}{r} 94\frac{1}{16} \\ +\ 31\frac{5}{8} \\ \hline \end{array} \qquad \begin{array}{r} 71\frac{1}{5} \\ +\ 79\frac{3}{10} \\ \hline \end{array}$$

Mixed Review!

Solve these story problems. Cross out any unnecessary information and underline the clue words. Reduce if necessary.

1. Charlie has 7 dollar bills and 2 quarters. He needs more quarters for the fair. If he changed one of his dollar bills into quarters, how many dollar bills and quarters will he have?

2. Natty and Charlotte worked at the library $4\frac{3}{4}$ hours last week. Mom told the girls she needed their help for some projects this week, so they will work only $2\frac{1}{4}$ hours. How much more time did they work last week than this week?

Name________________________________

Exercise 3 Day 103

Subtraction Review

Let's subtract fractions horizontally!

$\frac{11}{13} - \frac{5}{13} =$ $\frac{12}{17} - \frac{9}{17} =$ $\frac{16}{21} - \frac{8}{21} =$

$31\frac{4}{5} - 10\frac{1}{5} =$ $51\frac{2}{3} - 40\frac{1}{3} =$

Subtract and reduce the answer if necessary. Narrate to your teacher as you work through each of these problems.

$$\begin{array}{r} 45\frac{13}{20} \\ -\ 13\frac{2}{5} \\ \hline \end{array} \qquad \begin{array}{r} 58\frac{1}{2} \\ -\ 21\frac{1}{5} \\ \hline \end{array}$$

Mixed Practice!

Turn these improper fractions into mixed or whole numbers. Reduce if necessary.

$\frac{20}{4}$ $\frac{14}{3}$ $\frac{34}{12}$ $\frac{22}{11}$

Divide.

$12 \overline{)\ 2,460}$

Add.

$$\begin{array}{r} 99,158 \\ +\ 24,099 \\ \hline \end{array}$$

Subtract.

$$\begin{array}{r} 45,001 \\ -\ 23,689 \\ \hline \end{array}$$

Name________________________________

Add and Subtract!

Watch the denominators! Reduce if necessary!

$40\frac{7}{16} + 30\frac{1}{8}$

$73\frac{15}{20} - 52\frac{12}{20}$

$39\frac{3}{7} - 24\frac{1}{14}$

$99\frac{13}{16} - 92\frac{3}{4}$

$55\frac{15}{21} - 21\frac{3}{21}$

$59\frac{3}{10} - 12\frac{1}{4}$

Use your Least Common Multiple Chart to find the LCM of these groups of numbers. Narrate to your teacher any patterns you may see.

12, 3, 6 ________

5, 8, 40 ________

12, 36, 6 ________

4, 8, 16, 32 ________

Optional Review

Change the improper fractions into mixed numbers and the mixed numbers into improper fractions. Reduce if necessary.

$\frac{9}{6}$

$3\frac{7}{8}$

$\frac{11}{2}$

$5\frac{6}{7}$

Name________________________________

Review

Narrate each step to your teacher as you do this problem.

$$\begin{array}{r} 23\frac{3}{14} \\ -\ 8\frac{1}{7} \\ \hline \end{array}$$

Copy this concept on an index card and illustrate it on the backside.

1. Find the least common denominator of 2 and 10, which is 10. (If you need help, use your LCD Chart)
2. Make equivalent fractions with 10 as the denominator.
3. Subtract the fractions with the common denominators.
4. Turn any improper fractions into mixed numbers. Reduce if necessary.

$$\begin{array}{rl} \frac{1 \times 5}{2 \times 5} = & \frac{5}{10} \\ -\ \frac{3 \times 1}{10 \times 1} = & \frac{3}{10} \\ \hline & \frac{2}{10} = \frac{1}{5} \end{array}$$

Optional Review

Add.

$$\begin{array}{r} 14,623 \\ +\ 88,979 \\ \hline \end{array}$$

Subtract.

$$\begin{array}{r} 1,000,000 \\ -\ 896,672 \\ \hline \end{array}$$

Multiply.

$$\begin{array}{r} 52 \\ \times\ 62 \\ \hline \end{array}$$

Divide and check.

$$5 \overline{)\$79.85}$$

It's Sudoku Time Again!

By now, you should be getting even better at solving these puzzles! These are not just for fun – they are a wonderful logic- and skill-building challenge! While the examples in this book are simple, there are many variations of Sudoku that are available if you want to enjoy more.

Remember: Don't repeat numbers in a row, column, or 3 by 3 area (within the darker lines)!

				6			2	1
	5			4			9	
2	8	6		3	1	5		
	3	8	7		9			2
1					3			4
	9				8	7		3
		9	2			4	6	8
5		4	3	8	6		7	
8								

Adding and Subtracting Mixed Numbers with Common Denominators

Lesson 22

"Hey girls!" Charlie, Hairo, and Sean poked their heads around the corner of the girls' room door.

"Hay is for horses - straw is for cows, Charlie!" Natty giggled. "What is it?" She swung her legs around the side of the bed and sat up. The girls had been reading after playing outside.

"Haha, Natty," Charlie grinned at his sister. "We had an idea! Do you girls want to hear it?" All three girls nodded their heads, so he continued, "What do you think about having a fiesta? Dad and Uncle Justin will be back in the middle of next week, so we have time to plan it. We could even make a piñata! What do you think?"

"Oh, that would be so much fun!" Charlotte and Abby jumped up and squealed. "Let's go talk to Mom about it!" The kids hurried down the hall to the kitchen, where their mothers were sitting at the breakfast bar, drinking tea and chatting.

"Mom! Mom!" Abby stood at her mother's elbow and hopped from one foot to the other. She had a lot of energy. "Can we talk to you? MAY we talk to you?" she corrected herself.

"Yes, of course, Abby, go ahead!" her mom smiled at her.

"We want to put on a fiesta! We can do it all; you won't have to worry about a thing!" Abby said excitedly.

"Well, it's ok with me, if it's ok with Aunt Maddie — after all, this is her house," Kate said to her daughter.

"May we, Mom? May we?" asked Charlotte.

"Well, I don't see why not!" Maddie decided. "I think we probably have enough stuff around here to pull from. I tell you what, kids, if you go make a list of materials that you will need, I will tell you if we have it. If the list of needed material isn't too long, we will have ourselves a fiesta! But you kiddos will have to do it all!"

"Ok, Mom! We can do it!" Charlie agreed.

"Guys, come over here and sit down. Let's make our list!" Sean went to the table and pulled out the chairs. Abby and Charlotte gathered a pad of paper and pens.

"Ok, let's see..." Charlotte said.

"You know, children, this isn't that big a list of needed material! I think we can do this! I'm going to send some cash with Auntie Kate, so she can take you to the grocery store. I'll stay with the napping littles." The children watched as she pulled some money out of her wallet.

If you would like to have a fiesta like the children in the story, talk to your parent. Make a list of your favorite Mexican foods and find recipes (or if time is an issue, talk to your parent about purchasing them already to eat!) Start now gathering your ingredients and material!

Here are some ideas for your fiesta...

- Make a piñata (instructions are in Lesson 23!).
- Decorate with balloons and crepe-paper streamers.
- Make and eat a Mexican meal (delicious recipe in Lesson 23).
- Listen to Mexican music.

Name________________________________

Exercise 1 Day 106

Help Charlotte make a list for the fiesta!

These are the items I need to gather for my fiesta:

1.

2.

3.

4.

5.

6.

7.

8.

9.

10.

Mixed Review

Reduce and change any improper fractions to mixed numbers.

$$94\frac{7}{10} + 31\frac{7}{10}$$

$$36\frac{4}{5} + 14\frac{5}{8}$$

$$57\frac{9}{12} + 31\frac{5}{12}$$

Reduce.

$\frac{4}{8} =$ $\frac{3}{6} =$ $\frac{9}{12} =$ $\frac{5}{15} =$

Change these to a mixed number and reduce if necessary.

$\frac{5}{4} =$ $\frac{17}{9} =$ $\frac{8}{6} =$ $\frac{6}{5} =$

Name________________________________

Exercise 2 Day 107

New Concept for Copywork.

Sometimes we need to make a whole number into a fraction. To do this, simply use the same number in the numerator and in the denominator.

To write a whole number as a mixed number, we can take one whole and break it up into parts. Study the pictures below.

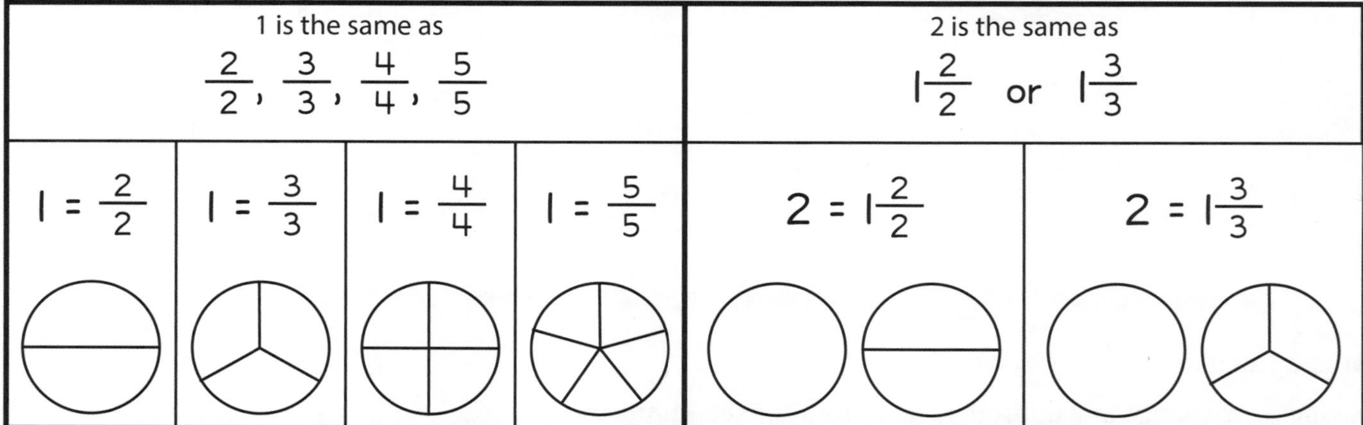

Try these! Fill in the blank with the correct number.

$1 = \frac{\quad}{7}$ $\qquad$ $1 = \frac{\quad}{12}$ $\qquad$ $1 = \frac{\quad}{9}$

Write as mixed numbers. The first one is done for you.

$2 = 1\frac{3}{3}$ $\qquad$ $4 = 3\frac{\quad}{5}$ $\qquad$ $6 = 5\frac{\quad}{3}$ $\qquad$ $11 = 10\frac{\quad}{12}$

Write as mixed numbers using one "unit" as an improper fraction. The first one is done for you.

$5 = 4\frac{5}{5}$ $\qquad$ $9 =$ $\qquad$ $4 =$ $\qquad$ $3 =$

Name________________________________

Exercise 3 Day 108

New Concept Practice

Look back at Exercise 2. Now let's begin to discover WHY we learned to write a whole number as an improper fraction!

This one is done for you.

$$\begin{array}{r} 1 = \frac{3}{3} \\ -\ \frac{2}{3} = \frac{2}{3} \\ \hline \frac{1}{3} \end{array}$$

Finish this one.

$$\begin{array}{r} 1 = \frac{\quad}{5} \\ -\ \frac{1}{5} = \frac{\quad}{5} \\ \hline \end{array}$$

Now do these.

$$\begin{array}{r} 1 = \underline{\quad} \\ -\ \frac{4}{15} = \underline{\quad} \\ \hline \end{array}$$

$$\begin{array}{r} 1 = \underline{\quad} \\ -\ \frac{7}{8} = \underline{\quad} \\ \hline \end{array}$$

Mixed Review!

Reduce if necessary.

$$\begin{array}{r} 7\frac{5}{8} \\ -\ 2\frac{1}{5} \\ \hline \end{array}$$

$$\begin{array}{r} 51\frac{6}{12} \\ +\ 16\frac{1}{3} \\ \hline \end{array}$$

Average these numbers:

23, 56, 78, 234, 98, 127

Name________________________________

Exercise 4 Day 109

Let's Build on That Concept!

Copywork:

Sometimes we need to borrow from the minuend (the top number in a subtraction problem) by taking 1 "unit" from the whole number and rewriting it as a fraction with a common denominator.

____

____

____

____

This one is done for you.

$$\begin{array}{rcr} 3 & = & 2\frac{3}{3} \\ -\ \frac{2}{3} & = & \frac{2}{3} \\ \hline & & 2\frac{1}{3} \end{array}$$

Finish this one.

$$\begin{array}{rcr} 8 & = & 7\frac{\ \ }{7} \\ -\ \frac{4}{7} & = & \frac{4}{7} \\ \hline \end{array}$$

Now do this one.

$$\begin{array}{rcr} 6 & = & \frac{\ \ }{\ \ } \\ -\ \frac{3}{8} & = & \frac{3}{8} \\ \hline \end{array}$$

And this one.

$$\begin{array}{rcr} 6 & = & \frac{\ \ }{\ \ } \\ -\ 2\frac{1}{2} & = & 2\frac{1}{2} \\ \hline \end{array}$$

Mixed Review!

Fill in the missing Roman numerals.

I, ______, ______, IV, ______, ______, ______, ______, IX, ______, XI, XII, ______, ______, XV, ______, XVII, ______, XIX, ______

Name____________________________

Copywork:

When we divide, we are taking a large group and breaking it into smaller groups. To divide with a two digit divisor, we use some mental math. When you have a two digit divisor, you will always use at least the first two digits of the dividend.

Divide and Check.

$6\overline{)\$47.04}$

Draw an obtuse angle, an acute angle, and a right angle. Label each.

Name______________________________

Exercise 5 Day 110

Review Time!

Solve. Reduce if necessary.

$32\frac{9}{15} + 24\frac{7}{15}$

$4 - \frac{3}{7}$

$4 - 1\frac{1}{6}$

$39\frac{7}{21} + 19\frac{1}{3}$

$15 - 2\frac{6}{7}$

$22\frac{7}{8} - 15\frac{2}{4}$

$32\frac{2}{3} + 78\frac{2}{3}$

Make equivalent fractions.

$\frac{1}{2} =$ $\frac{3}{4} =$ $\frac{2}{3} =$ $\frac{1}{4} =$

Convert.

2 years = _____ months

4,000 pounds = _____ tons

48 items = _____ dozen

60 inches = _____ feet

360 seconds = _____ minutes

27 feet = _____ yards

Adding Mixed Numbers with Uncommon Denominators

Lesson 23

"Charlie, can you grab that end of the streamer? We need to tape it up over there!" Charlotte was standing on a stool to reach the corner of the door.

"Sure. Here, Charlotte, let Hairo and me do that. We're tall enough to do it without falling," Charlie helped his twin sister down from the stool and took the end of the streamer. He and Hairo taped the strips of crepe paper as Natty, Charlotte, and Abby cut the pieces and handed them to the boys.

"I can't wait for our fiesta!" Abby said with shining eyes.

"I know! Me neither!" Natty agreed. They had worked hard all morning to make their special dish for the fiesta. Their mothers had only helped a few times!

The decorating was coming along really well, and they had even learned a new math concept — adding mixed numbers with uncommon denominators. They even had to carry a few times in their problems. Cooking and following a recipe used a lot of math skills!

"Uncle Sean and Dad will be home for our fiesta, right, Mom?" Abby asked her mother.

"Yes, I just got a call from them saying their flight landed on time, and they are in the car and on the way home. They should be here within the hour," Kate reassured her daughter.

"What do you think of our decorations, Mom?" Charlotte asked.

"They are just beautiful! You kids have done a spectacular job on preparing for this fiesta! I'm so excited to taste what you cooked!" Maddie Stevens answered.

Teacher

If you don't feel up to the challenges of a huge Mexican fiesta (with all of the food, etc...) please adjust this lesson to your needs. For example, allow your student(s) to focus on creating a piñata and decorations and substitute tortilla chips and salsa. Or purchase a piñata and make the recipe on the next page.

If you would like just ONE recipe for a delicious, one-dish Mexican meal, this is it!

This is a recipe for Cheesy Chicken Enchilada Bake. (This is from https://blogs.extension.iastate.edu/spendsmart/2012/04/09/cheesy-chicken-enchilada-bake/.)

CHEESY CHICKEN ENCHILADA BAKE

INGREDIENTS

- 1 pound boneless, skinless chicken breast (about 2 cups)
- ½ cup water
- 1 tablespoon chili powder
- 1 can (15-ounce) low sodium black beans, rinsed and drained
- 1 cup frozen corn
- 1 cup salsa
- 8 whole wheat tortillas
- Cooking spray
- ½ cup 2%-fat shredded cheddar cheese

DIRECTIONS:

1. Cut chicken breast into 4-5 chunks. Simmer in a medium saucepan with water and chili powder. Cook until internal temperature is 165° F (about 10 minutes).
2. Remove chicken from pan. Cut into smaller chunks or shred into small chunks and return to pan. Add beans, corn, and salsa to saucepan. Cook until hot, about 2 minutes. Remove from heat.
3. Spread ½ cup of chicken mixture down the center of each tortilla. Roll up and place seam-side down in greased 9×13 pan.
4. Spread any leftover chicken mixture over the top of the enchiladas.
5. Bake at 375° F for 12-15 minutes.
6. Sprinkle cheese on top of the enchiladas during the last 5 minutes of cooking.
7. Serve immediately.

Name________________________________

Exercise 1 Day 111

Review of Concept.

Sometimes when we add two or more mixed numbers, the fractional part of the sum is an improper fraction ($\frac{17}{15}$). To find the final answer, we must "set aside" the whole number part (84) while we turn the improper fraction into a mixed number. Finally, we add the two whole parts (84 and 1) and place our fractional part next to it ($85\frac{2}{15}$). Narrate what you are doing at each step.

$$\begin{array}{rcr} 23\frac{5}{15} & = & \frac{5}{15} \\ +\ 61\frac{4}{5} & = & \frac{12}{15} \\ \hline 84 & & \frac{17}{15} \end{array}$$

$$\begin{array}{r} 1\ \frac{2}{15} \\ 15\,\overline{)\,17} \\ -15 \\ \hline 2 \end{array}$$

$$84 + 1\frac{2}{15} = 85\frac{2}{15}$$

1. Find L.C.D.
2. Add (We see the fractional part of the sum is an improper fraction).
3. Turn that improper fraction into a mixed number.
4. Add the whole number part of your mixed number to the other whole number in your sum.
5. Place your fractional part next to the whole number. Your answer is $85\frac{2}{15}$.

Now you try it!

This one is done for you.

$$\begin{array}{rcr} 5\frac{13}{14} & = & \frac{13}{14} \\ +\ 4\frac{4}{7} & = & \frac{8}{14} \\ \hline 9 & & \frac{21}{14} \end{array}$$

$$\begin{array}{r} 1\ \frac{7}{14} \\ 14\,\overline{)\,21} \\ -14 \\ \hline 7 \end{array}$$

$$9 + 1\frac{7}{14} = 10\frac{7}{14} = 10\frac{1}{2}$$

Now try these.

$$\begin{array}{rcl} 4\frac{7}{9} & = & \text{—} \\ +\ 7\frac{2}{3} & = & \text{—} \\ \hline \end{array}$$

$$\begin{array}{rcl} 9\frac{2}{3} & = & \text{—} \\ +\ 2\frac{5}{12} & = & \text{—} \\ \hline \end{array}$$

$$\begin{array}{rcl} 7\frac{7}{10} & = & \text{—} \\ +\ 7\frac{3}{5} & = & \text{—} \\ \hline \end{array}$$

Name______________________________ Exercise 1 Day 111

Mixed Review!

1. The children were getting ready for their Mexican fiesta! Their moms told them to make a list of items they needed to purchase to make their piñata, as well as any ingredients they may need for their feast! Help them figure out how much it will all cost.

   Total cost: ________________

   - Large balloons (2 bags) $.79 each bag
   - Large bag of flour (1 bag) $3.89 each bag
   - Corn tortillas (2 packages) $2.65 each package
   - Flour tortillas (2 packages) $3.65 each package
   - Refried beans (3 cans) $1.65 each can
   - Mild salsa (1 container) $2.89 each container
   - Hot salsa (1 container) $2.89 each container

2. If the 6 older children divided the cost evenly amongst themselves, how much would they all have to pay?

3. The children's parents offered to pay half of the total. How much are they going to pay?

Name ________________________________

Exercise 2 Day 112

Let's Practice Some More!

Reduce if necessary.

$$3\frac{12}{16} = \text{—} \quad + 7\frac{3}{8} = \text{—}$$

$$6\frac{2}{9} = \text{—} \quad + 8\frac{17}{18} = \text{—}$$

$$4\frac{11}{15} = \text{—} \quad + 7\frac{1}{3} = \text{—}$$

Mixed Review!

Reduce if necessary.

$$3 - \frac{2}{7}$$

$$4 - \frac{9}{11}$$

$$53\frac{8}{10} - 18\frac{1}{3}$$

Write two factors for each of the following numbers.

36 _____, _____ 15 _____, _____ 9 _____, _____

1. What are prime numbers?
2. Write the number one million: ______________________
3. Subtract seven hundred from one thousand: ______________________
4. Write an equivalent fraction for $\frac{3}{9}$: ______________________
5. Change $\frac{35}{8}$ into a mixed number: ______________________
6. Average these three numbers: 54, 68, 22 ______________________
7. Write 45 as a Roman numeral: ______________________

Name________________________________

Exercise 3 Day 113

Work and Narrate!

Reduce if necessary.

$$\begin{array}{r} 7\frac{19}{24} = \text{—} \\ +\ 8\frac{3}{8} = \text{—} \\ \hline \end{array} \qquad \begin{array}{r} 9\frac{11}{12} = \text{—} \\ +\ 8\frac{1}{6} = \text{—} \\ \hline \end{array} \qquad \begin{array}{r} 1\frac{10}{21} = \text{—} \\ +\ 7\frac{5}{7} = \text{—} \\ \hline \end{array}$$

Concept Card

Copy this concept on an index card.

Sometimes when we add two or more mixed numbers, the fractional part of the sum is an improper fraction. To find the final answer, we must "set aside" the whole number part while we turn the improper fraction into a mixed number. Finally, we add the two whole parts and place our fractional part next to it.

Review.

Add.

$$\begin{array}{r} 78 \\ 85 \\ +\ 92 \\ \hline \end{array} \qquad \begin{array}{r} 10{,}565 \\ +\ 20{,}678 \\ \hline \end{array}$$

Subtract.

$$\begin{array}{r} 1{,}000{,}207 \\ -\ 872{,}198 \\ \hline \end{array}$$

Divide and check.

$$20 \overline{)\,6{,}000{,}320}$$

Fill in the blanks.

5 × _____ = 500

42 ÷ _____ = 7

480 ÷ _____ = 40

6 × _____ = 72

Name______________________________

Hands On!

Over the next two exercises, you will be building your own piñata. Here are some simple instructions!

You will need adult supervision for this project!

Materials you will need:

- Plastic tablecloth (or something else that is washable or toss-able!)
- Two bowls
- Flour
- Water
- Salt
- Balloons
- Newspaper
- Pin or needle
- Rope, twine, or strong string
- Scissors

Instructions:

- Cover your work area with newspaper or a plastic tablecloth.
- In a bowl, mix 2 cups of flour with 2 cups of water. Add a tablespoon of salt to create your papier-mâché mixture. With a spoon, combine until mixed to a batter-like texture.
- Blow up a balloon to the size you want your piñata to be, and knot the end.
- Tear up newspaper into strips about 1-2" inches in width.
- Dip each strip into the papier-mâché mixture, dragging it against the bowl's edge to remove excess moisture, and place each strip onto the balloon.
- Apply your strips in a crisscross pattern, leaving the knotted end of the balloon untouched.
- Once the balloon has been covered with about 3-4 layers of newspaper, allow the form to dry. This may take several days. To speed up the process, leave your piñata in a warm, dry place.
- When dried, hold the balloon's knot, and use a pin or needle to pop it. Poke two holes into opposite ends of the top of the piñata, and string twine, string, or rope through them to create your piñata's loop for hanging.
- Make another small batch of papier-mâché mixture (half the size of your first batch), and use your leftover newspaper strips to cover the top hole of your shape. Set the dry base in a clean bowl, and allow the wet area to stiffen.
- Once dried, your piñata is ready to fill and decorate!

To fill your piñata, use scissors to cut a small flap into the side of your finished piñata. Pull the flap up to fill, then press down to hide the opening.

Ideas to Decorate your Piñata

1. Use cupcake liners to decorate your piñata. Fold and glue these little liners all over your piñata in overlapping layers.
2. Tissue paper is also a fun and easy way to decorate your piñata. Simply cut out strips and squares and stack in layers and glue, leaving one edge loose like a ruffle!
3. Party hats also make fun decorations for your piñata! Simply glue them all over your piñata like spikes. You can even glue streamers on the end of each.

Subtracting Mixed Numbers with Uncommon Denominators

Lesson 24

"But I don't want them to go!" Ella's voice trembled with sadness. "I'll miss Danielle too much."

"I know, Honey. Goodbyes are so very hard. But we will see them again! Soon! I promise. Come out from under the bed. You need to say goodbye to your Auntie and Uncle and cousins. Come on, Honey. Out you come. Good girl. Come here, let me give you a hug," Maddie knelt in front of her small daughter and hugged her tightly. Goodbyes are so hard, she thought to herself.

"Goodbye, Uncle Justin. Goodbye, Aunt Kate!" Natty hugged first one and then the other. "I'll miss you!"

"We'll miss you, too, Natty. We'll miss all of you!" Kate said through her sniffling. She hugged each of her nephews and nieces and then started around again.

"Kate! We have to go, Honey! We have to be at the airport in an hour," Uncle Justin put his arm around his wife to try to steer her out the door. Ugh. Goodbyes are so hard, he thought to himself.

Maddie and all of the Stevens children stood at the door and waved goodbye to their family members. Sean Stevens was taking them to the airport.

The house seemed strangely quiet. Everyone was so sad!

"Come on guys. Let's try to cheer up! Should we play a game or something? What do you guys want to do? Games? Puzzles? Anything?" When no one answered Mom, she decided to take things into her own hands. "Ok, well, let's play this new game we got from Grandma and Grandpa for Christmas. It's a banking game! Look, it even has little checkbooks for each of the players. Doesn't this look fun?" she asked.

"Ok, I'll play," Charlie said sadly. "It won't be as much fun without Sean and Abby, but that's ok. We have to get use to them not being here."

"Ok, I'll play, too," Charlotte sighed and sat next to Charlie. One by one the children pulled out chairs and sat down around the table.

"Let me start by reading the directions," Mom said and tried to smile brightly at her children. Ella went to get her new coloring book and crayons.

"Here you go, kids; these are the little checkbooks we use to play the game," Mom slid the checkbooks and pencils across the table to each of the older kids. "This is a really cool game! Look at this list of skills covered in the game! It says, 'Writing checks, balancing bank accounts, addition/subtraction of decimals, and even work with fractions."

"Hey, that's what I was just teaching the girls the other day," Charlie said. "I'm going to like this game! I can already tell! And, what do you know, math was the answer to our problems again!" When everyone looked at him questioningly, he continued, "This game of math helped cheer us up!

Math saves the day again!" Everyone was giggling by now. Charlie and his math! What a silly boy!

Later that evening, the family was gathered in the family room for their bedtime devotion time. Dad looked at Mom with a questioning look, and she nodded her head at him. The children looked from one parent to the other. Something was up!

"Kids, Mom and I have a surprise for you!" Dad said, leaning forward with excitement. "We are going to go on a three week adventure! We are going to go to a wilderness camp! Mom and I have been asked to come run a children's survival awareness camp for children six to twelve years old. We have decided to go, and you all are coming with us!"

Whoops of excitement went up around the circle. Only Ella sat quietly.

"Daddy, I'm not old enough to go," Ella said with a quivering lower lip. "I'm not old enough to do anything the other kids can. It's like the game we got for Christmas! I'm too little to do anything." Ella's head hung down, and a single tear slipped off of the end of her nose.

"Oh Honey! You most certainly ARE going with us!" Dad picked Ella up and placed her on his knee. "Look at me, Ella. You are part of this family, and you are going! In fact, I told the camp owners that all of my children were coming, or none of us were coming. That's what Mom and I decided. And that is what has happened. We are all going, Ella. Including you!"

Ella smiled through her tears and snuggled against her daddy's chest. She didn't mind being small after all. She was the only one of the children who could still snuggle up under her daddy's chin. And that was a good thing!

Name________________________________

Exercise 1 Day 116

New Concept!

When we need to subtract $2\frac{4}{5}$ from $6\frac{1}{5}$, we need to borrow.

1. In this problem, we borrow from the 6. The 6 becomes $5\frac{5}{5}$.
2. The five-fifths we borrowed from the 6 is added to the $\frac{1}{5}$, making our new mixed number $5\frac{6}{5}$.
3. Now we can subtract.

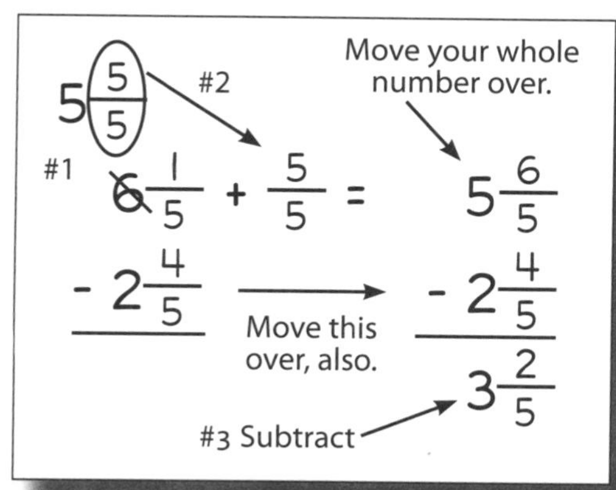

Copywork

When we need to subtract a mixed number problem and the top fraction is smaller than the bottom, we need to borrow just like any other subtraction problem. We borrow from the whole number, taking one "unit" from it and making it an equivalent fraction. We then subtract, using the new mixed number as the minuend (top number).

Name________________________________

Exercise 1 Day 116

You Try It Now!

The first one is done for you. Reduce if necessary.

$$\begin{array}{r} 4\frac{1}{3} = 3\frac{4}{3} \\ -\ 1\frac{2}{3} = 1\frac{2}{3} \\ \hline 2\frac{2}{3} \end{array} \qquad \begin{array}{r} 5\frac{3}{5} \\ -\ 2\frac{4}{5} \\ \hline \end{array} \qquad \begin{array}{r} 11\frac{1}{6} \\ -\ 9\frac{5}{6} \\ \hline \end{array}$$

Mixed Review!

Reduce and change improper fractions into mixed numbers.

$$\begin{array}{r} \frac{4}{9} \\ \frac{2}{3} \\ +\ \frac{5}{18} \\ \hline \end{array} \qquad \begin{array}{r} \frac{3}{9} \\ \frac{1}{3} \\ +\ \frac{1}{18} \\ \hline \end{array} \qquad \begin{array}{r} 11{,}050 \\ -\ 2{,}132 \\ \hline \end{array} \qquad \begin{array}{r} 57{,}459 \\ -\ 29{,}091 \\ \hline \end{array}$$

Solve

1,760 yards = ______ mile(s)

1 mile = ______ feet

3 miles = ______ yards

3 mile = ______ feet

108 items = ______ dozen

96 months = ______ years

Name________________________________

Exercise 2 Day 117

More Practice with the Concept!

Reduce if necessary. Choose one to narrate to your teacher.

$6\frac{3}{8} - 2\frac{5}{8}$

$5\frac{3}{7} - 4\frac{5}{7}$

$86\frac{1}{4} - 59\frac{3}{4}$

$10\frac{1}{9} - 3\frac{8}{9}$

Mixed Review!

Turn these improper fractions into mixed or whole numbers.

$\frac{42}{7}$ $\frac{63}{8}$ $\frac{25}{4}$

$\frac{17}{3}$ $\frac{33}{11}$ $\frac{75}{4}$

Reduce. Use your Reduce the Fraction! Chart if you need help.

$\frac{4}{8}$ $\frac{9}{27}$ $\frac{18}{32}$

$\frac{4}{14}$ $\frac{3}{15}$ $\frac{6}{20}$

Add.

$783 + 236 + 510$

$421 + 148 + 664$

Subtract.

$3,781 - 2,989$

$78 - 69$

Name________________________________

Adding onto the Concept

We have a mixed number problem with uncommon denominators.

$$8\frac{1}{3} = 8\frac{2}{6} = 7\frac{8}{6}$$
$$-\,5\frac{5}{6} = 5\frac{5}{6} = 5\frac{5}{6}$$
$$2\frac{3}{6} = 2\frac{1}{2}$$

$7\frac{6}{6}$

#1 Find a common denominator.

#2 Since the top fraction is smaller than the bottom, we need to borrow from the whole number to make a bigger fraction.

#3 Subtract.

#4 Reduce if necessary.

Study the problem above and try these. The first one is done for you. Reduce if necessary.

$$6\frac{1}{2} = 6\frac{2}{4} = 5\frac{6}{4}$$
$$-\,4\frac{3}{4} = 4\frac{3}{4} = 4\frac{3}{4}$$
$$1\frac{3}{4}$$

$$9\frac{3}{4} \quad - \, 5\frac{7}{8}$$

$$5\frac{1}{3} \quad - \, 3\frac{4}{9}$$

Mixed Review!

Write as decimals. The first one is done for you.

$\frac{51}{100}$ = .51 $\qquad$ $\frac{23}{100}$ = ______ $\qquad$ $\frac{1}{100}$ = ______

Copywork for Review!

The second place to the right of a decimal is the hundredths place.

____

____

Work with Your Fraction/Decimal/Percent Chart.

Show these fractions as decimals and percents on your chart.

☐ $\frac{4}{100}$ ☐ $\frac{78}{100}$ ☐ $\frac{92}{100}$ ☐ $\frac{28}{100}$ ☐ $\frac{16}{100}$

Name______________________________

Exercise 4 Day 119

Let's Review!

Reduce if necessary. Narrate to your teacher each step.

$$6\frac{1}{5} - 1\frac{4}{5}$$

$$9\frac{2}{7} - 1\frac{6}{7}$$

$$9\frac{3}{4} - 5\frac{7}{8}$$

$$391\frac{1}{6} - 187\frac{2}{3}$$

$$169\frac{8}{15} - 56\frac{4}{5}$$

Concept Card

Write the following on an index card and illustrate it.

When we need to subtract a mixed number problem and the top fraction is smaller than the bottom, we need to borrow just like any other subtraction problem We borrow from the whole number, taking one "unit" from it and making it an equivalent fraction (with the bottom fraction). We then subtract, using the new mixed number as the minuend (top number).

Review

Write these **numbers** in words.

301,568

____

34,560

____

2,001

____

$46.56

____

$782.10

____

Name________________________________

Sudoku!

Take your time — and see if it is getting easier to do these puzzles! The next time you are at the library or a store, look and see what kinds of Sudoku puzzles are available. If you want to know more, you can research the history of the puzzles!

5	6			8	7			4
		4				6		7
7			5	4				9
			8	9		3	1	
	5				1	2	9	
1	3	9			5			
	9	1	4	6			7	2
	2	5	7					1
		7					6	

Teacher

Have your student(s) work with any concepts he or she is having trouble with.

Review!

Reminders:

When you add or subtract fractions, you must find a common denominator to make equivalent fractions. Then you can add or subtract the fractions with the common denominators, reducing if you need to or turn any improper fractions into mixed numbers.

- An improper fraction is a fraction which has a larger numerator than denominator.
- A proper fraction is a fraction which has a larger denominator than numerator.

Examples

When we subtract fractions or mixed numbers with uncommon denominators, you need to find the least common denominator. Then you subtract as usual.

$$\begin{array}{rrcr} & \frac{2}{2} & = & \frac{4}{4} \\ - & \frac{2}{4} & = & \frac{2}{4} \\ \hline & & & \frac{2}{4} \end{array} \qquad \begin{array}{rrcr} & 2\frac{1}{2} & = & 2\frac{5}{10} \\ - & \frac{2}{5} & = & \frac{4}{10} \\ \hline & & & 2\frac{1}{10} \end{array}$$

In some mixed number addition problems, the answer is a whole number and an improper fraction. You cannot leave the answer this way! After you solve the problem, you "set aside" the whole number part of the answer. Next, you change the improper fraction part of the answer to a mixed number. Lastly, add the whole number to the mixed number.

$$\begin{array}{rrcr} & 2\frac{1}{2} & = & 2\frac{3}{6} \\ + & 2\frac{2}{3} & = & 2\frac{4}{6} \\ \hline & & & 4\frac{7}{6} = 5\frac{1}{6} \end{array}$$

Sometimes you need to make a whole number into a fraction. To do this, simply use the same number in the numerator and in the denominator.

$$1 = \frac{2}{2}, \frac{3}{3}, \frac{4}{4}, \frac{5}{5}$$

Sometimes you need to borrow from the minuend (the top number in a subtraction problem) by taking 1 "unit" from the whole number and rewriting it as a fraction with a common denominator.

$$\begin{array}{rrcr} & 3 & = & 2\frac{3}{3} \\ - & \frac{2}{3} & = & \frac{2}{3} \\ \hline & & & 2\frac{1}{3} \end{array}$$

Name______________________________

Review Time!

Review of all decimal concepts.

Copywork:

Fractions, decimals, and percents are three ways to name part of a whole. All three have numerators and denominators.

____

____

____

1 dollar (whole) has 100 cents (parts).
1 whole dollar is $\frac{100}{100}$.
1 whole dollar is 100%

____

____

____

Mixed Review

Divide and check.

$60\overline{)\$360.00}$

Add.

$$\begin{array}{r} \$\,6.13 \\ 3.56 \\ +\,7.13 \\ \hline \end{array}$$

Subtract.

$$\begin{array}{r} \$\,52.03 \\ -\,10.72 \\ \hline \end{array}$$

Name_______________________________

Exercise 2 Day 122

Bonus Concept! Writing Checks.

Have you ever watched your parents or older sibling write a check? Well, here's your chance to learn how to write one yourself!

Write the name of the store or person you are writing the check to on this line.

The amount written in words

Your signature goes here.

(Make sure you sign in cursive and that you use a blue or black ink pen when writing checks.)

Now you write one!

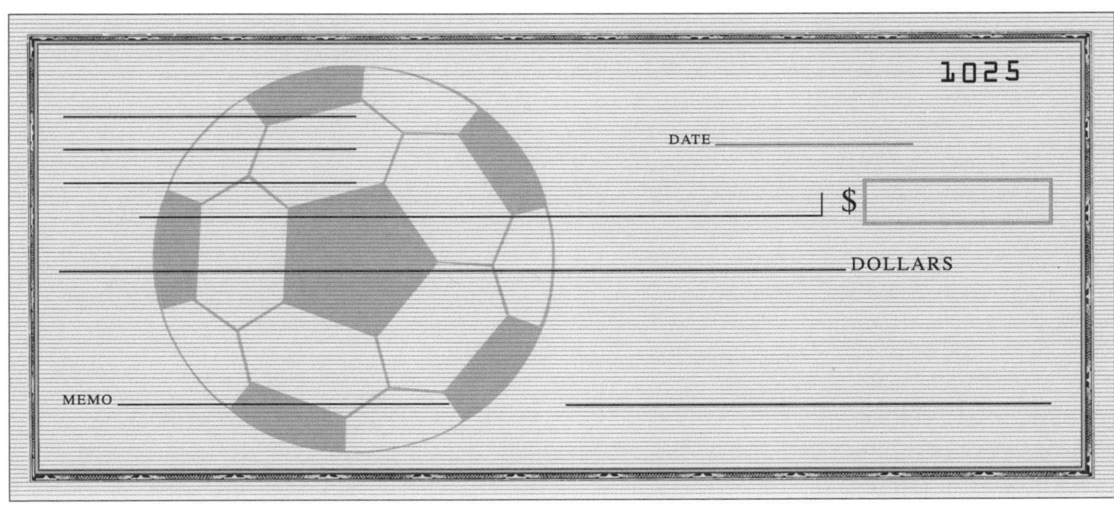

Review Time!

Review of addition and subtraction.

625	729	6,100	40,000
294	789	− 3,519	− 3,519
+ 723	+ 124		

Name______________________________

Exercise 3

Day 123

Review Time!

Review of averaging, geometry, and measurement.

Average these numbers:

567, 321, 672, 900

Copywork

A vertex is the point where two sides meet. For example, a triangle has three vertices.

____

____

In a three-dimensional shape, a vertex is where three or more edges meet, an edge is where two sides meet, and a face is the shape formed by the edges.

____

____

____

____

Fill in the blank

_______ feet = 1 yard

_______ cups = 1 pint

_______ seconds = 1 minute

_______ feet = 1 mile

_______ hours = 1 day

_______ pounds = 1 ton

_______ quarts = 1 gallon

_______ items = 1 dozen

_______ ounces = 1 pound

_______ days = 1 year

_______ pecks = 1 bushel

_______ quarts = 1 peck

Name________________________________

Exercise 4 Day 124

Review Time!

Review of place value and writing large numbers.

	Hundred Thousands	Ten Thousands	Thousands	Hundreds	Tens	Ones
823,221						
29,713						
645,001						
9,606						
450,230						
157						
9,001						
349,101						
761,851						
910,836						

Now choose four of the numbers from above to write in number words.

____

____

____

____

____

☐ Review your divisibility flashcards.

Name________________________________

Exercise 5

Day 125

Review Time!

Review your entire multiplication tables. Take note of any you need to practice.

x	1	2	3	4	5	6	7	8	9	10	11	12
1												
2												
3												
4												
5												
6												
7												
8												
9												
10												
11												
12												

Reduce

$\frac{36}{48} =$ $\frac{5}{10} =$ $\frac{108}{132} =$ $\frac{12}{144} =$

Multiplying Fractions

Lesson 26

"Dad, how much further is the camp?" Charlotte asked. They had been in the van for what seemed like an endless amount of time!

"Well, we have about sixty-two miles to go. The camp is one hundred and eighty-six miles from our drive-way according to the map online," Dad answered patiently. It had been a long trip, and the anticipation of the adventure at the wilderness training camp made it seem even longer.

The weather was starting to break, and the sun was noticeably warmer than even just the week before. It was going to be a fabulous three weeks with the family.

The van bumped along the rutted camp driveway. Frost was heaving the road, making large craters. Dad was driving slowly, weaving this way and that to avoid breaking an axle. Finally, the camp's lodge came into view — a beautiful building set amongst the pines.

"Wow! This place is amazing!" Charlie whistled from the back seat.

"Yes, it is! And the family who owns it is a wonderful family," Dad answered.

"Where are we staying, Dad?" Natty asked, peaking around the driver's seat in front of her. "Are we staying in that big lodge?"

"Yup, we sure are, Punkin!" Dad smiled at her in the rear view mirror. "We're staying right there on the very top floor!" Dad pointed up to the third floor of the lodge. It was a huge suite of rooms with a balcony running the entire length of it. Doors opened up from the separate rooms out onto the deck. Mom was imagining sitting out there early in the morning, watching the sun rise.

"Ok, gang! Let's get unloaded and settled in! The camp's opening meeting is in about $3\frac{1}{2}$ hours, so we have time to settle in and maybe even do some exploring," Dad instructed as he pulled open the side doors of the van.

The boys hopped out and started handing backpacks and duffle bags out to the girls. Everyone grabbed a couple of bags to carry, and they all walked into the lobby of the lodge.

The friendly looking, young girl behind the counter looked up and smiled. "Hello! You must be the Stevens family. I'm Nora Williams. My parents own this lodge. Dad said to show you to your suite — he and mom are out teaching the last snowshoeing lesson of the season." She grabbed keys off of a peg board behind her as she spoke and came around the counter to shake hands with Mom and Dad. "Hi, kids," she smiled at the children. "You are going to have so much fun here! Ok, come along with me..."

"Charlotte, have you ever seen a place like this?" Natty's eyes were round with astonishment. She ran her hand over the log wall next to her bed. It was smoothly peeled and varnished, and it glowed golden in the soft lamplight.

"Never. Isn't it just gorgeous?" Charlotte was stretched out on her bed. Everything in the lodge was made out of logs. Even their beds were made of varnished logs fitted together to make the bed frame. The quilts on each of the beds were unique and obviously home made. The whole lodge was cozy and absolutely the most amazing and rustic place they had ever seen!

"What an awesome place to live!" Ella said quietly from the balcony door. She was standing at the double, glass door, looking outside. She was still a little afraid to go out onto the deck, but from inside, the view outside was breathtaking!

"I am so excited to learn some of the survival skills Dad is going to be teaching the kids!" Natty commented. "He said the first class is about preparing a basic survival kit. Isn't that cool, Charlotte?"

"Yup, it sure is!" Charlotte answered. "This is going to be such a fun three weeks. You know, Natty, I was thinking... it's sure a good thing that we are homeschooled! We would never be able to just take off and go with our parents on a three week adventure if we went to regular school. Mom just said for us to keep up on our math and language lessons, and our reading while we are on the trip. Everything else is what we are learning from the survival camp. Yup, I'm sure glad we're homeschooled."

Name________________________________

Exercise 1 Day 126

New Concept!

In this exercise, we will be learning about multiplying fractions. This is one of the easiest fraction concepts!

Copywork

To multiply fractions, simply multiply the numerators together and the denominators together. Reduce if necessary.

____

____

____

____

This is what it looks like.

$$\frac{1}{2} \times \frac{2}{5} = \frac{1 \times 2}{2 \times 5} = \frac{2}{10} = \frac{1}{5}$$

Now You Try It!

Multiply and reduce if necessary.

$\frac{1}{3} \times \frac{4}{7}$ $\frac{2}{5} \times \frac{1}{3}$ $\frac{3}{5} \times \frac{1}{4}$

$\frac{1}{4} \times \frac{3}{8}$ $\frac{5}{7} \times \frac{2}{9}$ $\frac{3}{7} \times \frac{2}{5}$

Round these Numbers

Remember to look at the digit to the right of the place you are rounding to.

Number	One Million	One Thousand	Hundred
13,496,742			
9,057,391			
78,932,815			
16,284,935			

Name________________________________

Choose one of the numbers from **"Round these Numbers."** on the previous page, to write in number words.

____

____

Work Quickly.

$150 \div 10 =$

$\frac{15}{5} =$

$\frac{38}{2} =$

Multiplication in Story Problems

When we have a story problem that includes multiplying fractions, we watch for the clue word "of." In the following story problems, circle the word "of" and solve. Study the example.

Example:

Charlie's friend, Andrew, lives $\frac{3}{4}$ mile from the Stevens' house. Charlie usually walks $\frac{2}{3}$ of the distance to meet Andrew. What part of a mile does Charlie walk to meet Andrew?

$\frac{2}{3}$ of $\frac{3}{4}$ ----> $\frac{2}{3} \times \frac{3}{4} = \frac{6}{12}$ ---> reduced $\frac{1}{2}$

So Charlie walks $\frac{1}{2}$ mile to meet up with Andrew.

Story Problem

Natty asked Mr. Williams, the owner of the wilderness lodge, if all of the furniture was made of logs. Mr. Williams said that about $\frac{3}{4}$ of the lodge furnishings were, indeed, made out of logs like the ones in the girls' room. He told Natty that $\frac{1}{2}$ of the $\frac{3}{4}$ were made of pine logs, while the other $\frac{1}{2}$ were made from other types of logs. Natty multiplied $\frac{1}{2} \times \frac{3}{4}$ to find the fractional part of furniture made of pine logs. What is $\frac{1}{2}$ of $\frac{3}{4}$?

Name______________________________

More Practice!

Reduce if necessary.

$\frac{3}{8} \times \frac{5}{7}$ $\frac{2}{9} \times \frac{5}{11}$ $\frac{3}{4} \times \frac{7}{8}$

$\frac{1}{5} \times \frac{2}{3}$ $\frac{3}{4} \times \frac{8}{9}$ $\frac{2}{5} \times \frac{1}{6}$

Solve

Reduce if necessary.

1. Charlotte and Natty need $\frac{7}{8}$ yard of material to make pillows in sewing class. They will each use $\frac{1}{2}$ of the material. How much will they each use?

2. Dad bought $\frac{1}{2}$ gallon of frozen yogurt for the family to enjoy privately in their lodge rooms. They ate $\frac{2}{3}$ of it for dessert one night after supper. What part of a gallon of frozen yogurt did the family eat?

Multiply!

$$\begin{array}{r} 6{,}167 \\ \times \quad 6 \\ \hline \end{array} \qquad \begin{array}{r} 2{,}561 \\ \times \quad 23 \\ \hline \end{array} \qquad \begin{array}{r} 52 \\ \times \quad 21 \\ \hline \end{array}$$

Name________________________________

Exercise 3 Day 128

Adding onto the Concept!

Study this example. Read the explanation.

To multiply a fraction by a whole number, place the whole number over 1. Multiply as usual. Turn any improper fraction into a mixed number and reduce if necessary.

$$\frac{4}{5} \times 20 = \frac{4}{5} \times \frac{20}{1} = \frac{80}{5} = 16$$

$$\begin{array}{r} 16 \\ 5\overline{)80} \\ -5 \\ \hline 30 \\ -30 \\ \hline 0 \end{array}$$

In this example, the answer is a whole number. Sometimes you will have a mixed number answer.

Now you try it! Reduce if necessary.

$\frac{1}{5} \times 12 =$ $\frac{6}{7} \times 14 =$ $\frac{4}{9} \times 12 =$

$10 \times \frac{2}{5} =$ $6 \times \frac{3}{4} =$ $4 \times \frac{3}{5} =$

Mixed Review!

Circle the greater in each pair.

XXXIV; XC

$\frac{1}{2} \times \frac{1}{2}$; $\frac{1}{5} \times \frac{1}{2}$

$\frac{27}{8}$; $3\frac{5}{8}$

1,000,000; 1 billion

9 quarters; 32 nickels

$\frac{2}{7}$; $\frac{3}{14}$

Name ______________________________

More Mixed Review

1. What is the estimated cost:
   - a card $2.25
   - gift wrapping $1.75
   - puzzle $8.99

2. What is the actual cost?

3. What would the change be from a $20 bill?

Multiply.

Reduce if necessary.

$\frac{5}{10} \times \frac{2}{6} =$

$\frac{4}{7} \times \frac{3}{8} =$

$\frac{7}{8} \times \frac{1}{4} =$

$\frac{6}{9} \times \frac{1}{3} =$

Add.

$$\begin{array}{r} \$\ 525.05 \\ 623.04 \\ +\ 987.96 \\ \hline \end{array}$$

Subtract.

$$\begin{array}{r} \$\ 1{,}078.52 \\ -\ 682.78 \\ \hline \end{array}$$

Name________________________________

Exercise 4

Day 129

Reviewing Fraction Concepts

Let's work with the fraction concepts we have learned!

Change to improper fractions.

$3\frac{2}{3}$ $8\frac{4}{9}$ $6\frac{3}{5}$ $7\frac{5}{6}$

Multiply. Reduce if necessary.

$\frac{4}{7} \times \frac{1}{3} =$ $\frac{4}{9} \times \frac{3}{7} =$ $\frac{5}{7} \times \frac{8}{9} =$

$\frac{7}{11} \times 6 =$ $\frac{3}{4} \times 7 =$ $\frac{1}{3} \times 15 =$

Let's Add to the Concept.

$2\frac{2}{3} \times \frac{3}{4} =$

$\frac{8}{3} \times \frac{3}{4} = \frac{24}{12} = 2$

Do you see how we change the mixed number into an improper fraction? Then we multiply as usual. If the sum is an improper fraction, turn it into a whole or mixed number. Reduce the answer if necessary.

Now you try some! Reduce if necessary.

$3\frac{2}{3} \times \frac{3}{4} =$ $4\frac{1}{3} \times \frac{2}{5} =$ $2\frac{1}{8} \times \frac{1}{2} =$

Name______________________________

Exercise 5 Day 130

Review

#1 Copy this concept onto a new index card.

To multiply fractions we do not need to have common denominators. Simply multiply the numerators together and the denominators together. Reduce if necessary.

#2 Copy this onto a new index card.

To multiply a fraction by a whole number, place the whole number over 1. Multiply as usual. Turn any improper fraction into a mixed number and reduce if necessary.

$$\frac{4}{5} \times 20 = \frac{4}{5} \times \frac{20}{1} = \frac{80}{5} = 16$$

$$\begin{array}{r|l} & 16 \\ \hline 5 & 80 \\ & -5\downarrow \\ \hline & 30 \\ & -30 \\ \hline & 0 \end{array}$$

In this example, the answer is a whole number. Sometimes you will have a mixed number answer.

Reduce if necessary.

$5\frac{2}{3} \times \frac{4}{5} =$

$6\frac{1}{3} \times 1\frac{1}{3} =$

$\frac{6}{18} \times \frac{1}{2} =$

$8\frac{2}{3} \times 1\frac{1}{3} =$

$5 \times \frac{2}{3} =$

$\frac{4}{5} \times 2\frac{1}{5} =$

Bible Numbers Crossword Puzzle

Fill out the blanks in the sentences below to find the answers to the crossword puzzle. Look up answers in your Bible if needed.

ACROSS

2. Joseph's brothers received _______ pieces of silver when they sold him into slavery.

4. Starts out, "The Lord is my shepherd ..." The _______ Psalm.

7. The children of Israel were divided up into _______ Tribes.

8. Samson sent _____ foxes with burning tails into the Philistines' corn field.

DOWN

1. The children of Israel ate manna for _______ years?

3. Judas received _______ pieces of silver for his betrayal of Jesus.

5. The Ark had _______ people aboard?

6. Noah and his family enter the Ark in Genesis chapter _______.

Divisibility Rules & Dividing Fractions Lesson 27

"Ok, everyone needs to settle down now," Dad's voice rose above the noise in the room. There were eighteen children signed up for the survival camp. Everyone came and sat down on the floor. Dad stood in the front of the room and waited for quiet to settle over the room.

"Today we are going to learn about how to build a basic survival kit. My wife, Mrs. Stevens, is going to hand out the supplies for the kits. Please place the supplies in front of you as we go through what each is for. By the end of this class, you will have everything you need to have your very own basic survival kit. This kit needs to be in your backpack at all times when we go outside to do our survival classes."

Here are the items included in the survival kit. What do you think each one is for?

- 4 safety pins of various sizes
- 2 feet of thin, copper wire
- 4 fish hooks, with fishing floats
- 2 books of matches
- 1 very small candle
- 1 small compass
- 1 magnifying glass
- 1 small packet of Band-aids®
- 1 large (but thin) clear plastic bag
- 1 small metal tin with tight fitting lid to store all of the supplies in.

Name________________________________

Exercise 1 Day 131

Review of Divisibility Rules.

Use your Thinking Tools Cards with the divisibility rules to help you with this exercise.

Circle the numbers that are divisible by 2.

942 678 329 147 680 25

Circle the numbers that are divisible by 3.

29 4,332 138 691 87 432,864

Circle the numbers that are divisible by 4.

32,400 921 800 684 192 43,268,700

Circle the numbers that are divisible by 5.

673 480 95 82 115 332 900

Circle the numbers that are divisible by 9.

477 936 308 926

Word Problem

There were 35 students in the survival class. Find out how many of each item (listed on the previous page) will be needed to create 35 survival kits!

Solve

50 × 1,000 = ________

20 × 20 = ________

800 ÷ 10 = ________

4 × 12 = ________

16 − 8 + 10 + 2 = ________

Name____________________________

Exercise 2

Day 132

Practice the Concept

In this lesson we will be learning about dividing fractions. Don't worry! Dividing fractions is extremely simple. In fact, you don't ever divide fractions at all! Are you confused? Study this explanation.

> To divide a whole number by a fraction, place the whole number over a 1. Flip the second number and multiply. See! You never divide fractions.
>
> $9 \div \frac{2}{3} \rightarrow \frac{9}{1} \times \frac{3}{2} = \frac{27}{2} \rightarrow 13\frac{1}{2}$
>
> Change any improper fractions to a mixed number.

Now you try it!

Don't forget to reduce if necessary! The first one is done for you.

$6 \div \frac{1}{3} = \frac{6}{1} \times \frac{3}{1} = \frac{18}{1} = 18$

$5 \div \frac{2}{7} =$

$4 \div \frac{3}{5} =$

$7 \div \frac{4}{9} =$

Mixed Review!

Write the lowest common denominator for each. Use your Least Common Denominator (LCD) Chart if necessary. Solve. Reduce if necessary.

$\frac{1}{5} + \frac{1}{2} + \frac{1}{3}$ LCD = ______

$\frac{1}{8} + \frac{1}{4} + \frac{1}{3}$ LCD = ______

$\frac{1}{15} + \frac{1}{30} + \frac{1}{6}$ LCD = ______

$\frac{1}{6} + \frac{1}{8} + \frac{1}{4}$ LCD = ______

Write true or false in the blank.

______ 1,092 is divisible by 4

______ 24,111 is divisible by 9

______ 456 is divisible by 2

______ 4,320 is divisible by 5

______ 872 is divisible by 3

______ 342 is divisible by 10

______ 3,042 is divisible by 4

Name____________________________

Exercise 3 Day 133

Let's Add onto the Concept!

We have learned that we don't actually divide fractions. We multiply them by the reciprocal (which is the "flipped" second fraction). This is true for all fraction division problems.

$$\frac{1}{9} \div \frac{2}{3} = \frac{1}{9} \times \frac{3}{2} = \frac{3}{18} = \frac{1}{6}$$

Flip — Division problem — Multiply — Reduce

You Try It!

Reduce if necessary.

$\frac{1}{3} \div \frac{4}{7} =$ $\frac{2}{5} \div \frac{2}{3} =$ $\frac{5}{7} \div \frac{5}{9} =$

$\frac{6}{7} \div \frac{1}{4} =$ $\frac{3}{8} \div \frac{5}{6} =$ $\frac{4}{11} \div \frac{1}{5} =$

Review!

Put an x in the space if the number on the left of the chart is divisible by number at the top of the chart.

	2	3	4	5	9	10
432						
120						
900						
84						
40						
639						
135						

Name ______________________________

Exercise 4 Day 134

Let's Add onto the Concept Some More.

Now let's learn how to divide a mixed number by a fraction.

This is what it looks like!

$3\frac{3}{4} \div \frac{5}{6}$ Mixed number divided by a fraction

$\frac{15}{4} \div \frac{5}{6}$ Change mixed number into an improper fraction

$\frac{15}{4} \times \frac{6}{5}$ Flip second fraction and multiply

$\frac{90}{20} = \frac{9}{2} = 4\frac{1}{2}$ Reduce!

As you work this problem, fill in the blanks to explain what you are doing.

First, change ____________________ into an ______________ fraction.
Second, ______________ the second fraction to get its reciprocal.
Third, ______________ the numerator and the denominator as usual.
Lastly, change any improper fractions into a ______________ number and ______________ if necessary.

You try it! Reduce if necessary.

$3\frac{1}{3} \div \frac{4}{7} =$

$2\frac{3}{5} \div \frac{5}{9} =$

$6\frac{2}{3} \div \frac{5}{9} =$

$2\frac{4}{5} \div \frac{4}{7} =$

Mixed Review!

Solve and estimate.

$$\begin{array}{r} 5,011 \\ +\ 5,219 \\ \hline \end{array} \qquad \begin{array}{r} 199 \\ \times\ \ 2 \\ \hline \end{array} \qquad \begin{array}{r} 901 \\ -\ 699 \\ \hline \end{array}$$

Name____________________

☐ Thinking TOOL Cards

Copy these concepts on index cards and illustrate them.

To divide a whole number by a fraction, place the whole number over a 1. Flip the second number and multiply. See! You never divide fractions.

$$9 \div \frac{2}{3} \rightarrow \frac{9}{1} \times \frac{3}{2} = \frac{27}{2} \rightarrow 13\frac{1}{2}$$

Change any improper fractions to a mixed number.

$$\frac{1}{9} \div \frac{2}{3} = \frac{1}{9} \times \frac{3}{2} = \frac{3}{18} = \frac{1}{6}$$

Flip

Division problem

Multiply

Reduce

$3\frac{3}{4} \div \frac{5}{6}$ Mixed number divided by a fraction

$\frac{15}{4} \div \frac{5}{6}$ Change mixed number into an improper fraction

$\frac{15}{4} \times \frac{6}{5}$ Flip second fraction and multiply

$\frac{90}{20} = \frac{9}{2} = 4\frac{1}{2}$ Reduce!

Practice any of the concepts that you need extra help with.

Multiplying Decimals

"Today, we are going to be learning how to tie different types of survival knots. Everyone has a length of rope. I want all of you to follow my instructions carefully," Dad instructed from the middle of the group. The group stood watching Sean Stevens' hands move the rope around and through itself, until it was tied in an intricate knot.

"Let me do it again, and this time, do each step with me," he said and started over.

As Dad explained the procedure of tying knots, he wrote notes regarding the lengths of ropes needed for each type, on the whiteboard. He also worked out equations showing how much rope he would need to purchase for the class before they left on their survival expedition next week. Charlie noticed that when Dad multiplied whole numbers, the answer was a larger number — this made sense to Charlie, because he was familiar with multiplying. He also noticed that when his dad multiplied decimals, the answer was a smaller number! How odd! When he asked about it after class, this is what Dad explained: "When we multiply something by a whole number, like 1, we get a whole number answer. Like this 4 x 1 = 4, or 3 x 4 = 12. But if you multiply a number by a part of a whole number (which is what a decimal or a fraction is), like this, 4 x .3, your answer will 4 groups of .3, which is 1.2…do you understand?"

Charlie nodded his head, "Wow, Dad, this is going to take some practice! I understand what you showed me, but I'm used to multiplying whole numbers."

Later that evening Charlie asked Hario, "What do you think of the survival class?" Hairo was sitting on his bed in the boys' room at the lodge, practicing all of the knots that Dad had shown them in the class that morning. He couldn't seem to get the last step right. Each time he tried it, he seemed to just create a tangle!

"I like it a lot — except for this dumb knot!" Hairo said in disgust, as he tossed the rope onto Charlie's bed and turned off the lamp.

"Hairo, do you ever think about when you and Natty lived by yourselves in the shanty after your parents died?" Charlie asked quietly.

"Because Dad has been teaching us all of this cool survival stuff... and, well, you and Natty didn't have any of the supplies we say are necessary to be able to survive. You two just stayed alive by digging in garbage cans and begging." Charlie didn't want to upset his brother, but these questions had been rolling around in his head for quite some time.

"Natty and I did what we had to do to survive, Charlie. I really don't want to talk about it, okay? I would just as soon forget about that time in my life," Hairo's voice was a little shaky.

"Lord, please help Hairo be able to talk about his past," Charlie prayed silently. "Please show him that You have a plan to use it — even the hard stuff."

"I'm sorry if I upset you," Charlie said and sighed.

Name________________________________

Multiplying Decimals

Multiplying decimals is simple! Study the examples below.

Multiplying decimals...
We multiply as usual. Next, starting at the right, count the total number of decimal places in both factors and count off that many decimal places in the product.

```
  .5  ← 1 decimal place
        +
x .5  ← 1 decimal place
 .25  ← 2 decimal places
```

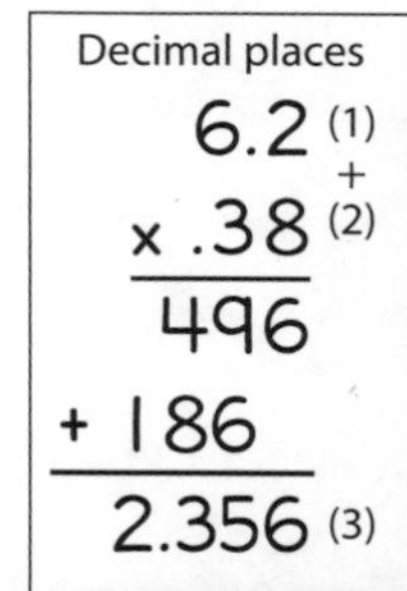


```
Decimal places
   1.52 (2)
         +
x   .41 (2)
    152
+  608
  .6232 (4)
```

Now you try it!

$$\begin{array}{r} .9 \\ \times\ .2 \\ \hline \end{array} \qquad \begin{array}{r} 3.45 \\ \times\ \ .3 \\ \hline \end{array} \qquad \begin{array}{r} 5.23 \\ \times\ .18 \\ \hline \end{array} \qquad \begin{array}{r} .572 \\ \times\ .42 \\ \hline \end{array}$$

Round!

Remember to look at the number to the right of the place you are rounding to.

Number	One Million	One Thousand	Hundred
12,456,120			
1,347,000			
875,351,902			
17,892,915			

Solve

Reduce if necessary.

$\frac{4}{9} \times \frac{6}{7} =$ $\qquad 8 \times \frac{1}{7} =$ $\qquad 7\frac{5}{8} \times \frac{1}{2} =$

Name______________________________

Exercise 2 Day 137

Multiplying Decimals

When we multiply decimals, we sometimes need to add a zero to the product to make enough decimal places. Like this. →

As you can see, we counted from the right the number of decimal places needed, but there were not enough places. This is where we added the zero to the left side of the product.

```
   .12 (2)
 x .13 (2)
 -----
    36
 + 12
 -----
 .0156 (4)
```

We need to add a zero to make enough decimal places.

You try it!

```
  .23        .41        .33        .36
x .16      x .17      x .16      x .21
-----      -----      -----      -----
```

More Work with Decimals.

Circle the decimal that is larger in each pair.

.003 or .3　　　6.4 or 6.45　　　.93 or .9　　　.18 or .194

Change these decimals to fractions. Reduce completely.

.50 =　　　.375 =　　　.400 =

Change these fractions to decimals and percents.

$\frac{25}{100}$ ______ ______%　　　$\frac{78}{100}$ ______ ______%

$\frac{54}{100}$ ______ ______%　　　$\frac{68}{100}$ ______ ______%

Solve

```
  5.09
+ 3.91
------
```

$8 \div \frac{5}{7} =$

Name________________________________

Multiplying Money

When we multiply money (with decimals), we use the same rules. When we find our product, however, we need to round to the hundredths place. Like this…

$$\begin{array}{r} \$\,5.15\ (2) \\ \times\ .65\ (2) \\ \hline 2575 \\ +\ 3090 \\ \hline 3.3475\ (4) \end{array}$$

$3.35 — Bigger than 5 round up!

Now you try it!

$$\begin{array}{r} \$\,4.85 \\ \times\ \ .23 \\ \hline \end{array} \qquad \begin{array}{r} \$\,7.23 \\ \times\ \ .16 \\ \hline \end{array} \qquad \begin{array}{r} \$\,2.91 \\ \times\ \ .82 \\ \hline \end{array} \qquad \begin{array}{r} \$\,5.18 \\ \times\ \ .28 \\ \hline \end{array}$$

Mixed Practice

Work through these problems and narrate to your teacher what you are doing. Don't forget to reduce all fractions to lowest terms.

$\frac{1}{3} \div \frac{9}{11} =$ $\qquad$ $\frac{1}{4} \div \frac{6}{7} =$ $\qquad$ $7\frac{1}{5} \div \frac{3}{7} =$

$5 \div \frac{2}{5} =$ $\qquad$ $\begin{array}{r} 6\frac{1}{5} \\ -\ 3\frac{3}{10} \\ \hline \end{array}$ $\qquad$ $\begin{array}{r} 7\frac{1}{5} \\ -\ 4\frac{4}{5} \\ \hline \end{array}$

Narrate your divisibility rules to your teacher. (Let them hold your cards to check you!)

Name____________________________

Exercise 4 Day 139

Review

More work with multiplying decimals.

$\begin{array}{r} .6 \\ \times\ .3 \\ \hline \end{array}$ $\begin{array}{r} .7 \\ \times\ .4 \\ \hline \end{array}$ $\begin{array}{r} 6.12 \\ \times\ .8 \\ \hline \end{array}$ $\begin{array}{r} .62 \\ \times\ .12 \\ \hline \end{array}$

$\begin{array}{r} \$\,5.13 \\ \times\ .18 \\ \hline \end{array}$ $\begin{array}{r} \$\,7.15 \\ \times\ .69 \\ \hline \end{array}$

Change these decimals to fractions. Reduce completely.

.42 = .315 = .601 = .37 =

Solve.

$\frac{5}{7} \div \frac{1}{7} =$ $4\frac{1}{3} \div 7 =$

$\frac{4}{5} \times \frac{7}{8} =$ $\frac{1}{5} \times \frac{1}{4} =$

$4\frac{1}{3} \div 1\frac{1}{3} =$ $2\frac{1}{2} \times \frac{6}{7} =$

Review These Concepts.

Multiplying decimals...

We multiply as usual. Next, starting at the right, count the total number of decimal places in both factors and count off that many decimal places in the product.

```
  .5  ← 1 decimal place
         +
x .5  ← 1 decimal place
 .25  ← 2 decimal places
```

Decimal places

```
    6.2  (1)
           +
  x .38  (2)
    496
+  186
  2.356  (3)
```

Decimal places

```
   1.52  (2)
           +
  x .41  (2)
    152
+  608
  .6232  (4)
```

When we multiply decimals, we sometimes need to add a zero to the product to make enough decimal places. Like this.

As you can see, we counted from the right the number of decimal places needed, but there were not enough places. This is where we added the zero to the left side of the product.

```
    .12  (2)
  x .13  (2)
     36
 + 12
  .0156  (4)
```

We need to add a zero to make enough decimal places.

When we multiply money (with decimals), we use the same rules. When we find our product, however, we need to round to the hundredths place

```
   $ 5.15  (2)
    x .65  (2)
     2575
 + 3090
   3.3475  (4)
        ↑
```

$3.35 Bigger than 5 round up!

Narrate to your teacher what you have learned about multiplying decimals in this lesson.

Dividing Decimals

Lesson 29

"Today, we are going to talk about a situation in which you can't find fresh water to drink," Dad addressed the class. It was raining outside, so the group was meeting in the lodge's large conference room. Everyone giggled over the irony of the topic of study on a day like today.

"I know. It's ironic that we are talking about finding water on a rainy day!" Dad smirked and then chuckled. "Ok, let's settle down and get started. Does anyone here know what to do if they can't find water to drink?" No one raised their hand, so Dad continued, "Well, there are a variety of ways to collect water from the elements around us. I've handed out worksheets showing some of these options. Let's work through them together, shall we? Charlie, you go first. Please choose one of the ways on the paper."

"Um. Ok, what about this one?" Charlie said, pointing to one of the illustrations on the paper hand-outs. "This one is about how to collect dew off of the grass at night. This looks pretty simple."

"That's a good one," Dad nodded in agreement. "Who here can explain how this would work?"

The morning went by quickly with a lively discussion on how to find water in an area that has no safe drinking water. The rain stopped after lunch, but there were still rivulets of water dripping from all of the trees.

The kids decided to take a break and work on some schoolwork and rest for a while. Mom had started teaching them some new concepts in their math books.

Hairo had been very quiet since his conversation with Charlie the night before. He hadn't seemed to want to be part of the class discussion that morning, and he seemed edgy. Charlie regretted even bringing up his question; he really wished he had just kept his mouth shut. All he could do was pray for his brother...and talk to his dad about it.

Dad explained to the class that drinking water is one of the biggest concerns in a survival situation. Clean water can be very rare in certain wilderness settings.

He showed the class some pictures he had taken of an experiment he had performed in order to gather data about water availability. He explained this to the class:

It took him 3.3 days to gather 6.9 quarts of water using the tarp/dew method.

He explained you had to divide the amount of water gathered by the number of days it took to gather it, like this: 6.9 ÷ 3.3.

Name______________________________

Exercise 1

Day 141

Review of Decimals and Fractions

Copywork:

In decimal place value, the place to the right of the decimal is the tenths place.

____

____

The second place to the right of a decimal is the hundredths place.

____

____

The third place to the right of the decimal is the thousandths place.

____

____

Circle the digit in the tenths place.

.234 782.56 .296 33.456

Circle the digit in the hundredths place.

45.892 122.902 3.91238 3.912

Circle the digit in the thousandths place.

23.5691 .7824 .91202 .41024

Turn these mixed numbers into improper fractions.

$2\frac{3}{4}$ $6\frac{2}{9}$ $1\frac{8}{11}$ $12\frac{1}{3}$

Name______________________________

New Concept!

When we divide decimals, we have to completely remove the decimal from the divisor. Study the explanation and example.

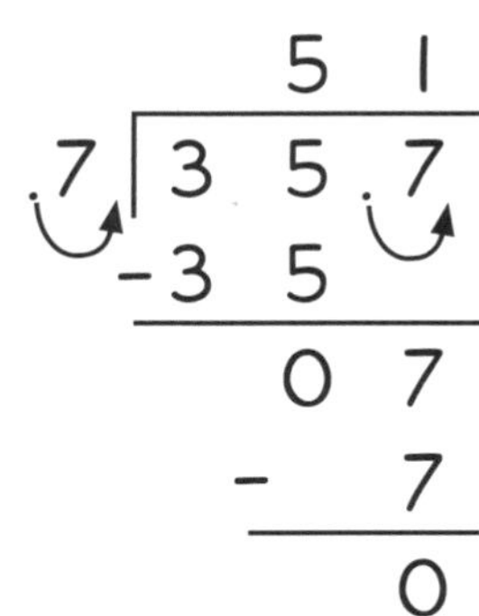

1. We need to remove the decimal from the divisor. Simply move it to the right until it is to the right of the divisor.

   .7 becomes 7. or 7

2. We have to do the same thing with the decimal in the dividend also.

   35.7 becomes 357. or 357

3. Now we simply divide as usual.

Now you try it!

$.8\overline{)40.8}$ $\qquad$ $.6\overline{)36.6}$ $\qquad$ $.5\overline{)60.5}$

Mixed Review!

Reduce these fractions. Use your Reduce that Fraction! Chart if you need help.

$\frac{3}{9}$ $\qquad$ $\frac{12}{36}$ $\qquad$ $\frac{9}{21}$ $\qquad$ $\frac{12}{33}$

Write the common denominator of these fractions.

$\frac{2}{3}, \frac{4}{18}$ $\qquad$ $\frac{4}{15}, \frac{3}{5}$ $\qquad$ $\frac{9}{12}, \frac{3}{36}$ $\qquad$ $\frac{1}{2}, \frac{3}{15}$

Find the perimeter of these shapes.

1. a square with 34 in. sides.

2. a rectangle that is 23 ft. long and 12 ft. wide

Name________________________________

Exercise 3 Day 143

Let's Practice Dividing Decimals!

$.9\overline{)36.9}$ $.7\overline{)14.7}$ $.4\overline{)10.4}$

Review

5.19	8.20	6.13
x .4	x .10	x .9

\$ 2.30	\$ 6.81
x .87	x .35

Copywork

The third place to the right of the decimal is the thousandths place.

____

____

Name________________________________

Exercise 4 Day 144

Dividing Decimals

Copy and illustrate this concept onto a new index card.

```
       5  1
.7 | 3 5 . 7
   - 3 5
     0 7
   -   7
       0
```

1. We need to remove the decimal from the divisor. Simply move it to the right until it is to the right of the divisor.

.7 becomes 7. or 7

2. We have to do the same thing with the decimal in the dividend also.

35.7 becomes 357. or 357

3. Now we simply divide as usual.

Hands On!

Go through Lessons 28 and 29 of this book and make a learning poster! Decorate your poster with stickers or illustrations. Use your poster to show and tell your family everything you have learned about multiplying and dividing fractions. If you can, take a picture of your poster and put it here!

Teacher

After today's exercise, discuss with your student(s) what needs to be gathered for Exercises 1 and 2 of the next lesson.

A Sudoku Challenge!

If you need to review the full instructions for how to solve the puzzle, review the instructions on pages 62 and 128.

				1	8	4		
	8	7		4				5
	1	4		9		2	8	
4	6	9	7	8				
	7					9	6	8
				6	1	7		
7				3	9		4	
8				2				6
2		3	1			8	5	

Just For Fun

Check out some wilderness survival guides from your local library. Make a list of poisonous trees, plants, and mushrooms that you may find in your area.

Making Change

Lesson 30

"Dad, Mom, may I come in?" Charlie asked from the door of his parents' room at the lodge.

"Sure, Charlie. What's up?" Sean and Maddie Stevens were seated on the small couch in the sitting area of the family's suite of lodge rooms. They had been discussing the up coming week and working on the budget for several special outings they had planned for their family. They had counted several stacks of bills and placed them in envelopes.

"Well, I need to talk to you about something. The other night, I asked Hairo about that time period in Peru that he and Natty lived by themselves in the shanty. You know, after their parents had died. Well, he got mad and said he didn't want to talk about it," Charlie looked down at his hands twisting in his lap and sniffed. "Now he's really mad and it's my fault."

"Charlie, the first thing you need to hear is, it's okay," his dad reassured him. "Hairo hasn't allowed himself to think about some of those hard times. And because of that, he hasn't worked through them. This survival camp is bringing back a lot of those hard memories for him, and with the memories, come the feelings. Charlie, Hairo would be struggling right now even if you hadn't said a word to him. Please know that. We are praying that God helps Hairo to face those memories and let God use them. Nothing happens to us that God can't use. He lets hard times to come to everyone, but He promises to use them to our good. Hairo - and ALL of us - have to learn to trust Him with our pasts as much as with our futures. Do you understand that, Charlie?"

"When is that going to happen, Dad? WHEN is God going to work all of this together for Hairo's good? Is it going to be soon? I want my brother back!" Charlie's eyes were moist. He missed his brother, and he wanted to tell God to hurry up and do the good stuff for Hairo.

"Honey, the Bible says that we have to wait on the Lord and be of good courage, and He will strengthen our hearts to follow Him," Mom reached out to Charlie with her soft words. "I know this is hard, Charlie, but you have God's word that He will work it all out. But, Charlie, He works on His own time. He sees the whole picture, while we only see the tiny, little sliver that we live in. We can't tell Him to get to work because it is inconvenient to us. That's where our faith comes into action. We have to have faith, especially when we cannot see. Do you understand that, Charlie?" Mom's words worked down through Charlie's chaotic emotions.

Charlie hung his head and nodded slowly. "But do you think it will be soon?" he asked lifting his head to look at his parents.

"We hope so. We truly hope so," Dad answered. In that moment, Charlie knew that his parents had been praying for Hairo for a long time. He decided right then and there that he, too, would start praying for his brother. He knew that God had a plan for Hairo — a good plan! Hairo needed to learn his part — seeking God with all of his heart.

Name______________________________ Exercise 1 Day 146

Making Change

Throughout this lesson, we are going to learn about counting change back. It is important that you know how many of each type of coin are in one dollar.

Let's review:

There are ________ pennies in a dollar. It is worth _______ cents

There are ________ nickels in a dollar. It is worth _______ cents

There are ________ dimes in a dollar. It is worth _______ cents

There are ________ quarters in a dollar. It is worth _______ cents

If you bought something that costs $3.35, and gave the cashier $5, how much would you get back in change? What bills and coins would you get back?

When we count back change, we start at the smallest denomination first. Draw the change you would receive in the problem above starting with the smallest amount.

Hands On!

Get your parent's permission before starting this project.

☐ Gather different types of small items from around your house.

☐ Make price tags for the items.

☐ Advertise to your household that you will be opening your very own (play) store.

☐ Organize your money (play money is fine!)

☐ Open your store.

Name________________________________

Word Problems

1. Sean and Maddie took Charlie, Charlotte, Natty, Hairo, Ella, and three of their friends from survival camp, out to see a movie on Saturday night. If adult tickets cost $8.25 and children's tickets cost $5.25, how much was the total?

2. If Sean paid with three $20 bills, how much did he receive in change?

3. Hairo and Charlie decided to use some of their spending money to buy popcorn, which cost $8 for a large bucket. Natty and Charlotte put their money together to purchase a large box of chocolate covered raisins, which cost $3.85. How much did the children spend on popcorn and candy?

4. If Charlie and Hairo paid with two $5 bills, what was their change?

5. If Charlotte and Natty paid with a $10 bill, what was their change?

6. Sean bought Maddie a chocolate bar and a small soda. The chocolate bar cost $2.75 and the soda was $3.50. Sean paid for the treat with a $5 bill and two $1 bills, what was his change?

7. What was the total amount spent by the entire family on Saturday night at the movie theater?

Hands On!

TACO HUT

Item	Price
Soft Shell Taco beef or chicken	$1.39
Hard Shell Taco beef or chicken	$.99
Nachos	$2.29
Quesadilla cheese, beef, or chicken	$3.50
Taco Bowl	$4.49
Fried Ice Cream	$1.59 (small)
	$2.89 (medium)
	$4.15 (large)
Iced Tea or Lemonade	$1.59 (small)
	$1.89 (medium)
	$2.15 (large)

1. Dad decided to take Mom and the five children out to the Taco Hut for dinner. He had $100 for the meal. They ordered 7 soft shell chicken tacos, 7 hard shell beef tacos, 3 nacho trays, and 7 small lemonades for dinner. How much did their total bill come to?

2. If Dad gives the cashier a $100 bill, how much change will he receive? What bills and coins will he get back?

3. Everyone except Ella ordered a small fried ice cream for dessert. How much did the 6 small fried ice creams come to?

4. If Dad gives the cashier a $20 bill how much change will he receive? What bills and coins will he get back?

5. How much money does Dad have left from his $100 bill?

6. If Dad decided to divide the remainder of his money five ways, how much would each person receive?

Name________________________________

Exercise 4 Day 149

Add

$$\begin{array}{r} 13.95 \\ 10.01 \\ +\ 12.62 \\ \hline \end{array}$$

$$\begin{array}{r} 73.12 \\ +\ 61.49 \\ \hline \end{array}$$

7.8 + 6.1 =

8.3 + 2.6 =

10.2 + 2.6 =

5.5 + 5.3 =

Multiply

$$\begin{array}{r} \$38.73 \\ \times\ \ 12 \\ \hline \end{array}$$

$$\begin{array}{r} 721.42 \\ \times\ \ 9 \\ \hline \end{array}$$

$$\begin{array}{r} 92.3 \\ \times\ .11 \\ \hline \end{array}$$

.3 × .4 =

.2 × 8 =

1.1 × .7 =

3.2 × .2 =

Name________________________________

Exercise 5 Day 150

Review Time!

Subtract.

10.2 - 7.1 =

156.4 - 42.2 =

2.5 - 1.5 =

232.8 - 12.6 =

$$\begin{array}{r} \$523.05 \\ -\ 293.67 \\ \hline \end{array} \qquad \begin{array}{r} 4,206.79 \\ -\ 526.75 \\ \hline \end{array} \qquad \begin{array}{r} 35,672.936 \\ -\ 6,893.797 \\ \hline \end{array}$$

Divide and check.

$.5 \overline{)\,.25}$ $\qquad .5 \overline{)\,2.5}$ $\qquad .06 \overline{)\,36.00}$

$.52 \overline{)\,5,200.52}$ $\qquad .6 \overline{)\,7,256.4}$

Review of All Division

Lesson 31

We have learned a lot about division. Let's take time to review.

When we divide, we are taking a large group and breaking it into smaller groups.

- There are three ways to show division. The fraction bar is one of the division symbols.
- When you have a two digit divisor, you will always use at least the first two digits of the dividend.
- When dividing money by a whole number (one without a decimal), we follow the same division rules. However, before beginning to divide, we bring the $ and the decimal point straight up.
- In a division problem, if both the divisor and the dividend end in a zero (or more than one zero), we can "cancel" the zero(s).
- We can write the remainder of a division problem as a fraction. The remainder becomes the numerator, and the divisor becomes the denominator.
- We don't actually divide fractions. We multiply them by the reciprocal (which is the "flipped" second fraction). This is true for all fraction division problems.

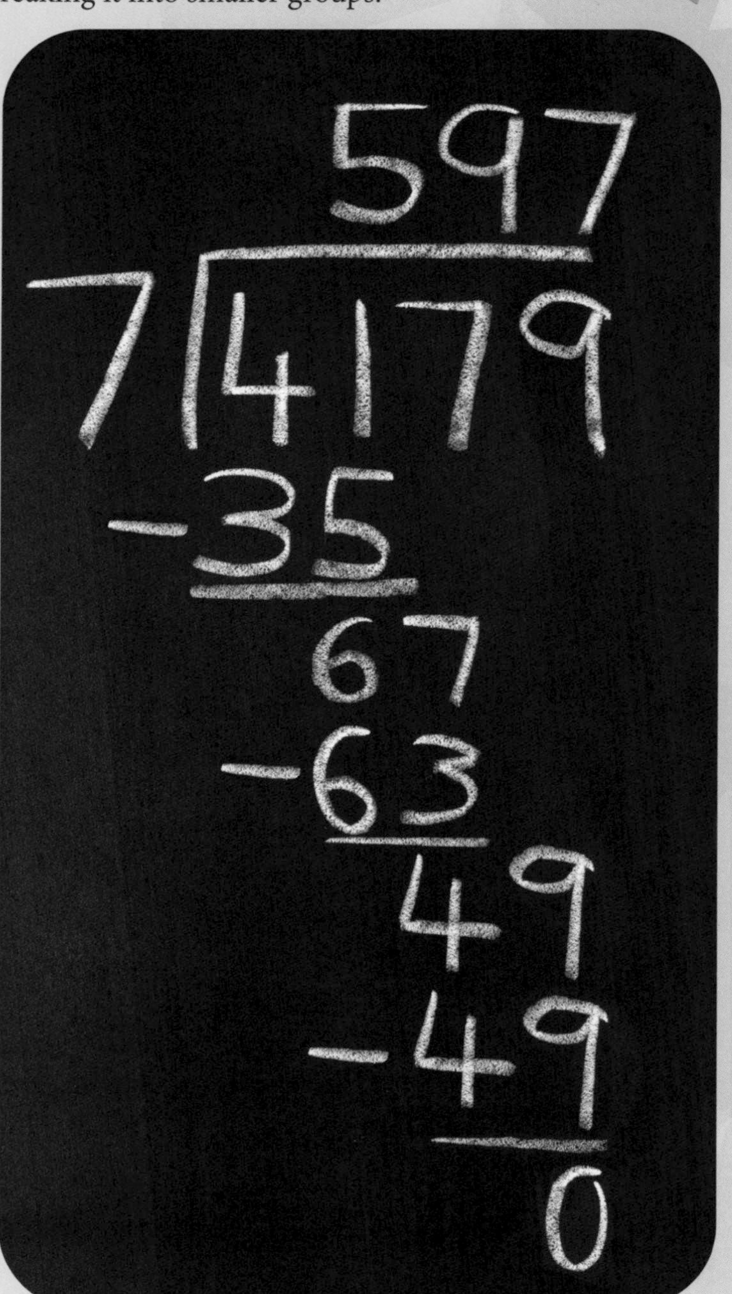

Name________________________________

Exercise 1 Day 151

Review Time!

Divide and check.

$30\overline{)600}$

$40\overline{)120}$

$50\overline{)200}$

$20\overline{)440}$

Circle the numbers that are divisible by the bolded numbers.

2: 45 62 103 464 901 1,036

4: 1,000 65 648 23 16 9,100

9: 810 969 333 432 17

Name________________________________

Exercise 2

Review Time!

Show the three ways to show division.

__________ __________ __________

Circle the numbers that are divisible by the bolded numbers.

3: 210 15 23 35 369

5: 63 10 1,015 725 92

10: 90 21 60 43 1,000

Show the three ways of division in each of these problems.

1. twenty-four divided by eight
2. eighty-one divided by nine
3. thirty-three divided by eleven
4. twelve divided by two
5. sixty-three divided by seven

Write the clue words that tell you to divide in a story problem.

Name________________________________ Exercise 3 Day 153

Review Time!

Copywork:

Sometimes we need to divide amounts of money. When dividing money by a whole number, we follow the same division rules. However, before beginning to divide, we bring the $ and the decimal point straight up.

Divide

$7 \overline{)\$63.07}$

$10 \overline{)\$806.30}$

$9 \overline{)\$72.09}$

$12 \overline{)\$486.36}$

Name______________________________

Exercise 4

Day 154

Review Time!

Divide these fractions. Reduce if necessary.

$\frac{1}{4} \div 2 =$

$\frac{7}{10} \div \frac{2}{3} =$

$\frac{2}{3} \div \frac{1}{3} =$

$\frac{6}{7} \div \frac{3}{4} =$

Convert these Measurements.

360 seconds = __________ minutes

5,280 feet = __________ miles(s)

108 months = __________ years

33 feet = __________ yards

730 days = __________ years

6,000 pounds = __________ tons

Word Problems

In survival class, Dad taught the students about maximizing all you have when in a survival situation. They also learned about how many calories the body burns doing various activities.

1. If the average person burns 360 calories per hour chopping wood, how many calories would you burn in fifteen minutes of wood chopping?

2. The group has 7 five-person tents. Each tent has 97.5 square feet of space. How many total square feet of space do all the tents have together?

3. If there are 35 people in the group, how many square feet of space does each person get in the tents?

Name________________________________

Exercise 5

Day 155

Review Time!

Copywork:

We can write the remainder of a division problem as a fraction. The remainder becomes the numerator, and the divisor becomes the denominator.

____

____

____

Divide

Write any remainders as fractions. Reduce if necessary.

$9\overline{)52}$ $8\overline{)79}$ $7\overline{)52}$

Divide and Check.

Narrate each step to your teacher.

$.4\overline{)36.4}$ $.8\overline{)16.8}$ $.5\overline{)10.5}$

Review of Factoring, Common Factors & Greatest Common Factors

Lesson 32

Factors are all of the different numbers that divide evenly (without a remainder) into a number.

- Factor trees are one way you can find factors of a number.
- Pairs of factors are two numbers that, when multiplied together, equal this number.
- When we list the factors, we write each one only once, from least to greatest.
- A common factor is a factor that two or more numbers share.
- In finding factors, divisibility rules are extremely useful!
- The greatest common factor (GCF) is the largest common factor any group of numbers have.

Name ____________________

Exercise 1

Day 156

Review Time!

Copywork:

Factors are all of the different numbers that divide evenly (without a remainder) into a number. Pairs of factors are two numbers that, when multiplied together, equal this number.

____

____

____

____

____

Complete the pairs of factors for these numbers.

14	20	45
1 × ______	1 × ______	1 × ______
2 × ______	2 × ______	5 × ______
7 × ______	4 × ______	9 × ______
14 × ______	5 × ______	15 × ______
	10 × ______	45 × ______
	20 × ______	

Now list the factors for each of the numbers above.

14 ____________________

20 ____________________

45 ____________________

Name______________________________

Review Time!

Copywork:

A common factor is a factor that two or more numbers share.

____

____

Use your Common Factors Chart to find the common factors for the following groups of numbers.

8, 16

15, 20

9, 21

6, 12

3, 6

Name________________________

Exercise 3 Day 158

Review Time!

Copywork:

The greatest common factor (GCF) is the largest common factor any group of numbers have.

___

___

___

Use your Greatest Common Factor Chart to find the greatest common factor for the following groups of numbers.

10 and 14

12, 18, and 24

36, 18, and 9

35, 20, and 15

☐ Write what you know about greatest common factors.

___

___

___

Name_______________________________

Exercise 4 Day 159

Review Time!

Use your Thinking TOOL Cards with the divisibility rules to help you with this exercise. Narrate to your teacher what you are doing.

Write six numbers that are divisible by 2.

____

Write six numbers that are divisible by 3.

____

Write six numbers that are divisible by 4.

____

Write six numbers that are divisible by 5.

____

Write six numbers that are divisible by 9.

____

☐ Write all of the divisibility rules in your own words.

____

____

____

____

____

____

____

Name________________________________

Sudoku Time!

See if you can complete the puzzle!

2			9	5				3
	9			7			6	
7	8			4			9	5
		9		1			8	
1		5						9
		8	6	9	7	4	5	
			8			7		
8	1	7		2		9	3	
9			7		1		4	

Review of Fractional Concepts Part 1

Lesson 33

This week we will be reviewing fractions. Let's see how much you remember.

- The top number in a fraction is the numerator.
- The bottom number is the denominator.
- The numerator tells us how many pieces of the whole we are talking about.
- The denominator tells us how many total pieces the whole was divided into.
- When you reduce a fraction, you aren't making it smaller. A fraction, which is reduced to its lowest terms, has the smallest numbers possible in the numerator and denominator.
- A reduced fraction is ALWAYS equivalent to the original, when divided by the greatest common factor of both numbers.

$$\frac{4}{4} = 1$$

Name______________________________

Review Time!

Copywork:

When you reduce a fraction, you aren't making it smaller. A fraction, which is reduced to its lowest terms, has the smallest numbers possible in the numerator and denominator. A reduced fraction is ALWAYS equivalent to the original, when divided by the greatest common factor of both numbers.

____

____

____

____

____

____

____

Hands On!

Use your Reduce that Fraction! Chart to reduce these fractions.

$\frac{3}{9}$ $\frac{8}{24}$ $\frac{10}{35}$

$\frac{9}{45}$ $\frac{5}{15}$ $\frac{36}{40}$

$\frac{4}{16}$

Name____________________________________

Exercise 2

Day 162

Review Time!

Copywork:

An improper fraction is a fraction which has a larger numerator than denominator. (Example: $\frac{7}{5}$) A proper fraction is a fraction which has a larger denominator than numerator. (Example: $\frac{2}{5}$)

____

____

____

____

____

Let's Practice!

Circle the improper fractions.

$\frac{4}{9}$ $\frac{7}{5}$ $\frac{2}{5}$ $\frac{9}{3}$

$\frac{5}{3}$ $\frac{10}{4}$ $\frac{12}{13}$

Change the improper fractions into mixed numbers and reduce them to the lowest terms. If you need help reducing, use your Reduce that Fraction! Chart.

Example:

$\frac{10}{6}$ $10 \div 6 = 1\frac{4}{6}$ reduced to lowest terms: $1\frac{2}{3}$

Now you do these:

$\frac{10}{2}$ $\frac{16}{5}$ $\frac{22}{7}$ $\frac{12}{10}$

$\frac{14}{4}$ $\frac{32}{8}$ $\frac{45}{8}$ $\frac{4}{3}$

Name______________________________

Exercise 3

Day 163

Review Time!

Explain in your own words how to change an improper fraction into a mixed number.

____

____

____

Solve. Show your work with these improper fractions.

$\frac{9}{4}$ $\frac{22}{7}$ $\frac{89}{9}$ $\frac{15}{2}$

Explain in your words how to change a mixed number into an improper fraction.

____

____

____

Solve. Show your work with these mixed numbers.

$3\frac{2}{3}$ $5\frac{1}{2}$ $10\frac{3}{5}$ $11\frac{3}{7}$

Word Problems

1. Each canteen contains $1\frac{1}{4}$ quarts of water. Write $1\frac{1}{4}$ as an improper fraction: __________

2. How many quarts of water would it take to fill 5 canteens? __________ (Show your work.)

Name______________________________

Exercise 4 Day 164

Review Time!

Change these mixed numbers into improper fractions.

$3\frac{1}{2}$ $1\frac{2}{3}$ $1\frac{1}{8}$ $5\frac{2}{3}$ $4\frac{3}{4}$

$5\frac{9}{10}$ $4\frac{3}{11}$ $3\frac{3}{4}$ $6\frac{1}{2}$ $5\frac{7}{8}$

Change these improper fractions into mixed numbers.

$\frac{17}{9}$ $\frac{14}{3}$ $\frac{23}{6}$ $\frac{82}{9}$ $\frac{16}{7}$

Word Problems

Each member of the survival group of 35 people needs to drink at least 2 canteens of water a day. If each canteen holds $1\frac{1}{4}$ quarts of water, how many quarts should each person drink per day?

How many quarts is that for the whole group?

Name________________________________

Review Time!

Reduce these fractions.

$\frac{3}{9}$ $\frac{7}{28}$ $\frac{3}{15}$

$\frac{9}{81}$ $\frac{10}{50}$

Change these improper fractions into mixed numbers. Reduce if needed.

$\frac{19}{4}$ $\frac{12}{8}$ $\frac{28}{9}$

$\frac{26}{5}$ $\frac{109}{8}$

Change these mixed numbers into improper fractions.

$9\frac{2}{3}$ $7\frac{2}{5}$ $5\frac{9}{10}$

$5\frac{2}{7}$ $11\frac{2}{18}$

Review of Fractional Concepts Part 2

Lesson 34

Let's continue our review of fractions.

In some mixed number addition problems, the answer is a whole number and an improper fraction. After we solve the problem, we "set aside" the whole number part of the answer. Next, we change the improper fraction part of the answer to a mixed number. Lastly, add the whole number to the mixed number.

- Finding the least common multiple in two or more numbers is helpful in finding the least common denominator in two or more fractions. To find the least common denominator in a group of fractions, we find the least common multiple of the denominators of those fractions.
- When we subtract fractions or mixed numbers with uncommon denominators, we need to find the least common denominator. Then we subtract as usual.
- Sometimes we need to make a whole number into a fraction. To do this, simply use the same number in the numerator and in the denominator.
- Sometimes we need to borrow from the minuend (the top number in a subtraction problem) by taking 1 "unit" from the whole number and rewriting it as a fraction with a common denominator.

$$\frac{1}{4} + \frac{1}{4} + \frac{1}{2} = 1$$

Name_______________________________

Exercise 1

Day 166

Review Time!

Copywork for review:

In some mixed number addition problems, the answer is a whole number and an improper fraction. We cannot leave the answer this way! After we solve the problem, we "set aside" the whole number part of the answer. Next, we change the improper fraction part of the answer to a mixed number. Lastly, add the whole number to the mixed number.

____

____

____

____

____

____

Add.

Reduce if necessary.

$\frac{2}{18} + \frac{4}{6}$

$\frac{1}{14} + \frac{2}{7}$

$\frac{3}{4} + \frac{3}{10}$

$\frac{4}{5} + \frac{3}{15}$

$5\frac{1}{2} + 4\frac{2}{3}$

$7\frac{1}{8} + 8\frac{1}{24}$

$4\frac{6}{7} + 2\frac{1}{14}$

$6\frac{1}{8} + 5\frac{3}{32}$

Name____________________

Exercise 2

Day 167

Review Time!

Copywork:

Just as we learned in adding fractions, when we subtract fractions or mixed numbers with uncommon denominators, we need to find the least common denominator. Then we subtract as usual.

Subtract.

Reduce if necessary.

$$\frac{13}{18} - \frac{4}{6}$$

$$\frac{3}{4} - \frac{2}{3}$$

$$17\frac{11}{14} - 8\frac{2}{7}$$

$$95\frac{9}{11} - 59\frac{3}{22}$$

$$93\frac{4}{5} - 42\frac{4}{10}$$

$$309\frac{7}{10} - 29\frac{4}{10}$$

Word Problem

One student from the survival class collected dew using a tarp. He collected 3 cups of water. Another student collected moisture that dripped from bushes. She collected $1\frac{1}{8}$ cups of water. How many more cups of water did the first student collect?

Name ______________________________

Exercise 3

Day 168

Review Time!

Copywork:

Sometimes we need to make a whole number into a fraction. To do this, simply use the same number in the numerator and in the denominator.

____

____

____

Solve.

Fill in the blank with the correct number.

$1 = \frac{\_\_}{4}$ $1 = \frac{\_\_}{15}$ $1 = \frac{\_\_}{7}$

Write as mixed numbers using one "unit" as an improper fraction. The first one is done for you.

$3 = 2\frac{3}{3}$ $7 =$ $4 =$ $10 =$ $11 =$

Subtract and then reduce fraction if necessary.

$4\frac{2}{3} - \frac{11}{12}$ $6 - 5\frac{1}{3}$ $7\frac{1}{3} + 6\frac{2}{8}$ $4\frac{6}{17} + 3\frac{10}{51}$

$\frac{5}{8} - \frac{1}{16}$ $\frac{6}{7} + \frac{8}{21}$ $1\frac{4}{5} - \frac{1}{10}$ $\frac{3}{8} - \frac{1}{16}$

Name________________________________

Exercise 4 Day 169

Review Time!

Copywork:

Sometimes we need to borrow from the minuend (the top number in a subtraction problem) by taking 1 "unit" from the whole number and rewriting it as a fraction with a common denominator.

Solve. Reduce if necessary. The first one is done for you.

$$\begin{array}{r} 6 = 5\frac{2}{2} \\ - \; 2\frac{1}{2} = 2\frac{1}{2} \\ \hline 3\frac{1}{2} \end{array} \qquad \begin{array}{r} 7 \\ - \; 1\frac{1}{6} \\ \hline \end{array} \qquad \begin{array}{r} 5 \\ - \; 1\frac{3}{4} \\ \hline \end{array}$$

$$\begin{array}{r} 8 \\ - \; \frac{3}{4} \\ \hline \end{array} \qquad \begin{array}{r} 16 \\ - \; 4\frac{3}{4} \\ \hline \end{array} \qquad \begin{array}{r} 18 \\ - \; 6\frac{7}{8} \\ \hline \end{array}$$

Word Problems

1. Look back at Exercise 2. How much water did the two students collect together?

2. A third student collected $4\frac{1}{3}$ cups of rainwater. How many cups do the 3 students have altogether?

Name________________________________

Exercise 5 Day 170

Review Time!

Solve. Reduce if necessary.

$12\frac{9}{13} + 26\frac{7}{13}$

$14\frac{1}{2} + 6\frac{2}{3}$

$5 - \frac{4}{7}$

$17\frac{1}{2} - 6\frac{3}{8}$

$9 + 1\frac{5}{6}$

$32\frac{6}{7} - 17\frac{1}{8}$

$39\frac{6}{21} + 17\frac{1}{3}$

$\frac{3}{4} - \frac{1}{8}$

In your own words, explain the process of subtracting fractions with borrowing.

____

____

____

Review of Multiplying and Dividing Fractions

Lesson 35

- To multiply fractions we do not need to have common denominators. Simply, multiply the numerators together and the denominators together. Reduce if necessary.
- When we have a story problem that includes multiplying fractions, we watch for the clue word "of." In story problems, circle the word of and solve.
- To multiply a fraction by a whole number, simply place the whole number over 1. Multiply as usual. Turn any improper fraction into a mixed number and reduce if necessary.
- We don't actually divide fractions. We multiply them by the reciprocal (which is the "flipped" second fraction). This is true for all fraction division problems.
- To divide a whole number by a fraction, place the whole number over a 1. Flip the second number and multiply.
- To divide a mixed number by a fraction, change mixed number into an improper fraction. Flip the second fraction and multiply. Change any improper fractions to a mixed number.

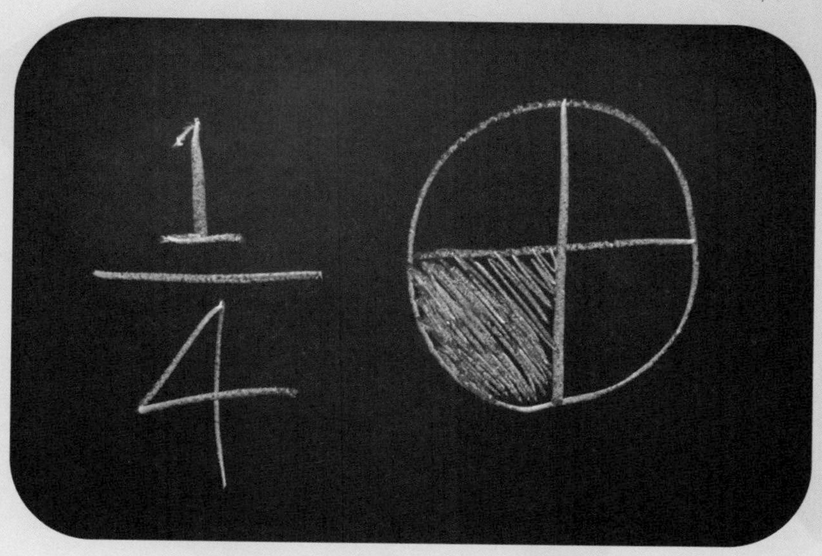

Name______________________________

Exercise 1 Day 171

Review Time!

Copywork:

To multiply fractions we do not need to have common denominators. Simply, multiply the numerators together and the denominators together. Reduce if necessary.

____

____

____

____

Solve

Reduce if necessary.

$\frac{2}{3} \times \frac{3}{7} =$ $\frac{5}{8} \times \frac{1}{3} =$ $\frac{6}{5} \times \frac{1}{5} =$

$\frac{3}{4} \times \frac{3}{9} =$ $\frac{2}{7} \times \frac{2}{7} =$ $\frac{6}{7} \times \frac{2}{8} =$

Write what you learned about multiplying fractions.

____

____

____

Name________________________________

Review Time!

More Practice!

$\frac{1}{8} \times \frac{2}{5} =$ $\frac{6}{4} \times \frac{1}{9} =$ $\frac{3}{5} \times \frac{1}{7} =$

$\frac{5}{6} \times \frac{1}{4} =$ $\frac{1}{3} \times \frac{2}{3} =$ $\frac{2}{3} \times \frac{6}{7} =$

When we have a story problem that includes multiplying fractions, we watch for the clue word "of."

Write two story problems that use multiplying fractions. Did you use the word "of" in it? Solve your story problems, or see if your teacher can solve them.

1.

2.

Name_______________________________

Exercise 3

Day 173

Review Time!

Copywork:

We change the mixed number into an improper fraction. Then we multiply as usual. If the sum is an improper fraction, turn it into a whole or mixed number. Reduce the answer if necessary.

____

____

____

____

Solve. Reduce if necessary.

$3\frac{2}{3} \times \frac{3}{4} =$

$7\frac{1}{3} \times \frac{3}{5} =$

$6\frac{1}{8} \times \frac{3}{7} =$

$12 \times \frac{2}{5} =$

$6 \times \frac{3}{8} =$

$7 \times \frac{4}{7} =$

Write a story problem using two mixed numbers with multiplying fractions. Solve your story problem or have your teacher solve it.

____

____

____

Name________________________________

Exercise 4 Day 174

Review Time!

Copywork:

We have learned that we don't actually divide fractions. We multiply them by the reciprocal (which is the "flipped" second fraction). This is true for all fraction division problems.

___

___

___

Solve.

$6 \div \frac{1}{3} =$ $\frac{2}{5} \div \frac{4}{5} =$ $\frac{3}{7} \div \frac{1}{9} =$

$\frac{3}{7} \div \frac{2}{5} =$ $\frac{2}{7} \div \frac{5}{8} =$ $\frac{7}{13} \div \frac{1}{6} =$

$3\frac{1}{3} \div \frac{5}{7} =$ $2\frac{3}{5} \div \frac{4}{7} =$ $6\frac{8}{11} \div \frac{5}{7} =$

$7\frac{4}{5} \div \frac{3}{7} =$ $6\frac{1}{4} \div \frac{5}{8} =$ $\frac{2}{3} \div \frac{1}{2} =$

As you work these problems, fill in the blanks to explain what you are doing.

First, change ______________________________ into an __________________ fraction.

Second, __________ the second fraction to get its reciprocal.

Third, __________ the numerator and the denominator as usual.

Lastly, change any improper fractions into a ____________ number and ____________ if necessary.

Name________________________________

Optional Math Crossword Puzzle

Solve the math problems below to find the answers to the crossword puzzle.

ACROSS

1. 5,341 + 9,520 + 5,165 = ______________
5. 765 + 964 + 82 = ______________
6. 535 ÷ 5 = ______________
7. 620 x 4 = ______________
9. 215 + 365 + 624 = ______________
11. 42,262 + 52,799 = ______________
14. 2,678 + 7,322 = ______________
15. 9,428 x 4 = ______________

DOWN

2. 11,529 – 5,312 = ______________
3. 3,584 ÷ 7 = ______________
4. 4,374 x 5 = ______________
8. 10,001 x 8 = ______________
10. 90,000 – 68,130 = ______________
11. 81,000 ÷ 9 = ______________
12. 40,002 + 60,520 = ______________
13. 140 x 75 = ______________

Review of Multiplying and Dividing Decimals

Lesson 36

Our last week of review is all about decimals!

- In decimal place value, the place to the right of the decimal is the tenths place.
- Multiply as usual. Next, starting at the right, count the total number of decimal places in both factors and count off that many decimal places in the product.
- When we multiply decimals, we sometimes need to add a zero to the product to make enough decimal places. Count from the right the number of decimal places needed. When there are not enough places, this is where a zero is added to the left side of the product.
- When we multiply money (with decimals), we use the same rules. When we find our product, however, we need to round to the hundredths place.
- When we divide decimals, we have to completely remove the decimal from the divisor.

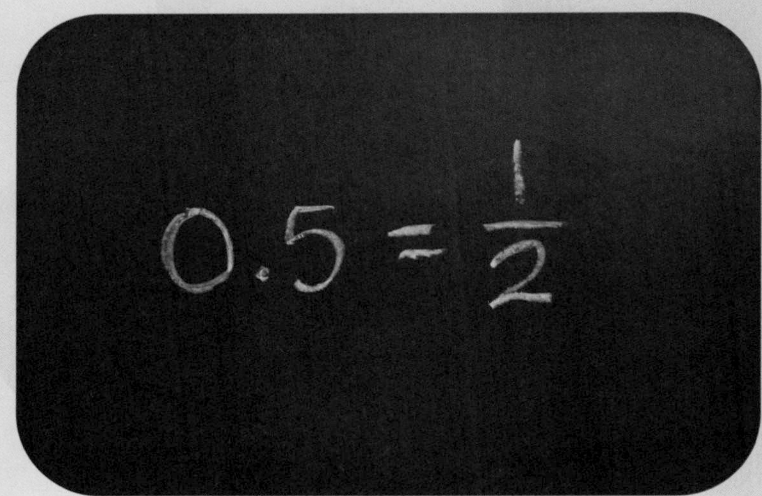

Name________________________________ Exercise 1 Day 176

Review Time!

Copywork:

When we multiply decimals, we multiply as usual. Next, starting at the right, count the total number of decimal places in both factors and count off that many decimal places from the right in the product.

Solve.

$$\begin{array}{r} .9 \\ \times\ .4 \\ \hline \end{array} \qquad \begin{array}{r} 7.25 \\ \times\ .3 \\ \hline \end{array} \qquad \begin{array}{r} 3.42 \\ \times\ .88 \\ \hline \end{array} \qquad \begin{array}{r} .642 \\ \times\ .11 \\ \hline \end{array}$$

Write, in your own words, what you have learned about multiplying decimals.

Name____________________

Exercise 2 Day 177

Review Time!

When we multiply decimals, we sometimes need to add a zero to the product to make enough decimal places. Like this.

As you can see, we counted from the right the number of decimal places needed, but there were not enough places. This is where we added the zero to the left side of the product.

$$\begin{array}{r} .12 \ (2) \\ \times\ .13 \ (2) \\ \hline 36 \\ +\ 12 \\ \hline .\underline{0}156 \ (4) \end{array}$$

We need to add a zero to make enough decimal places.

$$\begin{array}{r} .23 \\ \times\ .15 \\ \hline \end{array} \qquad \begin{array}{r} .31 \\ \times\ .17 \\ \hline \end{array} \qquad \begin{array}{r} .43 \\ \times\ .16 \\ \hline \end{array} \qquad \begin{array}{r} .25 \\ \times\ .21 \\ \hline \end{array}$$

$$\begin{array}{r} .5 \\ \times\ .3 \\ \hline \end{array} \qquad \begin{array}{r} .12 \\ \times\ .6 \\ \hline \end{array} \qquad \begin{array}{r} 17.1 \\ \times\ 6 \\ \hline \end{array} \qquad \begin{array}{r} 14.2 \\ \times\ .8 \\ \hline \end{array}$$

Write what you have learned about adding zero to the product when multiplying decimals.

____

____

____

Name______________________________

Exercise 3 Day 178

Review Time!

Copywork:

When we multiply money (with decimals), we use the same rules. When we find our product, however, we need to round to the hundredths place.

____

____

____

Multiply

$\begin{array}{r} \$\,3.85 \\ \times\ .43 \\ \hline \end{array}$	$\begin{array}{r} \$\,7.13 \\ \times\ .18 \\ \hline \end{array}$	$\begin{array}{r} \$\,2.11 \\ \times\ .80 \\ \hline \end{array}$	$\begin{array}{r} \$\,2.38 \\ \times\ .27 \\ \hline \end{array}$

Write what you have learned about multiplying money.

____

____

____

Name______________________________

Exercise 4 Day 179

Review Time!

Copywork:

When we divide decimals, we have to completely remove the decimal from the divisor.

____

____

____

Divide and Check

$.9\overline{)18.9}$ $\qquad$ $.4\overline{)13.6}$ $\qquad$ $.5\overline{)20.5}$

The Double Sudoku Challenge!

Here is a variation on the simple Sudoku puzzles you have been completing. This is a Double Sudoku – which just means there are two Sudoku puzzles in one overlapped puzzle. We have outlined one puzzle in blue, and the other in green.

When solving this kind of Sudoku, the same rules that you have learned still apply. You just have to take into account both puzzles when finding the solutions for each. The most challenge portion of the puzzle will be the four 3 x 3 squares in the overlapped area (it is the shaded portion). **Hint** – use the numbers outside of the overlapped area as clues to find the missing numbers for each Sudoku!

When solved, both puzzles will be complete with no repeated numbers in the rows, columns, or 3 x 3 squares within the 9 x 9 green and blue puzzles. As always, if you are not sure about what to do, talk to your teacher and ask for help.

4	5	6	8					1			
3	8	2				4	7				
9	7	1	3		2	5	6	8			
5		3	9	8	7			6	5		4
				3	1		5			2	
6		7		2		9				7	
	2		7				3		4		2
	3			1		6	9				
8		9			3	1	4	7	6		8
			1			4		9	2	8	3
				6	2				9	4	5
			3		9	5		8	7	6	1

Manipulative Section

Note: Charts may be laminated or put in sheet protectors and used with dry erase markers.

Roman Numerals
I = one
V = five
X = ten
L = fifty
C = one hundred
D = five hundred
M = one thousand

Fraction/Decimal/Percent Chart			
What it looks like...	Fraction	Decimal	Percent

Geometry Chart

A triangle has 3 sides.

A square has 4 equal sides and 90° angles.

A rectangle has 4 sides and 90° angles.

A pentagon has 5 sides.

A hexagon has 6 sides.

A heptagon has 7 sides.

An octagon has 8 sides.

A nonagon has 9 sides.

Three-dimensional shapes are solid shapes

rectangular prism

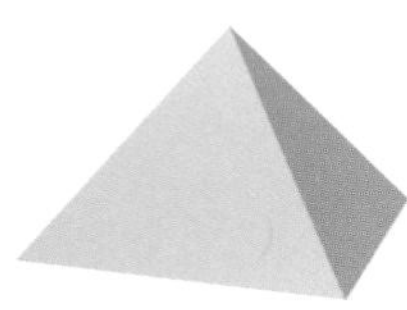

square pyramid

cone

cube

sphere

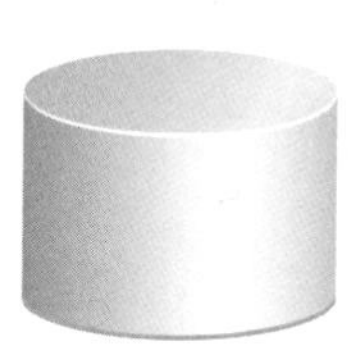

cylinder

Geometry Chart

These are three basic types of lines

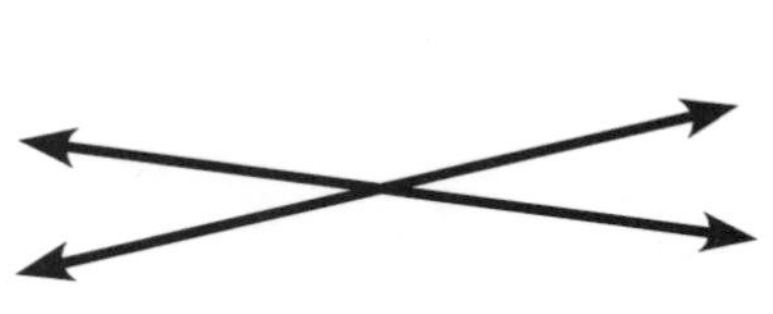

Lines that cross one another are called intersecting lines

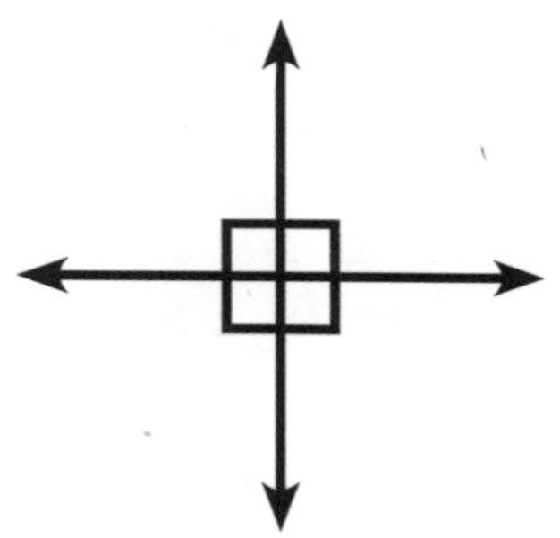

Intersecting lines that form right angles are called perpendicular lines.

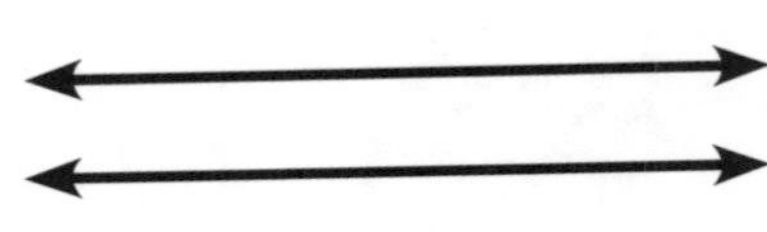

Lines that never intersect and are the same distance apart are called parallel lines.

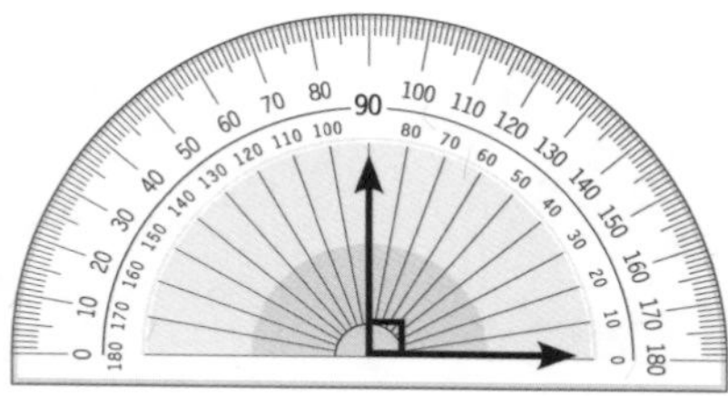

A right angle measures 90° and is shown by the ∟.

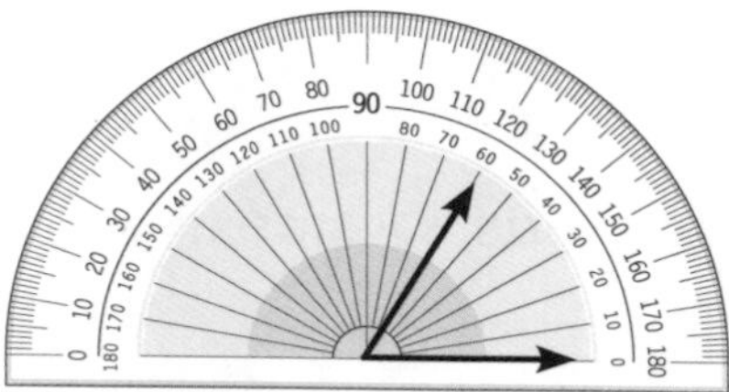

An acute angle is any angle which measures less than 90°.

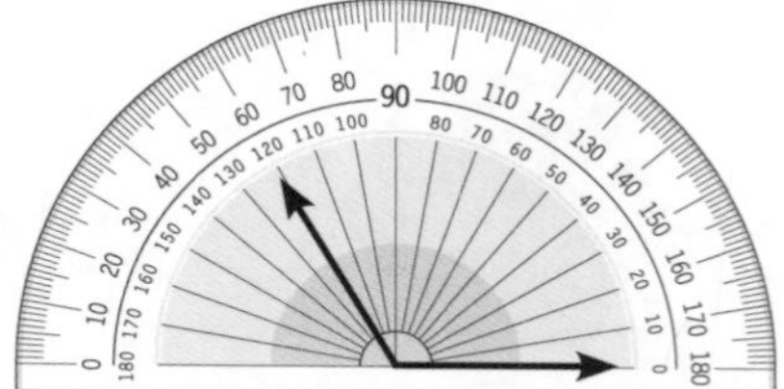

An obtuse angle is any angle which measures more than 90°.

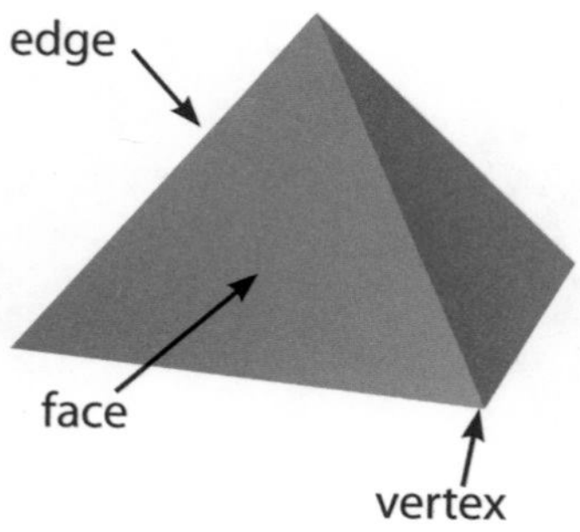

In a three-dimensional shape, a vertex is where three or more edges meet, an edge is where two sides meet, and a face is the shape formed by the edges. In this square pyramid, see if you can find the 5 vertices, the 8 edges, and the 5 faces. Notice that there are 4 triangle faces and 1 square face.

Common Factors Chart

Number	Pairs of Factors	Factors	Common Factors

Greatest Common Factor Chart

Number	Pairs of Factors	Factors	Common Factors	Greatest Common Factor

Least Common Multiple (LCM) Chart

Number	Multiples	Common Multiples	LCM

Least Common Denominator Chart

Write the Fraction, Circle the Denominator	Multiples of Denominators	Least Common Multiple	Least Common Denominator

Reduce that Fraction! Chart

This is a sample of how to use the Reduce that Fraction! Chart.

Fraction	Factors of the Numerator and Denominator	Greatest Common Factor (divide the numerator and denominator by this number to reduce)	Reduced Fraction
$\frac{4}{8}$	(1), (2), (4) (1), (2), (4), 8	4	$\frac{1}{2}$

Reduce that Fraction! Chart

Fraction	Factors of the Numerator and Denominator	Greatest Common Factor (divide the numerator and denominator by this number to reduce)	Reduced Fraction

Measurement Chart: English

Length
12 inches = 1 foot
3 feet = 1 yard
5,280 feet = 1 mile
1,760 yards = 1 mile

Volume
2 cups = 1 pint
2 pints = 1 quart
4 quarts = 1 gallon
8 quarts = 1 peck
4 pecks = 1 bushel

Time
60 seconds = 1 minute
60 minutes = 1 hour
24 hours = 1 day
7 days = 1 week
365 days = 1 year
366 days = 1 leap year
12 months = 1 year

Items
12 items = 1 dozen

Weight
16 ounces = 1 pound
2,000 pounds = 1 ton

Measurement Chart: Metric

Prefix	Meaning	Length	Mass	Capacity
kilo-	thousand (1,000)	kilometer	kilogram	kiloliter
hecto-	hundred (100)	hectometer	hectogram	hectoliter
deka-	ten (10)	dekameter	dekagram	dekaliter
base unit	ones (1)	meter	gram	liter
deci-	tenths (0.1)	decimeter	decigram	deciliter
centi-	hundreds (0.01)	centimeter	centigram	centiliter
milli-	thousands (0.001)	millimeter	milligram	milliliter

Multiplication Grid

x	1	2	3	4	5	6	7	8	9	10	11	12
1	1	2	3	4	5	6	7	8	9	10	11	12
2	2	4	6	8	10	12	14	16	18	20	22	24
3	3	6	9	12	15	18	21	24	27	30	33	36
4	4	8	12	16	20	24	28	32	36	40	44	48
5	5	10	15	20	25	30	35	40	45	50	55	60
6	6	12	18	24	30	36	42	48	54	60	66	72
7	7	14	21	28	35	42	49	56	63	70	77	84
8	8	16	24	32	40	48	56	64	72	80	88	96
9	9	18	27	36	45	54	63	72	81	90	99	108
10	10	20	30	40	50	60	70	80	90	100	110	120
11	11	22	33	44	55	66	77	88	99	110	121	132
12	12	24	36	48	60	72	84	96	108	120	132	144

Long Division Practice Mat

Put a check next to each step as you complete it.

STEPS OF DIVISION:

1. ☐ Divide
2. ☐ Multiply
3. ☐ Subtract
4. ☐ Compare
5. ☐ Bring down
6. ☐ Start over if needed

Name________________________ **Exercise 1** Day 1

Mental Math

20 + 8 + 6 + 11 + 3 + 5 = 53

110 + 120 + 350 = 580

1,090 + 10 + 100 = 1,200

650 + 40 + 8 + 2 = 700

200 + 60 + 9 + 10 = 279

4,001 + 9 + 80 = 4,090

Facts review. Work quickly.

+	4	6	10	8	2	3	5	1	9	7	0
6	10	12	16	14	8	9	11	7	15	13	6

+	6	4	8	0	1	2	9	3	5	7	10
9	15	13	17	9	10	11	18	12	14	16	19

+	2	5	8	1	10	3	6	4	0	7	9
8	10	13	16	9	18	11	14	12	8	15	17

+	8	2	9	6	0	7	1	4	3	10	5
7	15	9	16	13	7	14	8	11	10	17	12

16 Math Level 5 – Lesson 1

Name________________________ **Exercise 2** Day 2

Addition review.

520 + 294 + 24 = 838

613 + 356 + 713 = 1,682

95,011 + 15,219 = 110,230

90,345 + 43,821 = 134,166

38 + 25 + 35 + 14 = 112

24 + 31 + 26 + 15 = 96

41 + 86 + 26 + 38 = 191

Fill in the blanks. Write the subtraction equation you used to solve the problem underneath it. The first one is done for you.

8 + <u>7</u> = 15
15 − 8 = 7

5 + <u>6</u> = 11
11 − 5 = 6

4 + <u>10</u> = 14
14 − 4 = 10

9 + <u>8</u> = 17
17 − 9 = 8

7 + <u>5</u> = 12
12 − 7 = 5

9 + <u>3</u> = 12
12 − 9 = 3

10 + <u>10</u> = 20
20 − 10 = 10

8 + <u>8</u> = 16
16 − 8 = 8

8 + <u>9</u> = 17
17 − 8 = 9

3 + <u>8</u> = 11
11 − 3 = 8

2 + <u>10</u> = 12
12 − 2 = 10

7 + <u>9</u> = 16
16 − 7 = 9

Math Level 5 – Lesson 1 17

Name________________________ **Exercise 3** Day 3

Subtraction review.

9,000 − 6,826 = 2,174

3,055 − 2,245 = 810

20,020 − 12,172 = 7,848

52,031 − 10,729 = 41,302

Need more practice?

300 − 144 = 156

600 − 149 = 451

300 − 226 = 74

Fill in the blanks. Write the addition equation you used to solve the problem underneath it. The first one is done for you.

17 − <u>8</u> = 9
8 + 9 = 17

12 − <u>6</u> = 6
6 + 6 = 12

16 − <u>9</u> = 7
7 + 9 = 16

16 − <u>8</u> = 8
8 + 8 = 16

20 − <u>10</u> = 10
10 + 10 = 20

15 − <u>6</u> = 9
9 + 6 = 15

14 − <u>5</u> = 9
9 + 5 = 14

13 − <u>5</u> = 8
8 + 5 = 13

5 − <u>0</u> = 5
5 + 0 = 5

21 − <u>10</u> = 11
11 + 10 = 21

19 − <u>8</u> = 11
11 + 8 = 19

18 − <u>3</u> = 15
15 + 3 = 18

18 Math Level 5 – Lesson 1

Name________________________ **Exercise 4** Day 4

Word Problems:

1. When Grandpa Stevens took the children to the State Fair, they counted 24 big rides in one area of the midway, 19 smaller rides in the children's area, and 15 rides along the old-fashioned board walks in the "Ole' Western Days" area. How many rides did they count all together at the fair?
   24 + 19 + 15 = 58 rides all together
2. How many more rides did they count in the midway than the children's area?
   24 − 19 = 5 more rides
3. At the fair, Charlie bought cotton candy for $1.75, Hairo bought an ice-cream cone for $2.25, and Charlotte and Natty combined their money to buy a funnel cake for $5.90. How much money did they all spend together?
   $1.75 + 2.25 + 5.90 = $9.90 all together
4. How much more did the girls pay for the funnel cake than Charlie paid for his cotton candy?
   $5.90 − 1.75 = $4.15
5. What addition clue words do you look for in a word problem?
   "How many rides did they count all together?"
   "How much did they spend all together?"
6. What subtraction clue words do you look for in a word problem?
   "How many more rides…"
   "How much more did…"

Math Level 5 – Lesson 1 19

Solutions Manual: Lesson 2

Name________________________ **Exercise 1** Day 6

Multiplication review.

x	1	2	3	4	5	6	7	8	9	10
0	0	0	0	0	0	0	0	0	0	0
1	1	2	3	4	5	6	7	8	9	10
2	2	4	6	8	10	12	14	16	18	20
3	3	6	9	12	15	18	21	24	27	30
4	4	8	12	16	20	24	28	32	36	40
5	5	10	15	20	25	30	35	40	45	50
6	6	12	18	24	30	36	42	48	54	60
7	7	14	21	28	35	42	49	56	63	70
8	8	16	24	32	40	48	56	64	72	80
9	9	18	27	36	45	54	63	72	81	90
10	10	20	30	40	50	60	70	80	90	100
11	11	22	33	44	55	66	77	88	99	110
12	12	24	36	48	60	72	84	96	108	120

Division Review. Write the multiplication equation you used to solve each problem. The first one is done for you.

21 ÷ 3 = 7 — 7 x 3 = 21

36 ÷ 4 = 9 — 9 x 4 = 36

42 ÷ 6 = 7 — 7 x 6 = 42

40 ÷ 5 = 8 — 8 x 5 = 40

12 ÷ 4 = 3 — 3 x 4 = 12

56 ÷ 7 = 8 — 8 x 7 = 56

22 Math Level 5 – Lesson 2

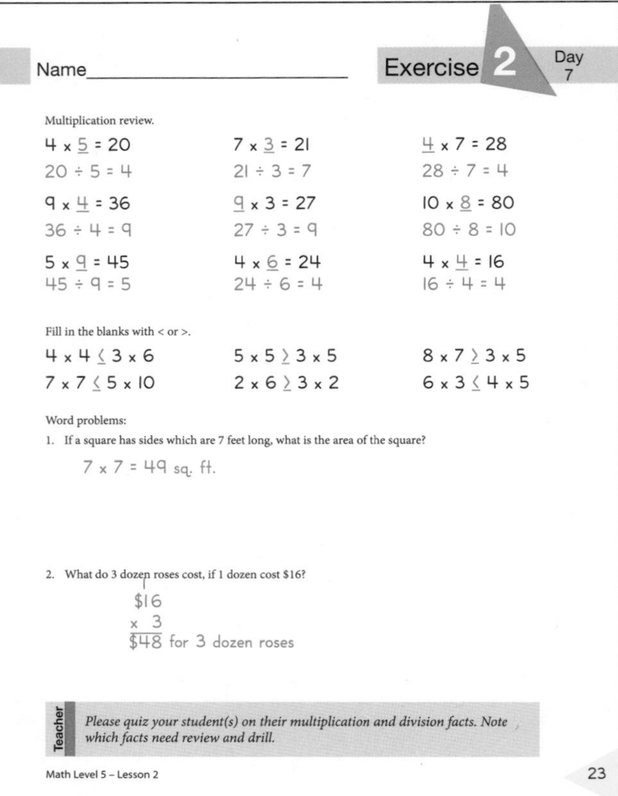

Name________________________ **Exercise 2** Day 7

Multiplication review.

4 x 5 = 20 / 20 ÷ 5 = 4 — 7 x 3 = 21 / 21 ÷ 3 = 7 — 4 x 7 = 28 / 28 ÷ 7 = 4

9 x 4 = 36 / 36 ÷ 4 = 9 — 9 x 3 = 27 / 27 ÷ 3 = 9 — 10 x 8 = 80 / 80 ÷ 8 = 10

5 x 9 = 45 / 45 ÷ 9 = 5 — 4 x 6 = 24 / 24 ÷ 6 = 4 — 4 x 4 = 16 / 16 ÷ 4 = 4

Fill in the blanks with < or >.

4 x 4 < 3 x 6 — 5 x 5 > 3 x 5 — 8 x 7 > 3 x 5

7 x 7 < 5 x 10 — 2 x 6 > 3 x 2 — 6 x 3 < 4 x 5

Word problems:

1. If a square has sides which are 7 feet long, what is the area of the square?
   7 x 7 = 49 sq. ft.

2. What do 3 dozen roses cost, if 1 dozen cost $16?
   $16 x 3 = $48 for 3 dozen roses

Teacher *Please quiz your student(s) on their multiplication and division facts. Note which facts need review and drill.*

Math Level 5 – Lesson 2 23

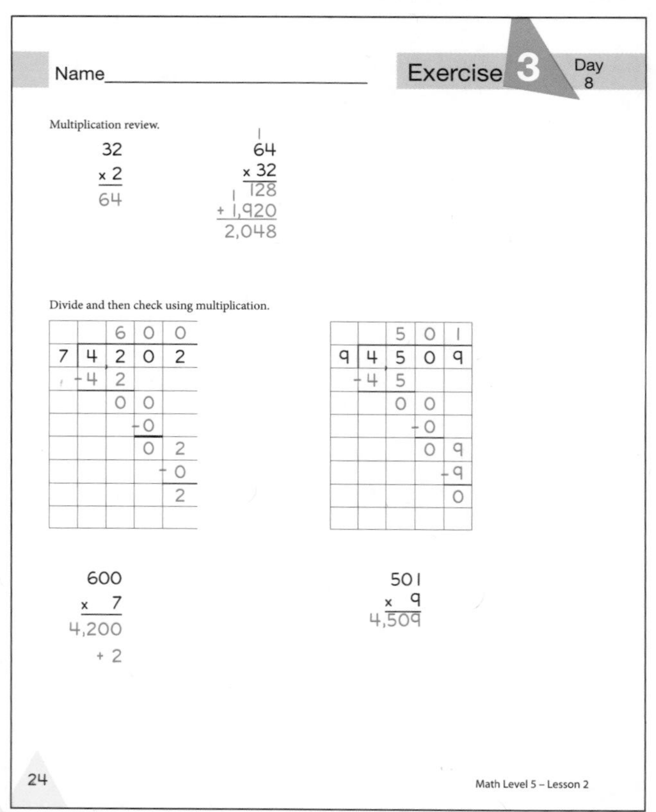

Name________________________ **Exercise 3** Day 8

Multiplication review.

32 x 2 = 64

64 x 32: 128 + 1,920 = 2,048

Divide and then check using multiplication.

4,202 ÷ 7 = 600 r 2 (−42, 00, −0, 02, −0, 2)

4,509 ÷ 9 = 501 (−45, 00, −0, 09, −9, 0)

600 x 7 = 4,200 + 2

501 x 9 = 4,509

24 Math Level 5 – Lesson 2

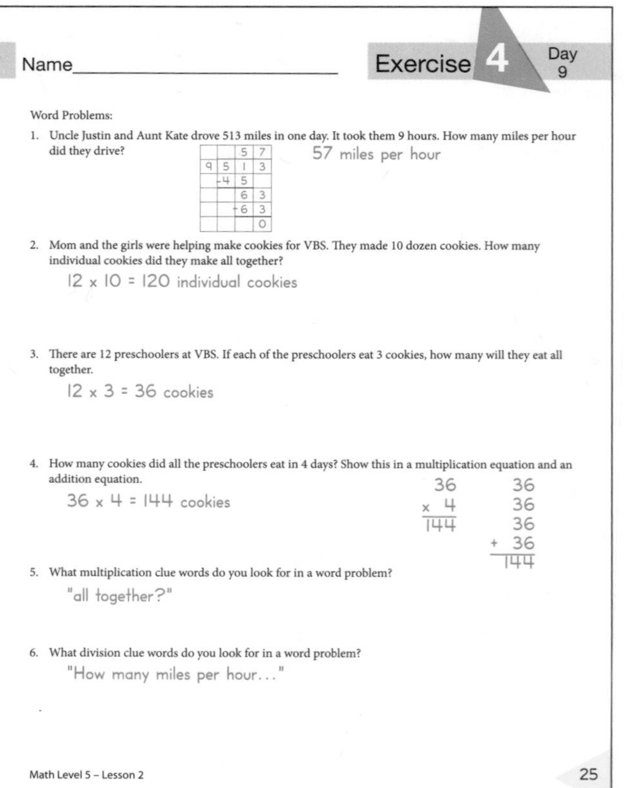

Name________________________ **Exercise 4** Day 9

Word Problems:

1. Uncle Justin and Aunt Kate drove 513 miles in one day. It took them 9 hours. How many miles per hour did they drive?
   513 ÷ 9 = 57 (−45, 63, −63, 0) — 57 miles per hour
2. Mom and the girls were helping make cookies for VBS. They made 10 dozen cookies. How many individual cookies did they make all together?
   12 x 10 = 120 individual cookies
3. There are 12 preschoolers at VBS. If each of the preschoolers eat 3 cookies, how many will they eat all together.
   12 x 3 = 36 cookies
4. How many cookies did all the preschoolers eat in 4 days? Show this in a multiplication equation and an addition equation.
   36 x 4 = 144 cookies
   36 x 4 = 144; 36 + 36 + 36 + 36 = 144
5. What multiplication clue words do you look for in a word problem?
   "all together?"
6. What division clue words do you look for in a word problem?
   "How many miles per hour..."

Math Level 5 – Lesson 2 25

Solutions Manual: Lesson 3

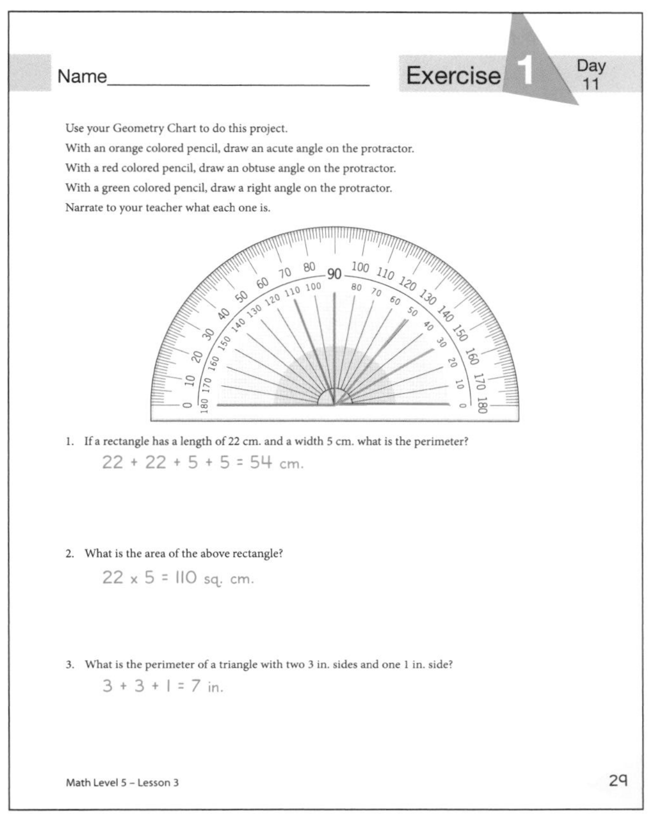

Name________________________ Exercise 1 Day 11

Use your Geometry Chart to do this project.
With an orange colored pencil, draw an acute angle on the protractor.
With a red colored pencil, draw an obtuse angle on the protractor.
With a green colored pencil, draw a right angle on the protractor.
Narrate to your teacher what each one is.

1. If a rectangle has a length of 22 cm. and a width 5 cm. what is the perimeter?
   22 + 22 + 5 + 5 = 54 cm.

2. What is the area of the above rectangle?
   22 x 5 = 110 sq. cm.

3. What is the perimeter of a triangle with two 3 in. sides and one 1 in. side?
   3 + 3 + 1 = 7 in.

Math Level 5 – Lesson 3 29

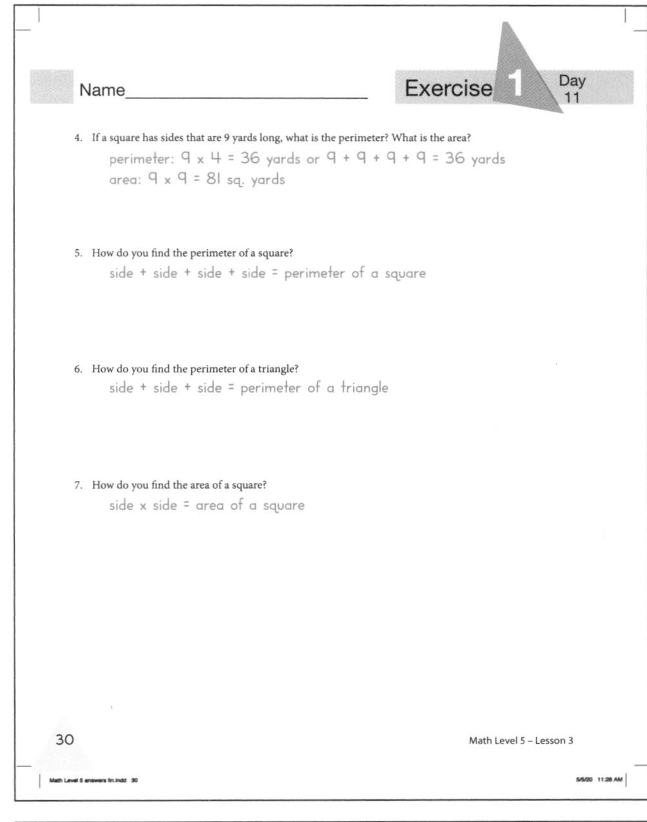

Name________________________ Exercise 1 Day 11

4. If a square has sides that are 9 yards long, what is the perimeter? What is the area?
   perimeter: 9 x 4 = 36 yards or 9 + 9 + 9 + 9 = 36 yards
   area: 9 x 9 = 81 sq. yards

5. How do you find the perimeter of a square?
   side + side + side + side = perimeter of a square

6. How do you find the perimeter of a triangle?
   side + side + side = perimeter of a triangle

7. How do you find the area of a square?
   side x side = area of a square

30 Math Level 5 – Lesson 3

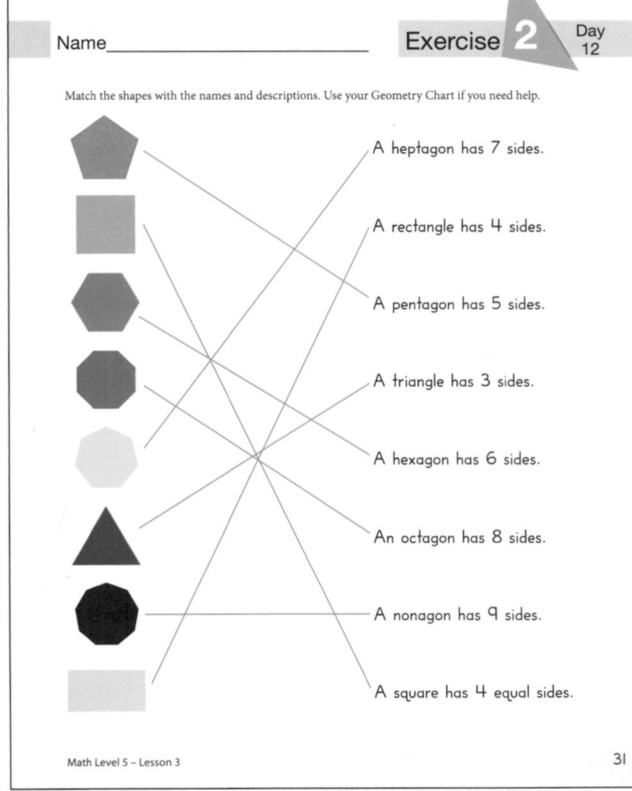

Name________________________ Exercise 2 Day 12

Match the shapes with the names and descriptions. Use your Geometry Chart if you need help.

A heptagon has 7 sides.
A rectangle has 4 sides.
A pentagon has 5 sides.
A triangle has 3 sides.
A hexagon has 6 sides.
An octagon has 8 sides.
A nonagon has 9 sides.
A square has 4 equal sides.

Math Level 5 – Lesson 3 31

Name________________________ Exercise 3 Day 13

Copywork:

A vertex is the point where two sides meet. For example, a triangle has three vertices.

Copywork

1 — 3 vertices — 2 — 3

Draw! Use your Geometry Chart if you need help! Write how many sides each shape has.

hexagon	octagon	pentagon	nonagon	heptagon
6	8	5	9	7

Tell your teacher what kinds of angles make up each shape. For instance, a square is made up of 4 right angles.

- ☐ triangle (3) can be right, obtuse, or acute angles
- ☐ nonagon (9) obtuse angle
- ☐ octagon (8) obtuse angles
- ☐ heptagon (7) obtuse angles
- ☐ rectangle (4) right angles
- ☐ pentagon (5) obtuse angles
- ☐ hexagon (6) obtuse angles

32 Math Level 5 – Lesson 3

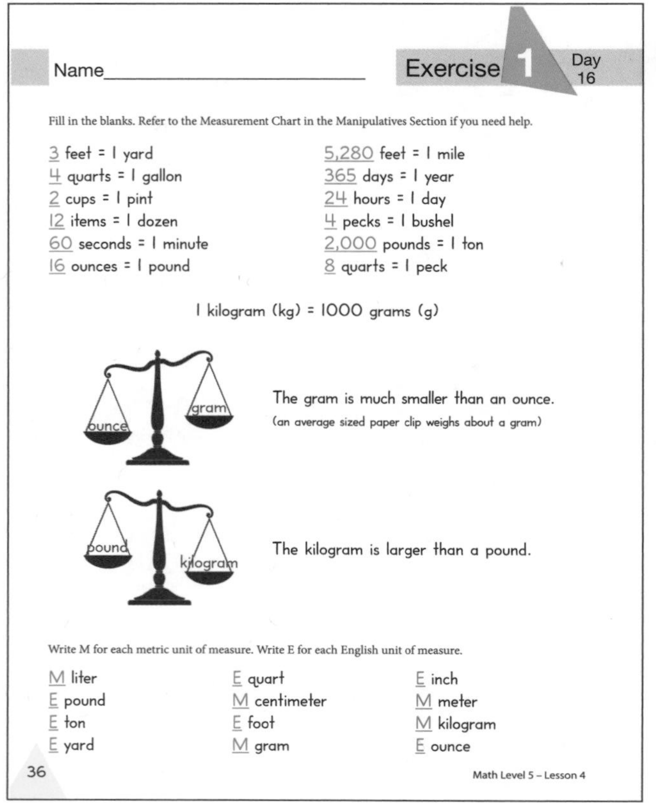
Name______________________ Exercise 1 Day 16

Fill in the blanks. Refer to the Measurement Chart in the Manipulatives Section if you need help.

3 feet = 1 yard
4 quarts = 1 gallon
2 cups = 1 pint
12 items = 1 dozen
60 seconds = 1 minute
16 ounces = 1 pound
5,280 feet = 1 mile
365 days = 1 year
24 hours = 1 day
4 pecks = 1 bushel
2,000 pounds = 1 ton
8 quarts = 1 peck

1 kilogram (kg) = 1000 grams (g)

The gram is much smaller than an ounce.
(an average sized paper clip weighs about a gram)

The kilogram is larger than a pound.

Write M for each metric unit of measure. Write E for each English unit of measure.

M liter
E pound
E ton
E yard
E quart
M centimeter
E foot
M gram
E inch
M meter
M kilogram
E ounce

36 Math Level 5 – Lesson 4

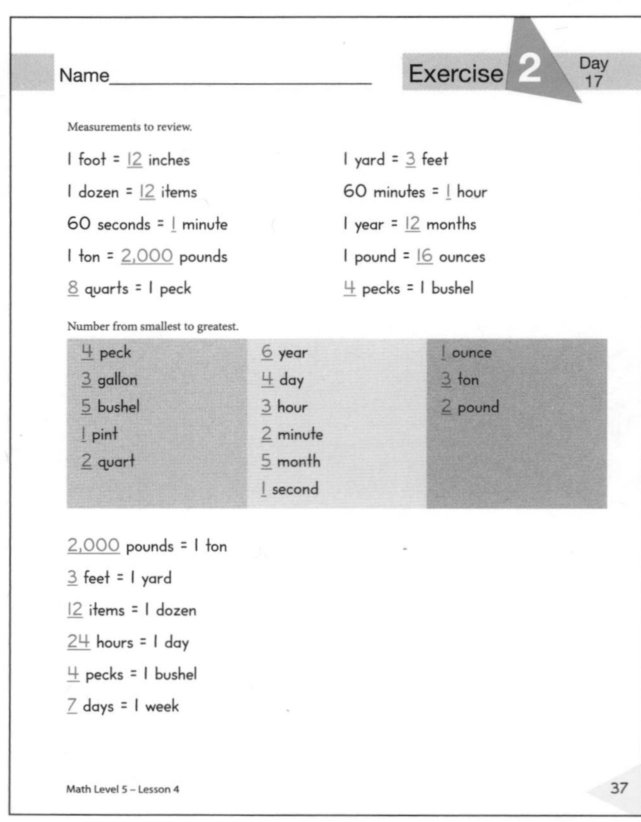
Name______________________ Exercise 2 Day 17

Measurements to review.

1 foot = 12 inches
1 dozen = 12 items
60 seconds = 1 minute
1 ton = 2,000 pounds
8 quarts = 1 peck
1 yard = 3 feet
60 minutes = 1 hour
1 year = 12 months
1 pound = 16 ounces
4 pecks = 1 bushel

Number from smallest to greatest.

4 peck	6 year	1 ounce
3 gallon	4 day	3 ton
5 bushel	3 hour	2 pound
1 pint	2 minute	
2 quart	5 month	
	1 second	

2,000 pounds = 1 ton
3 feet = 1 yard
12 items = 1 dozen
24 hours = 1 day
4 pecks = 1 bushel
7 days = 1 week

Math Level 5 – Lesson 4 37

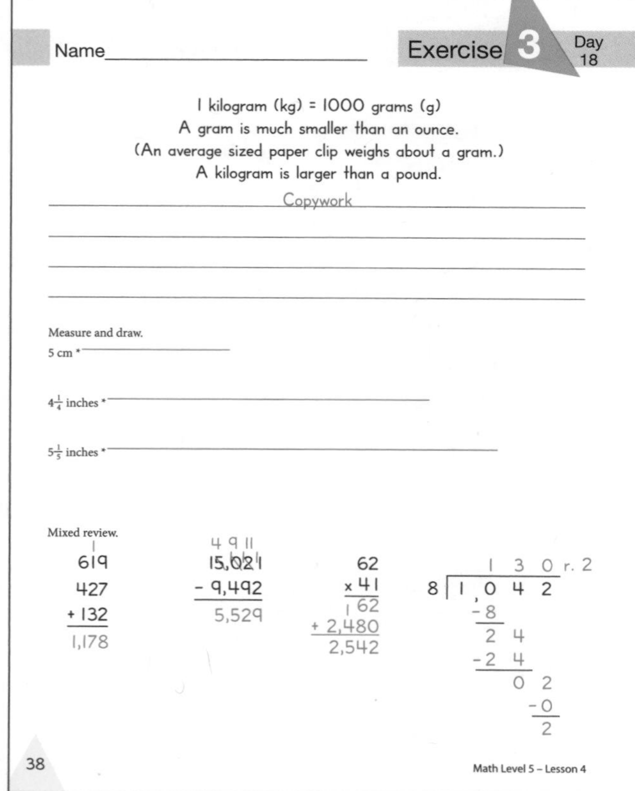
Name______________________ Exercise 3 Day 18

1 kilogram (kg) = 1000 grams (g)
A gram is much smaller than an ounce.
(An average sized paper clip weighs about a gram.)
A kilogram is larger than a pound.

Copywork

Measure and draw.

5 cm •

$4\frac{1}{4}$ inches •

$5\frac{1}{2}$ inches •

Mixed review.

619 + 427 + 132 = 1,178

15,021 − 9,492 = 5,529

62 × 41: 62 + 2,480 = 2,542

1,042 ÷ 8 = 130 r. 2 (− 8, 24, − 24, 02, − 0, 2)

38 Math Level 5 – Lesson 4

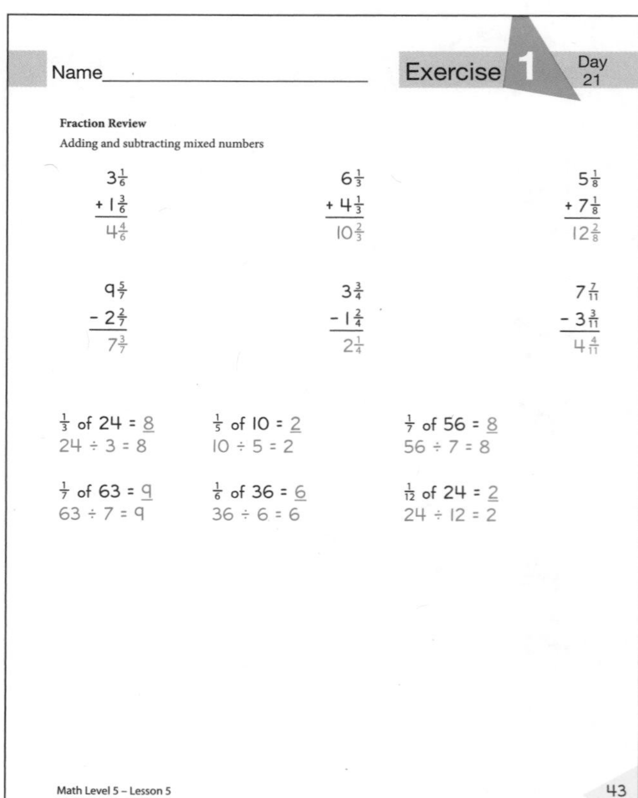
Name______________________ Exercise 1 Day 21

Fraction Review
Adding and subtracting mixed numbers

$3\frac{1}{6} + 1\frac{3}{6} = 4\frac{4}{6}$

$6\frac{1}{3} + 4\frac{1}{3} = 10\frac{2}{3}$

$5\frac{1}{8} + 7\frac{1}{8} = 12\frac{2}{8}$

$9\frac{5}{7} - 2\frac{2}{7} = 7\frac{3}{7}$

$3\frac{3}{4} - 1\frac{2}{4} = 2\frac{1}{4}$

$7\frac{7}{11} - 3\frac{3}{11} = 4\frac{4}{11}$

$\frac{1}{3}$ of 24 = 8; 24 ÷ 3 = 8

$\frac{1}{5}$ of 10 = 2; 10 ÷ 5 = 2

$\frac{1}{7}$ of 56 = 8; 56 ÷ 7 = 8

$\frac{1}{7}$ of 63 = 9; 63 ÷ 7 = 9

$\frac{1}{6}$ of 36 = 6; 36 ÷ 6 = 6

$\frac{1}{12}$ of 24 = 2; 24 ÷ 12 = 2

Math Level 5 – Lesson 5 43

Name____________________ **Exercise 2** Day 22

Multiply each numerator and denominator by 4 to find equivalent fractions.

$\frac{1}{5} = \frac{4}{20}$ $\frac{2}{6} = \frac{8}{24}$ $\frac{4}{5} = \frac{16}{20}$

$\frac{1 \times 4}{5 \times 4} = \frac{4}{20}$ $\frac{2 \times 4}{6 \times 4} = \frac{8}{24}$ $\frac{4 \times 4}{5 \times 4} = \frac{16}{20}$

$\frac{5}{8} = \frac{20}{32}$ $\frac{3}{9} = \frac{12}{36}$ $\frac{2}{7} = \frac{8}{28}$

$\frac{5 \times 4}{8 \times 4} = \frac{20}{32}$ $\frac{3 \times 4}{9 \times 4} = \frac{12}{36}$ $\frac{2 \times 4}{7 \times 4} = \frac{8}{28}$

Divide each numerator and denominator by 3 to find equivalent fractions. This is called reducing.

$\frac{3}{9} = \frac{1}{3}$ $\frac{6}{18} = \frac{2}{6}$ $\frac{3}{15} = \frac{1}{5}$

$\frac{3 \div 3}{9 \div 3} = \frac{1}{3}$ $\frac{6 \div 3}{18 \div 3} = \frac{2}{6}$ $\frac{3 \div 3}{15 \div 3} = \frac{1}{5}$

$\frac{12}{36} = \frac{4}{12}$ $\frac{9}{27} = \frac{3}{9}$ $\frac{9}{18} = \frac{3}{6}$

$\frac{12 \div 3}{36 \div 3} = \frac{4}{12}$ $\frac{9 \div 3}{27 \div 3} = \frac{3}{9}$ $\frac{9 \div 3}{18 \div 3} = \frac{3}{6}$

Solve.

$\frac{2}{8} + \frac{3}{8} = \frac{5}{8}$ $\frac{1}{7} + \frac{4}{7} = \frac{5}{7}$ $\frac{4}{19} + \frac{15}{19} = \frac{19}{19}$ (or 1)

$\frac{10}{13} - \frac{7}{13} = \frac{3}{13}$ $\frac{4}{11} - \frac{3}{11} = \frac{1}{11}$ $\frac{18}{30} - \frac{9}{30} = \frac{9}{30}$

Name____________________ **Exercise 3** Day 23

Read these mixed numbers to your teacher. Choose two to illustrate. The first one is done for you.

$5\frac{1}{4}$ (Example) $8\frac{1}{2}$ $7\frac{7}{8}$ $10\frac{2}{3}$

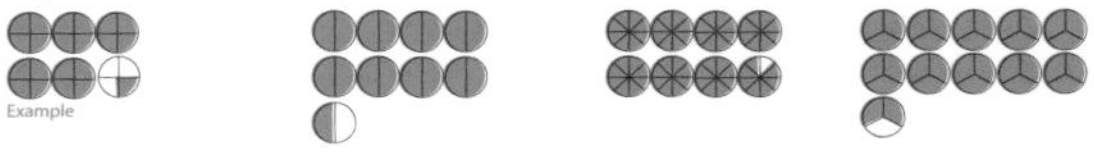

$2\frac{4}{5}$ $1\frac{8}{10}$ $3\frac{1}{6}$

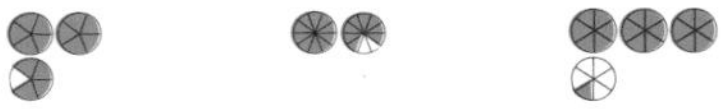

$\frac{1}{4}$ of 32 = 8 $\frac{1}{2}$ of 22 = 11 $\frac{1}{8}$ of 64 = 8

32 ÷ 4 = 8   22 ÷ 2 = 11   64 ÷ 8 = 8

$\frac{1}{3}$ of 63 = 21 $\frac{1}{9}$ of 36 = 4 $\frac{1}{2}$ of 120 = 60

63 ÷ 3 = 21   36 ÷ 9 = 4   120 ÷ 2 = 60

$801\frac{4}{7} + 719\frac{2}{7} = 1{,}520\frac{6}{7}$ $915\frac{5}{12} + 647\frac{3}{12} = 1{,}562\frac{8}{12}$ $292\frac{6}{11} + 188\frac{3}{11} = 480\frac{9}{11}$

$442\frac{14}{15} - 378\frac{6}{15} = 64\frac{8}{15}$ $200\frac{9}{10} - 196\frac{1}{10} = 4\frac{8}{10}$ $763\frac{2}{10} - 196\frac{1}{10} = 567\frac{1}{10}$

Name____________________ **Exercise 2** Day 27

Solve.

4.7 + 0.2 = 4.9   5.2 + 1.4 = 6.6   14.23 + 1.3 = 15.53

$30.91 − 19.32 = $11.59 $260.95 − 216.20 = $44.75 $460.00 − 15.63 = 444.37

Use your **Fractions, Decimal, Percent Chart** in the back of the book to write these as fractions and decimals.

- ☐ eight hundredths $\frac{8}{100}$ .08
- ☐ eighty-three hundredths $\frac{83}{100}$ .83
- ☐ twenty-one hundredths $\frac{21}{100}$ .21
- ☐ sixty hundredths $\frac{60}{100}$ .60
- ☐ fifty-three hundredths $\frac{53}{100}$ .53
- ☐ six hundredths $\frac{6}{100}$ .06

Name____________________ **Exercise 3** Day 28

Copywork:

Fractions, decimals, and percents are three ways to name part of a whole. All three have numerators and denominators.

Copywork

$\frac{50}{100}$ shows 50 parts of 100.
The decimal 0.50 is read 50 hundredths and shows 50 parts of 100.
Percent means hundredths, so 50% also means 50 parts of 100.

Copywork

Use your **Fractions, Decimal, Percent Chart** to show these fractions as decimals and percents.

☐	$\frac{36}{100}$ .36	36%		☐	$\frac{34}{100}$ .34	34%	
☐	$\frac{12}{100}$ .12	12%		☐	$\frac{87}{100}$ .87	87%	
☐	$\frac{67}{100}$ .67	67%		☐	$\frac{5}{100}$ .05	5%	
☐	$\frac{86}{100}$ .86	86%		☐	$\frac{52}{100}$ .52	52%	

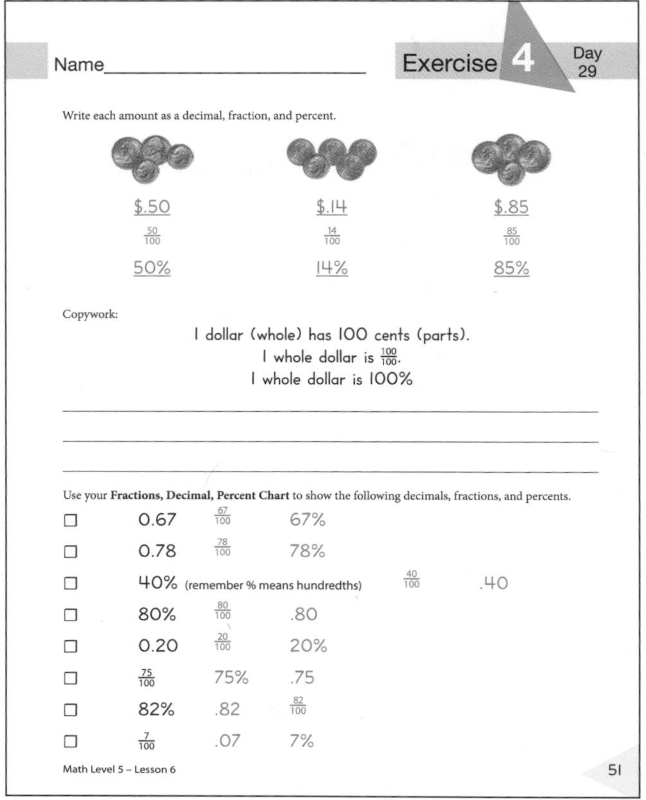
Name____________________ Exercise 4 Day 29

Write each amount as a decimal, fraction, and percent.

$.50	$.14	$.85
$\frac{50}{100}$	$\frac{14}{100}$	$\frac{85}{100}$
50%	14%	85%

Copywork:

I dollar (whole) has 100 cents (parts).
I whole dollar is $\frac{100}{100}$.
I whole dollar is 100%

Use your **Fractions, Decimal, Percent Chart** to show the following decimals, fractions, and percents.

- ☐ 0.67 $\frac{67}{100}$ 67%
- ☐ 0.78 $\frac{78}{100}$ 78%
- ☐ 40% (remember % means hundredths) $\frac{40}{100}$ .40
- ☐ 80% $\frac{80}{100}$ .80
- ☐ 0.20 $\frac{20}{100}$ 20%
- ☐ $\frac{75}{100}$ 75% .75
- ☐ 82% .82 $\frac{82}{100}$
- ☐ $\frac{7}{100}$ .07 7%

Math Level 5 – Lesson 6 51

Name____________________ Exercise 1 Day 31

Let's Practice a New Concept!

We have learned the 10's multiplication table. You have probably noticed that each of the 10's facts ends in zero. When we multiply any number by 10, we simply add a zero. When we multiply any number by 100, we simply add two zeros. When we multiply any number by 1,000, we simply add three zeros.

Example:

2 x 10 = 20	6 x 10 = 60	9 x 10 = 90
2 x 100 = 200	6 x 100 = 600	9 x 100 = 900
2 x 1,000 = 2,000	6 x 1,000 = 6,000	9 x 1,000 = 9,000

Here is another way of showing this type of problem:

21 x 100 = 2100 — This is called "letting the zeros hang!"

126, x 1,000 = 126,000 — Wow! I hung all three zeros!

Now you try!

x	10	100	1,000
4	40	400	4,000
8	80	800	8,000
22	220	2,200	22,000
30	300	3,000	30,000
126	1,260	12,600	126,000

In this space, use the "hanging zero" method to show one of these.

Example: 30 x 100 = 3,000

Math Review!

852 + 514 + 699 = 2,065

390 + 354 + 42 = 786

8,000 − 3,816 = 4,184

75 + 45 + 23 + 41 = 184

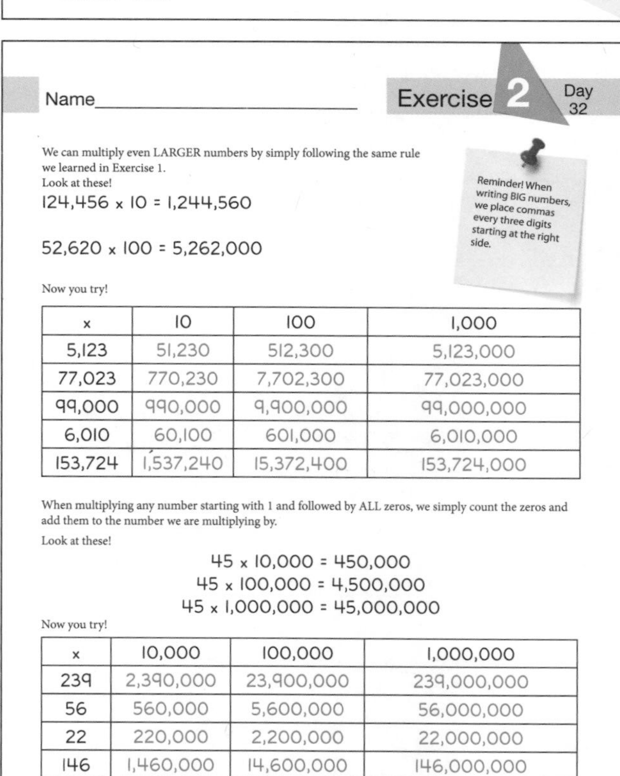
Name____________________ Exercise 2 Day 32

We can multiply even LARGER numbers by simply following the same rule we learned in Exercise 1.
Look at these!

124,456 x 10 = 1,244,560

52,620 x 100 = 5,262,000

Reminder! When writing BIG numbers, we place commas every three digits starting at the right side.

Now you try!

x	10	100	1,000
5,123	51,230	512,300	5,123,000
77,023	770,230	7,702,300	77,023,000
99,000	990,000	9,900,000	99,000,000
6,010	60,100	601,000	6,010,000
153,724	1,537,240	15,372,400	153,724,000

When multiplying any number starting with 1 and followed by ALL zeros, we simply count the zeros and add them to the number we are multiplying by.

Look at these!

45 x 10,000 = 450,000
45 x 100,000 = 4,500,000
45 x 1,000,000 = 45,000,000

Now you try!

x	10,000	100,000	1,000,000
239	2,390,000	23,900,000	239,000,000
56	560,000	5,600,000	56,000,000
22	220,000	2,200,000	22,000,000
146	1,460,000	14,600,000	146,000,000
600	6,000,000	60,000,000	600,000,000

56 Math Level 5 – Lesson 7

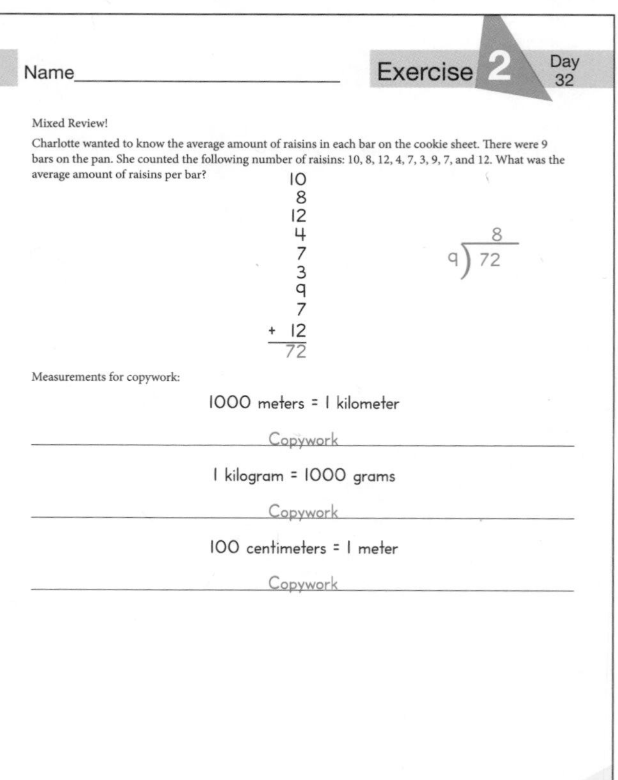
Name____________________ Exercise 2 Day 32

Mixed Review!

Charlotte wanted to know the average amount of raisins in each bar on the cookie sheet. There were 9 bars on the pan. She counted the following number of raisins: 10, 8, 12, 4, 7, 3, 9, 7, and 12. What was the average amount of raisins per bar?

10 + 8 + 12 + 4 + 7 + 3 + 9 + 7 + 12 = 72

72 ÷ 9 = 8

Measurements for copywork:

1000 meters = 1 kilometer

Copywork

1 kilogram = 1000 grams

Copywork

100 centimeters = 1 meter

Copywork

Math Level 5 – Lesson 7 57

Name____________________ **Exercise 3** Day 33

Let's build on this concept again...
What happens when we want to multiply a number by more than one group of 10?
Look at these and tell your teacher the pattern.

3 x 3 = 9	4 x 2 = 8
3 x 30 = 90	4 x 20 = 80
3 x 300 = 900	4 x 200 = 800
3 x 3,000 = 9,000	4 x 2,000 = 8,000

Now you try!

2 x 3 = 6	2 x 2 = 4	4 x 3 = 12
2 x 30 = 60	2 x 20 = 40	4 x 30 = 120
2 x 300 = 600	2 x 200 = 400	4 x 300 = 1,200
2 x 3,000 = 6,000	2 x 2,000 = 4,000	4 x 3,000 = 12,000

We know division is the opposite of multiplication. Starting in column a. let's reverse the multiplication problems to make them division problems. Pay special attention to any patterns you see. Narrate to your teacher. Write them on the lines below.

6 ÷ 3 = 2	4 ÷ 2 = 2	12 ÷ 3 = 4
60 ÷ 2 = 30 or 60 ÷ 30 = 2	40 ÷ 2 = 20 or 40 ÷ 20 = 2	120 ÷ 30 = 4
600 ÷ 2 = 300 or 600 ÷ 300 = 2	400 ÷ 2 = 200 or 400 ÷ 200 = 2	1,200 ÷ 4 = 300 or 1,200 ÷ 300 = 4
6,000 ÷ 2 = 3,000 or 6,000 ÷ 3,000 = 2	4,000 ÷ 2 = 2,000 or 4,000 ÷ 2,000 = 2	12,000 ÷ 4 = 3,000 or 12,000 ÷ 3,000 = 4

58 Math Level 5 – Lesson 7

Name____________________ **Exercise 3** Day 33

Mixed Review!
Solve these.

20 cups = 10 pints (20 ÷ 2)	18 cups = 9 pints (18 ÷ 2)
16 cups = 8 pints (16 ÷ 2)	10 cups = 5 pints (10 ÷ 2)
12 cups = 6 pints (12 ÷ 2)	6 cups = 3 pints (6 ÷ 2)

Solve and match with the problems that show the solution with division.

2 x 3 = 6	15 ÷ 3 = 5
4 x 10 = 40	6 ÷ 2 = 3
3 x 5 = 15	40 ÷ 4 = 10
6 x 3 = 18	18 ÷ 3 = 6
7 x 3 = 21	21 ÷ 7 = 3
4 x 3 = 12	12 ÷ 3 = 4
3 x 3 = 9	20 ÷ 2 = 10
9 x 3 = 27	27 ÷ 3 =
2 x 10 = 20	9 ÷ 3 = 3

Solve and check.

5) 5,005 = 1,001 (−5, 0 0 0 5, −5, 0); check: 1,001 x 5 = 5,005

4) 600 = 150 (−4, 20, −20, 00); check: 150 x 4 = 600

Math Level 5 – Lesson 7 59

Name____________________ **Exercise 4** Day 34

Let's Practice!

2 x 8 = 16	5 x 3 = 15
2 x 80 = 160	5 x 30 = 150
2 x 800 = 1,600	5 x 300 = 1,500
2 x 8,000 = 16,000	5 x 3,000 = 15,000

Now write the division problems for each of the problems in the table.

16 ÷ 2 = 8	15 ÷ 5 = 3
160 ÷ 2 = 80 or 160 ÷ 80 = 2	150 ÷ 5 = 30 or 150 ÷ 30 = 5
1,600 ÷ 2 = 800 or 1,600 ÷ 800 = 2	1,500 ÷ 5 = 300 or 1,500 ÷ 300 = 5
16,000 ÷ 2 = 8,000 or 16,000 ÷ 8,000 = 2	15,000 ÷ 5 = 3,000 or 15,000 ÷ 3,000 = 5

Review!

8) 240 = 30 (−24, 00)

5) 357 = 71 r. 2 (−35, 07, −5, 2)

4) 8136 = 2034 (−8, 013, −12, 16, −16, 0)

60 Math Level 5 – Lesson 7

Name____________________ **Exercise 5** Day 35

Puzzle Time.

Sudoku is a very popular type of math puzzle! It has varying designs but it is usually seen in a 9 x 9 grid.

The puzzle below features a 9 x 9 box (count the first row of blocks = 9 and then count the first column of blocks = 9) divided into three 3 x 3 grids. The game requires the player to use the numbers 1–9 only one time per 3 x 3 square, on each column, and each row. So when you read the numbers by row or by column or within the 3 x 3 squares, the numbers 1–9 appear only once.

See if you can solve the 3 x 3 square in the center of the puzzle. (Hint: Look at the numbers that already exist in the rows that are missing a number. Write down the missing numbers for each row and column. Now, compare those numbers to the numbers that already are either in the 3 x 3 square, row, or column. Then see how you can place the missing numbers and not repeat numbers 1–9 in the 3 x 3 area, the column, or the row.) It's a little hard at first, but remember this is a fun way to learn! (If you're not sure what to do, ask your teacher for help.)

3 x 3 = 9 Rows

3 x 3 = 9 Columns

8	7	6	5	4	3	1	9	2
5	4	3	2	1	9	7	6	8
2	1	9	8	7	6	4	3	5
1	9	8	7	6	5	3	2	4
4	3	2	1	9	8	6	5	7
7	6	5	4	3	2	9	8	1
3	2	1	9	8	7	5	4	6
6	5	4	3	2	1	8	7	9
9	8	7	6	5	4	2	1	3

62 Math Level 5 – Lesson 7

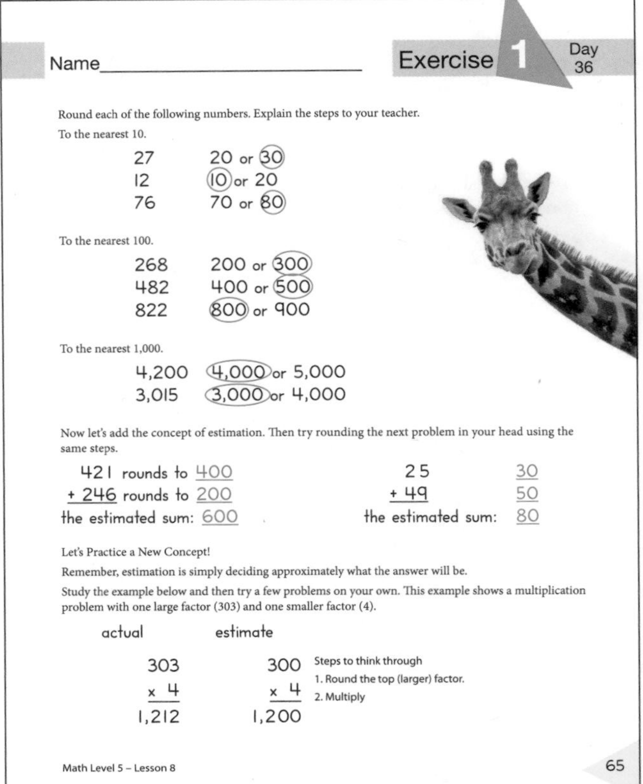

Name____________________ Exercise 1 Day 36

Round each of the following numbers. Explain the steps to your teacher.

To the nearest 10.

27 — 20 or (30)
12 — (10) or 20
76 — 70 or (80)

To the nearest 100.

268 — 200 or (300)
482 — 400 or (500)
822 — (800) or 900

To the nearest 1,000.

4,200 — (4,000) or 5,000
3,015 — (3,000) or 4,000

Now let's add the concept of estimation. Then try rounding the next problem in your head using the same steps.

421 rounds to 400
\+ 246 rounds to 200
the estimated sum: 600

25 — 30
\+ 49 — 50
the estimated sum: 80

Let's Practice a New Concept!

Remember, estimation is simply deciding approximately what the answer will be.

Study the example below and then try a few problems on your own. This example shows a multiplication problem with one large factor (303) and one smaller factor (4).

actual: 303 × 4 = 1,212

estimate: 300 × 4 = 1,200

Steps to think through
1. Round the top (larger) factor.
2. Multiply

Math Level 5 – Lesson 8 65

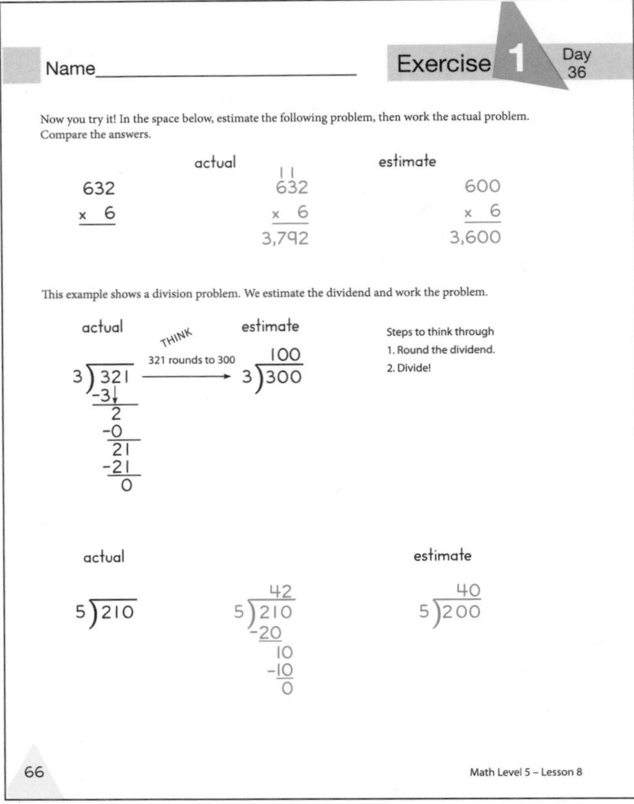

Name____________________ Exercise 1 Day 36

Now you try it! In the space below, estimate the following problem, then work the actual problem. Compare the answers.

632 × 6

actual: 632 × 6 = 3,792

estimate: 600 × 6 = 3,600

This example shows a division problem. We estimate the dividend and work the problem.

actual: 3)321 — −3, 2, −0, 21, −21, 0 — quotient 107

THINK: 321 rounds to 300

estimate: 3)300 = 100

Steps to think through
1. Round the dividend.
2. Divide!

actual: 5)210

5)210 = 42 — −20, 10, −10, 0

estimate: 5)200 = 40

66 Math Level 5 – Lesson 8

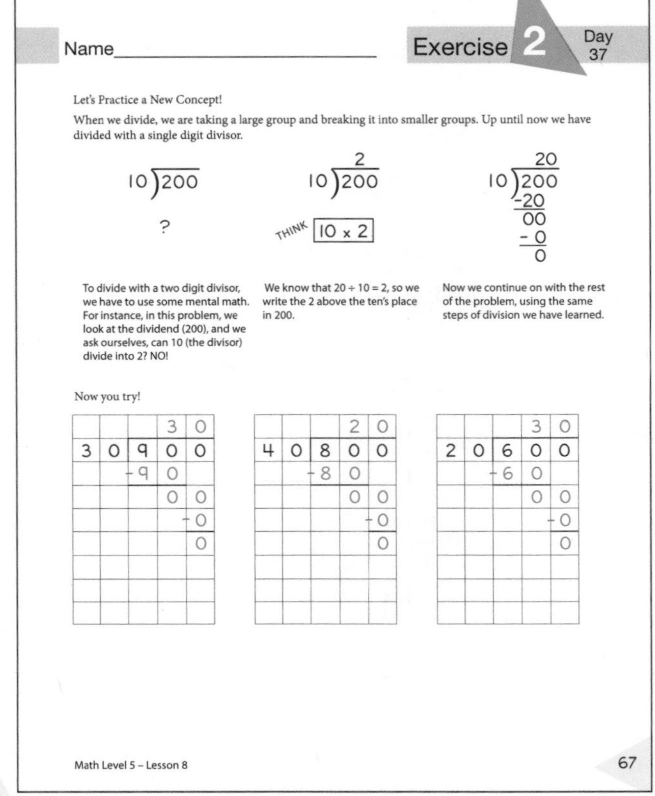

Name____________________ Exercise 2 Day 37

Let's Practice a New Concept!

When we divide, we are taking a large group and breaking it into smaller groups. Up until now we have divided with a single digit divisor.

10)200 ?

10)200 = 2 — THINK 10 x 2

10)200 = 20 — −20, 00, −0, 0

To divide with a two digit divisor, we have to use some mental math. For instance, in this problem, we look at the dividend (200), and we ask ourselves, can 10 (the divisor) divide into 2? NO!

We know that 20 ÷ 10 = 2, so we write the 2 above the ten's place in 200.

Now we continue on with the rest of the problem, using the same steps of division we have learned.

Now you try!

			3	0
3	0	9	0	0
		−9	0	
			0	0
				−0
				0

			2	0
4	0	8	0	0
		−8	0	
			0	0
				−0
				0

			3	0
2	0	6	0	0
		−6	0	
			0	0
				−0
				0

Math Level 5 – Lesson 8 67

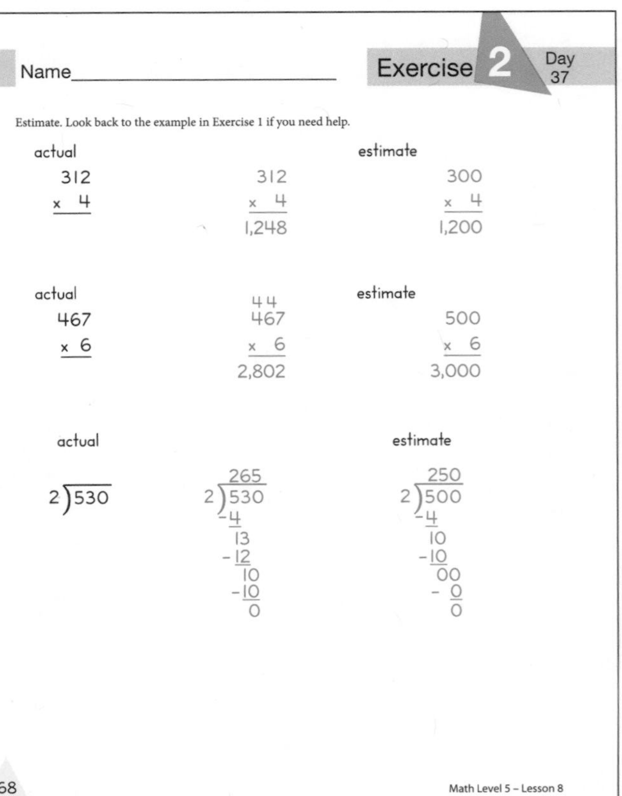

Name____________________ Exercise 2 Day 37

Estimate. Look back to the example in Exercise 1 if you need help.

actual: 312 × 4 = 1,248

estimate: 300 × 4 = 1,200

actual: 467 × 6 = 2,802

estimate: 500 × 6 = 3,000

actual: 2)530 = 265 — −4, 13, −12, 10, −10, 0

estimate: 2)500 = 250 — −4, 10, −10, 00, −0, 0

68 Math Level 5 – Lesson 8

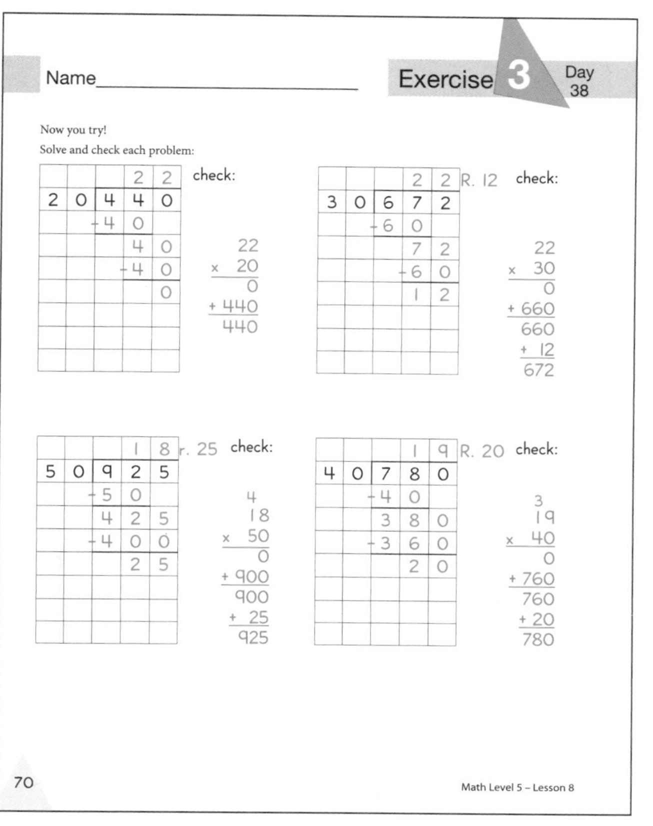
Name____________________ **Exercise 3** Day 38

Now you try!
Solve and check each problem.

20) 440 = 22
−40, 40, −40, 0

check: 22 × 20 = 0 + 440 = 440

30) 672 = 22 R. 12
−60, 72, −60, 12

check: 22 × 30 = 0 + 660 = 660 + 12 = 672

50) 925 = 18 r. 25
−50, 425, −400, 25

check: 18 × 50 = 0 + 900 = 900 + 25 = 925

40) 780 = 19 R. 20
−40, 380, −360, 20

check: 19 × 40 = 0 + 760 = 760 + 20 = 780

70 Math Level 5 – Lesson 8

Name____________________ **Exercise 4-5** Day 39-40

Watch your estimation!
Solve and check each problem.

5) 510 = 102
−5, 010, −10, 0

check: 102 × 5 = 510

60) 760 = 12 R. 40
−60, 160, −120, 40

check: 12 × 60 = 0 + 720 = 720 + 40 = 760

9) 270 = 30
−27, 00, −0, 0

check: 30 × 9 = 270

70) 800 = 11 R. 30
−70, 100, −70, 30

check: 11 × 70 = 0 + 770 = 770 + 30 = 800

Actual: 758 × 4 = 3,032

Estimate: 800 × 4 = 3,200

Narrate to your teacher everything you have learned this week.

Math Level 5 – Lesson 8 71

Name____________________ **Exercise 4-5** Day 39-40

Puzzle Time.

The **Sudoku** puzzle below features a 9 x 9 box (count the first row of blocks = 9 and then count the first column of blocks = 9) divided into three 3 x 3 grids. The game requires the player to use the numbers 1–9 only one time per 3 x 3 square, on each column, and each row. So when you read the numbers by row or by column or within the 3 x 3 squares, the numbers 1–9 appear only once.

See if you can solve the 3 x 3 square in the center of the puzzle. (Hint: Look at the numbers that already exist in the rows that are missing a number. Write down the missing numbers for each row and column. Now, compare those numbers to the numbers that already are either in the 3 x 3 square, row, or column. Then see how you can place the missing numbers and not repeat numbers 1–9 in the 3 x 3 area, the column, or the row.) It's a little hard at first, but remember this is a fun way to learn! (If you're not sure what to do, ask your teacher for help.)

2	1	9	5	4	3	6	7	8
5	4	3	8	7	6	9	1	2
8	7	6	2	1	9	3	4	5
4	3	2	7	6	5	8	9	1
7	6	5	1	9	8	2	3	4
1	9	8	4	3	2	5	6	7
3	2	1	6	5	4	7	8	9
6	5	4	9	8	7	1	2	3
9	8	7	3	2	1	4	5	6

72 Math Level 5 – Lesson 8

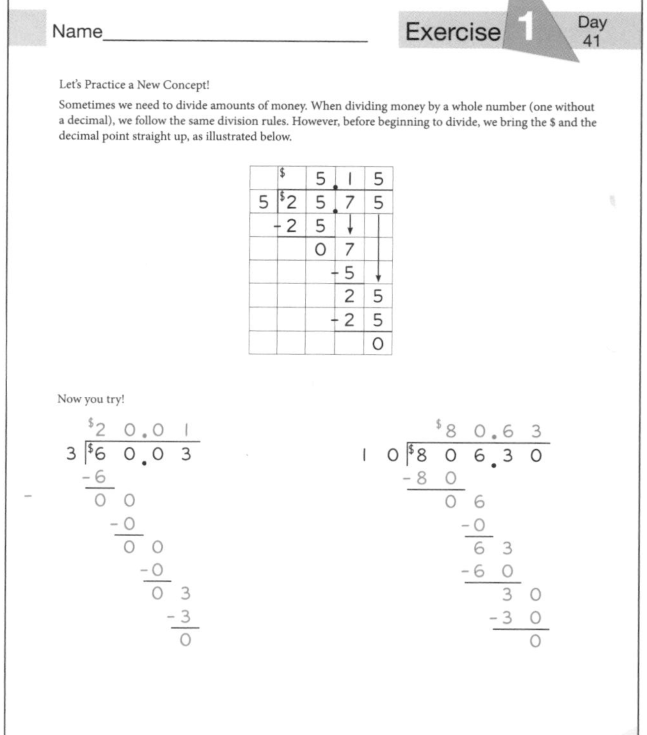
Name____________________ **Exercise 1** Day 41

Let's Practice a New Concept!

Sometimes we need to divide amounts of money. When dividing money by a whole number (one without a decimal), we follow the same division rules. However, before beginning to divide, we bring the $ and the decimal point straight up, as illustrated below.

5) $25.75 = $5.15
−25, 07, −5, 25, −25, 0

Now you try!

3) $60.03 = $20.01
−6, 00, −0, 00, −0, 03, −3, 0

10) $806.30 = $80.63
−80, 06, −0, 63, −60, 30, −30, 0

Math Level 5 – Lesson 9 75

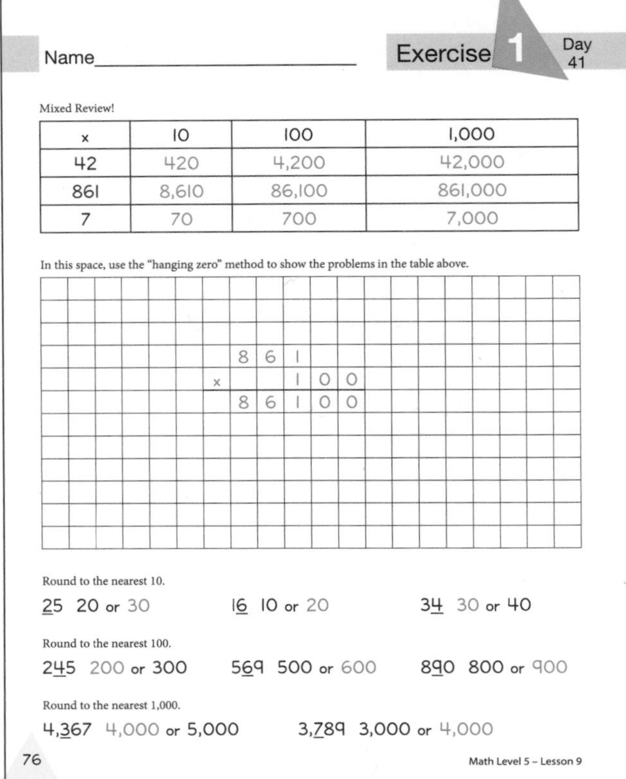

Name________________________ Exercise 1 Day 41

Mixed Review!

x	10	100	1,000
42	420	4,200	42,000
861	8,610	86,100	861,000
7	70	700	7,000

In this space, use the "hanging zero" method to show the problems in the table above.

```
   8 6 1
 x   1 0 0
   8 6 1 0 0
```

Round to the nearest 10.

25 20 or 30   16 10 or 20   34 30 or 40

Round to the nearest 100.

245 200 or 300   569 500 or 600   890 800 or 900

Round to the nearest 1,000.

4,367 4,000 or 5,000   3,789 3,000 or 4,000

76 Math Level 5 – Lesson 9

Name________________________ Exercise 2 Day 42

Copywork:

When we divide, we are taking a large group and breaking it into smaller groups. To divide with a two digit divisor, we have to use some mental math. When you have a two digit divisor, you will always use at least the first two digits of the dividend.

Copywork

Orally narrate to your teacher what you are doing, as you work through the problems.

```
        4 0 r. 10
 2 1 | 8 5 0
     - 8 4
         1 0
       -   0
         1 0
```

```
   831        7,015       518
   386      - 2,649     x  14
 + 702        4,366     2,072
 1,919                + 5,180
                        7,252
```

Math Level 5 – Lesson 9 77

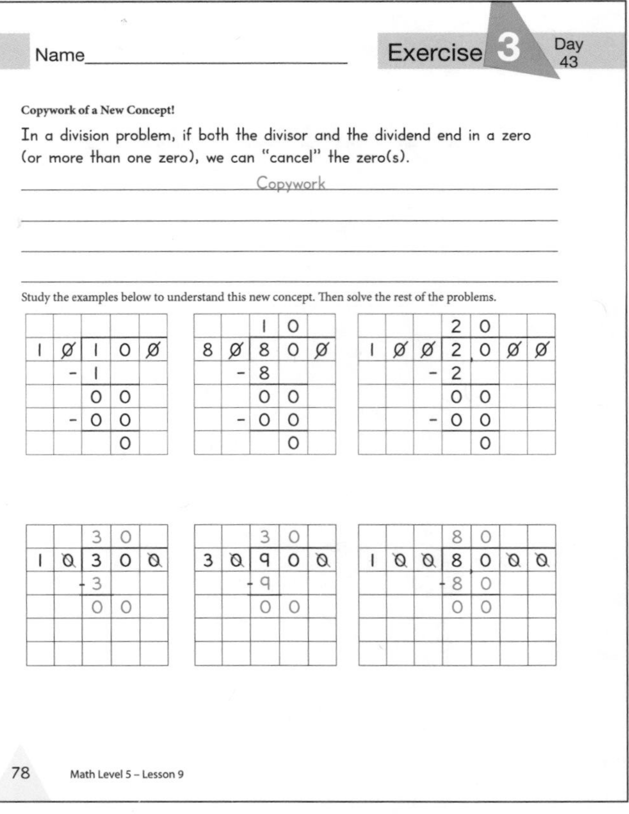

Name________________________ Exercise 3 Day 43

Copywork of a New Concept!

In a division problem, if both the divisor and the dividend end in a zero (or more than one zero), we can "cancel" the zero(s).

Copywork

Study the examples below to understand this new concept. Then solve the rest of the problems.

```
     1 0          1 0            2 0
1 0 | 1 0 0   8 0 | 8 0 0   1 0 0 | 2 0 0 0
   - 1           - 8             - 2
     0 0           0 0             0 0
   - 0 0         - 0 0           - 0 0
       0             0               0
```

```
     3 0          3 0              8 0
1 0 | 3 0 0   3 0 | 9 0 0   1 0 0 | 8 0 0 0
   - 3           - 9               - 8
     0 0           0 0               0 0
```

78 Math Level 5 – Lesson 9

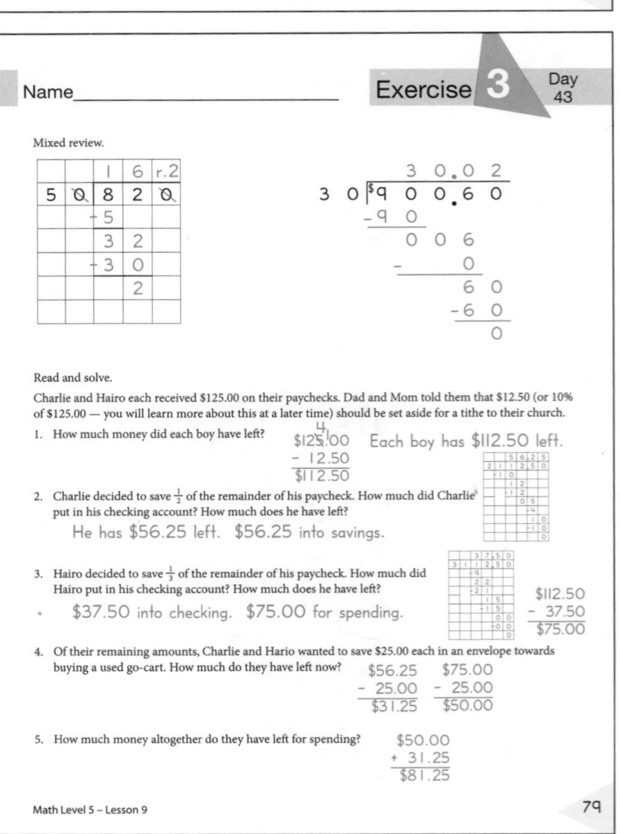

Name________________________ Exercise 3 Day 43

Mixed review.

```
       1 6 r.2
 5 0 | 8 2 0
     - 5
       3 2
     - 3 0
         2
```

```
          3 0 . 0 2
 3 0 | $9 0 0 . 6 0
      - 9 0
          0 0 6
        -     0
              6 0
            - 6 0
                0
```

Read and solve.

Charlie and Hairo each received $125.00 on their paychecks. Dad and Mom told them that $12.50 (or 10% of $125.00 — you will learn more about this at a later time) should be set aside for a tithe to their church.

1. How much money did each boy have left? $125.00 − 12.50 = $112.50 Each boy has $112.50 left.
2. Charlie decided to save $\frac{1}{2}$ of the remainder of his paycheck. How much did Charlie put in his checking account? How much does he have left?
   He has $56.25 left. $56.25 into savings.
3. Hairo decided to save $\frac{1}{3}$ of the remainder of his paycheck. How much did Hairo put in his checking account? How much does he have left?
   $37.50 into checking. $75.00 for spending. ($112.50 − 37.50 = $75.00)
4. Of their remaining amounts, Charlie and Hario wanted to save $25.00 each in an envelope towards buying a used go-cart. How much do they have left now? $56.25 − 25.00 = $31.25 $75.00 − 25.00 = $50.00
5. How much money altogether do they have left for spending? $50.00 + 31.25 = $81.25

Math Level 5 – Lesson 9 79

Solutions Manual: Lesson 10

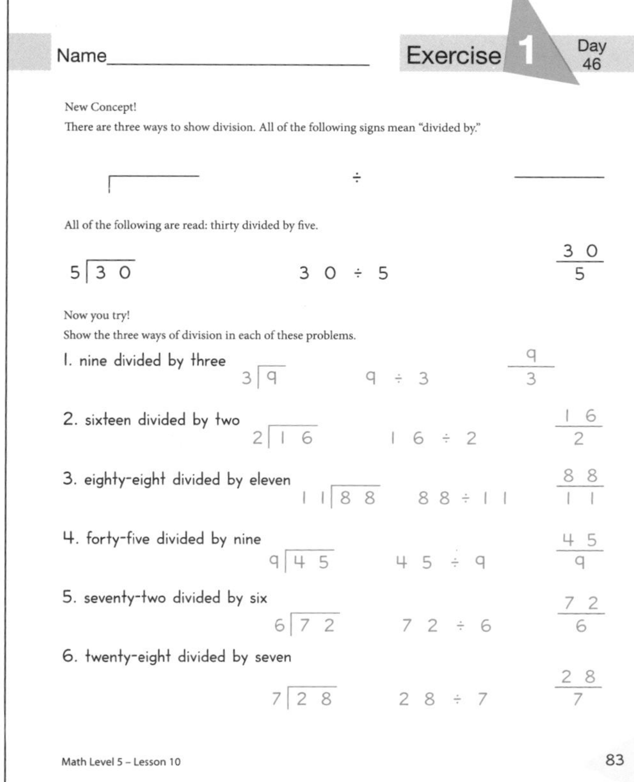

Name__________ **Exercise 1** Day 46

New Concept!

There are three ways to show division. All of the following signs mean "divided by."

$\overline{)\ \ }$ ÷ —

All of the following are read: thirty divided by five.

$5\overline{)30}$ 30 ÷ 5 $\frac{30}{5}$

Now you try!

Show the three ways of division in each of these problems.

1. nine divided by three $3\overline{)9}$ 9 ÷ 3 $\frac{9}{3}$
2. sixteen divided by two $2\overline{)16}$ 16 ÷ 2 $\frac{16}{2}$
3. eighty-eight divided by eleven $11\overline{)88}$ 88 ÷ 11 $\frac{88}{11}$
4. forty-five divided by nine $9\overline{)45}$ 45 ÷ 9 $\frac{45}{9}$
5. seventy-two divided by six $6\overline{)72}$ 72 ÷ 6 $\frac{72}{6}$
6. twenty-eight divided by seven $7\overline{)28}$ 28 ÷ 7 $\frac{28}{7}$

Math Level 5 – Lesson 10 83

Name__________ **Exercise 1** Day 46

Review!

x	1	2	3	4	5	6	7	8	9	10	11	12
1	1	2	3	4	5	6	7	8	9	10	11	12
2	2	4	6	8	10	12	14	16	18	20	22	24
3	3	6	9	12	15	18	21	24	27	30	33	36
4	4	8	12	16	20	24	28	32	36	40	44	48
5	5	10	15	20	25	30	35	40	45	50	55	60
6	6	12	18	24	30	36	42	48	54	60	66	72
7	7	14	21	28	35	42	49	56	63	70	77	84
8	8	16	24	32	40	48	56	64	72	80	88	96
9	9	18	27	36	45	54	63	72	81	90	99	108
10	10	20	30	40	50	60	70	80	90	100	110	120
11	11	22	33	44	55	66	77	88	99	110	121	132
12	12	24	36	48	60	72	84	96	108	120	132	144

84 Math Level 5 – Lesson 10

Name__________ **Exercise 2** Day 47

Quick Review! What is a mixed number?

Copywork!

When reading mixed numbers, such as $2\frac{1}{2}$, we read the whole number first, then the word "and," lastly, the fraction.

Copywork

New Concept! Writing remainders as fractions.

We can write the remainder of a division problem as a fraction. The remainder (in this problem, 1) becomes the numerator, and the divisor (in this problem, 8) becomes the denominator.

$8\overline{)41} = 5\frac{1}{8}$; -40; 1

Now you try!

$8\overline{)41} = 5\frac{1}{8}$ (−40, 1)

$3\overline{)91} = 30\frac{1}{3}$ (−9, 01, −0, 1)

$5\overline{)66} = 13\frac{1}{5}$ (−5, 16, −15, 1)

Mixed Review!

Read these mixed numbers to your teacher.

$2\frac{1}{7}$ $4\frac{1}{3}$ $1\frac{1}{16}$ $7\frac{7}{8}$ $9\frac{4}{6}$

When we solve word problems, we notice the "clue word" that tell us what operation to use. Write subtract, add, multiply, or divide beside each of these "clue words."

in all add

have left subtract

times multiply

altogether add (or sometimes multiply)

share equally divide

more than subtract

less subtract

both add (or sometimes multiply)

Math Level 5 – Lesson 10 85

Name__________ **Exercise 3** Day 48

More Practice! Write the remainders as fractions.

$3\overline{)49} = 16\frac{1}{3}$ (−3, 19, −18, 1)

$6\overline{)11} = 1\frac{5}{6}$ (−6, 5)

$9\overline{)20} = 2\frac{2}{9}$ (−18, 2)

Copywork!

There are three ways to show division.

Copywork

Draw the three ways to show "divided by."

$\overline{)\ \ }$ ÷ —

Solve.

$610\frac{4}{9} + 518\frac{2}{9} = 1{,}128\frac{6}{9}$

$421\frac{9}{17} + 299\frac{6}{17} = 720\frac{15}{17}$

$57\frac{7}{12} - 43\frac{5}{12} = 14\frac{2}{12}$

$961\frac{8}{10} - 750\frac{6}{10} = 211\frac{2}{10}$

Copywork!

A heptagon has 7 sides.

Copywork

A rectangle has 4 sides.

Copywork

86 Math Level 5 – Lesson 10

Name________________________ Exercise  4 Day 49

Copywork!

We can write the remainder of a division problem as a fraction. The remainder becomes the numerator, and the divisor becomes the denominator.

Mixed Review!

Write the remainder as a fraction.

$$\begin{array}{r} 45\ R.\tfrac{2}{11} \\ 11\overline{)497} \\ -44 \\ 57 \\ -55 \\ 2 \end{array}$$

Divide.

$$\begin{array}{r} 30\ R.\tfrac{16}{32} \\ 32\overline{)976} \\ -96 \\ 16 \end{array}$$

Cancel your zeros and divide.

$$\begin{array}{r} 7 \\ 70\overline{)490} \\ 490 \\ 0 \end{array}$$

Word Problems

1. Dad asked the boys how big Mr. Smith's garage was. The boys knew that it was 25 feet deep and 40 feet wide. They sat down to figure out the square footage of the garage. What should their answer be? Remember to label your answer in square feet. When you are finished completing the problem, read through the story problem and circle all of the clue words and phrases.

$$\begin{array}{r} 40 \\ \times\ 25 \\ \hline 200 \\ +\ 800 \\ \hline 1{,}000 \end{array}$$ sq. feet

You know you multiply because the garage is a rectangle, 40 feet by 25 feet. Area of a rectangle is length x width (or side x side).

Name________________________ Exercise  4 Day 49

2. What is the perimeter of the garage from story problem 1?

40 + 40 + 25 + 25 = 130

or

40 x 2 = 80
25 x 2 = 50

$$\begin{array}{r} 80 \\ +\ 50 \\ \hline 130 \end{array}$$ feet

3. The boys came across 129 bent, rusty, old bike tire rims while cleaning out Mr. Smith's garage. Mr. Smith told them to divide them into piles of 12 each. How many piles of bent, rusty, old bike tire rims did they have? How many were left over? When you are finished completing the problem, read through the story problem and circle all of the clue words and phrases.

$$\begin{array}{r} 10\ R.9 \\ 12\overline{)129} \\ -12 \\ 09 \\ -0 \\ 9 \end{array}$$

10 piles with 9 left over

Name________________________ Exercise  5 Day 50

Show the three ways of division in each of these problems.

six divided by two

$2\overline{)6}$ $6 \div 2$ $\frac{6}{2}$

thirty-six divided by six

$6\overline{)36}$ $36 \div 6$ $\frac{36}{6}$

two hundred twenty divided by ten

$10\overline{)220}$ $220 \div 10$ $\frac{220}{10}$

Mixed review.

5 x 7 + 6 = 41
35 + 6

30 x 10 + 36 = 336
300 + 36

42 x 100 + 7 = 4207
4,200 + 7

6 x 6 − 30 = 6
36 − 30

5 x 4 + 20 = 40
20 + 20

3 x 8 x 2 − 48 = 0
24 x 2 = 48 − 48

$$\begin{array}{r} 14 \\ \times\ 16 \\ \hline 84 \\ +\ 140 \\ \hline 224 \end{array} \qquad \begin{array}{r} 42 \\ \times\ 8 \\ \hline 336 \end{array} \qquad \begin{array}{r} 13 \\ \times\ 22 \\ \hline 26 \\ +\ 260 \\ \hline 286 \end{array}$$

			7	1	R. 6
1	1	7	8	7	
	−	7	7		
			1	7	
		−	1	1	
				6	

Name________________________ Exercise 1 Day 51

With a blue colored pencil, draw a right angle on the protractor.
With a green colored pencil, draw an acute angle on the protractor.
With a yellow colored pencil, draw an obtuse angle on the protractor.
Narrate to your teacher what each one is.

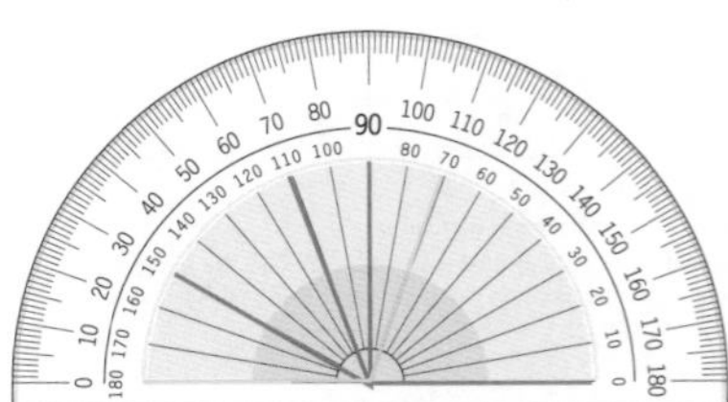

Mixed division review. Solve and check.

$$\begin{array}{r} 122\ R.6 \\ 21\overline{)2{,}568} \\ -21 \\ 46 \\ -42 \\ 48 \\ -42 \\ 6 \end{array} \qquad \begin{array}{r} 122 \\ \times\ 21 \\ \hline 122 \\ +\ 2440 \\ \hline 2562 \\ +\ 6 \\ \hline 2568 \end{array}$$

$$\begin{array}{r} 29 \\ 30\overline{)870} \\ -60 \\ 270 \\ -270 \\ 0 \end{array} \qquad \begin{array}{r} 29 \\ \times\ 30 \\ \hline 870 \end{array}$$

Solutions Manual: Lesson 11

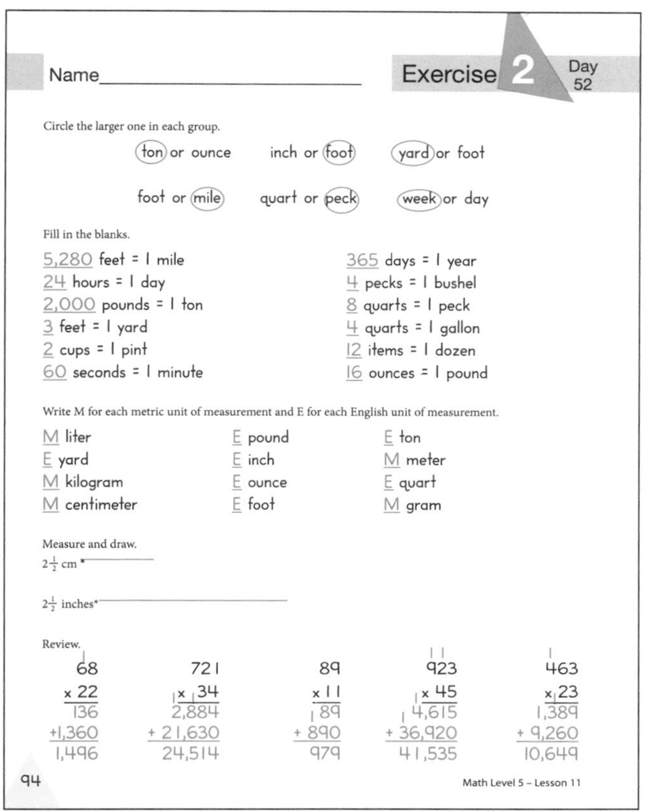

Name______________________ **Exercise 2** Day 52

Circle the larger one in each group.

(ton) or ounce — inch or (foot) — (yard) or foot

foot or (mile) — quart or (peck) — (week) or day

Fill in the blanks.

5,280 feet = 1 mile
24 hours = 1 day
2,000 pounds = 1 ton
3 feet = 1 yard
2 cups = 1 pint
60 seconds = 1 minute
365 days = 1 year
4 pecks = 1 bushel
8 quarts = 1 peck
4 quarts = 1 gallon
12 items = 1 dozen
16 ounces = 1 pound

Write M for each metric unit of measurement and E for each English unit of measurement.

M liter
E yard
M kilogram
M centimeter
E pound
E inch
E ounce
E foot
E ton
M meter
E quart
M gram

Measure and draw.

$2\frac{1}{2}$ cm

$2\frac{1}{2}$ inches

Review.

68 × 22	721 × 34	89 × 11	923 × 45	463 × 23
136	2,884	89	4,615	1,389
+1,360	+ 21,630	+ 890	+ 36,920	+ 9,260
1,496	24,514	979	41,535	10,649

94 Math Level 5 – Lesson 11

Name______________________ **Exercise 3** Day 53

Copywork:

In decimal place value, the place to the right of the decimal is the tenths place.

Copywork

The second place to the right of a decimal is the hundredths place.

Copywork

When we add or subtract decimals, we need to line up the decimal points; this includes money problems. In division, we move the decimal point straight up into the answer.

Copywork

0.3 is read three tenths, and 0.03 is read three hundredths

Copywork

Solve.

52 × 48	613 × 21	82 × 10	1,468 × 100	32,052 × 1,000
416	613	820	146,800	32,052,000
+ 2,080	+ 12,260			
2,496	12,873			

Math Level 5 – Lesson 11 95

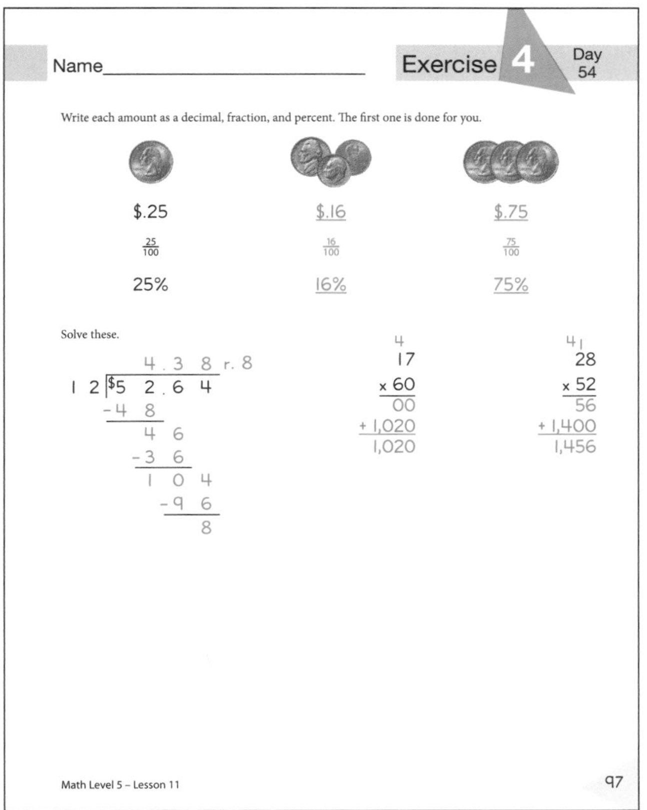

Name______________________ **Exercise 4** Day 54

Write each amount as a decimal, fraction, and percent. The first one is done for you.

$.25	$.16	$.75
$\frac{25}{100}$	$\frac{16}{100}$	$\frac{75}{100}$
25%	16%	75%

Solve these.

$5.264 ÷ 12 = 4.38 r. 8
−48
46
−36
104
−96
8

17 × 60 = 00 + 1,020 = 1,020

28 × 52 = 56 + 1,400 = 1,456

Math Level 5 – Lesson 11 97

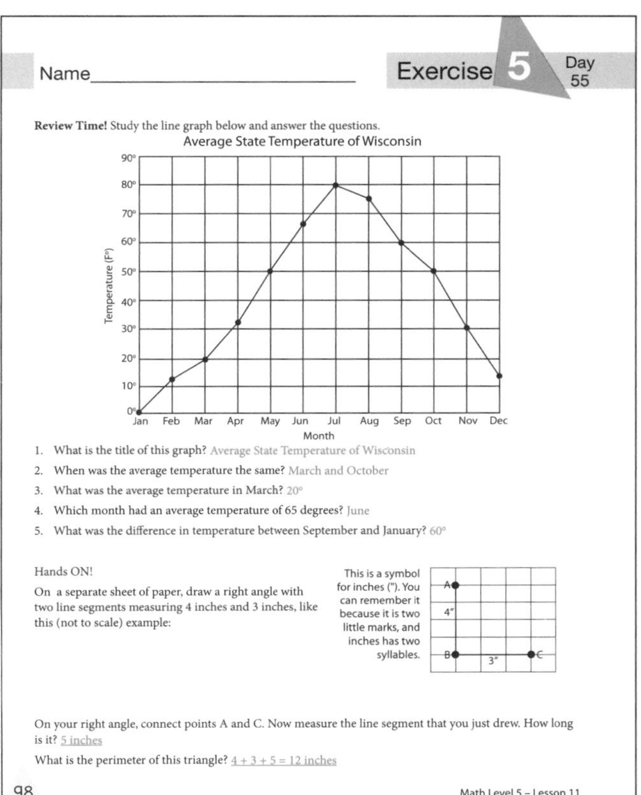

Name______________________ **Exercise 5** Day 55

Review Time! Study the line graph below and answer the questions.

1. What is the title of this graph? Average State Temperature of Wisconsin
2. When was the average temperature the same? March and October
3. What was the average temperature in March? 20°
4. Which month had an average temperature of 65 degrees? June
5. What was the difference in temperature between September and January? 60°

Hands ON!

On a separate sheet of paper, draw a right angle with two line segments measuring 4 inches and 3 inches, like this (not to scale) example:

This is a symbol for inches ("). You can remember it because it is two little marks, and inches has two syllables.

On your right angle, connect points A and C. Now measure the line segment that you just drew. How long is it? 5 inches

What is the perimeter of this triangle? 4 + 3 + 5 = 12 inches

98 Math Level 5 – Lesson 11

Solutions Manual: Lesson 12

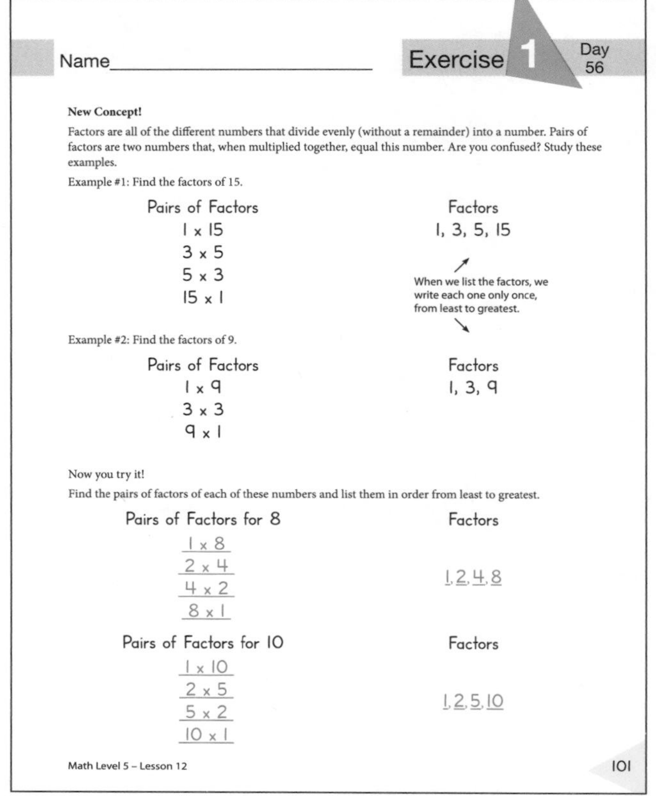

Name______________________ **Exercise 1** Day 56

New Concept!

Factors are all of the different numbers that divide evenly (without a remainder) into a number. Pairs of factors are two numbers that, when multiplied together, equal this number. Are you confused? Study these examples.

Example #1: Find the factors of 15.

Pairs of Factors	Factors
1 x 15	1, 3, 5, 15
3 x 5	
5 x 3	
15 x 1	

When we list the factors, we write each one only once, from least to greatest.

Example #2: Find the factors of 9.

Pairs of Factors	Factors
1 x 9	1, 3, 9
3 x 3	
9 x 1	

Now you try it!

Find the pairs of factors of each of these numbers and list them in order from least to greatest.

Pairs of Factors for 8	Factors
1 x 8	
2 x 4	1, 2, 4, 8
4 x 2	
8 x 1	

Pairs of Factors for 10	Factors
1 x 10	
2 x 5	1, 2, 5, 10
5 x 2	
10 x 1	

Math Level 5 – Lesson 12 101

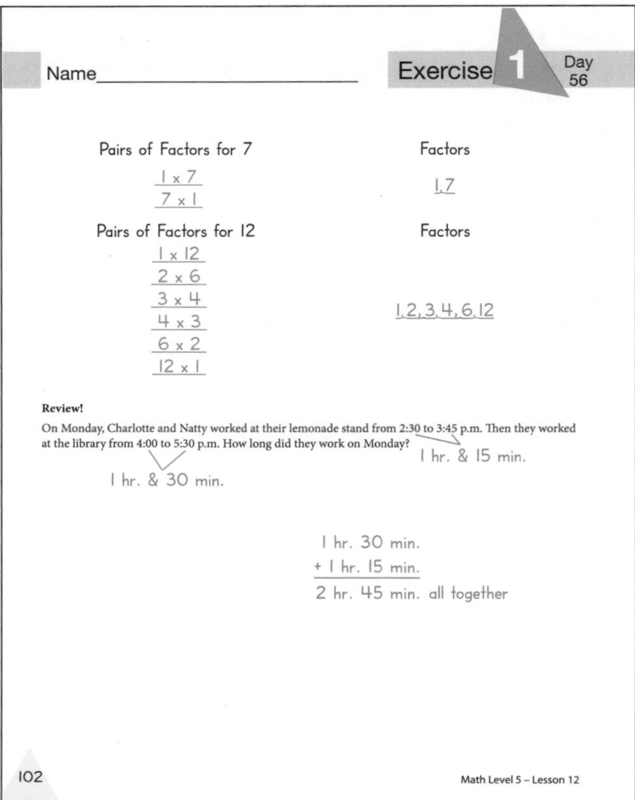

Name______________________ **Exercise 1** Day 56

Pairs of Factors for 7	Factors
1 x 7	1, 7
7 x 1	

Pairs of Factors for 12	Factors
1 x 12	
2 x 6	
3 x 4	1, 2, 3, 4, 6, 12
4 x 3	
6 x 2	
12 x 1	

Review!

On Monday, Charlotte and Natty worked at their lemonade stand from 2:30 to 3:45 p.m. Then they worked at the library from 4:00 to 5:30 p.m. How long did they work on Monday?

1 hr. & 15 min.

1 hr. & 30 min.

1 hr. 30 min.
\+ 1 hr. 15 min.
2 hr. 45 min. all together

102 Math Level 5 – Lesson 12

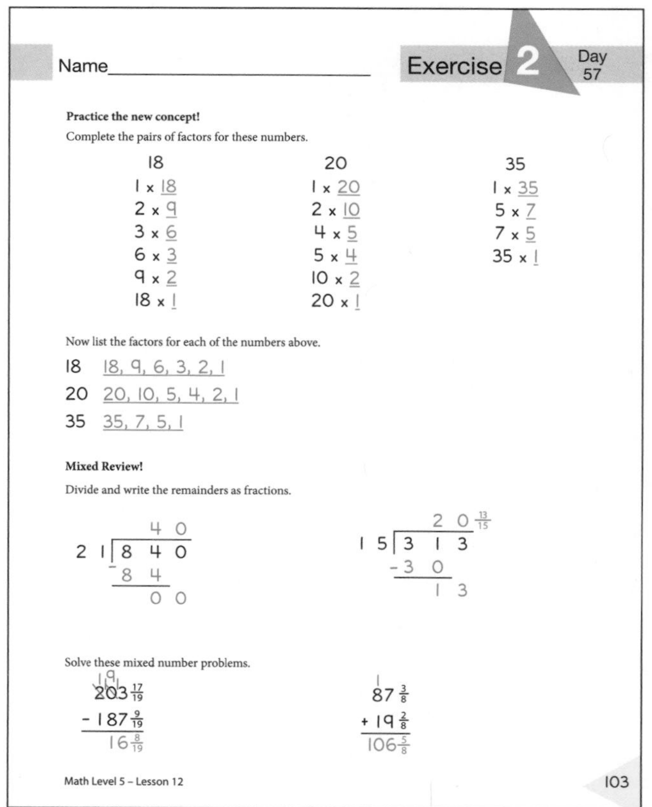

Name______________________ **Exercise 2** Day 57

Practice the new concept!

Complete the pairs of factors for these numbers.

18	20	35
1 x 18	1 x 20	1 x 35
2 x 9	2 x 10	5 x 7
3 x 6	4 x 5	7 x 5
6 x 3	5 x 4	35 x 1
9 x 2	10 x 2	
18 x 1	20 x 1	

Now list the factors for each of the numbers above.

18 18, 9, 6, 3, 2, 1
20 20, 10, 5, 4, 2, 1
35 35, 7, 5, 1

Mixed Review!

Divide and write the remainders as fractions.

$840 \div 21 = 40$ (−84, 00)

$313 \div 15 = 20\frac{13}{15}$ (−30, 13)

Solve these mixed number problems.

$203\frac{17}{19} - 187\frac{9}{19} = 16\frac{8}{19}$

$87\frac{3}{8} + 19\frac{2}{8} = 106\frac{5}{8}$

Math Level 5 – Lesson 12 103

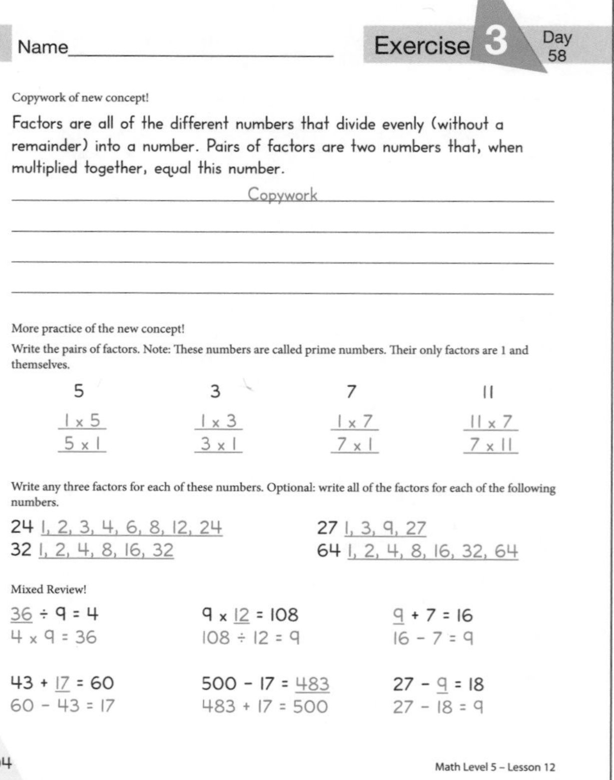

Name______________________ **Exercise 3** Day 58

Copywork of new concept!

Factors are all of the different numbers that divide evenly (without a remainder) into a number. Pairs of factors are two numbers that, when multiplied together, equal this number.

Copywork

More practice of the new concept!

Write the pairs of factors. Note: These numbers are called prime numbers. Their only factors are 1 and themselves.

5	3	7	11
1 x 5	1 x 3	1 x 7	11 x 7
5 x 1	3 x 1	7 x 1	7 x 11

Write any three factors for each of these numbers. Optional: write all of the factors for each of the following numbers.

24 1, 2, 3, 4, 6, 8, 12, 24
27 1, 3, 9, 27
32 1, 2, 4, 8, 16, 32
64 1, 2, 4, 8, 16, 32, 64

Mixed Review!

36 ÷ 9 = 4	9 x 12 = 108	9 + 7 = 16
4 x 9 = 36	108 ÷ 12 = 9	16 − 7 = 9
43 + 17 = 60	500 − 17 = 483	27 − 9 = 18
60 − 43 = 17	483 + 17 = 500	27 − 18 = 9

104 Math Level 5 – Lesson 12

Name________________________

Exercise 4 Day 59

Practice with factoring!

Fill in this chart. The first one is done for you.

Number	Pairs of Factors	Factors
6	1 x 6 2 x 3	1, 2, 3, 6
12	1 x 12 2 x 6 3 x 4 12 x 1 6 x 2 4 x 3	1, 2, 3, 4, 6, 12
18	1 x 18 2 x 9 3 x 6 18 x 1 9 x 2 6 x 3	1, 2, 3, 6, 9, 18
25	25 x 1 5 x 5 1 x 25	1, 3, 25
27	27 x 1 9 x 3 1 x 27 3 x 9	1, 3, 9, 27
49	49 x 1 7 x 7 1 x 49	1, 7, 49
64	64 x 1 2 x 32 4 x 16 8 x 8 1 x 64 32 x 2 16 x 4	1, 2, 4, 8, 16, 32, 64
72	72 x 1 2 x 36 3 x 24 4 x 18 6 x 12 8 x 9 1 x 72 36 x 2 24 x 3 18 x 4 12 x 6 9 x 8	1, 2, 3, 4, 6, 8, 9, 12, 18, 24, 36, 72
84	84 x 1 42 x 2 28 x 3 21 x 4 14 x 6 12 x 7 1 x 84 2 x 42 3 x 28 4 x 21 6 x 14 7 x 12	1, 2, 3, 4, 6, 7, 12, 14, 21, 28, 42, 84
96	96 x 1 48 x 2 32 x 3 24 x 4 16 x 6 12 x 8 1 x 96 2 x 48 3 x 32 4 x 24 6 x 16 8 x 12	1, 2, 3, 4, 6, 8, 12, 16, 24, 32, 48, 96
66	66 x 1 2 x 33 3 x 22 6 x 11 1 x 66 33 x 2 22 x 3 11 x 6	1, 2, 3, 6, 11, 22, 33, 66
50	50 x 1 2 x 25 5 x 10 1 x 50 25 x 2 10 x 5	1, 2, 5, 10, 25, 50
100	100 x 1 2 x 50 4 x 25 5 x 20 10 x 10 1 x 100 50 x 2 25 x 4 20 x 5	1, 2, 4, 5, 10, 20, 25, 50, 100
42	42 x 1 2 x 21 3 x 14 6 x 7 1 x 42 21 x 2 14 x 3 7 x 6	1, 2, 3, 6, 7, 14, 21, 42
48	48 x 1 24 x 2 3 x 16 4 x 12 6 x 8 1 x 48 2 x 24 16 x 3 12 x 4 8 x 6	1, 2, 3, 4, 6, 8, 12, 16, 24, 48
11	11 x 1 11 x 1	1, 11

Name________________________

Exercise 5 Day 60

Review Time!

☐ Take the time now to narrate to your teacher everything you have learned about factoring.

Bonus Concept!

In Lesson 7, we discussed converting measurements. When we are going from larger units of measure to smaller units of measure, we multiply, as seen in the example:

3 yards = 9 feet

Since we know that 3 feet = 1 yard, we can multiply 3 x 3. So think: 3 groups of 3 yards.

1 foot | 1 foot | 1 foot | 1 foot | 1 foot | 1 foot | 1 foot | 1 foot | 1 foot
1 yard | 1 yard | 1 yard

Now you try it!

There are 5,280 feet in 1 mile.
5,280 x 2
10,560 feet = 2 miles

There are 12 items in 1 dozen.
12 x 3
36 items = 3 dozen

There are 60 minutes in 1 hour.
60 x 24
1,440 minutes = 24 hours

There are 1,760 yards in 1 mile.
1,760 x 8
14,080 yards = 8 miles

There are 12 items in 1 dozen.
36 ÷ 13
36 items = 3 dozen

There are 60 seconds in a minute.
3,600 ÷ 60
3,600 seconds = 60 minutes

There are 2,000 pounds in 1 ton
10,000 ÷ 2,000
10,000 pounds = 5 tons

There are 12 months in 1 year
132 ÷ 12
132 months = 11 years

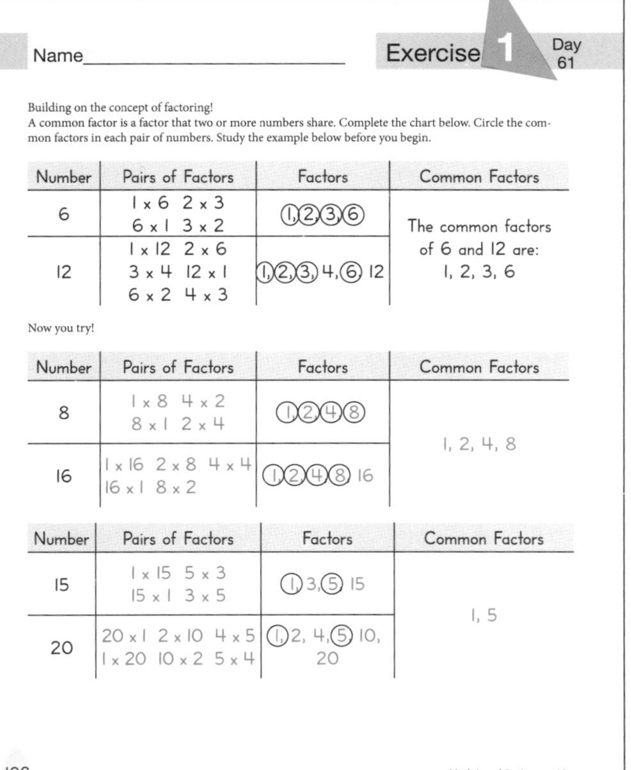
Name________________________

Exercise 1 Day 61

Building on the concept of factoring!

A common factor is a factor that two or more numbers share. Complete the chart below. Circle the common factors in each pair of numbers. Study the example below before you begin.

Number	Pairs of Factors	Factors	Common Factors
6	1 x 6 2 x 3 6 x 1 3 x 2	(1) (2) (3) (6)	The common factors of 6 and 12 are: 1, 2, 3, 6
12	1 x 12 2 x 6 3 x 4 12 x 1 6 x 2 4 x 3	(1) (2) (3) 4, (6) 12	

Now you try!

Number	Pairs of Factors	Factors	Common Factors
8	1 x 8 4 x 2 8 x 1 2 x 4	(1) (2) (4) (8)	1, 2, 4, 8
16	1 x 16 2 x 8 4 x 4 16 x 1 8 x 2	(1) (2) (4) (8) 16	

Number	Pairs of Factors	Factors	Common Factors
15	1 x 15 5 x 3 15 x 1 3 x 5	(1) 3, (5) 15	1, 5
20	20 x 1 2 x 10 4 x 5 1 x 20 10 x 2 5 x 4	(1) 2, 4, (5) 10, 20	

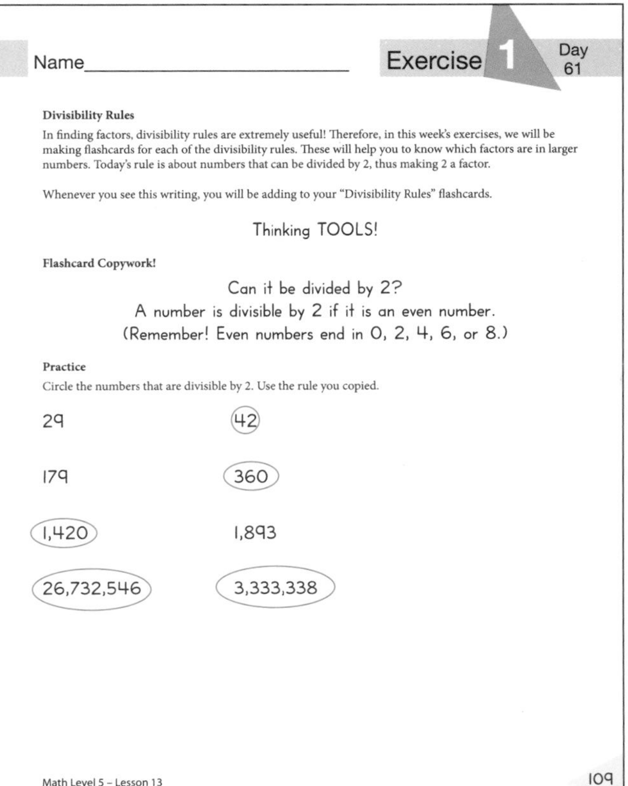
Name________________________

Exercise 1 Day 61

Divisibility Rules

In finding factors, divisibility rules are extremely useful! Therefore, in this week's exercises, we will be making flashcards for each of the divisibility rules. These will help you to know which factors are in larger numbers. Today's rule is about numbers that can be divided by 2, thus making 2 a factor.

Whenever you see this writing, you will be adding to your "Divisibility Rules" flashcards.

Thinking TOOLS!

Flashcard Copywork!

Can it be divided by 2?
A number is divisible by 2 if it is an even number.
(Remember! Even numbers end in 0, 2, 4, 6, or 8.)

Practice

Circle the numbers that are divisible by 2. Use the rule you copied.

29 (42)

179 (360)

(1,420) 1,893

(26,732,546) (3,333,338)

Name________________________ Exercise 2 Day 62

Hands ON!
Remove your Common Factor/Greatest Common Factor Chart and the Reduce that Fraction! Chart from the back of this book. Trim the rough edge and laminate your chart. You will be using the Common Factor side of the chart today. Using a washable marker, find the common factors for the following groups of numbers.

10 and 14
10 (1)(2) 5, 10
14 (1)(2) 7, 14

12, 18, and 24
12 (1)(2)(3) 4, (6) 12
18 (1)(2)(3)(6) 9, 18
24 (1)(2)(3) 4, (6) 8, 12, 24

36, 18, and 9
36 (1) 2, (3) 4, 6, (9) 12, 18, 36
18 (1) 2, (3) 6, (9) 18
9 (1)(3)(9)

35, 20, and 15
35 (1)(5) 7, 35
20 (1) 2, 4, (5) 10, 20
15 (1) 3, (5) 15

Thinking TOOLS!

Flashcard copywork! (Today, you will be making two flashcards.)

Can it be divided by 5?
A number is divisible by 5 if the one's digit is 0 or 5.

Can it be divided by 10?
A number is divisible by 10 if the one's digit is 0.

Flashcard exercise!
Circle the numbers that are divisible by 5. Use the rule you copied.

16 (150) (25) (2,000)
254 (75) 3,210,062 4,001

Circle the numbers that are divisible by 10. Use the rule you copied.

(210) (16,210) 10,004 107
16,222,005 (1,400) (550) (2,000)

110 Math Level 5 – Lesson 13

Name________________________ Exercise 3 Day 63

New Concept! The Greatest Common Factor (GCF) is the largest common factor any group of numbers have.

Hands ON!
You will be using the Greatest Common Factor Chart side of the chart you made in Exercise 2. Using a washable marker, find the greatest common factor for the following groups of numbers. Study the example.

Number	Pairs of Factors	Factors	Common Factors	Greatest Common Factor
6	1 x 6, 2 x 3, 6 x 1, 3 x 2	(1)(2)(3)(6)	The common factors of 6 and 12 are: 1, 2, 3, 6	6
12	1 x 12, 2 x 6, 3 x 4, 12 x 1, 6 x 2, 4 x 3	(1)(2)(3) 4, (6) 12		

10 and 14 2
10 (1)(2) 5, 10
14 (1)(2) 7, 14

12, 18, and 24 6
12 (1)(2)(3) 4, (6) 12
18 (1)(2)(3)(6) 9, 18
24 (1)(2)(3) 4, (6) 8, 12, 24

36, 18, and 9 3
36 (1) 2, (3) 4, 6, (9) 12, 18, 36
18 (1) 2, (3) 6, (9) 18
9 (1)(3)(9)

35, 20, and 15 5
35 (1)(5) 7, 35
20 (1) 2, 4, (5) 10, 20
15 (1) 3, (5) 15

Circle the numbers that are divisible by 3.

608 (894) (1,008) (42) 58

Can it be divided by 9?
A number is divisible by 9 if the sum of the digits is divisible by 9.
Example: the number 909 is divisible by 9
because 9 + 0 + 9 = 18, and 18 is divisible by 9.

Circle the numbers that are divisible by 9.

(72) 807 10,500 5,222 (603)

Math Level 5 – Lesson 13 111

Name________________________ Exercise 4 Day 64

MYSTERY SOLVED! Have you been wondering WHY we have been spending so much time on factors, common factors, and greatest common factors? In this exercise, we will be showing you how to reduce fractions using the greatest common factor. Study the example on the back of your Reduce that Fraction! Chart which you prepared in Exercise 2. First, copy this important fact!

Copywork!
When you reduce a fraction, you aren't making it smaller. A fraction, which is reduced to its lowest terms, has the smallest numbers possible in the numerator and denominator. A reduced fraction is ALWAYS equivalent to the original, when divided by the Greatest Common Factor of both numbers.

Copywork

Hands ON!
Use your "Reduce that Fraction! Chart" to reduce these fractions.

$\frac{6}{12} = \frac{1}{2}$ $\frac{7}{21} = \frac{1}{3}$ $\frac{10}{45} = \frac{2}{9}$ $\frac{45}{50} = \frac{9}{10}$

$\frac{15}{18} = \frac{5}{6}$ $\frac{36}{40} = \frac{9}{10}$ $\frac{2}{10} = \frac{1}{5}$

112 Math Level 5 – Lesson 13

Name________________________ Exercise 5 Day 65

Thinking TOOLS!

Flashcard copywork!

Can it be divided by 4?
A number is divisible by 4 if the last two digits are both zeros, or if they are divisible by 4.
Example: the number 400 is divisible by 4 because it ends in two zeros. The number 248 is also divisible by 4 because 48 (the last two digits) is divisible by 4.

Circle the numbers that are divisible by 4. Use the rule you copied.

(800) 242 (680) 375 (1,424)

Narration Quiz
Use your Reduce that Fraction! Chart to narrate to your teacher what you are doing as you reduce these fractions.

- ☐ $\frac{12}{14}$ $\frac{6}{7}$
- ☐ $\frac{42}{54}$ $\frac{7}{9}$
- ☐ $\frac{6}{12}$ $\frac{1}{2}$
- ☐ $\frac{18}{30}$ $\frac{3}{5}$
- ☐ $\frac{21}{24}$ $\frac{7}{8}$

Math Level 5 – Lesson 13 113

Solutions Manual: Lesson 14

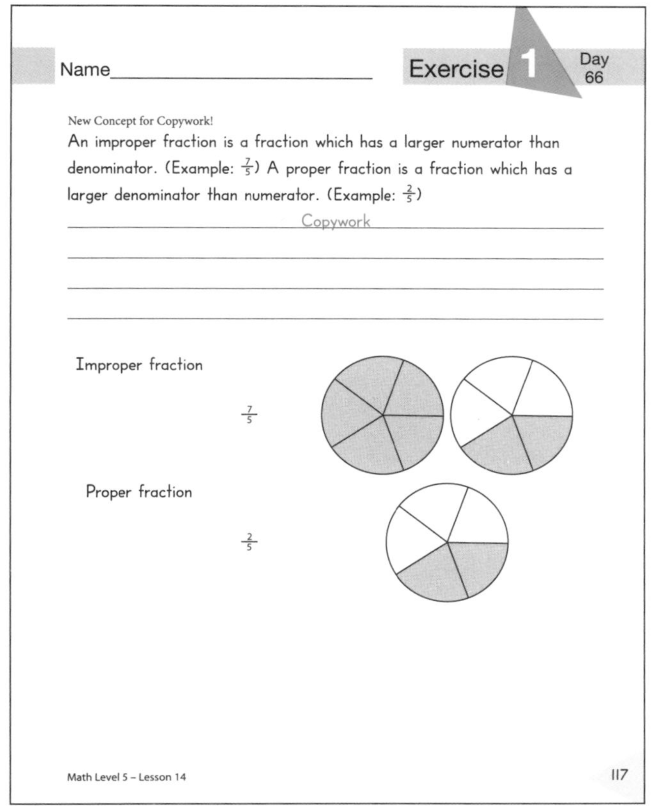

Name__________________ Exercise 1 Day 66

New Concept for Copywork!

An improper fraction is a fraction which has a larger numerator than denominator. (Example: $\frac{7}{5}$) A proper fraction is a fraction which has a larger denominator than numerator. (Example: $\frac{2}{5}$)

Copywork

Improper fraction $\frac{7}{5}$

Proper fraction $\frac{2}{5}$

Math Level 5 – Lesson 14 117

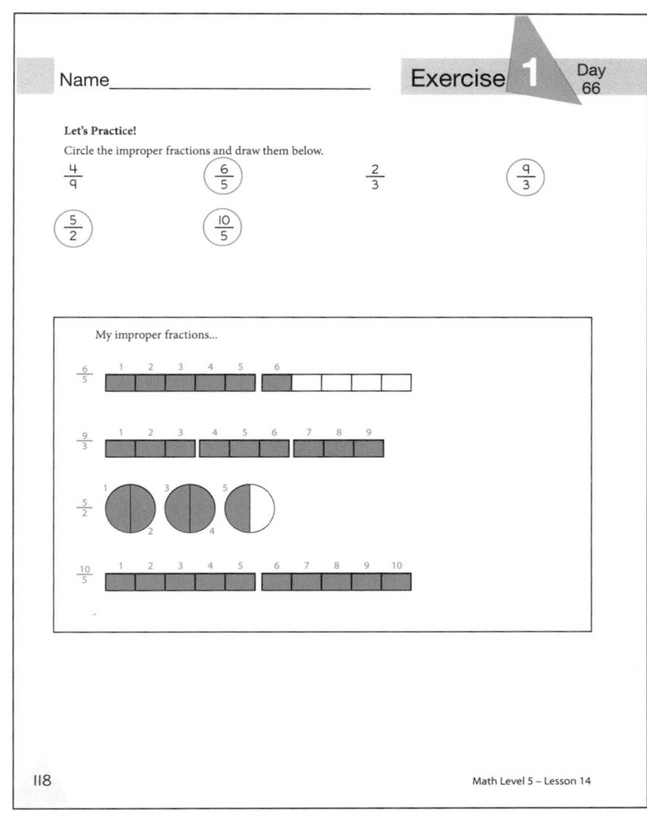

Name__________________ Exercise 1 Day 66

Let's Practice!

Circle the improper fractions and draw them below.

$\frac{4}{9}$ (circled: $\frac{6}{5}$) $\frac{2}{3}$ (circled: $\frac{9}{3}$)

(circled: $\frac{5}{2}$) (circled: $\frac{10}{5}$)

My improper fractions...

$\frac{6}{5}$ 1 2 3 4 5 6

$\frac{9}{3}$ 1 2 3 4 5 6 7 8 9

$\frac{5}{2}$ 1 2 3 4 5

$\frac{10}{5}$ 1 2 3 4 5 6 7 8 9 10

118 Math Level 5 – Lesson 14

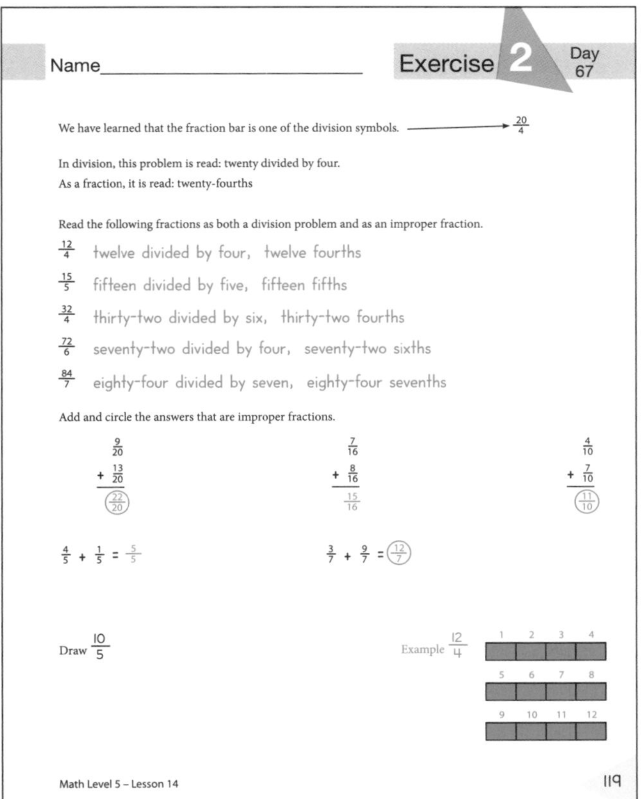

Name__________________ Exercise 2 Day 67

We have learned that the fraction bar is one of the division symbols. → $\frac{20}{4}$

In division, this problem is read: twenty divided by four.
As a fraction, it is read: twenty-fourths

Read the following fractions as both a division problem and as an improper fraction.

$\frac{12}{4}$ twelve divided by four, twelve fourths

$\frac{15}{5}$ fifteen divided by five, fifteen fifths

$\frac{32}{4}$ thirty-two divided by six, thirty-two fourths

$\frac{72}{6}$ seventy-two divided by four, seventy-two sixths

$\frac{84}{7}$ eighty-four divided by seven, eighty-four sevenths

Add and circle the answers that are improper fractions.

$\frac{9}{20} + \frac{13}{20} = \frac{22}{20}$ (circled) $\frac{7}{16} + \frac{8}{16} = \frac{15}{16}$ $\frac{4}{10} + \frac{7}{10} = \frac{11}{10}$ (circled)

$\frac{4}{5} + \frac{1}{5} = \frac{5}{5}$ $\frac{3}{7} + \frac{9}{7} = \frac{12}{7}$ (circled)

Draw $\frac{10}{5}$ Example $\frac{12}{4}$ 1 2 3 4 / 5 6 7 8 / 9 10 11 12

Math Level 5 – Lesson 14 119

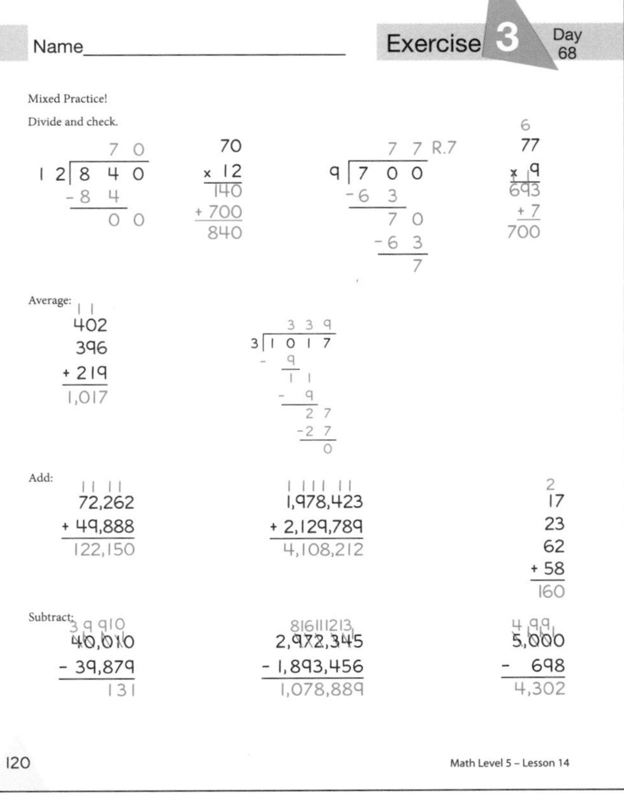

Name__________________ Exercise 3 Day 68

Mixed Practice!

Divide and check.

840 ÷ 12 = 70; check: 70 × 12 = 140 + 700 = 840

700 ÷ 9 = 77 R.7; check: 77 × 9 = 693 + 7 = 700

Average: 402 + 396 + 219 = 1,017; 1,017 ÷ 3 = 339

Add: 72,262 + 49,888 = 122,150; 1,978,423 + 2,129,789 = 4,108,212; 17 + 23 + 62 + 58 = 160

Subtract: 40,010 − 39,879 = 131; 2,972,345 − 1,893,456 = 1,078,889; 5,000 − 698 = 4,302

120 Math Level 5 – Lesson 14

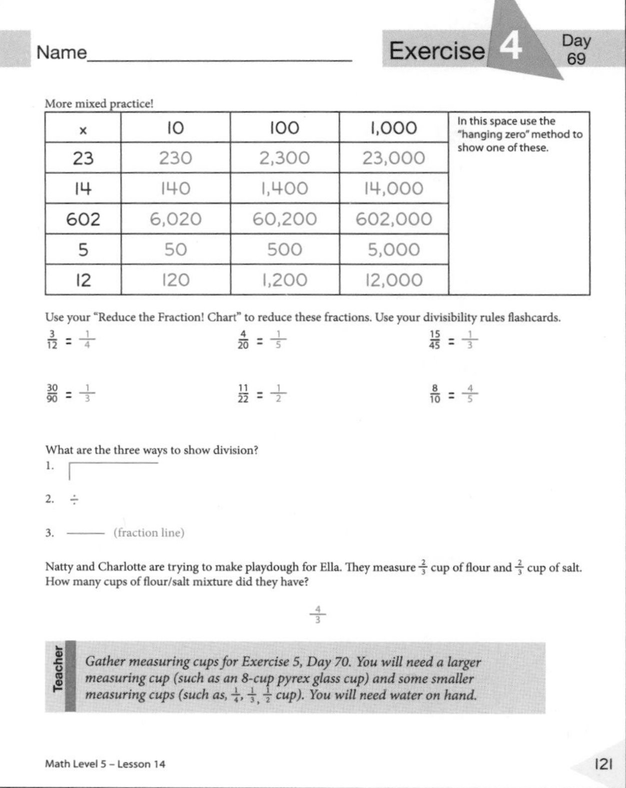

Name________________ **Exercise 4** Day 69

More mixed practice!

x	10	100	1,000
23	230	2,300	23,000
14	140	1,400	14,000
602	6,020	60,200	602,000
5	50	500	5,000
12	120	1,200	12,000

In this space use the "hanging zero" method to show one of these.

Use your "Reduce the Fraction! Chart" to reduce these fractions. Use your divisibility rules flashcards.

$\frac{3}{12} = \frac{1}{4}$ $\frac{4}{20} = \frac{1}{5}$ $\frac{15}{45} = \frac{1}{3}$

$\frac{30}{90} = \frac{1}{3}$ $\frac{11}{22} = \frac{1}{2}$ $\frac{8}{10} = \frac{4}{5}$

What are the three ways to show division?

1. ⟌
2. ÷
3. ——— (fraction line)

Natty and Charlotte are trying to make playdough for Ella. They measure $\frac{2}{3}$ cup of flour and $\frac{2}{3}$ cup of salt. How many cups of flour/salt mixture did they have?

$\frac{4}{3}$

Teacher *Gather measuring cups for Exercise 5, Day 70. You will need a larger measuring cup (such as an 8-cup pyrex glass cup) and some smaller measuring cups (such as, $\frac{1}{4}$, $\frac{1}{3}$, $\frac{1}{2}$ cup). You will need water on hand.*

Math Level 5 – Lesson 14 121

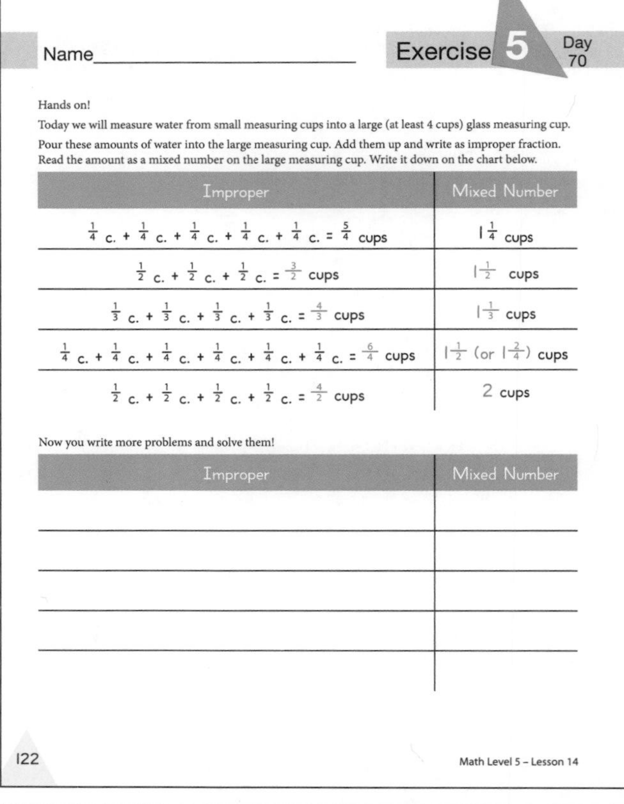

Name________________ **Exercise 5** Day 70

Hands on!

Today we will measure water from small measuring cups into a large (at least 4 cups) glass measuring cup.

Pour these amounts of water into the large measuring cup. Add them up and write as improper fraction. Read the amount as a mixed number on the large measuring cup. Write it down on the chart below.

Improper	Mixed Number
$\frac{1}{4}$ c. + $\frac{1}{4}$ c. + $\frac{1}{4}$ c. + $\frac{1}{4}$ c. + $\frac{1}{4}$ c. = $\frac{5}{4}$ cups	$1\frac{1}{4}$ cups
$\frac{1}{2}$ c. + $\frac{1}{2}$ c. + $\frac{1}{2}$ c. = $\frac{3}{2}$ cups	$1\frac{1}{2}$ cups
$\frac{1}{3}$ c. + $\frac{1}{3}$ c. + $\frac{1}{3}$ c. + $\frac{1}{3}$ c. = $\frac{4}{3}$ cups	$1\frac{1}{3}$ cups
$\frac{1}{4}$ c. + $\frac{1}{4}$ c. + $\frac{1}{4}$ c. + $\frac{1}{4}$ c. + $\frac{1}{4}$ c. + $\frac{1}{4}$ c. = $\frac{6}{4}$ cups	$1\frac{1}{2}$ (or $1\frac{2}{4}$) cups
$\frac{1}{2}$ c. + $\frac{1}{2}$ c. + $\frac{1}{2}$ c. + $\frac{1}{2}$ c. = $\frac{4}{2}$ cups	2 cups

Now you write more problems and solve them!

Improper	Mixed Number

122 Math Level 5 – Lesson 14

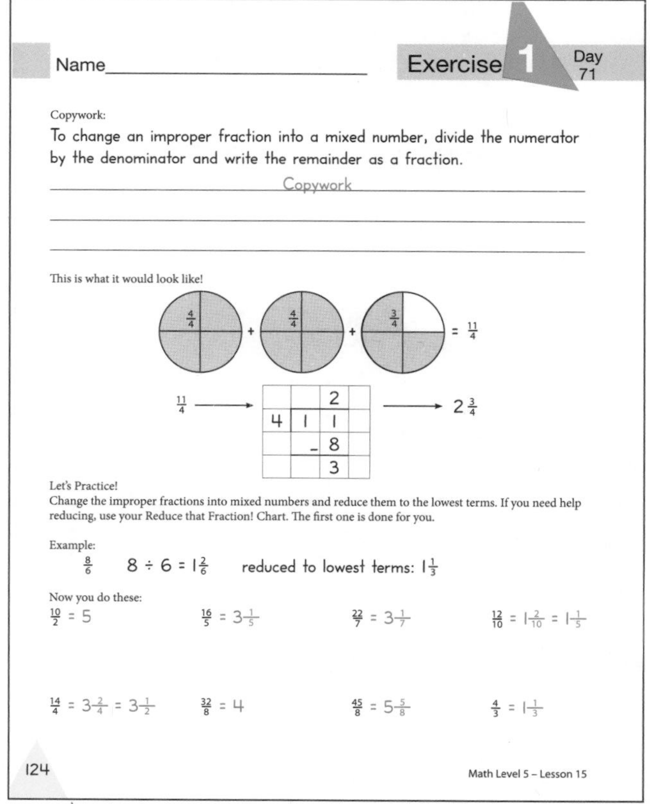

Name________________ **Exercise 1** Day 71

Copywork:

To change an improper fraction into a mixed number, divide the numerator by the denominator and write the remainder as a fraction.

Copywork

This is what it would look like!

$\frac{4}{4} + \frac{4}{4} + \frac{3}{4} = \frac{11}{4}$

$\frac{11}{4}$ ⟶ $11 \div 4 = 2$ R 3 ⟶ $2\frac{3}{4}$

Let's Practice!

Change the improper fractions into mixed numbers and reduce them to the lowest terms. If you need help reducing, use your Reduce that Fraction! Chart. The first one is done for you.

Example:

$\frac{8}{6}$ $8 \div 6 = 1\frac{2}{6}$ reduced to lowest terms: $1\frac{1}{3}$

Now you do these:

$\frac{10}{2} = 5$ $\frac{16}{5} = 3\frac{1}{5}$ $\frac{22}{7} = 3\frac{1}{7}$ $\frac{12}{10} = 1\frac{2}{10} = 1\frac{1}{5}$

$\frac{14}{4} = 3\frac{2}{4} = 3\frac{1}{2}$ $\frac{32}{8} = 4$ $\frac{45}{8} = 5\frac{5}{8}$ $\frac{4}{3} = 1\frac{1}{3}$

124 Math Level 5 – Lesson 15

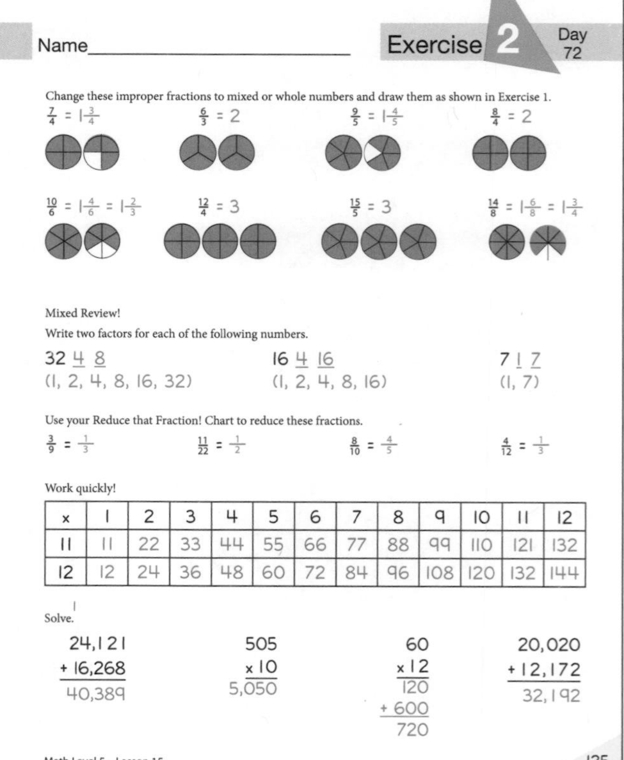

Name________________ **Exercise 2** Day 72

Change these improper fractions to mixed or whole numbers and draw them as shown in Exercise 1.

$\frac{7}{4} = 1\frac{3}{4}$ $\frac{6}{3} = 2$ $\frac{9}{5} = 1\frac{4}{5}$ $\frac{8}{4} = 2$

$\frac{10}{6} = 1\frac{4}{6} = 1\frac{2}{3}$ $\frac{12}{4} = 3$ $\frac{15}{5} = 3$ $\frac{14}{8} = 1\frac{6}{8} = 1\frac{3}{4}$

Mixed Review!

Write two factors for each of the following numbers.

32 4 8 (1, 2, 4, 8, 16, 32) 16 4 16 (1, 2, 4, 8, 16) 7 1 7 (1, 7)

Use your Reduce that Fraction! Chart to reduce these fractions.

$\frac{3}{9} = \frac{1}{3}$ $\frac{11}{22} = \frac{1}{2}$ $\frac{8}{10} = \frac{4}{5}$ $\frac{4}{12} = \frac{1}{3}$

Work quickly!

x	1	2	3	4	5	6	7	8	9	10	11	12
11	11	22	33	44	55	66	77	88	99	110	121	132
12	12	24	36	48	60	72	84	96	108	120	132	144

Solve.

24,121 + 16,268 = 40,389

505 x 10 = 5,050

60 x 12 = 120 + 600 = 720

20,020 + 12,172 = 32,192

Math Level 5 – Lesson 15 125

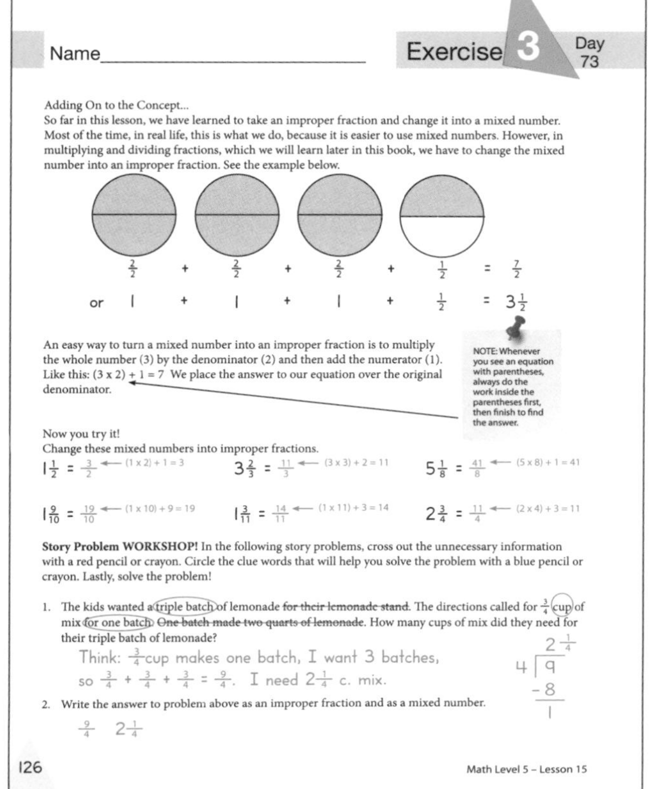

Name________________________ **Exercise 3** Day 73

Adding On to the Concept...
So far in this lesson, we have learned to take an improper fraction and change it into a mixed number. Most of the time, in real life, this is what we do, because it is easier to use mixed numbers. However, in multiplying and dividing fractions, which we will learn later in this book, we have to change the mixed number into an improper fraction. See the example below.

$\frac{2}{2} + \frac{2}{2} + \frac{2}{2} + \frac{1}{2} = \frac{7}{2}$

or $1 + 1 + 1 + \frac{1}{2} = 3\frac{1}{2}$

An easy way to turn a mixed number into an improper fraction is to multiply the whole number (3) by the denominator (2) and then add the numerator (1). Like this: (3 x 2) + 1 = 7 We place the answer to our equation over the original denominator.

NOTE: Whenever you see an equation with parentheses, always do the work inside the parentheses first, then finish to find the answer.

Now you try it!
Change these mixed numbers into improper fractions.

$1\frac{1}{2} = \frac{3}{2}$ ← (1 x 2) + 1 = 3 $3\frac{2}{3} = \frac{11}{3}$ ← (3 x 3) + 2 = 11 $5\frac{1}{8} = \frac{41}{8}$ ← (5 x 8) + 1 = 41

$1\frac{9}{10} = \frac{19}{10}$ ← (1 x 10) + 9 = 19 $1\frac{3}{11} = \frac{14}{11}$ ← (1 x 11) + 3 = 14 $2\frac{3}{4} = \frac{11}{4}$ ← (2 x 4) + 3 = 11

Story Problem WORKSHOP! In the following story problems, cross out the unnecessary information with a red pencil or crayon. Circle the clue words that will help you solve the problem with a blue pencil or crayon. Lastly, solve the problem!

1. The kids wanted a triple batch of lemonade ~~for their lemonade stand~~. The directions called for $\frac{3}{4}$ cup of mix for one batch. ~~One batch made two quarts of lemonade~~. How many cups of mix did they need for their triple batch of lemonade?

   Think: $\frac{3}{4}$ cup makes one batch, I want 3 batches, so $\frac{3}{4} + \frac{3}{4} + \frac{3}{4} = \frac{9}{4}$. I need $2\frac{1}{4}$ c. mix.

   $9 \div 4 = 2\frac{1}{4}$ (9 − 8 = 1)

2. Write the answer to problem above as an improper fraction and as a mixed number.

   $\frac{9}{4}$ $2\frac{1}{4}$

126 Math Level 5 – Lesson 15

Name________________________ **Exercise 4** Day 74

Today, you are going to make your own fraction circles. Use whatever size bowl, plate, or cup you want to make your circles. Make sure your circles are all the same size. Use a ruler to draw lines on your circles to make fractions. Make fraction circles to show these mixed numbers and improper fractions.

- ☐ $2\frac{1}{2}$
- ☐ $4\frac{2}{3}$
- ☐ $1\frac{3}{4}$
- ☐ $\frac{11}{5}$
- ☐ $\frac{16}{8}$
- ☐ $\frac{13}{6}$

Show and narrate to your family what you learned about improper fractions and mixed numbers.

Optional review for Day 74 or Day 75.
Change these improper fractions into mixed numbers.

$\frac{11}{3} = 3\frac{2}{3}$ $\frac{12}{7} = 1\frac{5}{7}$

$\frac{19}{8} = 2\frac{3}{8}$ $\frac{22}{3} = 7\frac{1}{3}$

Change these mixed numbers into improper fractions.

$5\frac{1}{3} = \frac{16}{3}$ ← (5 x 3) + 1 = 16 $7\frac{1}{8} = \frac{57}{8}$ ← (7 x 8) + 1 = 57

$4\frac{3}{4} = \frac{19}{4}$ ← (4 x 4) + 3 = 19 $9\frac{2}{5} = \frac{47}{5}$ ← (7 x 8) + 1 = 57

Math Level 5 – Lesson 15 127

Name________________________ **Exercise 5** Day 75

It's time to solve another Sudoku!

You may have noticed the Sudoku puzzles becoming more of a challenge as you see examples with more of the numbers missing. While these are a bigger challenge, remember that the process to solve them remains simple.

See if you can solve the 3 x 3 square in the center of the puzzle. Remember:

1. Look at the numbers already in the rows that are missing a number.
2. Write down the missing numbers for each row and column. (Hint: Writing on the edges of the puzzle in line with the columns or rows are a good way to keep these numbers in mind.
3. Compare those numbers to the numbers that already in the 3 x 3 square, row, or column.
4. See if you can place the missing numbers and not repeat numbers 1–9 in the 3 x 3 area, the column, or the row.
5. Confused or not sure what to do? Ask your teacher for help.

8	7	6	5	4	3	1	9	2
5	4	3	2	1	9	7	6	8
2	1	9	8	7	6	4	3	5
1	9	8	7	6	5	3	2	4
4	3	2	1	9	8	6	5	7
7	6	5	4	3	2	9	8	1
3	2	1	9	8	7	5	4	6
6	5	4	3	2	1	8	7	9
9	8	7	6	5	4	2	1	3

128 Math Level 5 – Lesson 15

Name________________________ **Exercise 1** Day 76

New Concept for Copywork!
When we add a group of fractions together, sometimes the sum is an improper fraction. When this happens, we change the sum into a mixed number and reduce if necessary.

Copywork

This is how it looks:

$\frac{3}{10} + \frac{4}{10} + \frac{5}{10} = \frac{12}{10} = 1\frac{2}{10} = 1\frac{1}{5}$

Our answer is an improper fraction ($\frac{12}{10}$), so we change it to a mixed number ($1\frac{2}{10}$). Our mixed number needs to be reduced to lowest terms ($1\frac{1}{5}$).

Now you try it!
Add the fractions. If the sum is an improper fraction, change it to a mixed number, and reduce as necessary. If you need help reducing, use your "Reduce that Fraction! Chart."

$\frac{7}{8} + \frac{7}{8} = \frac{14}{8} = 1\frac{6}{8} = 1\frac{3}{4}$

$\frac{4}{10} + \frac{7}{10} = \frac{11}{10} = 1\frac{1}{10}$

$\frac{4}{5} + \frac{3}{5} = \frac{7}{5} = 1\frac{2}{5}$

$\frac{6}{11} + \frac{5}{11} + \frac{3}{11} = \frac{14}{11} = 1\frac{3}{11}$

$\frac{2}{15} + \frac{7}{15} + \frac{11}{15} = \frac{20}{15} = 1\frac{5}{15} = 1\frac{1}{3}$

Math Level 5 – Lesson 16 131

Solutions Manual: Lesson 16

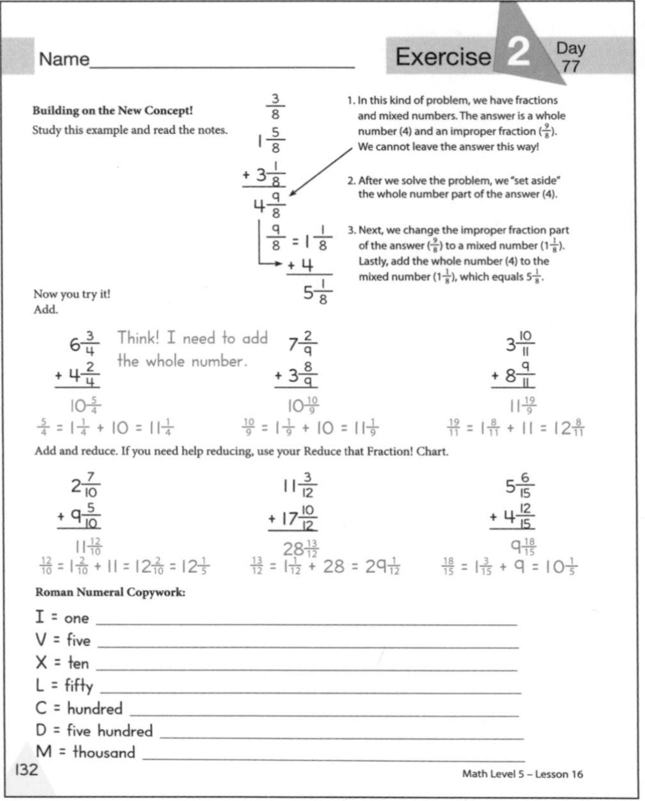

Name________________ **Exercise 2** Day 77

Building on the New Concept!
Study this example and read the notes.

$$\frac{3}{8} + 1\frac{5}{8} + 3\frac{1}{8} = 4\frac{9}{8} \qquad \frac{9}{8} = 1\frac{1}{8} \qquad 1\frac{1}{8} + 4 = 5\frac{1}{8}$$

1. In this kind of problem, we have fractions and mixed numbers. The answer is a whole number (4) and an improper fraction ($\frac{9}{8}$). We cannot leave the answer this way!
2. After we solve the problem, we "set aside" the whole number part of the answer (4).
3. Next, we change the improper fraction part of the answer ($\frac{9}{8}$) to a mixed number ($1\frac{1}{8}$). Lastly, add the whole number (4) to the mixed number ($1\frac{1}{8}$), which equals $5\frac{1}{8}$.

Now you try it!
Add.

$6\frac{3}{4} + 4\frac{2}{4} = 10\frac{5}{4}$ Think! I need to add the whole number. $\frac{5}{4} = 1\frac{1}{4} + 10 = 11\frac{1}{4}$

$7\frac{2}{9} + 3\frac{8}{9} = 10\frac{10}{9}$; $\frac{10}{9} = 1\frac{1}{9} + 10 = 11\frac{1}{9}$

$3\frac{10}{11} + 8\frac{9}{11} = 11\frac{19}{11}$; $\frac{19}{11} = 1\frac{8}{11} + 11 = 12\frac{8}{11}$

Add and reduce. If you need help reducing, use your Reduce that Fraction! Chart.

$2\frac{7}{10} + 9\frac{5}{10} = 11\frac{12}{10}$; $\frac{12}{10} = 1\frac{2}{10} + 11 = 12\frac{2}{10} = 12\frac{1}{5}$

$11\frac{3}{12} + 17\frac{10}{12} = 28\frac{13}{12}$; $\frac{13}{12} = 1\frac{1}{12} + 28 = 29\frac{1}{12}$

$5\frac{6}{15} + 4\frac{12}{15} = 9\frac{18}{15}$; $\frac{18}{15} = 1\frac{3}{15} + 9 = 10\frac{1}{5}$

Roman Numeral Copywork:

I = one ________________
V = five ________________
X = ten ________________
L = fifty ________________
C = hundred ________________
D = five hundred ________________
M = thousand ________________

132 Math Level 5 – Lesson 16

Name________________ **Exercise 3** Day 78

Copywork!

In some mixed number addition problems, the answer is a whole number and an improper fraction. Solve the problem, "set aside" the whole number part of the answer, change the improper fraction part of the answer to a mixed number, and add the whole number to the mixed number.

Copywork

Solve.

$1\frac{8}{9} + 1\frac{2}{9} = 2\frac{10}{9}$; $\frac{10}{9} = 1\frac{1}{9} + 2 = 3\frac{1}{9}$

$3\frac{4}{7} + 4\frac{6}{7} = 7\frac{10}{7}$; $\frac{10}{7} = 1\frac{3}{7} + 7 = 8\frac{3}{7}$

$8\frac{1}{2} + 3\frac{1}{2} = 11\frac{2}{2}$; $\frac{2}{2} = 1 + 11 = 12$

$13\frac{1}{10} + 17\frac{4}{10} = 30\frac{5}{10}$; $30\frac{5}{10} = 30\frac{1}{2}$

Fill in the Missing Roman Numerals.

I, II, III, IV, V, VI, VII, VIII, IX, X, XI, XII, XIII, XIV, XV, XVI, XVII, XVIII, XIX, XX

Math Level 5 – Lesson 16 133

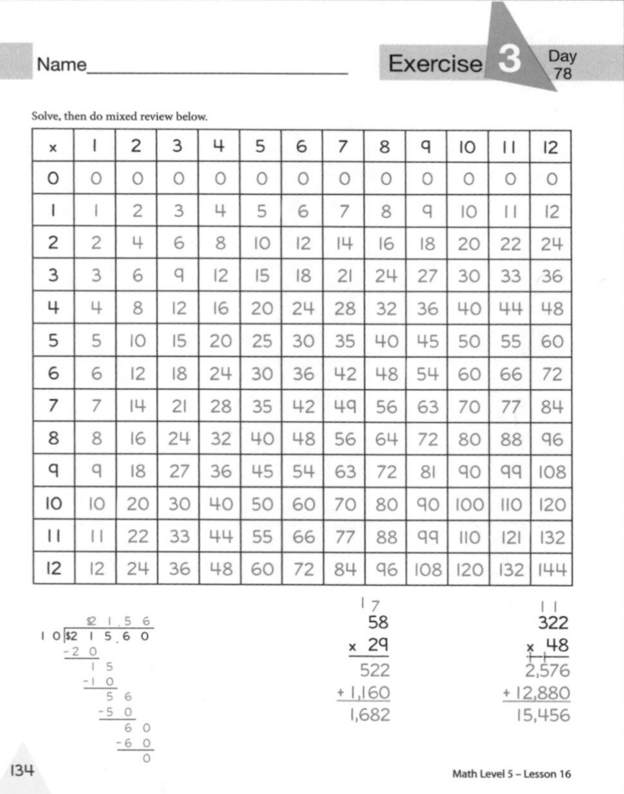

Name________________ **Exercise 3** Day 78

Solve, then do mixed review below.

x	1	2	3	4	5	6	7	8	9	10	11	12
0	0	0	0	0	0	0	0	0	0	0	0	0
1	1	2	3	4	5	6	7	8	9	10	11	12
2	2	4	6	8	10	12	14	16	18	20	22	24
3	3	6	9	12	15	18	21	24	27	30	33	36
4	4	8	12	16	20	24	28	32	36	40	44	48
5	5	10	15	20	25	30	35	40	45	50	55	60
6	6	12	18	24	30	36	42	48	54	60	66	72
7	7	14	21	28	35	42	49	56	63	70	77	84
8	8	16	24	32	40	48	56	64	72	80	88	96
9	9	18	27	36	45	54	63	72	81	90	99	108
10	10	20	30	40	50	60	70	80	90	100	110	120
11	11	22	33	44	55	66	77	88	99	110	121	132
12	12	24	36	48	60	72	84	96	108	120	132	144

$\$215.60 \div 10 = \$21.56$ (−20, 15, −10, 56, −50, 60, −60, 0)

58×29: 522 + 1,160 = 1,682

322×48: 2,576 + 12,880 = 15,456

134 Math Level 5 – Lesson 16

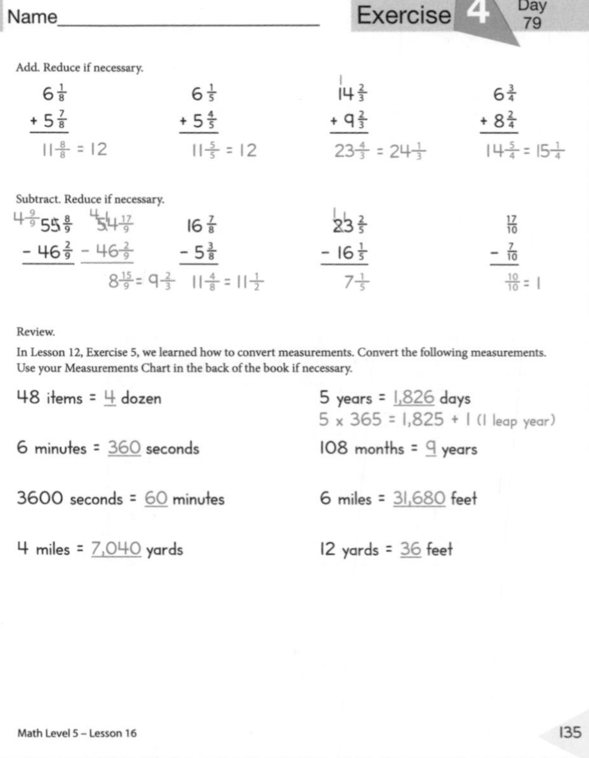

Name________________ **Exercise 4** Day 79

Add. Reduce if necessary.

$6\frac{1}{8} + 5\frac{7}{8} = 11\frac{8}{8} = 12$

$6\frac{1}{5} + 5\frac{4}{5} = 11\frac{5}{5} = 12$

$14\frac{2}{3} + 9\frac{2}{3} = 23\frac{4}{3} = 24\frac{1}{3}$

$6\frac{3}{4} + 8\frac{2}{4} = 14\frac{5}{4} = 15\frac{1}{4}$

Subtract. Reduce if necessary.

$55\frac{8}{9} - 46\frac{2}{9}$ ($4\frac{9}{9}$; $54\frac{17}{9} - 46\frac{2}{9}$) $= 8\frac{15}{9} = 9\frac{2}{3}$

$16\frac{7}{8} - 5\frac{3}{8} = 11\frac{4}{8} = 11\frac{1}{2}$

$23\frac{2}{5} - 16\frac{1}{5} = 7\frac{1}{5}$

$\frac{17}{10} - \frac{7}{10} = \frac{10}{10} = 1$

Review.

In Lesson 12, Exercise 5, we learned how to convert measurements. Convert the following measurements. Use your Measurements Chart in the back of the book if necessary.

48 items = 4 dozen

5 years = 1,826 days
5 x 365 = 1,825 + 1 (1 leap year)

6 minutes = 360 seconds

108 months = 9 years

3600 seconds = 60 minutes

6 miles = 31,680 feet

4 miles = 7,040 yards

12 yards = 36 feet

Math Level 5 – Lesson 16 135

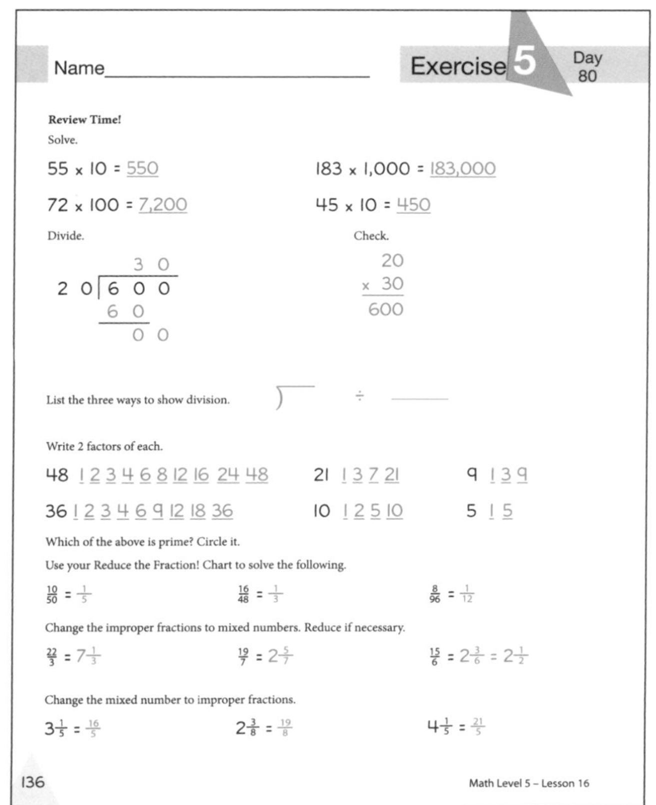

Name________________ **Exercise 5** Day 80

Review Time!
Solve.

55 x 10 = 550 183 x 1,000 = 183,000

72 x 100 = 7,200 45 x 10 = 450

Divide.

$$20\overline{)600} = 30$$

60
00

Check.

20
x 30
600

List the three ways to show division. $\overline{)\quad}$ ÷ ____

Write 2 factors of each.

48 1 2 3 4 6 8 12 16 24 48 21 1 3 7 21 9 1 3 9

36 1 2 3 4 6 9 12 18 36 10 1 2 5 10 5 1 5

Which of the above is prime? Circle it.

Use your Reduce the Fraction! Chart to solve the following.

$\frac{10}{50} = \frac{1}{5}$ $\frac{16}{48} = \frac{1}{3}$ $\frac{8}{96} = \frac{1}{12}$

Change the improper fractions to mixed numbers. Reduce if necessary.

$\frac{22}{3} = 7\frac{1}{3}$ $\frac{19}{7} = 2\frac{5}{7}$ $\frac{15}{6} = 2\frac{3}{6} = 2\frac{1}{2}$

Change the mixed number to improper fractions.

$3\frac{1}{5} = \frac{16}{5}$ $2\frac{3}{8} = \frac{19}{8}$ $4\frac{1}{5} = \frac{21}{5}$

136 Math Level 5 – Lesson 16

Name________________ **Exercise 1** Day 81

New Concept!

What is a multiple? Do you know how to skip count by 2s, by 3s, by 4s, etc? The numbers you say when you count by 2s, for example, are all the multiples of 2. Therefore, when we write the multiples of 2, we write them this way: 2, 4, 6, 8, 10. . . A number has endless multiples, which is why we wrote . . .

Now you try it!

List the next five multiples of each number. Remember, you are skip counting! The first one is done for you.

7: 7, 14, 21, 28, 35, 42, . . .

5: 5, 10, 15, 20, 25, 30, . . .

4: 4, 8, 12, 16, 20, 24, . . .

8: 8, 16, 24, 32, 40, 48, . . .

10: 10, 20, 30, 40, 50, 60, . . .

12: 12, 24, 36, 48, 60, 72, . . .

6: 6, 12, 18, 24, 30, 36, . . .

Mixed Review:

Write the number one million:
1,000,000

Subtract six hundred from one thousand:
1000 − 600 = 400

Write an equivalent fraction for $\frac{7}{8}$:
$\frac{14}{16}, \frac{21}{24}, \frac{28}{32}$

Change $\frac{21}{5}$ into a mixed number:
$\frac{21}{5} = 4\frac{1}{5}$

Average these three numbers: 38, 67, 99
38 + 67 + 99 = 204 204 ÷ 3 = 68

Write 21 as a Roman Numeral:
XXI

Add.
Reduce as necessary.

$$14\frac{16}{17} + 1\frac{2}{17} = 15\frac{18}{17} = 16\frac{1}{17}$$

$$13\frac{15}{16} + 14\frac{3}{16} = 27\frac{18}{16} = 28\frac{2}{16} = 28\frac{1}{8}$$

Math Level 5 – Lesson 17 139

Name________________ **Exercise 2** Day 82

Building on the concept!
Copywork:

Common multiples are multiples shared by two or more numbers.

Copywork

The least common multiple (LCM) is the smallest multiple shared by two or more numbers. We use the LCM to find common denominators between two or more fractions.

Copywork

Now you try it!
Fill in the following chart. The first one is done for you.

Number	Multiples	Common Multiples	Least Common Multiple
6	6, 12, 18, 24, 30, 36, ...	12, 24, 36, ...	12
12	12, 24, 36, 48, 60, 72, ...		
5	5, 10, 15, ..., 35, (40) ...	40	40
8	8, 16, 24, 32, (40) 48, ...		
3	3, 6, 9, (12), 15, 18, 21, (24) ...	12, 24	12
4	4, 8, (12), 16, 20, (24) ...		

140 Math Level 5 – Lesson 17

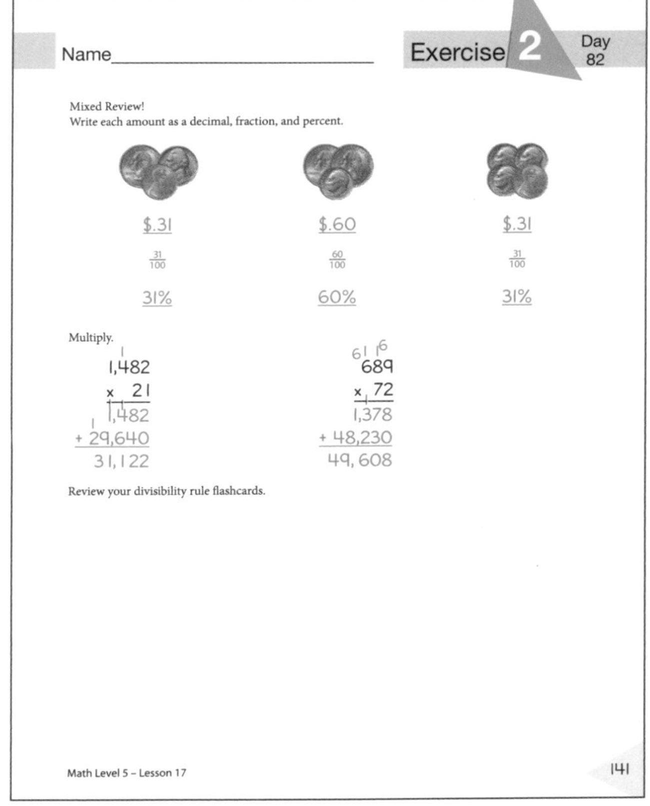

Name________________ **Exercise 2** Day 82

Mixed Review!
Write each amount as a decimal, fraction, and percent.

$.31 $.60 $.31

$\frac{31}{100}$ $\frac{60}{100}$ $\frac{31}{100}$

31% 60% 31%

Multiply.

1,482
x 21
1,482
+ 29,640
31,122

689
x 72
1,378
+ 48,230
49,608

Review your divisibility rule flashcards.

Math Level 5 – Lesson 17 141

Name____________________ **Exercise 3** Day 83

Hands ON!

Remove, trim the rough edge, and laminate your Least Common Multiple Chart in the back of this book. Using your chart find the least common multiple of these numbers.

4, 6	12	4 | 4, 8, (12) 16, ... 6 | 6, (12) 18, 24, ...
8, 12	24	8 | 8, 16, (24) 32, ... 12 | 12, (24) 36, 48, ...
5, 10	10	5 | 5, (10) 15, 20, ... 10 | (10) 20, 30, 40, ...
9, 12	36	9 | 9, 18, 27, (36) ... 12 | 12, 24, (36) 48, ...
2, 3, 4	12	2 | 2, 4, 6, 8, 10, (12) ... 3 | 3, 6, 9, (12) 15, 18, ... 4 | 4, 8, (12) 16, 20, ...

Mixed Review!

Solve and check these problems.

$32 \overline{)913}$ = 28 R. 17: -64, 273, -256, 17

Check: $28 \times 32 = 56 + 840 = 896$; $896 + 17 = 913$

$28 \overline{)892}$ = 31 R. 24: -84, 52, -28, 24

Check: $31 \times 28 = 248 + 620 = 868$; $868 + 24 = 892$

Story Problems:

1. Charlotte and Natty used a recipe that they needed to double. The recipe called for $1\frac{3}{4}$ cups of sugar. How many cups of sugar do the girls need when they double the recipe? Reduce if necessary.

   $1\frac{3}{4} + 1\frac{3}{4} = 2\frac{6}{4} = 3\frac{1}{2}$ cups of sugar

2. Mom gave the girls 2 packages that each contained $12\frac{1}{2}$ feet of blanket trim to use on their memory quilt. The quilt is 4 feet wide and 5 feet long. What is the perimeter of their quilt?

   4 + 4 + 5 + 5 = 18 feet

   How much blanket trim will they have left over?

   $12\frac{1}{2} + 12\frac{1}{2} = 24\frac{2}{2} = 25$ ft.

   $25 - 18 = 7$ feet left over

Name____________________ **Exercise 4** Day 84

Practicing the concept!

Circle the numbers that are multiples of the bolded numbers.

5: 2 (40) (10) (5) 12 62 (70) (15)

11: 14 (55) 108 (22) 10 (33) (132) 66

8: 36 (64) 66 (72) 46 54 (96) 84

9: 21 (18) (108) 96 (81) 71 (54) 67

Use your LCM chart to find the least common multiple of these numbers.

8, 10	40	8 | 8, 16, 24, 32, (40) ... 10 | 10, 20, 30, (40) 50, ...
3, 7	21	3 | 3, 6, 9, 12, 15, 18, (21) 24 ... 7 | 7, 14, (21) 28, 35, 42, ...
4, 11	44	4 | 4, 8, 12, 16, 20, 24, 28, 32, 36, 40, (44) ... 11 | 11, 22, 33, (44) 55, 66, 77, ...
6, 9	18	6 | 6, 12, (18) 24, ... 9 | 9, (18) 27, 36, ...
5, 8, 4	40	5 | 5, 10, 15, 20, 25, 30, 35, (40) 45, ... 8 | 8, 16, 24, 32, (40) 48, 56, 64, ... 4 | 4, 8, 12, 16, 20, 24, 28, 32, 36, (40) ...

Review Copywork!

In some mixed number addition problems, the answer is a whole number and an improper fraction. After we solve the problem, we "set aside" the whole number part of the answer. Next, we change the improper fraction part of the answer to a mixed number. Lastly, add the whole number to the mixed number.

Copywork

Name____________________ **Exercise 5** Day 85

Review Time!

Use your Least Common Multiple Chart to find the least common multiple of the following numbers. Narrate to your teacher what you are doing.

☐ 3, 12	12	3 | 3, 6, 9, (12) 15, 18, 21, 24 ... 12 | (12) 24, 36, 48, 60, ...
☐ 8, 16	16	8 | 8, (16) 24, 32, 40, ... 16 | (16) 32, 48, 64, ...
☐ 3, 5	15	3 | 3, 6, 9, 12, (15) 18, 21, 24 ... 5 | 5, 10, (15) 20, 25, 30, ...
☐ 7, 8	56	7 | 7, 14, 21, 28, 35, 42, 49, (56) 63, ... 8 | 8, 16, 24, 32, 40, 48, (56) 64, ...
☐ 9, 18	18	9 | 9, (18) 27, 36, ... 18 | (18) 36, 54, 72, ...
☐ 10, 50	50	10 | 10, 20, 30, 40, (50) ... 50 | (50) 100, 150, 200, ...
☐ 3, 6, 30	30	3 | 3, 6, 9, 12, 15, 18, 21, 24, 27, (30) ... 6 | 6, 12, 18, 24, (30) 36, 42, 48, ... 30 | (30) 60, 90, 120, 150, 180, ...

Add.
Reduce as necessary.

$22\frac{5}{8} + 3\frac{7}{8} = 25\frac{12}{8} = 26\frac{4}{8} = 26\frac{1}{2}$

$15\frac{4}{9} + 6\frac{7}{9} = 21\frac{11}{9} = 22\frac{2}{9}$

$17\frac{2}{3} + 8\frac{1}{3} = 25\frac{3}{3} = 26$

NOTE: Please make sure you have a measuring tape for a project in our next lesson.

Name____________________ **Exercise 1** Day 86

Now you try it! Fill in the chart!

Use your Least Common Denominator Chart which is on the other side of your Least Common Multiple Chart to find the least common denominators of these fractions.

Circle the Denominator	Multiples of Denominators (circle the common multiples)	Least Common Multiple	Least Common Denominator
$\frac{1}{5}$	5, (10) 15, (20) 25, (30) ...	10, 20, ...	10
$\frac{1}{10}$	(10) (20) (30) (40) (50) ...		
$\frac{1}{3}$	3, (6) 9, (12) 15, (18) ...	6, 12, 18, ...	6
$\frac{1}{6}$	(6) (12) (18) (24) (30) (36) ...		
$\frac{1}{2}$	2, 4, 6, 8, 10, (12) ...	12, 24, ...	12
$\frac{3}{12}$	(12) (24) (36) (48) (60) ...		
$\frac{1}{4}$	4, 8, 12, 16, (20) 24, ...	20, 40, ...	20
$\frac{1}{5}$	5, 10, 15, (20) 25, 30, ...		
$\frac{1}{2}$	2, 4, (6) 8, 10, (12) ...	6, 12, 18, ...	6
$\frac{2}{3}$	3, (6) 9, (12) 15, (18) ...		
$\frac{6}{7}$	7, 14, 21, ..., 49, (56) ...	56, ...	56
$\frac{7}{8}$	8, 16, ..., 48, (56) ...		

Solutions Manual: Lesson 18

Name____________________ **Exercise 2** Day 87

Let's Review!

Write the missing numbers to make equivalent fractions. Make sure to multiply both the numerator and the denominator by the same number. The first one is done for you.

$\frac{2 \times 3}{3 \times 3} = \frac{6}{9}$ $\frac{5}{7} = \frac{15}{21}$ $\frac{4}{5} = \frac{16}{20}$

$\frac{3}{4} = \frac{12}{16}$ $\frac{4}{9} = \frac{8}{18}$ $\frac{6}{7} = \frac{18}{21}$

Let's Practice the concept!

Use your Least Common Denominator Chart to find the least common denominators of these fractions. Narrate to your teacher what you are doing.

$\frac{3}{8}, \frac{1}{2}$ 8

$\frac{4}{11}, \frac{5}{22}$ 22

$\frac{3}{7}, \frac{3}{14}, \frac{1}{2}$ 14

$\frac{1}{3}, \frac{2}{9}, \frac{5}{18}$ 18

$\frac{3}{10}, \frac{7}{20}$ 20

Solve this word problem.

When mom and the girls made the cranberry Christmas punch, they did not want to add as much sugar as the recipe called for. They decided to use $\frac{1}{4}$ cup per recipe instead of $\frac{1}{3}$ cup.

If they made the recipe 10 times, how many cups of sugar did they use?

$\frac{1}{4} + \frac{1}{4} + \frac{1}{4} + \frac{1}{4} + \frac{1}{4} + \frac{1}{4} + \frac{1}{4} + \frac{1}{4} + \frac{1}{4} + \frac{1}{4} = \frac{10}{4} = 2\frac{2}{4} = 2\frac{1}{2}$

What is the least common denominator of $\frac{1}{4}$ and $\frac{1}{3}$ cup?

$\frac{1}{3}$	3, 4, 9, (12), 15, 18, ...
$\frac{1}{4}$	4, 8, (12), 16, 20, 24, ...

12

Name____________________ **Exercise 2** Day 87

Solve:

x	1	2	3	4	5	6	7	8	9	10	11	12
0	0	0	0	0	0	0	0	0	0	0	0	0
1	1	2	3	4	5	6	7	8	9	10	11	12
2	2	4	6	8	10	12	14	16	18	20	22	24
3	3	6	9	12	15	18	21	24	27	30	33	36
4	4	8	12	16	20	24	28	32	36	40	44	48
5	5	10	15	20	25	30	35	40	45	50	55	60
6	6	12	18	24	30	36	42	48	54	60	66	72
7	7	14	21	28	35	42	49	56	63	70	77	84
8	8	16	24	32	40	48	56	64	72	80	88	96
9	9	18	27	36	45	54	63	72	81	90	99	108
10	10	20	30	40	50	60	70	80	90	100	110	120
11	11	22	33	44	55	66	77	88	99	110	121	132
12	12	24	36	48	60	72	84	96	108	120	132	144

Name____________________ **Exercise 3** Day 88

More Practice!

Use your Least Common Denominator Chart to find the least common denominators of these fractions.

$\frac{2}{10}, \frac{7}{20}$ 20
- 10 | 10, (20), 30, 40, 50, ...
- 20 | (20), 40, 50, 60, ...

$\frac{4}{5}, \frac{3}{7}$ 35
- 5 | 5, 10, 15, 20, 25, 30, (35) ...
- 7 | 7, 14, 21, 28, (35), 42, 49, ...

$\frac{3}{5}, \frac{4}{5}, \frac{5}{6}$ 30
- 5 | 5, 10, 15, 20, 25, (30), 35, ...
- 6 | 6, 12, 18, 24, (30), 36, 42, ...

$\frac{5}{12}, \frac{13}{108}$ 108
- 12 | 12, 24, 36, 48, 60, 72, 84, 96, (108) ...
- 108 | (108), 216, 324, 432, ...

$\frac{2}{11}, \frac{21}{121}$ 121
- 11 | 11, 22,33 44, 55, ... (121,) ...
- 121 | (121,) 242, 363, 484, ...

Remember!

Use your Least Common Multiple Chart to find the least common multiple of the following numbers.

☐ 5, 11 55
- 5 | 5, 10, 15, 20, 25, 30, 35, 40, 45, 50, (55) ...
- 11 | 11, 22, 33, 44, (55), 66, 77, 88, 99, ...

☐ 2, 7 14
- 2 | 2, 4, 6, 8, 10, 12, (14) 16, ...
- 7 | 7, (14) 21, 28, 35, 42, 49, ...

☐ 6, 8 24
- 6 | 6, 12, 18, (24) 30, 36, 42, ...
- 8 | 8, 16, (24) 32, 40, 48, 56, ...

☐ 9, 12 36
- 9 | 9, 18, 27, (36) 45, 54, 63, 72, 81, ...
- 12 | 12, 24, (36) 48, 60, 72, 84, 96, 108, ...

☐ 3, 10 30
- 3 | 3, 6, 9, 12, 15, 18, 21, 24, 27, (30) ...
- 10 | 10, 20, (30) 40, 50, 60, 70, 80, ...

☐ 4, 10 20
- 4 | 4, 8, 12, 16, (20) 24, ...
- 10 | 10, (20) 30, 40, 50, ...

☐ 4, 6, 9 36
- 4 | 4, 8, 12, 16, 20, 24, 28, 32, (36) ...
- 6 | 6, 12, 18, 24, 30, (36) 42, 48, ...
- 9 | 9, 18, 27, (36) 45, 54, 63, 72, 81, ...

Mixed Review!

Solve.

$$\begin{array}{r} 619 \\ 226 \\ +\ 214 \\ \hline 1{,}059 \end{array} \qquad \begin{array}{r} 365 \\ \times\ 32 \\ \hline 730 \\ +\ 10{,}950 \\ \hline 11{,}680 \end{array} \qquad \begin{array}{r} 22 \\ \times\ 69 \\ \hline 198 \\ +\ 1{,}320 \\ \hline 1{,}518 \end{array} \qquad \begin{array}{r} 3{,}000 \\ +\ 1{,}846 \\ \hline 4{,}846 \end{array}$$

Name____________________ **Exercise 4** Day 89

Let's work with fractions!

Solve these story problems. Cross out any information that is not necessary. Use a green pencil or crayon to circle any clue words.

1. Mom and the girls gathered up the leftover desserts ~~after the Christmas outreach dinner to take to the nursing home the next day. They planned to serve tea with dessert for an elderly ladies' Christmas tea.~~ They gathered $2\frac{3}{4}$ pans of brownies, $1\frac{1}{4}$ pans of butterscotch bars, (and) $3\frac{1}{4}$ pans of peppermint cocoa bars. How many pans of dessert were (left over?)

   $2\frac{3}{4} + 1\frac{1}{4} + 3\frac{1}{4} = 6\frac{5}{4}$ $6 + 1\frac{1}{4} = 7\frac{1}{4}$ pans of bars

2. The girls used $\frac{2}{3}$ spool of white thread to hem stitch their quilt's edges (and) $1\frac{2}{3}$ spool of medium blue to sew quilting designs on the squares. ~~Charlotte liked the dark blue better, but there wasn't enough of it to complete the job~~. How many spools did they use (altogether?)

   $1\frac{2}{3} + \frac{2}{3} = 1\frac{4}{3}$ $1 + 1\frac{1}{3} = 2\frac{1}{3}$ spools

Review of Decimals, Fractions, and Percents Copywork:

In decimal place value, the place to the right of the decimal is the tenths place.

Copywork

The second place to the right of a decimal is the hundredths place.

Copywork

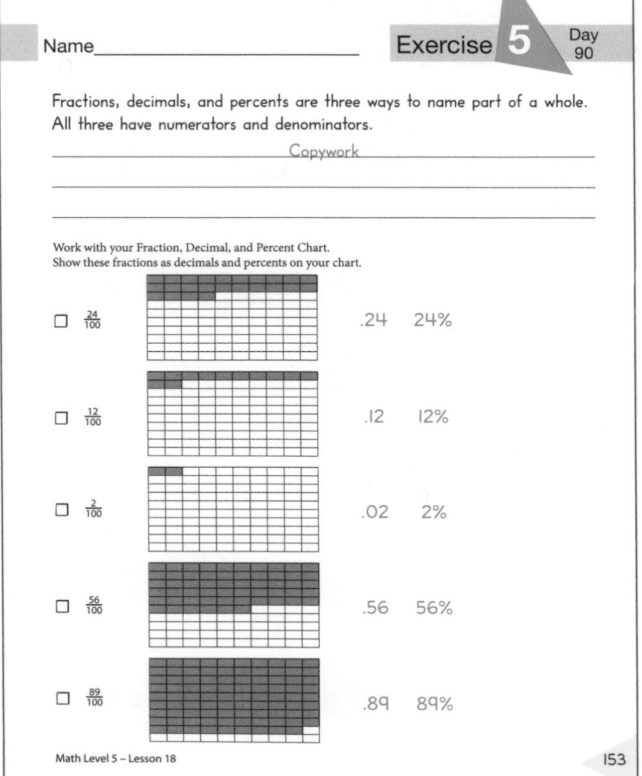

Name________________________ **Exercise 5** Day 90

Fractions, decimals, and percents are three ways to name part of a whole. All three have numerators and denominators.

Copywork

Work with your Fraction, Decimal, and Percent Chart.
Show these fractions as decimals and percents on your chart.

- ☐ $\frac{24}{100}$ .24 24%
- ☐ $\frac{12}{100}$ .12 12%
- ☐ $\frac{2}{100}$ .02 2%
- ☐ $\frac{56}{100}$ .56 56%
- ☐ $\frac{89}{100}$ .89 89%

Math Level 5 – Lesson 18 153

Name________________________ **Exercise 5** Day 90

Review Time! Narration Quiz

Use your Least Common Denominator Chart to find the least common denominators of these fractions. Narrate to your teacher what you are doing. Narrate to your teacher the difference between the greatest common factor (GCF) and the least common multiple (LCM).

Circle the Denominator	Multiples of Denominators (circle the common multiples)	Least Common Multiple	Least Common Denominator
$\frac{2}{3}$	3, 6, 9, 12, (15) 18, ...	15, 30, ...	15
$\frac{4}{5}$	5, 10, (15) 20, 25, 30, ...		
$\frac{1}{2}$	2, 4, 6, 8, 10, (12) ...	12, 24, ...	12
$\frac{1}{3}$	3, 6, 9, (12) 15, 18, ...		
$\frac{1}{4}$	4, 8, (12) 16, 20, 24, ...		
$\frac{3}{5}$	5, 10, 15, 20, 25, (30), ...	30, 60, ...	30
$\frac{1}{10}$	10, 20, (30), 40, 50, ...		
$\frac{2}{15}$	15, (30), 45, 60, 75 ...		
$\frac{3}{4}$	4, 8, 12, 16, (20), 24, ...	20, 40, ...	20
$\frac{7}{20}$	(20), 40, 60, 80 ...		

Hands ON!

One of Ella's favorite Christmas gifts was the book, *The Giraffe that Walked to Paris* by Nancy Milton. (If you are able to locate a copy of this book*, I highly recommend reading it!) This is the true story of a giraffe that was a gift from the ruler of Egypt to the king of France. The giraffe in the story was 11 feet tall; she was short for a giraffe. Do some research and find out the average height of a giraffe. Now use a measuring tape to measure that length on the floor or outside. Write it here: Answers will vary feet. Now measure yourself and compare it to the average giraffe. How much taller is a giraffe? Answers will vary feet taller.

*Zarafa, the Giraffe who Walked to the King is an alternative book about the same giraffe and is a bit easier to find.

154 Math Level 5 – Lesson 19

Name________________________ **Exercise 1** Day 91

☐ Review your divisibility rule flash cards.

☐ Copy the following concepts, each on a new index card.

Thinking TOOL #1 Factors are all of the different numbers that divide evenly (without a remainder) into a number. Pairs of factors are two numbers that, when multiplied together, equal this number.

Thinking TOOL #2 The Greatest Common Factor (GCF) is the largest common factor any group of numbers have.

☐ Narrate!

Optional review.

$5 \times 100 = 500$ $6 \times 60 = 360$

$100 \times 100 = 10{,}000$ $55 \times 1{,}000 = 55{,}000$

$5\frac{2}{3} = \frac{17}{3}$ $6\frac{7}{8} = \frac{55}{8}$ $6\frac{2}{3} = \frac{20}{3}$

$\frac{15}{2} = 7\frac{1}{2}$ $\frac{17}{2} = 8\frac{1}{2}$ $\frac{33}{5} = 6\frac{3}{5}$

```
      2 0 0 1 0 R. 23
3 0 ) 6 0 0,3 2 3
      6 0
        0 0 3 2
            3 0
              2 3
```

```
   33
  555
x  60
33,300
```

156 Math Level 5 – Lesson 19

Name________________________ **Exercise 2** Day 92

☐ Use your Reduce that Fraction! Chart to reduce these fractions:

$\frac{3}{12} = \frac{1}{4}$ $\frac{4}{16} = \frac{1}{4}$ $\frac{6}{24} = \frac{1}{4}$ $\frac{9}{45} = \frac{1}{5}$ $\frac{4}{18} = \frac{2}{9}$

☐ Copy the following concepts, each on a new index card.

Thinking TOOL #3 An improper fraction is a fraction which has a larger numerator than denominator.

Thinking TOOL #4 To change an improper fraction into a mixed number, divide the numerator by the denominator and write the remainder as a fraction. An easy way to turn a mixed number into an improper fraction is to multiply the whole number by the denominator and then add the numerator.

☐ Narrate!

Optional review.

Write an equivalent fraction for each.

$\frac{7}{8} = \frac{14}{16}, \frac{21}{24},\ldots$ $\frac{5}{9} = \frac{10}{18}, \frac{15}{27},\ldots$ $\frac{1}{2} = \frac{2}{4}, \frac{4}{8},\ldots$ $\frac{3}{4} = \frac{6}{8}, \frac{9}{12},\ldots$

Change the improper fractions into mixed numbers.

$\frac{109}{12} = 9\frac{1}{12}$ $\frac{200}{4} = 50$ $\frac{39}{8} = 4\frac{7}{8}$

Change the mixed numbers into improper fractions.

$7\frac{2}{3} = \frac{23}{3}$ $8\frac{7}{9} = \frac{79}{9}$ $14\frac{2}{3} = \frac{44}{3}$

Math Level 5 – Lesson 19 157

Name________________ **Exercise 3** Day 93

☐ Use your **Greatest Common Factor Chart** to find the Greatest Common Factor for these groups of numbers:

Number	Pairs of Factors	Factors	Common Factors	Greatest Common Factors
9	1 x 9 3 x 3	①③⑨		
36	1 x 36 2 x 18 3 x 12 4 x 9 6 x 6 4 x 3	① 2,③ 4, 6,⑨ 12, 18, 36	1, 3, 9	9
4	1 x 4 2 x 2	①② 4		
18	1 x 18 2 x 9 3 x 6	①② 3, 6, 9, 18	1, 2	2
15	1 x 15 3 x 5	①③ 5, 15		
18	1 x 18 2 x 9 3 x 6	① 2,③ 6, 9, 18	1, 3	3
16	1 x 16 2 x 8 4 x 4	①②④⑧ 16		
24	1 x 24 2 x 12 3 x 8 4 x 6	①② 3,④ 6,⑧ 12, 24	1, 2, 4, 8	8

☐ Copy this concept on a new index card.

Thinking TOOL #5 In some mixed number addition problems, the answer is a whole number and an improper fraction. We cannot leave the answer this way! After we solve the problem, we "set aside" the whole number part of the answer. Next, we change the improper fraction part of the answer to a mixed number. Lastly, add the whole number to the mixed number.

Optional Review. Reduce if necessary.

$7\frac{7}{8} + 8\frac{3}{8} = 15\frac{10}{8}$; $15 + 1\frac{2}{8} = 16\frac{1}{4}$

$14\frac{2}{3} + 2\frac{2}{3} = 16\frac{4}{3}$; $16 + 1\frac{1}{3} = 17\frac{1}{3}$

$7\frac{6}{7} + 2\frac{2}{7} = 9\frac{8}{7}$; $9 + 1\frac{1}{7} = 10\frac{1}{7}$

$6\frac{2}{9} + 2\frac{8}{9} = 8\frac{10}{9}$; $8 + 1\frac{1}{9} = 9\frac{1}{9}$

158 Math Level 5 – Lesson 19

Name________________ **Exercise 4** Day 94

☐ Use your **Least Common Multiple Chart** to find the Least Common Multiple for these groups of numbers:

Number	Multiples	Least Common Multiple	Least Common Denominator
5	5, 10, 15, 20, 25, 30, ...	35, 70, ...	35
35	35, 70, 105, 140, ...		
6	6, 12, 18, 24, 30 ...	24, 36, ...	24
8	8, 16, 24, 32, 40, ...		
10	10, 20, 30, 40, 50, 60 ...	60, 120, ...	60
12	12, 24, 36, 48, 60, ...		
3	3, 6, 9, 12, 15, 18, ...	21, 42, ...	21
7	7, 14, 21, 28, 35, ...		

☐ Copy the following concepts, each on a new index card.

Thinking TOOL #6 Common multiples are multiples shared by two or more numbers.

Thinking TOOL #7 The least common multiple (LCM) is the smallest multiple shared by two or more numbers. We use the LCM to find common denominators between two or more fractions.

Optional Review.

Circle the multiples for the following.

8: 35 (16) 49 (24) (40)

12: (108) 133 148 (96) (36)

5: 78 (100) (35) 76 (40)

4: 14 (24) 78 (16) (32)

Math Level 5 – Lesson 19 159

Name________________ **Exercise 5** Day 95

☐ Copy the following concepts, each on a new index card.

Thinking TOOL #8 There are three ways to show division. All of the signs mean "divided by."

) ÷ —

Thinking TOOL #9 We can write the remainder of a division problem as a fraction. The remainder becomes the numerator, and the divisor becomes the denominator.

☐ Narrate!

Optional Review.

Divide, write remainder as a fraction.

$1,478 \div 5 = 295\frac{3}{5}$

```
     2 9 5 3/5
5 | 1,4 7 8
   -1 0
     4 7
    -4 5
       2 8
      -2 5
         3
```

Check.

```
  42
  295
x   5
1,475
+   3
1,478
```

Multiply.

```
   142
x   21
   142
+2,840
 2,982
```

Add.

```
  1,472
  6,342
+ 5,978
 13,792
```

Average.

```
   5
   4
   6
   3
   2
+ 10
  30
```

```
     5
6 | 3 0
   -3 0
      0
```

160 Math Level 5 – Lesson 19

Name________________ **Exercise 1** Day 96

New Concept for Copywork!

When we add or subtract fractions, they must have a common denominator.

Copywork

Let's Practice!

1. I need to find the Least Common Denominator of 2 and 10, which is 10. (If you need help, use your LCD Chart)
2. So I know I need to make equivalent fractions with 10 as the denominator.
3. Add (or subtract) the fractions with the common denominators.
4. Reduce if necessary. Turn any improper fractions into mixed numbers.

The first one is done for you.

$\frac{1}{2}\frac{\times 5}{\times 5} = \frac{5}{10}$; $+\ \frac{3}{10}\frac{\times 1}{\times 1} = \frac{3}{10}$; $\frac{8}{10} = \frac{4}{5}$

Finish this one.

$\frac{1}{3}\frac{\times 3}{\times 3} = \frac{3}{9}$; $+\ \frac{2}{9}\frac{\times 1}{\times 1} = \frac{2}{9}$; $\frac{5}{9}$

Solve. Reduce as necessary.

$\frac{1}{3}\frac{\times 4}{\times 4} = \frac{4}{12}$; $+\ \frac{3}{4}\frac{\times 3}{\times 3} = \frac{9}{12}$; $\frac{13}{12} = 1\frac{1}{12}$

$\frac{2}{5}\frac{\times 2}{\times 2} = \frac{4}{10}$; $+\ \frac{3}{10}\frac{\times 1}{\times 1} = \frac{3}{10}$; $\frac{7}{10}$

$\frac{4}{15}\frac{\times 1}{\times 1} = \frac{4}{15}$; $+\ \frac{2}{5}\frac{\times 3}{\times 3} = \frac{6}{15}$; $\frac{10}{15} = \frac{2}{3}$

$\frac{1}{9}\frac{\times 4}{\times 4} = \frac{4}{36}$; $+\ \frac{3}{4}\frac{\times 9}{\times 9} = \frac{27}{36}$; $\frac{31}{36}$

Math Level 5 – Lesson 20 163

Name________________________ **Exercise 2** Day 97

More practice with the new concept! Reduce if necessary. Change any improper fractions into mixed numbers.

$\frac{1}{4}\times\frac{2}{2}=\frac{2}{8}$, $+\ \frac{3}{8}\times\frac{1}{1}=\frac{3}{8}$, $\frac{5}{8}$

$\frac{3}{7}\times\frac{2}{2}=\frac{6}{14}$, $+\ \frac{2}{14}\times\frac{1}{1}=\frac{2}{14}$, $\frac{8}{14}=\frac{4}{7}$

$\frac{6}{18}\times\frac{1}{1}=\frac{6}{18}$, $+\ \frac{1}{6}\times\frac{3}{3}=\frac{3}{18}$, $\frac{9}{18}=\frac{1}{2}$

$\frac{3}{4}\times\frac{5}{5}=\frac{15}{20}$, $+\ \frac{3}{10}\times\frac{2}{2}=\frac{6}{20}$, $\frac{21}{20}=1\frac{1}{20}$

Mixed Review!

Reduce these fractions. Use your Reduce that Fraction! Chart if you need help.

$\frac{5}{30}=\frac{1}{6}$ $\frac{3}{33}=\frac{1}{11}$ $\frac{2}{22}=\frac{1}{11}$ $\frac{6}{18}=\frac{1}{3}$

Write the least common denominator of these fractions.

$\frac{3}{8},\frac{1}{2}$ 8 $\frac{3}{11},\frac{1}{22}$ 22 $\frac{1}{2},\frac{1}{10}$ 10

Work quickly.

Solve.

x	1	2	3	4	5	6	7	8	9	10	11	12
7	7	14	21	28	35	42	49	56	63	70	77	84
8	8	16	24	32	40	48	56	64	72	80	88	96
9	9	18	27	36	45	54	63	72	81	90	99	108
10	10	20	30	40	50	60	70	80	90	100	110	120
11	11	22	33	44	55	66	77	88	99	110	121	132
12	12	24	36	48	60	72	84	96	108	120	132	144

164 Math Level 5 – Lesson 20

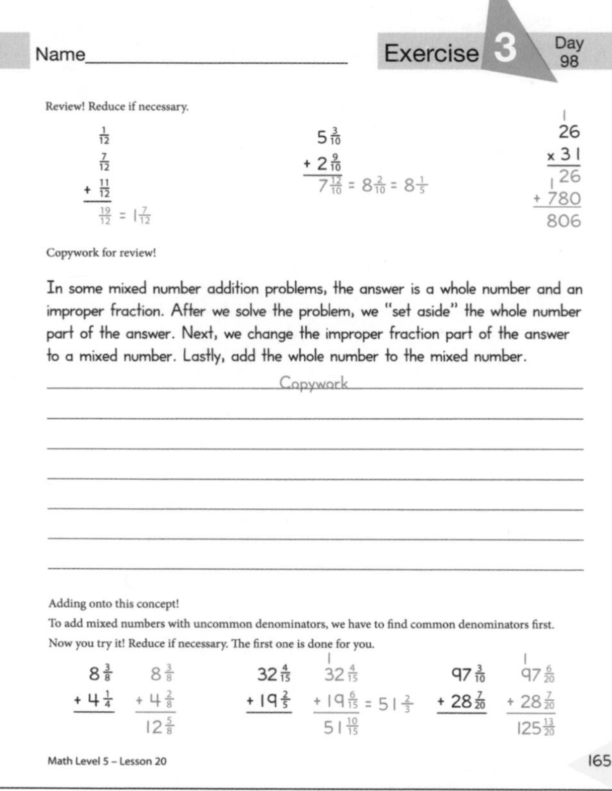
Name________________________ **Exercise 3** Day 98

Review! Reduce if necessary.

$\frac{1}{12} + \frac{7}{12} + \frac{11}{12} = \frac{19}{12} = 1\frac{7}{12}$

$5\frac{3}{10} + 2\frac{9}{10} = 7\frac{12}{10} = 8\frac{2}{10} = 8\frac{1}{5}$

26×31: 26 + 780 = 806

Copywork for review!

In some mixed number addition problems, the answer is a whole number and an improper fraction. After we solve the problem, we "set aside" the whole number part of the answer. Next, we change the improper fraction part of the answer to a mixed number. Lastly, add the whole number to the mixed number.

Copywork

Adding onto this concept!

To add mixed numbers with uncommon denominators, we have to find common denominators first.

Now you try it! Reduce if necessary. The first one is done for you.

$8\frac{3}{8} + 4\frac{1}{4}$ → $8\frac{3}{8} + 4\frac{2}{8} = 12\frac{5}{8}$

$32\frac{4}{15} + 19\frac{2}{5}$ → $32\frac{4}{15} + 19\frac{6}{15} = 51\frac{10}{15} = 51\frac{2}{3}$

$97\frac{3}{10} + 28\frac{7}{20}$ → $97\frac{6}{20} + 28\frac{7}{20} = 125\frac{13}{20}$

Math Level 5 – Lesson 20 165

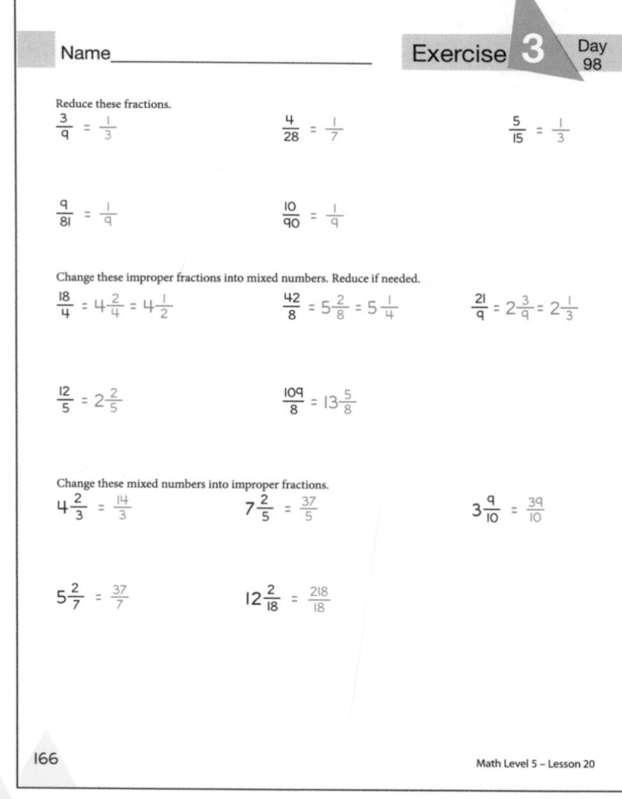
Name________________________ **Exercise 3** Day 98

Reduce these fractions.

$\frac{3}{9}=\frac{1}{3}$ $\frac{4}{28}=\frac{1}{7}$ $\frac{5}{15}=\frac{1}{3}$

$\frac{9}{81}=\frac{1}{9}$ $\frac{10}{90}=\frac{1}{9}$

Change these improper fractions into mixed numbers. Reduce if needed.

$\frac{18}{4}=4\frac{2}{4}=4\frac{1}{2}$ $\frac{42}{8}=5\frac{2}{8}=5\frac{1}{4}$ $\frac{21}{9}=2\frac{3}{9}=2\frac{1}{3}$

$\frac{12}{5}=2\frac{2}{5}$ $\frac{109}{8}=13\frac{5}{8}$

Change these mixed numbers into improper fractions.

$4\frac{2}{3}=\frac{14}{3}$ $7\frac{2}{5}=\frac{37}{5}$ $3\frac{9}{10}=\frac{39}{10}$

$5\frac{2}{7}=\frac{37}{7}$ $12\frac{2}{18}=\frac{218}{18}$

166 Math Level 5 – Lesson 20

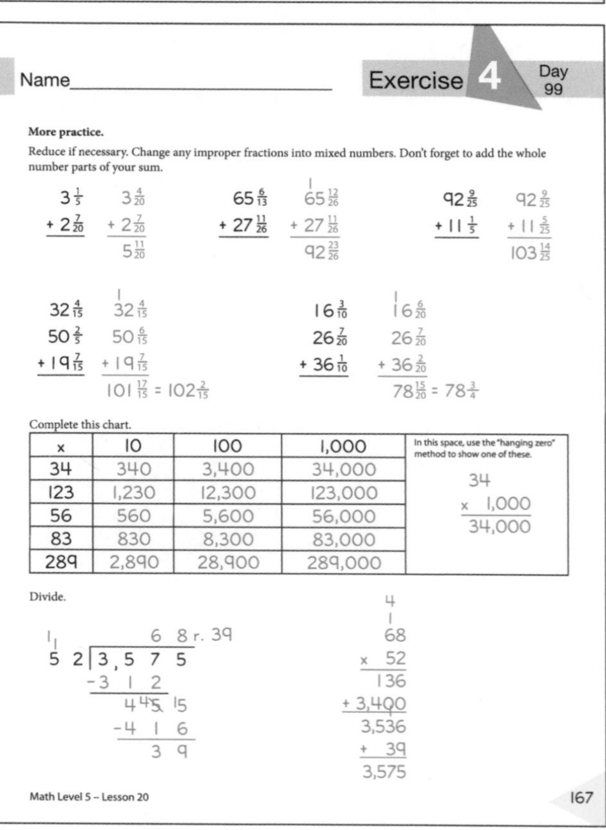
Name________________________ **Exercise 4** Day 99

More practice.

Reduce if necessary. Change any improper fractions into mixed numbers. Don't forget to add the whole number parts of your sum.

$3\frac{1}{5} + 2\frac{7}{20}$ → $3\frac{4}{20} + 2\frac{7}{20} = 5\frac{11}{20}$

$65\frac{6}{13} + 27\frac{11}{26}$ → $65\frac{12}{26} + 27\frac{11}{26} = 92\frac{23}{26}$

$92\frac{9}{25} + 11\frac{1}{5}$ → $92\frac{9}{25} + 11\frac{5}{25} = 103\frac{14}{25}$

$32\frac{4}{15} + 50\frac{2}{5} + 19\frac{7}{15}$ → $32\frac{4}{15} + 50\frac{6}{15} + 19\frac{7}{15} = 101\frac{17}{15} = 102\frac{2}{15}$

$16\frac{3}{10} + 26\frac{7}{20} + 36\frac{1}{10}$ → $16\frac{6}{20} + 26\frac{7}{20} + 36\frac{2}{20} = 78\frac{15}{20} = 78\frac{3}{4}$

Complete this chart.

x	10	100	1,000
34	340	3,400	34,000
123	1,230	12,300	123,000
56	560	5,600	56,000
83	830	8,300	83,000
289	2,890	28,900	289,000

In this space, use the "hanging zero" method to show one of these.

34 x 1,000 = 34,000

Divide.

3,575 ÷ 52 = 68 r. 39 (−312, 455, −416, 39)

Check: 68 x 52 = 136 + 3,400 = 3,536; 3,536 + 39 = 3,575

Math Level 5 – Lesson 20 167

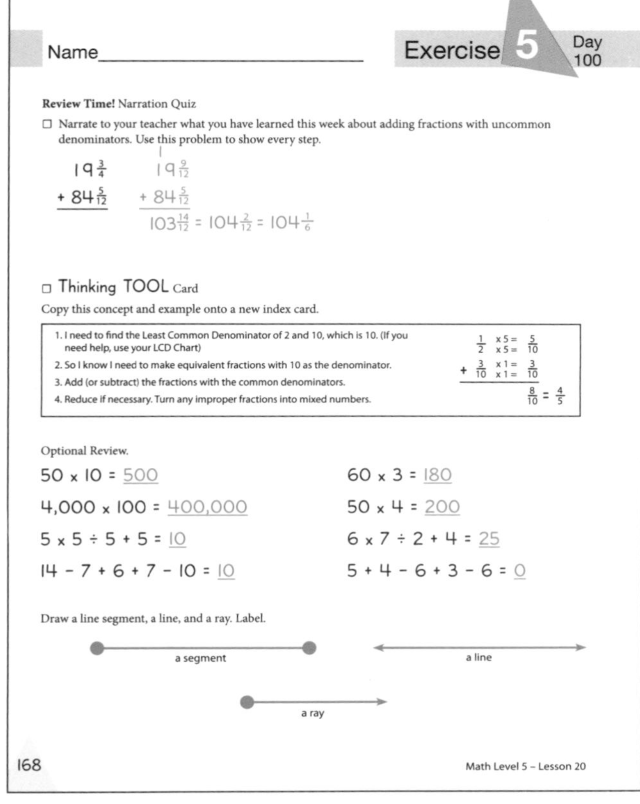

Name______________________ **Exercise 5** Day 100

Review Time! Narration Quiz

☐ Narrate to your teacher what you have learned this week about adding fractions with uncommon denominators. Use this problem to show every step.

$19\frac{3}{4} + 84\frac{5}{12}$

$19\frac{9}{12} + 84\frac{5}{12} = 103\frac{14}{12} = 104\frac{2}{12} = 104\frac{1}{6}$

☐ Thinking TOOL Card

Copy this concept and example onto a new index card.

1. I need to find the Least Common Denominator of 2 and 10, which is 10. (If you need help, use your LCD Chart)
2. So I know I need to make equivalent fractions with 10 as the denominator.
3. Add (or subtract) the fractions with the common denominators.
4. Reduce if necessary. Turn any improper fractions into mixed numbers.

$\frac{1}{2}\frac{\times 5}{\times 5} = \frac{5}{10}$, $+\ \frac{3}{10}\frac{\times 1}{\times 1} = \frac{3}{10}$, $\frac{8}{10} = \frac{4}{5}$

Optional Review.

50 x 10 = 500

4,000 x 100 = 400,000

5 x 5 ÷ 5 + 5 = 10

14 − 7 + 6 + 7 − 10 = 10

60 x 3 = 180

50 x 4 = 200

6 x 7 ÷ 2 + 4 = 25

5 + 4 − 6 + 3 − 6 = 0

Draw a line segment, a line, and a ray. Label.

a segment — a line — a ray

168 — Math Level 5 – Lesson 20

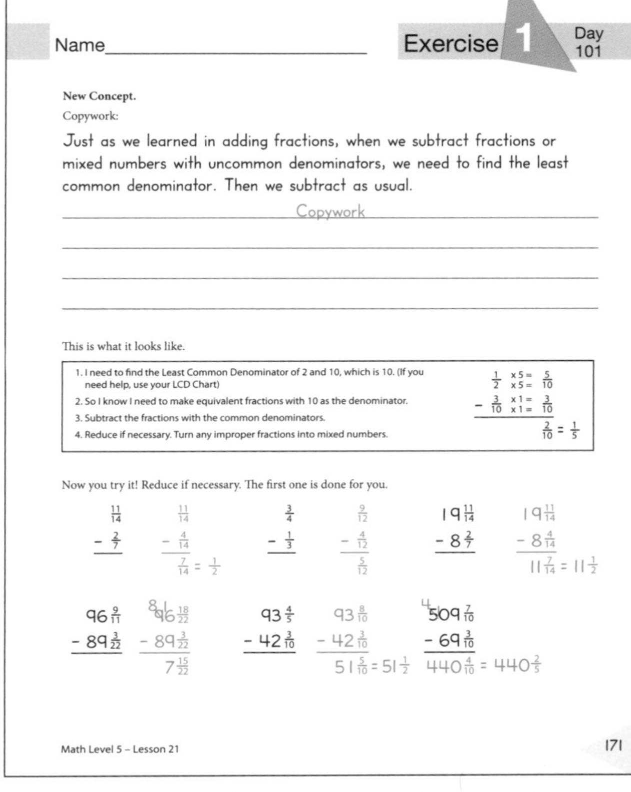

Name______________________ **Exercise 1** Day 101

New Concept.

Copywork:

Just as we learned in adding fractions, when we subtract fractions or mixed numbers with uncommon denominators, we need to find the least common denominator. Then we subtract as usual.

Copywork

This is what it looks like.

1. I need to find the Least Common Denominator of 2 and 10, which is 10. (If you need help, use your LCD Chart)
2. So I know I need to make equivalent fractions with 10 as the denominator.
3. Subtract the fractions with the common denominators.
4. Reduce if necessary. Turn any improper fractions into mixed numbers.

$\frac{1}{2}\frac{\times 5}{\times 5} = \frac{5}{10}$, $-\ \frac{3}{10}\frac{\times 1}{\times 1} = \frac{3}{10}$, $\frac{2}{10} = \frac{1}{5}$

Now you try it! Reduce if necessary. The first one is done for you.

$\frac{11}{14} - \frac{2}{7}$: $\frac{11}{14} - \frac{4}{14} = \frac{7}{14} = \frac{1}{2}$

$\frac{3}{4} - \frac{1}{3}$: $\frac{9}{12} - \frac{4}{12} = \frac{5}{12}$

$19\frac{11}{14} - 8\frac{2}{7}$: $19\frac{11}{14} - 8\frac{4}{14} = 11\frac{7}{14} = 11\frac{1}{2}$

$96\frac{9}{11} - 89\frac{3}{22}$: $96\frac{18}{22} - 89\frac{3}{22} = 7\frac{15}{22}$

$93\frac{4}{5} - 42\frac{3}{10}$: $93\frac{8}{10} - 42\frac{3}{10} = 51\frac{5}{10} = 51\frac{1}{2}$

$509\frac{7}{10} - 69\frac{3}{10} = 440\frac{4}{10} = 440\frac{2}{5}$

Math Level 5 – Lesson 21 — 171

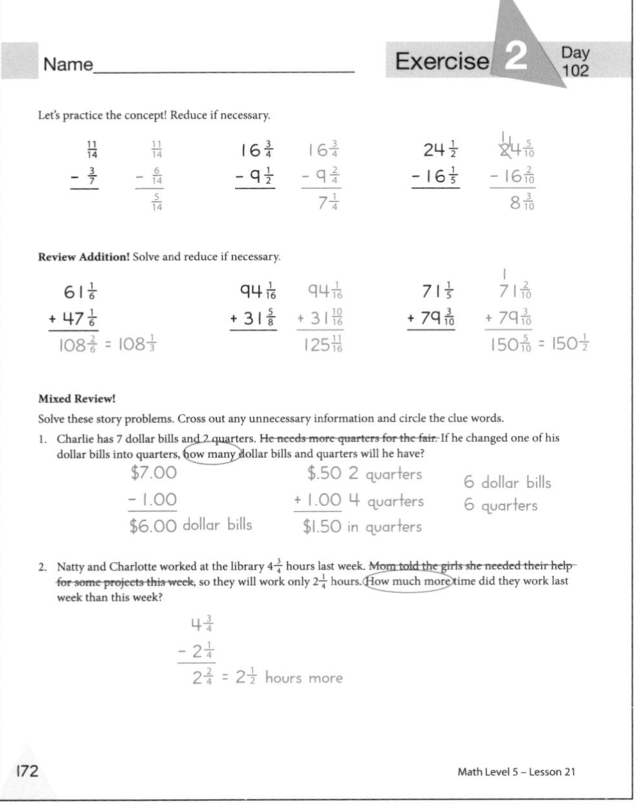

Name______________________ **Exercise 2** Day 102

Let's practice the concept! Reduce if necessary.

$\frac{11}{14} - \frac{3}{7}$: $\frac{11}{14} - \frac{6}{14} = \frac{5}{14}$

$16\frac{3}{4} - 9\frac{1}{2}$: $16\frac{3}{4} - 9\frac{2}{4} = 7\frac{1}{4}$

$24\frac{1}{2} - 16\frac{1}{5}$: $24\frac{5}{10} - 16\frac{2}{10} = 8\frac{3}{10}$

Review Addition! Solve and reduce if necessary.

$61\frac{1}{6} + 47\frac{1}{6} = 108\frac{2}{6} = 108\frac{1}{3}$

$94\frac{1}{16} + 31\frac{5}{8}$: $94\frac{1}{16} + 31\frac{10}{16} = 125\frac{11}{16}$

$71\frac{1}{5} + 79\frac{3}{10}$: $71\frac{2}{10} + 79\frac{3}{10} = 150\frac{5}{10} = 150\frac{1}{2}$

Mixed Review!

Solve these story problems. Cross out any unnecessary information and circle the clue words.

1. Charlie has 7 dollar bills and 2 quarters. ~~He needs more quarters for the fair.~~ If he changed one of his dollar bills into quarters, how many dollar bills and quarters will he have?

   \$7.00 − 1.00 = \$6.00 dollar bills
   \$.50 2 quarters + 1.00 4 quarters = \$1.50 in quarters
   6 dollar bills, 6 quarters

2. Natty and Charlotte worked at the library $4\frac{3}{4}$ hours last week. ~~Mom told the girls she needed their help for some projects this week,~~ so they will work only $2\frac{1}{4}$ hours. How much more time did they work last week than this week?

   $4\frac{3}{4} - 2\frac{1}{4} = 2\frac{2}{4} = 2\frac{1}{2}$ hours more

172 — Math Level 5 – Lesson 21

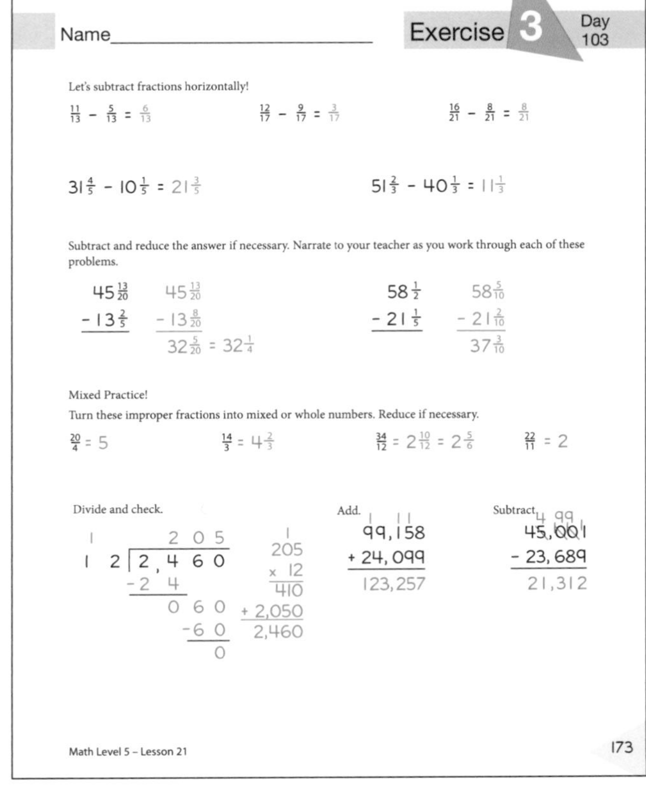

Name______________________ **Exercise 3** Day 103

Let's subtract fractions horizontally!

$\frac{11}{13} - \frac{5}{13} = \frac{6}{13}$ $\frac{12}{17} - \frac{9}{17} = \frac{3}{17}$ $\frac{16}{21} - \frac{8}{21} = \frac{8}{21}$

$31\frac{4}{5} - 10\frac{1}{5} = 21\frac{3}{5}$ $51\frac{2}{3} - 40\frac{1}{3} = 11\frac{1}{3}$

Subtract and reduce the answer if necessary. Narrate to your teacher as you work through each of these problems.

$45\frac{13}{20} - 13\frac{2}{5}$: $45\frac{13}{20} - 13\frac{8}{20} = 32\frac{5}{20} = 32\frac{1}{4}$

$58\frac{1}{2} - 21\frac{1}{5}$: $58\frac{5}{10} - 21\frac{2}{10} = 37\frac{3}{10}$

Mixed Practice!

Turn these improper fractions into mixed or whole numbers. Reduce if necessary.

$\frac{20}{4} = 5$ $\frac{14}{3} = 4\frac{2}{3}$ $\frac{34}{12} = 2\frac{10}{12} = 2\frac{5}{6}$ $\frac{22}{11} = 2$

Divide and check.

2,460 ÷ 12 = 205; check: 205 x 12 = 410 + 2,050 = 2,460

Add.

99,158 + 24,099 = 123,257

Subtract.

45,001 − 23,689 = 21,312

Math Level 5 – Lesson 21 — 173

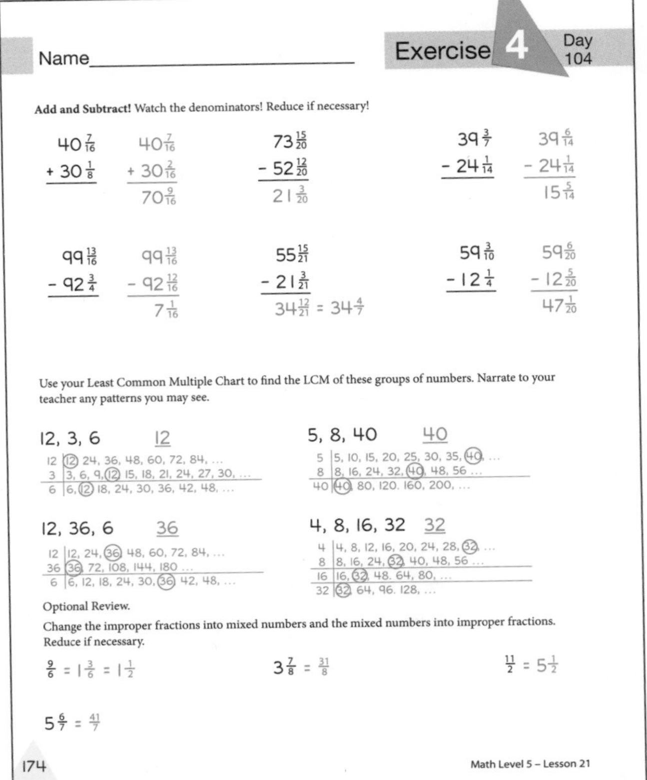

Name________________ Exercise 4 Day 104

Add and Subtract! Watch the denominators! Reduce if necessary!

$40\frac{7}{16} + 30\frac{1}{8}$ → $40\frac{7}{16} + 30\frac{2}{16} = 70\frac{9}{16}$

$73\frac{15}{20} - 52\frac{12}{20} = 21\frac{3}{20}$

$39\frac{3}{7} - 24\frac{1}{14}$ → $39\frac{6}{14} - 24\frac{1}{14} = 15\frac{5}{14}$

$99\frac{13}{16} - 92\frac{3}{4}$ → $99\frac{13}{16} - 92\frac{12}{16} = 7\frac{1}{16}$

$55\frac{15}{21} - 21\frac{3}{21} = 34\frac{12}{21} = 34\frac{4}{7}$

$59\frac{3}{10} - 12\frac{1}{4}$ → $59\frac{6}{20} - 12\frac{5}{20} = 47\frac{1}{20}$

Use your Least Common Multiple Chart to find the LCM of these groups of numbers. Narrate to your teacher any patterns you may see.

12, 3, 6 — 12

12 | (12) 24, 36, 48, 60, 72, 84, …
3 | 3, 6, 9, (12) 15, 18, 21, 24, 27, 30, …
6 | 6, (12) 18, 24, 30, 36, 42, 48, …

5, 8, 40 — 40

5 | 5, 10, 15, 20, 25, 30, 35, (40), …
8 | 8, 16, 24, 32, (40), 48, 56 …
40 | (40), 80, 120. 160, 200, …

12, 36, 6 — 36

12 | 12, 24, (36), 48, 60, 72, 84, …
36 | (36), 72, 108, 144, 180 …
6 | 6, 12, 18, 24, 30, (36), 42, 48, …

4, 8, 16, 32 — 32

4 | 4, 8, 12, 16, 20, 24, 28, (32), …
8 | 8, 16, 24, (32), 40, 48, 56 …
16 | 16, (32), 48. 64, 80, …
32 | (32), 64, 96. 128, …

Optional Review.

Change the improper fractions into mixed numbers and the mixed numbers into improper fractions. Reduce if necessary.

$\frac{9}{6} = 1\frac{3}{6} = 1\frac{1}{2}$ $3\frac{7}{8} = \frac{31}{8}$ $\frac{11}{2} = 5\frac{1}{2}$

$5\frac{6}{7} = \frac{41}{7}$

174 Math Level 5 – Lesson 21

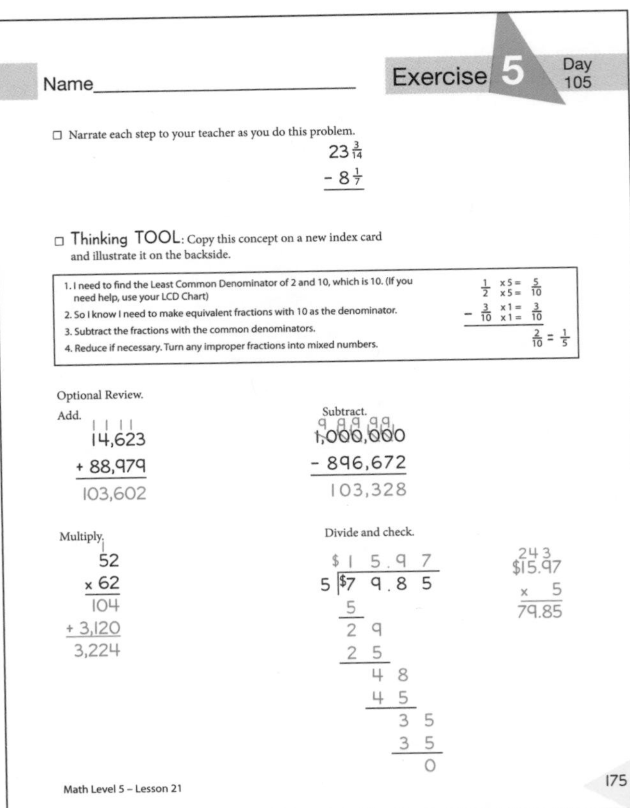

Name________________ Exercise 5 Day 105

☐ Narrate each step to your teacher as you do this problem.

$23\frac{3}{14} - 8\frac{1}{7}$

☐ Thinking TOOL: Copy this concept on a new index card and illustrate it on the backside.

1. I need to find the Least Common Denominator of 2 and 10, which is 10. (If you need help, use your LCD Chart)
2. So I know I need to make equivalent fractions with 10 as the denominator.
3. Subtract the fractions with the common denominators.
4. Reduce if necessary. Turn any improper fractions into mixed numbers.

$\frac{1}{2}\ \frac{\times 5}{\times 5} = \frac{5}{10}$
$-\frac{3}{10}\ \frac{\times 1}{\times 1} = \frac{3}{10}$
$\frac{2}{10} = \frac{1}{5}$

Optional Review.

Add.
14,623 + 88,979 = 103,602

Subtract.
1,000,000 − 896,672 = 103,328

Multiply.
52 × 62: 104 + 3,120 = 3,224

Divide and check.
$79.85 ÷ 5 = $15.97 (5, 29, 25, 48, 45, 35, 35, 0)
Check: $15.97 × 5 = 79.85

Math Level 5 – Lesson 21 175

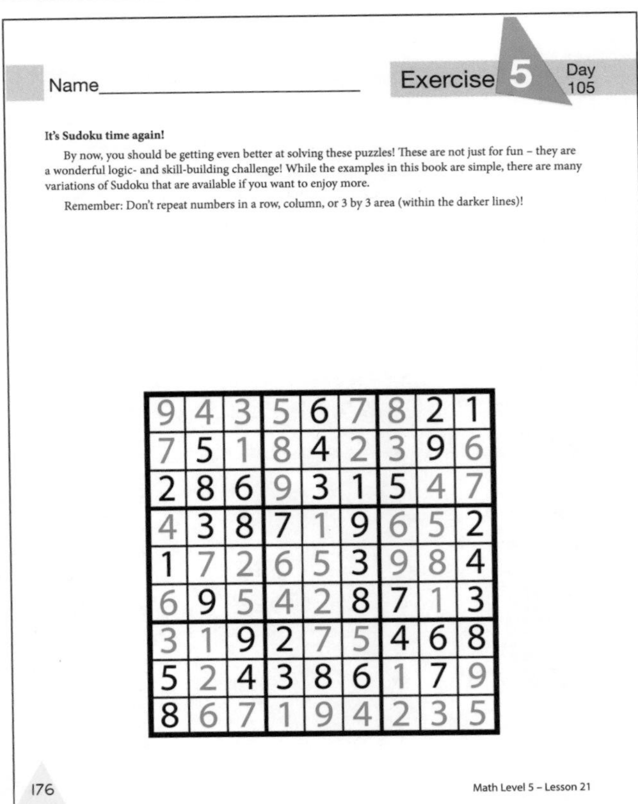

Name________________ Exercise 5 Day 105

It's Sudoku time again!

By now, you should be getting even better at solving these puzzles! These are not just for fun – they are a wonderful logic- and skill-building challenge! While the examples in this book are simple, there are many variations of Sudoku that are available if you want to enjoy more.

Remember: Don't repeat numbers in a row, column, or 3 by 3 area (within the darker lines)!

9	4	3	5	6	7	8	2	1
7	5	1	8	4	2	3	9	6
2	8	6	9	3	1	5	4	7
4	3	8	7	1	9	6	5	2
1	7	2	6	5	3	9	8	4
6	9	5	4	2	8	7	1	3
3	1	9	2	7	5	4	6	8
5	2	4	3	8	6	1	7	9
8	6	7	1	9	4	2	3	5

176 Math Level 5 – Lesson 21

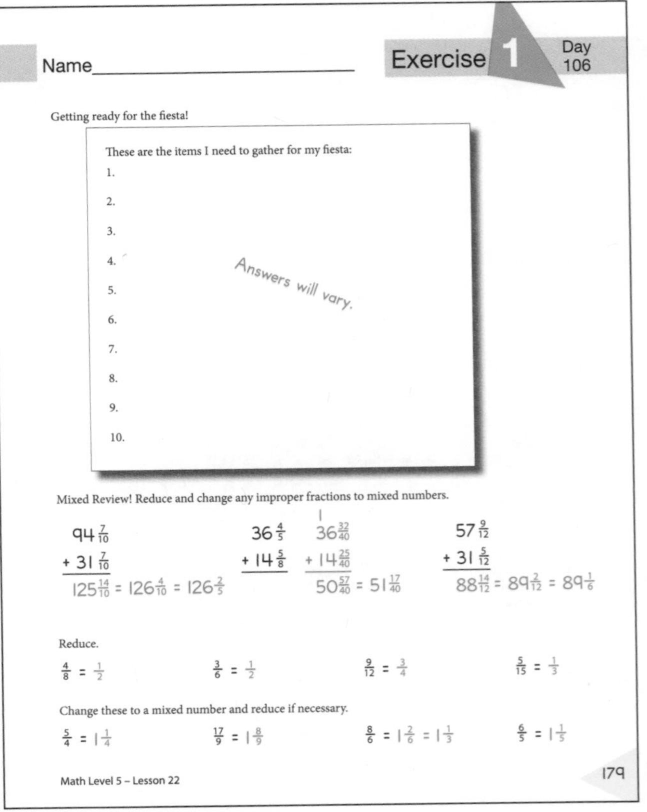

Name________________ Exercise 1 Day 106

Getting ready for the fiesta!

These are the items I need to gather for my fiesta:

1.
2.
3.
4.
5.
6.
7.
8.
9.
10.

Answers will vary.

Mixed Review! Reduce and change any improper fractions to mixed numbers.

$94\frac{7}{10} + 31\frac{7}{10} = 125\frac{14}{10} = 126\frac{4}{10} = 126\frac{2}{5}$

$36\frac{4}{5} + 14\frac{5}{8}$ → $36\frac{32}{40} + 14\frac{25}{40} = 50\frac{57}{40} = 51\frac{17}{40}$

$57\frac{9}{12} + 31\frac{5}{12} = 88\frac{14}{12} = 89\frac{2}{12} = 89\frac{1}{6}$

Reduce.

$\frac{4}{8} = \frac{1}{2}$ $\frac{3}{6} = \frac{1}{2}$ $\frac{9}{12} = \frac{3}{4}$ $\frac{5}{15} = \frac{1}{3}$

Change these to a mixed number and reduce if necessary.

$\frac{5}{4} = 1\frac{1}{4}$ $\frac{17}{9} = 1\frac{8}{9}$ $\frac{8}{6} = 1\frac{2}{6} = 1\frac{1}{3}$ $\frac{6}{5} = 1\frac{1}{5}$

Math Level 5 – Lesson 22 179

Solutions Manual: Lesson 22

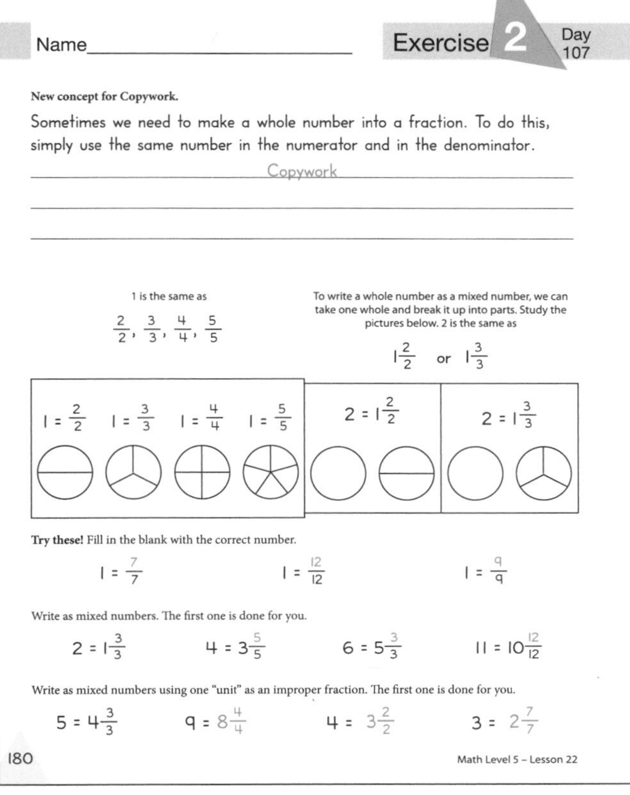

Name____________ **Exercise 2** Day 107

New concept for Copywork.

Sometimes we need to make a whole number into a fraction. To do this, simply use the same number in the numerator and in the denominator.

Copywork

1 is the same as $\frac{2}{2}, \frac{3}{3}, \frac{4}{4}, \frac{5}{5}$

To write a whole number as a mixed number, we can take one whole and break it up into parts. Study the pictures below. 2 is the same as $1\frac{2}{2}$ or $1\frac{3}{3}$

$1 = \frac{2}{2}$ $1 = \frac{3}{3}$ $1 = \frac{4}{4}$ $1 = \frac{5}{5}$ $2 = 1\frac{2}{2}$ $2 = 1\frac{3}{3}$

Try these! Fill in the blank with the correct number.

$1 = \frac{7}{7}$ $1 = \frac{12}{12}$ $1 = \frac{9}{9}$

Write as mixed numbers. The first one is done for you.

$2 = 1\frac{3}{3}$ $4 = 3\frac{5}{5}$ $6 = 5\frac{3}{3}$ $11 = 10\frac{12}{12}$

Write as mixed numbers using one "unit" as an improper fraction. The first one is done for you.

$5 = 4\frac{3}{3}$ $9 = 8\frac{4}{4}$ $4 = 3\frac{2}{2}$ $3 = 2\frac{7}{7}$

180 Math Level 5 – Lesson 22

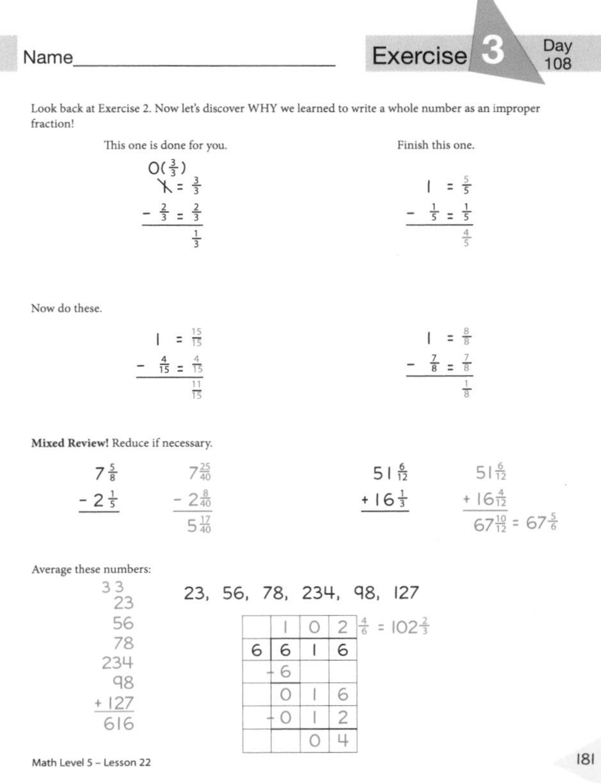

Name____________ **Exercise 3** Day 108

Look back at Exercise 2. Now let's discover WHY we learned to write a whole number as an improper fraction!

This one is done for you.

$0(\frac{3}{3})$ $1 = \frac{3}{3}$; $-\frac{2}{3} = \frac{2}{3}$; $\frac{1}{3}$

Finish this one.

$1 = \frac{5}{5}$; $-\frac{1}{5} = \frac{1}{5}$; $\frac{4}{5}$

Now do these.

$1 = \frac{15}{15}$; $-\frac{4}{15} = \frac{4}{15}$; $\frac{11}{15}$

$1 = \frac{8}{8}$; $-\frac{7}{8} = \frac{7}{8}$; $\frac{1}{8}$

Mixed Review! Reduce if necessary.

$7\frac{5}{8} - 2\frac{1}{5}$ → $7\frac{25}{40} - 2\frac{8}{40} = 5\frac{17}{40}$

$51\frac{6}{12} + 16\frac{1}{3}$ → $51\frac{6}{12} + 16\frac{4}{12} = 67\frac{10}{12} = 67\frac{5}{6}$

Average these numbers: 23, 56, 78, 234, 98, 127

23 + 56 + 78 + 234 + 98 + 127 = 616

$616 \div 6 = 102\frac{4}{6} = 102\frac{2}{3}$ (6) 616; −6; 01; 016; −012; 04)

Math Level 5 – Lesson 22 181

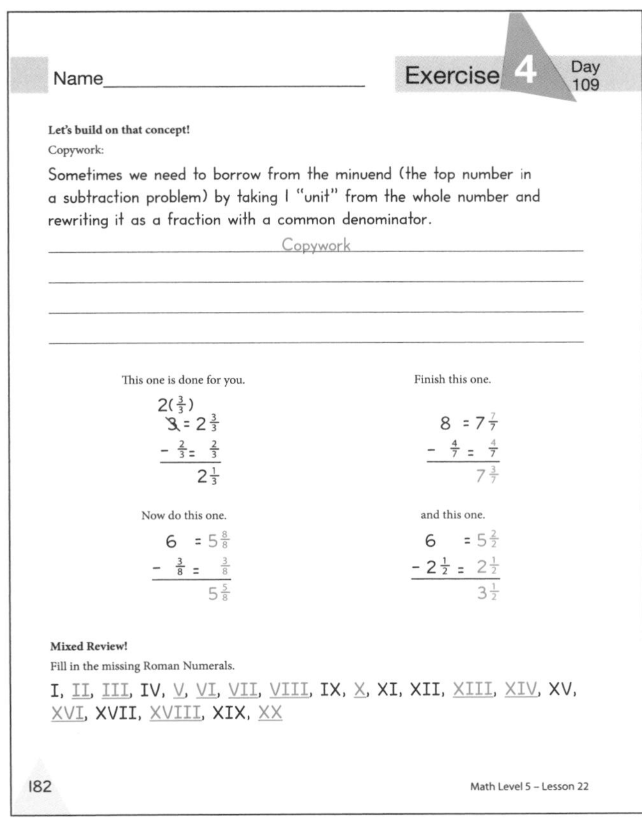

Name____________ **Exercise 4** Day 109

Let's build on that concept!

Copywork:

Sometimes we need to borrow from the minuend (the top number in a subtraction problem) by taking 1 "unit" from the whole number and rewriting it as a fraction with a common denominator.

Copywork

This one is done for you.

$2(\frac{3}{3})$ $3 = 2\frac{3}{3}$; $-\frac{2}{3} = \frac{2}{3}$; $2\frac{1}{3}$

Finish this one.

$8 = 7\frac{7}{7}$; $-\frac{4}{7} = \frac{4}{7}$; $7\frac{3}{7}$

Now do this one.

$6 = 5\frac{8}{8}$; $-\frac{3}{8} = \frac{3}{8}$; $5\frac{5}{8}$

and this one.

$6 = 5\frac{2}{2}$; $-2\frac{1}{2} = 2\frac{1}{2}$; $3\frac{1}{2}$

Mixed Review!

Fill in the missing Roman Numerals.

I, II, III, IV, V, VI, VII, VIII, IX, X, XI, XII, XIII, XIV, XV, XVI, XVII, XVIII, XIX, XX

182 Math Level 5 – Lesson 22

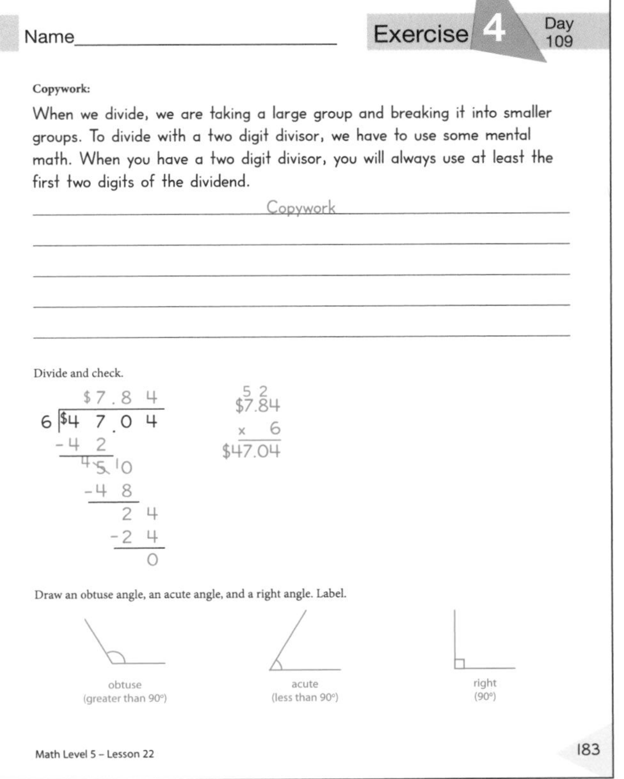

Name____________ **Exercise 4** Day 109

Copywork:

When we divide, we are taking a large group and breaking it into smaller groups. To divide with a two digit divisor, we have to use some mental math. When you have a two digit divisor, you will always use at least the first two digits of the dividend.

Copywork

Divide and check.

$\$47.04 \div 6 = \$7.84$ (−42; 50; −48; 24; −24; 0)

Check: $\$7.84 \times 6 = \$47.04$

Draw an obtuse angle, an acute angle, and a right angle. Label.

Math Level 5 – Lesson 22 183

Name________________ **Exercise 5** Day 110

Review Time!

$32\frac{9}{15} + 24\frac{7}{15} = 56\frac{16}{15} = 57\frac{1}{15}$

$4 = 3\frac{7}{7}$; $-\frac{3}{7} = \frac{3}{7}$; $3\frac{4}{7}$

$4 = 3\frac{6}{6}$; $-1\frac{1}{6} = 1\frac{1}{6}$; $2\frac{5}{6}$

$39\frac{7}{21} = 39\frac{7}{21}$; $+19\frac{1}{3} = 19\frac{7}{21}$; $58\frac{14}{21} = 58\frac{2}{3}$

Review. Reduce if necessary.

$15 = 14\frac{7}{7}$; $-2\frac{6}{7} = 2\frac{6}{7}$; $12\frac{1}{7}$

$22\frac{7}{8} = 22\frac{7}{8}$; $-15\frac{2}{4} = 15\frac{4}{8}$; $7\frac{3}{8}$

$32\frac{2}{3} + 78\frac{2}{3} = 110\frac{4}{3} = 111\frac{1}{3}$

Make equivalent fractions.

$\frac{1}{2} = \frac{2}{4}, \frac{3}{6}, \ldots$ $\frac{3}{4} = \frac{6}{8}, \frac{9}{12}, \ldots$ $\frac{2}{3} = \frac{4}{6}, \frac{6}{9}, \ldots$ $\frac{1}{4} = \frac{2}{8}, \frac{3}{12}, \ldots$

Convert.

2 years = 24 months 4,000 pounds = 2 tons

48 items = 4 dozen 60 inches = 5 feet

360 seconds = 6 minutes 27 feet = 9 yards

184 Math Level 5 – Lesson 22

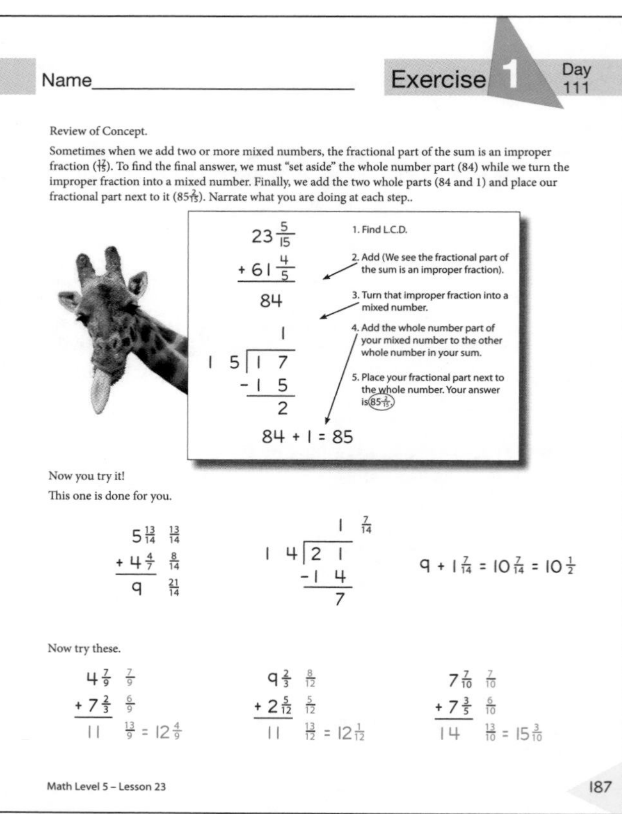

Name________________ **Exercise 1** Day 111

Review of Concept.

Sometimes when we add two or more mixed numbers, the fractional part of the sum is an improper fraction ($\frac{17}{15}$). To find the final answer, we must "set aside" the whole number part (84) while we turn the improper fraction into a mixed number. Finally, we add the two whole parts (84 and 1) and place our fractional part next to it ($85\frac{2}{15}$). Narrate what you are doing at each step..

$23\frac{5}{15} + 61\frac{4}{5} = 84 \frac{17}{15}$; $17 \div 15 = 1$ r 2; $84 + 1 = 85$

Now you try it!

This one is done for you.

$5\frac{13}{14} + 4\frac{4}{7}\left(\frac{8}{14}\right) = 9\frac{21}{14}$; $21 \div 14 = 1\frac{7}{14}$; $9 + 1\frac{7}{14} = 10\frac{7}{14} = 10\frac{1}{2}$

Now try these.

$4\frac{7}{9} + 7\frac{2}{3}\left(\frac{6}{9}\right) = 11\frac{13}{9} = 12\frac{4}{9}$

$9\frac{2}{3}\left(\frac{8}{12}\right) + 2\frac{5}{12} = 11\frac{13}{12} = 12\frac{1}{12}$

$7\frac{7}{10} + 7\frac{3}{5}\left(\frac{6}{10}\right) = 14\frac{13}{10} = 15\frac{3}{10}$

Math Level 5 – Lesson 23 187

Name________________ **Exercise 1** Day 111

Mixed Review!

1. The children were getting ready for their Mexican Fiesta! Their moms told them to make a list of items they needed to purchase to make their Piñata, as well as any ingredients they may need for their feast! Help them figure out how much it will all cost. Total cost: $28.80
   - Corn tortillas (2 packages) $2.65 each package = $2.65 x 2 = $5.30 — $5.30
   - Flour tortillas (2 packages) $3.65 each package = $3.65 x 2 = $7.30 — $7.30
   - Refried beans (3 cans) $1.65 each can = $1.65 x 3 = $4.95 — $4.95
   - Mild salsa (1 container) $2.89 each container = $2.89 — $2.89
   - Hot salsa (1 container) $2.89 each container = $2.89 — $2.89
   - Large balloons (2 bags) $.79 each bag = $.79 x 2 = $1.58 — $1.58
   - Large bag of flour (1 bag) $3.89 each bag = $3.89 — + $3.89

   $28.80

2. If the 6 older children divided the cost evenly amongst themselves, how much would they all have to pay?

   $\$28.80 \div 6 = \$4.80$ (−24, 48, −48, 00)

3. The children's parents offered to pay half of the total. How much are they going to pay?

   $\$28.80 \div 2 = \$14.40$ (−2, 08, −8, 08, −8, 00)

188 Math Level 5 – Lesson 23

Name________________ **Exercise 2** Day 112

Let's practice some more! Reduce if necessary.

$3\frac{12}{16} + 7\frac{3}{8}\left(\frac{6}{16}\right) = 10\frac{18}{16} = 11\frac{2}{16} = 11\frac{1}{8}$

$6\frac{2}{9}\left(\frac{4}{18}\right) + 8\frac{17}{18} = 14\frac{21}{18} = 15\frac{3}{18} = 15\frac{1}{6}$

$4\frac{11}{15} + 7\frac{1}{3}\left(\frac{5}{15}\right) = 11\frac{16}{15} = 12\frac{1}{15}$

Mixed Review! Reduce if necessary.

$3 - \frac{2}{7}$: $2\frac{7}{7} - \frac{2}{7} = 2\frac{5}{7}$

$4 - \frac{9}{11}$: $3\frac{11}{11} - \frac{9}{11} = 3\frac{2}{11}$

$53\frac{8}{10} - 18\frac{1}{3}$: $53\frac{24}{30} - 18\frac{10}{30} = 35\frac{14}{30} = 35\frac{7}{15}$

Write two factors for each of the following numbers.

36 9 4 15 3 5 9 3 9

1. What are prime numbers? Any number that is only divisible by one and itself.
2. Write the number one million: 1,000,000
3. Subtract seven hundred from one thousand: 300
4. Write an equivalent fraction for $\frac{3}{5}$: Answers will vary.
5. Change $\frac{35}{8}$ into a mixed number: $4\frac{3}{8}$
6. Average these three numbers: 54, 68, 22 $54 + 68 + 22 = 144 \div 3 = 48$
7. Write 45 as a Roman Numeral: XLV

Math Level 5 – Lesson 23 189

Solutions Manual: Lesson 23 — Lesson 24

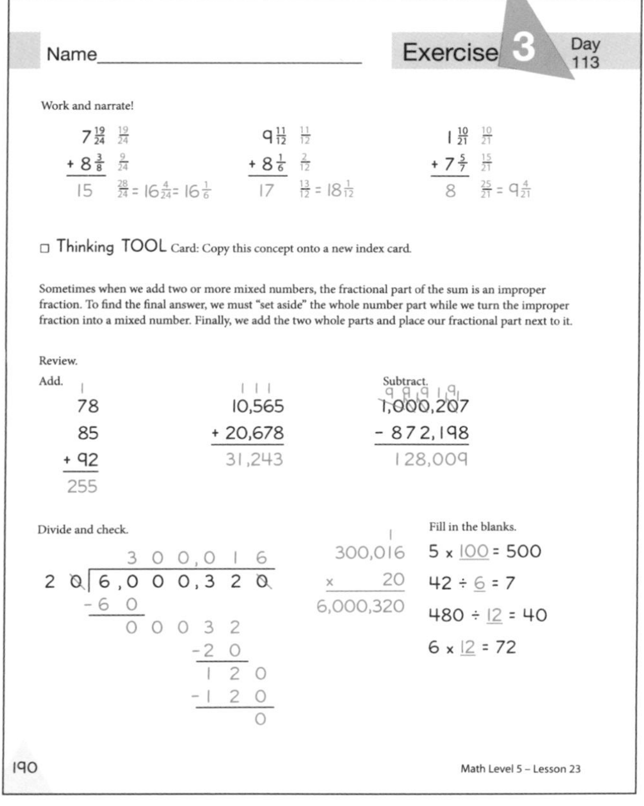
Name__________ **Exercise 3** Day 113

Work and narrate!

$7\frac{19}{24}$ → $\frac{19}{24}$; $+8\frac{3}{8}$ → $\frac{9}{24}$; 15, $\frac{28}{24} = 16\frac{4}{24} = 16\frac{1}{6}$

$9\frac{11}{12}$ → $\frac{11}{12}$; $+8\frac{1}{6}$ → $\frac{2}{12}$; 17, $\frac{13}{12} = 18\frac{1}{12}$

$1\frac{10}{21}$ → $\frac{10}{21}$; $+7\frac{5}{7}$ → $\frac{15}{21}$; 8, $\frac{25}{21} = 9\frac{4}{21}$

□ Thinking TOOL Card: Copy this concept onto a new index card.

Sometimes when we add two or more mixed numbers, the fractional part of the sum is an improper fraction. To find the final answer, we must "set aside" the whole number part while we turn the improper fraction into a mixed number. Finally, we add the two whole parts and place our fractional part next to it.

Review.

Add. 78 + 85 + 92 = 255   10,565 + 20,678 = 31,243

Subtract. 1,000,207 − 872,198 = 128,009

Divide and check. 6,000,320 ÷ 20 = 300,016 (−60, 0032, −20, 120, −120, 0)   Check: 300,016 × 20 = 6,000,320

Fill in the blanks.

5 x 100 = 500

42 ÷ 6 = 7

480 ÷ 12 = 40

6 x 12 = 72

190   Math Level 5 – Lesson 23

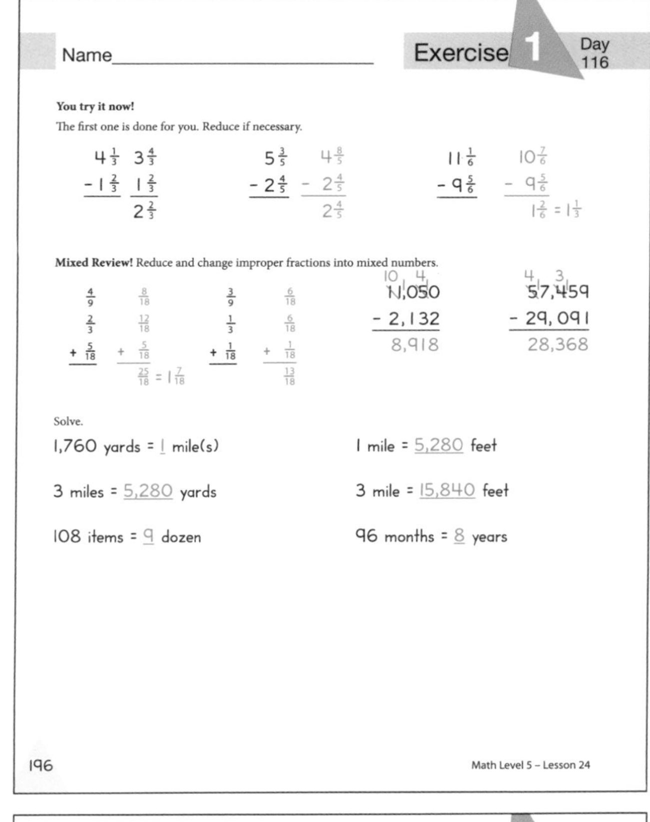
Name__________ **Exercise 1** Day 116

You try it now!
The first one is done for you. Reduce if necessary.

$4\frac{1}{3} = 3\frac{4}{3}$; $-1\frac{2}{3} = 1\frac{2}{3}$; $2\frac{2}{3}$

$5\frac{3}{5} = 4\frac{8}{5}$; $-2\frac{4}{5} = 2\frac{4}{5}$; $2\frac{4}{5}$

$11\frac{1}{6} = 10\frac{7}{6}$; $-9\frac{5}{6} = 9\frac{5}{6}$; $1\frac{2}{6} = 1\frac{1}{3}$

Mixed Review! Reduce and change improper fractions into mixed numbers.

$\frac{4}{9} = \frac{8}{18}$, $\frac{2}{3} = \frac{12}{18}$, $+\frac{5}{18} = \frac{5}{18}$; $\frac{25}{18} = 1\frac{7}{18}$

$\frac{3}{9} = \frac{6}{18}$, $\frac{1}{3} = \frac{6}{18}$, $+\frac{1}{18} = \frac{1}{18}$; $\frac{13}{18}$

11,050 − 2,132 = 8,918   57,459 − 29,091 = 28,368

Solve.

1,760 yards = 1 mile(s)   1 mile = 5,280 feet

3 miles = 5,280 yards   3 mile = 15,840 feet

108 items = 9 dozen   96 months = 8 years

196   Math Level 5 – Lesson 24

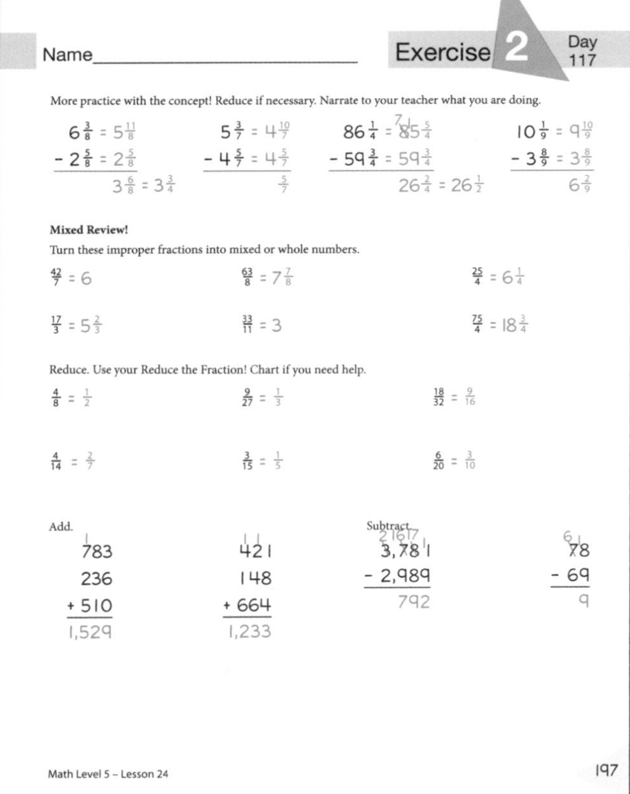
Name__________ **Exercise 2** Day 117

More practice with the concept! Reduce if necessary. Narrate to your teacher what you are doing.

$6\frac{3}{8} = 5\frac{11}{8}$; $-2\frac{5}{8} = 2\frac{5}{8}$; $3\frac{6}{8} = 3\frac{3}{4}$

$5\frac{3}{7} = 4\frac{10}{7}$; $-4\frac{5}{7} = 4\frac{5}{7}$; $\frac{5}{7}$

$86\frac{1}{4} = 85\frac{5}{4}$; $-59\frac{3}{4} = 59\frac{3}{4}$; $26\frac{2}{4} = 26\frac{1}{2}$

$10\frac{1}{9} = 9\frac{10}{9}$; $-3\frac{8}{9} = 3\frac{8}{9}$; $6\frac{2}{9}$

Mixed Review!
Turn these improper fractions into mixed or whole numbers.

$\frac{42}{7} = 6$ $\frac{63}{8} = 7\frac{7}{8}$ $\frac{25}{4} = 6\frac{1}{4}$

$\frac{17}{3} = 5\frac{2}{3}$ $\frac{33}{11} = 3$ $\frac{75}{4} = 18\frac{3}{4}$

Reduce. Use your Reduce the Fraction! Chart if you need help.

$\frac{4}{8} = \frac{1}{2}$ $\frac{9}{27} = \frac{1}{3}$ $\frac{18}{32} = \frac{9}{16}$

$\frac{4}{14} = \frac{2}{7}$ $\frac{3}{15} = \frac{1}{5}$ $\frac{6}{20} = \frac{3}{10}$

Add. 783 + 236 + 510 = 1,529   421 + 148 + 664 = 1,233

Subtract. 3,781 − 2,989 = 792   78 − 69 = 9

Math Level 5 – Lesson 24   197

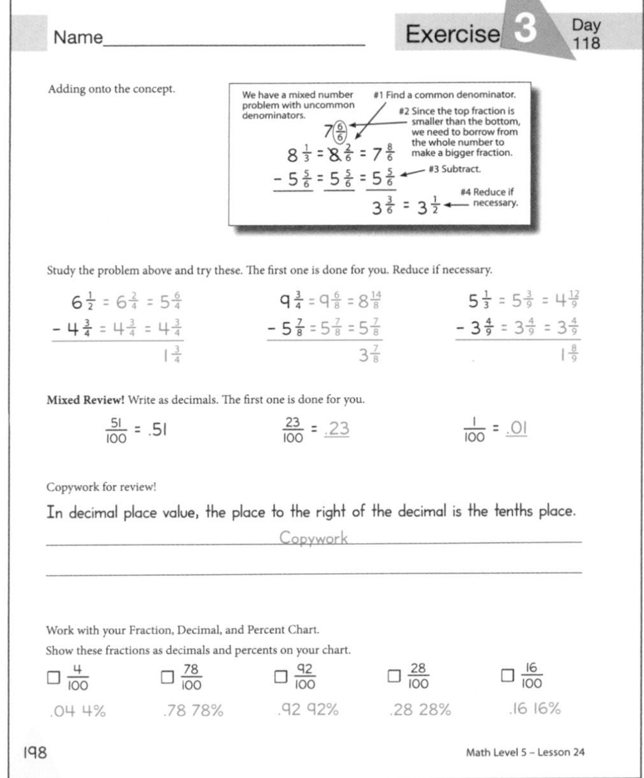
Name__________ **Exercise 3** Day 118

Adding onto the concept.

We have a mixed number problem with uncommon denominators.
#1 Find a common denominator.
#2 Since the top fraction is smaller than the bottom, we need to borrow from the whole number to make a bigger fraction.
#3 Subtract.
#4 Reduce if necessary.

$8\frac{1}{3} = 8\frac{2}{6} = 7\frac{8}{6}$; $-5\frac{5}{6} = 5\frac{5}{6} = 5\frac{5}{6}$; $3\frac{3}{6} = 3\frac{1}{2}$

Study the problem above and try these. The first one is done for you. Reduce if necessary.

$6\frac{1}{2} = 6\frac{2}{4} = 5\frac{6}{4}$; $-4\frac{3}{4} = 4\frac{3}{4} = 4\frac{3}{4}$; $1\frac{3}{4}$

$9\frac{3}{4} = 9\frac{6}{8} = 8\frac{14}{8}$; $-5\frac{7}{8} = 5\frac{7}{8} = 5\frac{7}{8}$; $3\frac{7}{8}$

$5\frac{1}{3} = 5\frac{3}{9} = 4\frac{12}{9}$; $-3\frac{4}{9} = 3\frac{4}{9} = 3\frac{4}{9}$; $1\frac{8}{9}$

Mixed Review! Write as decimals. The first one is done for you.

$\frac{51}{100} = .51$ $\frac{23}{100} = .23$ $\frac{1}{100} = .01$

Copywork for review!

In decimal place value, the place to the right of the decimal is the tenths place.

Copywork

Work with your Fraction, Decimal, and Percent Chart.
Show these fractions as decimals and percents on your chart.

□ $\frac{4}{100}$ .04 4%   □ $\frac{78}{100}$ .78 78%   □ $\frac{92}{100}$ .92 92%   □ $\frac{28}{100}$ .28 28%   □ $\frac{16}{100}$ .16 16%

198   Math Level 5 – Lesson 24

Solutions Manual: Lesson 24 — Lesson 25

Name________________ **Exercise 4** Day 119

Let's Review! Reduce if necessary. Narrate to your teacher each step.

$6\frac{1}{5} = 5\frac{6}{5}$
$-1\frac{4}{5} = 1\frac{4}{5}$
$4\frac{2}{5}$

$9\frac{2}{7} = 8\frac{9}{7}$
$-1\frac{6}{7} = 1\frac{6}{7}$
$7\frac{3}{7}$

$9\frac{3}{4} = 9\frac{6}{8} = 8\frac{14}{8}$
$-5\frac{7}{8} = 5\frac{7}{8} = 5\frac{7}{8}$
$3\frac{7}{8}$

$391\frac{1}{6} = 391\frac{1}{6} = 390\frac{7}{6}$
$-187\frac{2}{3} = 187\frac{4}{6} = 187\frac{4}{6}$
$203\frac{3}{6} = 203\frac{1}{2}$

$169\frac{8}{15} = 169\frac{8}{15} = 168\frac{23}{15}$
$-56\frac{4}{5} = 56\frac{12}{15} = 56\frac{12}{15}$
$112\frac{11}{15}$

□ Thinking TOOL Card Copywork (Write the following on a new index card and illustrate it.)

We cannot subtract a mixed number problem when the top fraction is smaller than the bottom. Therefore, just like any other subtraction problem, we need to borrow. We borrow from the whole number, taking one "unit" from it and making it an equivalent fraction(with the bottom fraction). We then subtract, using the new mixed number as the minuend (top number).

Write these **numbers** in words.

301,568
Three hundred thousand one, five hundred sixty-eight

34,560
Thirty-four thousand, five hundred sixty

2,001
Two thousand, one

$46.56
Forty-six dollars and fifty-six cents

$782.10
Seven hundred eighty-two dollars and ten cents

Math Level 5 – Lesson 24 199

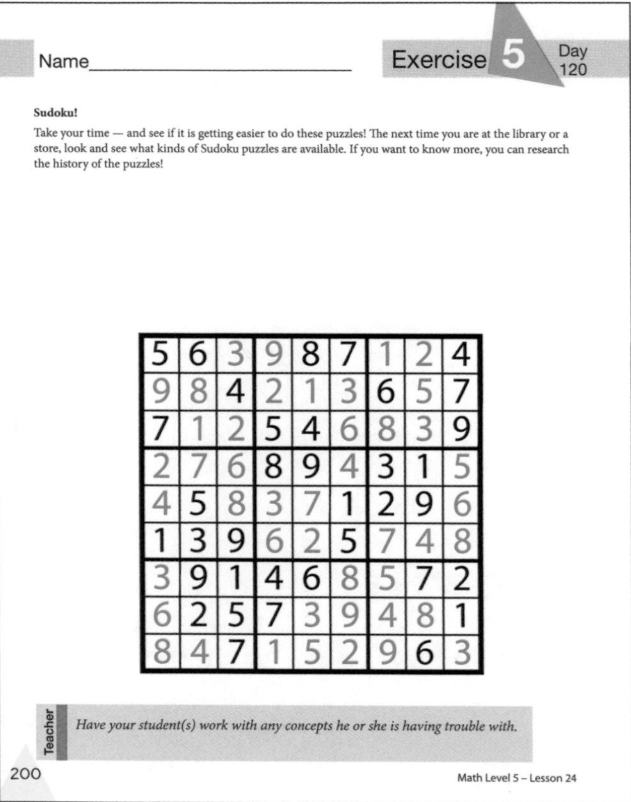

Name________________ **Exercise 5** Day 120

Sudoku!

Take your time — and see if it is getting easier to do these puzzles! The next time you are at the library or a store, look and see what kinds of Sudoku puzzles are available. If you want to know more, you can research the history of the puzzles!

5	6	3	9	8	7	1	2	4
9	8	4	2	1	3	6	5	7
7	1	2	5	4	6	8	3	9
2	7	6	8	9	4	3	1	5
4	5	8	3	7	1	2	9	6
1	3	9	6	2	5	7	4	8
3	9	1	4	6	8	5	7	2
6	2	5	7	3	9	4	8	1
8	4	7	1	5	2	9	6	3

Teacher: *Have your student(s) work with any concepts he or she is having trouble with.*

200 Math Level 5 – Lesson 24

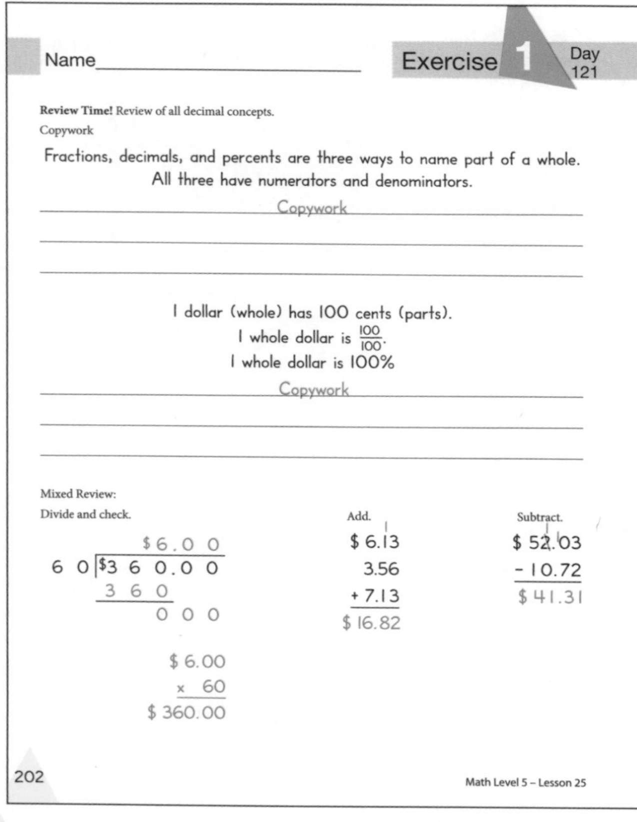

Name________________ **Exercise 1** Day 121

Review Time! Review of all decimal concepts.

Copywork

Fractions, decimals, and percents are three ways to name part of a whole.
All three have numerators and denominators.

Copywork

I dollar (whole) has 100 cents (parts).
I whole dollar is $\frac{100}{100}$.
I whole dollar is 100%

Copywork

Mixed Review:

Divide and check.

$$\begin{array}{r} \$6.00 \\ 60\overline{)\$360.00} \\ 360 \\ \hline 000 \end{array}$$

$$\begin{array}{r} \$6.00 \\ \times\ 60 \\ \hline \$360.00 \end{array}$$

Add.

$$\begin{array}{r} \$6.13 \\ 3.56 \\ +\ 7.13 \\ \hline \$16.82 \end{array}$$

Subtract.

$$\begin{array}{r} \$52.03 \\ -\ 10.72 \\ \hline \$41.31 \end{array}$$

202 Math Level 5 – Lesson 25

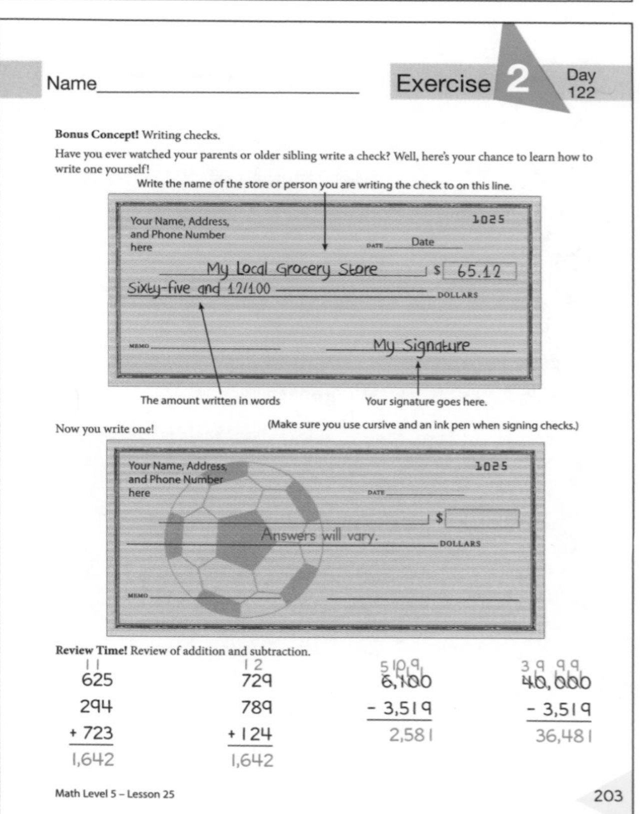

Name________________ **Exercise 2** Day 122

Bonus Concept! Writing checks.

Have you ever watched your parents or older sibling write a check? Well, here's your chance to learn how to write one yourself!

Write the name of the store or person you are writing the check to on this line.

Your Name, Address, and Phone Number here 1025
DATE Date
My Local Grocery Store $ 65.12
Sixty-five and 12/100 DOLLARS
MEMO My Signature

The amount written in words

Your signature goes here.

Now you write one! (Make sure you use cursive and an ink pen when signing checks.)

Your Name, Address, and Phone Number here 1025
DATE
$
Answers will vary. DOLLARS
MEMO

Review Time! Review of addition and subtraction.

$$\begin{array}{r} 625 \\ 294 \\ +\ 723 \\ \hline 1{,}642 \end{array} \quad \begin{array}{r} 729 \\ 789 \\ +\ 124 \\ \hline 1{,}642 \end{array} \quad \begin{array}{r} 6{,}100 \\ -\ 3{,}519 \\ \hline 2{,}581 \end{array} \quad \begin{array}{r} 40{,}000 \\ -\ 3{,}519 \\ \hline 36{,}481 \end{array}$$

Math Level 5 – Lesson 25 203

Name____________________ **Exercise 3** Day 123

Review Time! Review of averaging, geometry, and measurement.

Average these numbers: → 615

567, 321, 672, 900

```
  567          6 1 5
  321      4 ) 2 4 6 0
  672         -2 4
+ 900            0 6
2,460            - 4
                   2 0
                  -2 0
                     0
```

Copywork:

A vertex is the point where two sides meet. For example, a triangle has three vertices.

Copywork

In a three-dimensional shape, a vertex is where three or more edges meet, an edge is where two sides meet, and a face is the shape formed by the edges.

Copywork

3 feet = 1 yard	4 quarts = 1 gallon
2 cups = 1 pint	12 items = 1 dozen
60 seconds = 1 minute	16 ounces = 1 pound
5,280 feet = 1 mile	365 days = 1 year
24 hours = 1 day	4 pecks = 1 bushel
2,000 pounds = 1 ton	8 quarts = 1 peck

204 Math Level 5 – Lesson 25

Name____________________ **Exercise 4** Day 124

Review Time! Review of Place Value and writing large numbers.

	Hundred Thousands	Ten Thousands	Thousands	Hundreds	Tens	Ones
823,221	8	2	3	2	2	1
29,713		2	9	7	1	3
645,001	6	4	5	0	0	1
9,606			9	6	0	6
450,230	4	5	0	2	3	0
157				1	5	7
9,001			9	0	0	1
349,101	3	4	9	1	0	1
761,851	7	6	1	8	5	1
910,836	9	1	0	8	3	6

Now choose four of the numbers from above to write in number words.

Answers will vary.

Review your divisibility flashcards.

Math Level 5 – Lesson 25 205

Name____________________ **Exercise 5** Day 125

Review Time! Review your entire multiplication tables. Take note of any you need to practice.

x	1	2	3	4	5	6	7	8	9	10	11	12
0	0	0	0	0	0	0	0	0	0	0	0	0
1	1	2	3	4	5	6	7	8	9	10	11	12
2	2	4	6	8	10	12	14	16	18	20	22	24
3	3	6	9	12	15	18	21	24	27	30	33	36
4	4	8	12	16	20	24	28	32	36	40	44	48
5	5	10	15	20	25	30	35	40	45	50	55	60
6	6	12	18	24	30	36	42	48	54	60	66	72
7	7	14	21	28	35	42	49	56	63	70	77	84
8	8	16	24	32	40	48	56	64	72	80	88	96
9	9	18	27	36	45	54	63	72	81	90	99	108
10	10	20	30	40	50	60	70	80	90	100	110	120
11	11	22	33	44	55	66	77	88	99	110	121	132
12	12	24	36	48	60	72	84	96	108	120	132	144

Reduce.

$\frac{36}{48} = \frac{3}{4}$ $\frac{5}{10} = \frac{1}{2}$ $\frac{108}{132} = \frac{9}{11}$ $\frac{12}{144} = \frac{1}{12}$

206 Math Level 5 – Lesson 25

Name____________________ **Exercise 1** Day 126

New Concept!

In this exercise, we will be learning about multiplying fractions. This is one of the easiest fraction concepts!

Copywork...

To multiply fractions we do not need to have common denominators. Simply, multiply the numerators together and the denominators together. Reduce if necessary.

Copywork

This is what it looks like.

$$\frac{1}{2} \times \frac{2}{5} = \frac{1 \times 2}{2 \times 5} = \frac{2}{10} = \frac{1}{5}$$

Now you try it! Multiply and reduce if necessary.

$\frac{1}{3} \times \frac{4}{7} = \frac{4}{21}$ $\frac{2}{5} \times \frac{1}{3} = \frac{2}{15}$ $\frac{3}{5} \times \frac{1}{4} = \frac{3}{20}$

$\frac{1}{4} \times \frac{3}{8} = \frac{3}{32}$ $\frac{5}{7} \times \frac{2}{9} = \frac{10}{63}$ $\frac{3}{7} \times \frac{2}{5} = \frac{6}{35}$

Mixed Review! Round these numbers. Remember to look at the digit to the right of the place you are rounding to.

Number	One Million	One Thousand	Hundred
13,496,742	13,000,000	13,497,000	13,496,700
9,057,391	9,000,000	9,057,000	9,057,400
78,932,815	79,000,000	78,933,000	78,932,800
16,284,935	16,000,000	16,285,000	16,284,900

Math Level 5 – Lesson 26 209

Solutions Manual: Lesson 26

Name______________________ **Exercise 1** Day 126

Choose one of the numbers from **"Round these numbers."** on the previous page, to write in number words.

Answers will vary.

Work quickly.

$150 \div 10 = 15$

$\frac{15}{5} = 3$

$\frac{38}{2} = 19$

When we have a story problem that includes multiplying fractions, we watch for the clue word "of." In the following story problems, circle the word of and solve. Study the example.

Example:

Charlie's friend, Andrew, lives $\frac{3}{4}$ mile from the Stevens' house. Charlie usually walks $\frac{2}{3}$ of the distance to meet Andrew. What part of a mile does Charlie walk to meet Andrew?

$\frac{2}{3}$ of $\frac{3}{4}$ ----> $\frac{2}{3} \times \frac{3}{4} = \frac{6}{12}$ ---> reduced $\frac{1}{2}$ So Charlie walks $\frac{1}{2}$ mile to meet up with Andrew.

Story problems.

Natty asked Mr. Williams, the owner of the wilderness lodge, if all of the furniture was made of logs. Mr. Williams said that about $\frac{3}{4}$ of the lodge furnishings were, indeed, made out of logs like the ones in the girls' room. He told Natty that $\frac{1}{2}$ of the $\frac{3}{4}$ were made of pine logs, while the other $\frac{1}{2}$ were made from other types of logs. Natty multiplied $\frac{1}{2} \times \frac{3}{4}$ to find the fractional part. What is $\frac{1}{2}$ of $\frac{3}{4}$?

$\frac{1}{2} \times \frac{3}{4} = \frac{3}{8}$ is $\frac{1}{2}$ of $\frac{3}{4}$

210 Math Level 5 – Lesson 26

Name______________________ **Exercise 2** Day 127

More Practice!

$\frac{3}{8} \times \frac{5}{7} = \frac{15}{56}$ $\frac{2}{9} \times \frac{5}{11} = \frac{10}{99}$ $\frac{3}{4} \times \frac{7}{8} = \frac{21}{32}$

$\frac{1}{5} \times \frac{2}{3} = \frac{2}{15}$ $\frac{3}{4} \times \frac{8}{9} = \frac{24}{36} = \frac{2}{3}$ $\frac{2}{5} \times \frac{1}{6} = \frac{2}{30} = \frac{1}{15}$

Solve. Reduce if necessary.

1. Charlotte and Natty need $\frac{7}{8}$ yard of material to make pillows in sewing class. They will each use $\frac{1}{2}$ of the material. How much do they each use?

   $\frac{7}{8} \times \frac{1}{2} = \frac{7}{16}$ yards of material

2. Dad bought $\frac{1}{2}$ gallon of frozen yogurt for the family to enjoy privately in their lodge rooms. They ate $\frac{2}{3}$ of it for dessert one night after supper. What part of a gallon of frozen yogurt did the family eat?

   $\frac{1}{2} \times \frac{2}{3} = \frac{2}{6} = \frac{1}{3}$ gallon of frozed yogurt

Multiply!

6,167	2,561	52
x 6	x 23	x 21
37,002	7,683	52
	+ 51,220	+ 1,040
	58,903	1,092

Math Level 5 – Lesson 26 211

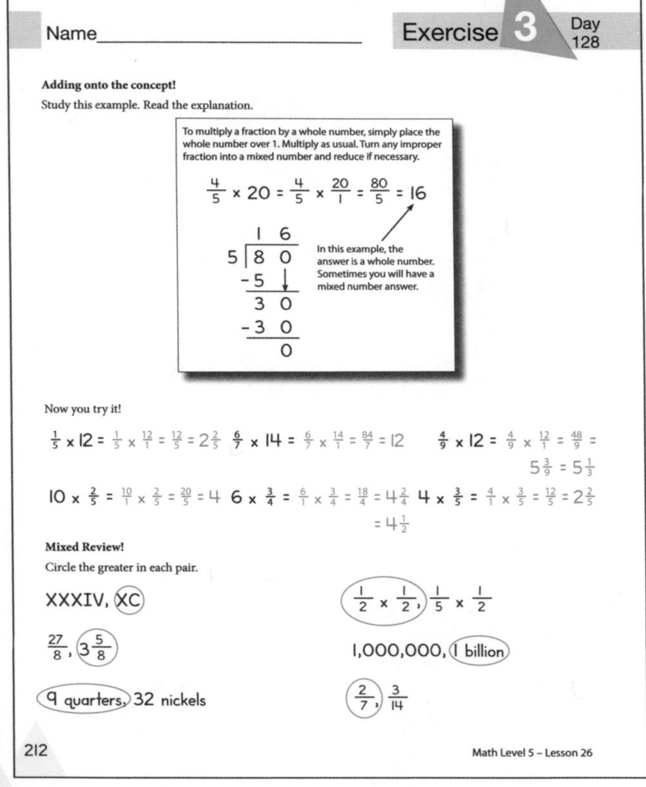

Name______________________ **Exercise 3** Day 128

Adding onto the concept!

Study this example. Read the explanation.

To multiply a fraction by a whole number, simply place the whole number over 1. Multiply as usual. Turn any improper fraction into a mixed number and reduce if necessary.

$\frac{4}{5} \times 20 = \frac{4}{5} \times \frac{20}{1} = \frac{80}{5} = 16$

$80 \div 5 = 16$: -5, 30, -30, 0

In this example, the answer is a whole number. Sometimes you will have a mixed number answer.

Now you try it!

$\frac{1}{5} \times 12 = \frac{1}{5} \times \frac{12}{1} = \frac{12}{5} = 2\frac{2}{5}$ $\frac{6}{7} \times 14 = \frac{6}{7} \times \frac{14}{1} = \frac{84}{7} = 12$ $\frac{4}{9} \times 12 = \frac{4}{9} \times \frac{12}{1} = \frac{48}{9} = 5\frac{3}{9} = 5\frac{1}{3}$

$10 \times \frac{2}{5} = \frac{10}{1} \times \frac{2}{5} = \frac{20}{5} = 4$ $6 \times \frac{3}{4} = \frac{6}{1} \times \frac{3}{4} = \frac{18}{4} = 4\frac{2}{4} = 4\frac{1}{2}$ $4 \times \frac{3}{5} = \frac{4}{1} \times \frac{3}{5} = \frac{12}{5} = 2\frac{2}{5}$

Mixed Review!

Circle the greater in each pair.

XXXIV, (XC)

$\left(\frac{1}{2} \times \frac{1}{2}\right)$, $\frac{1}{5} \times \frac{1}{2}$

$\frac{27}{8}$, $\left(3\frac{5}{8}\right)$

1,000,000, (1 billion)

(9 quarters), 32 nickels

$\left(\frac{2}{7}\right)$, $\frac{3}{14}$

212 Math Level 5 – Lesson 26

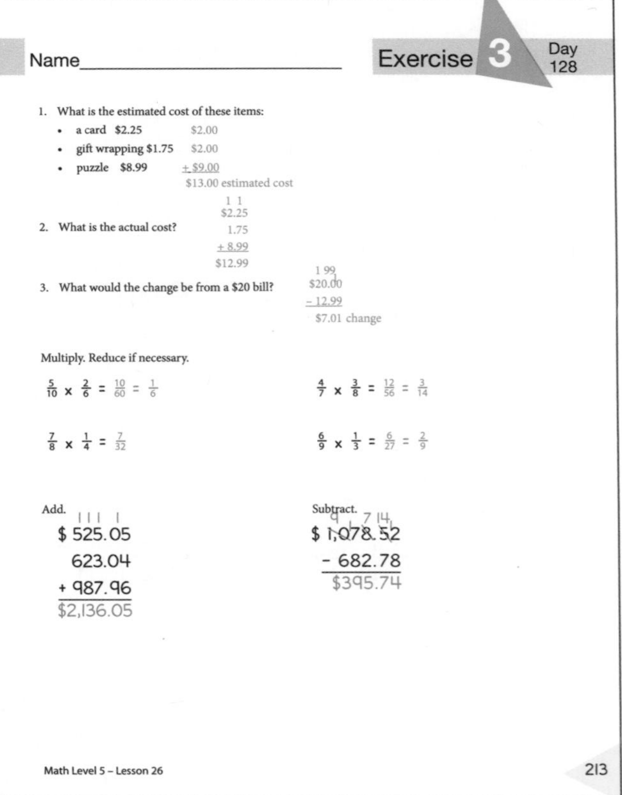

Name______________________ **Exercise 3** Day 128

1. What is the estimated cost of these items:
   - a card $2.25 — $2.00
   - gift wrapping $1.75 — $2.00
   - puzzle $8.99 — + $9.00

   $13.00 estimated cost

2. What is the actual cost?

   $2.25 + 1.75 + 8.99 = $12.99

3. What would the change be from a $20 bill?

   $20.00 − 12.99 = $7.01 change

Multiply. Reduce if necessary.

$\frac{5}{10} \times \frac{2}{6} = \frac{10}{60} = \frac{1}{6}$ $\frac{4}{7} \times \frac{3}{8} = \frac{12}{56} = \frac{3}{14}$

$\frac{7}{8} \times \frac{1}{4} = \frac{7}{32}$ $\frac{6}{9} \times \frac{1}{3} = \frac{6}{27} = \frac{2}{9}$

Add.

$ 525.05
623.04
+ 987.96
$2,136.05

Subtract.

$ 1,078.52
− 682.78
$395.74

Math Level 5 – Lesson 26 213

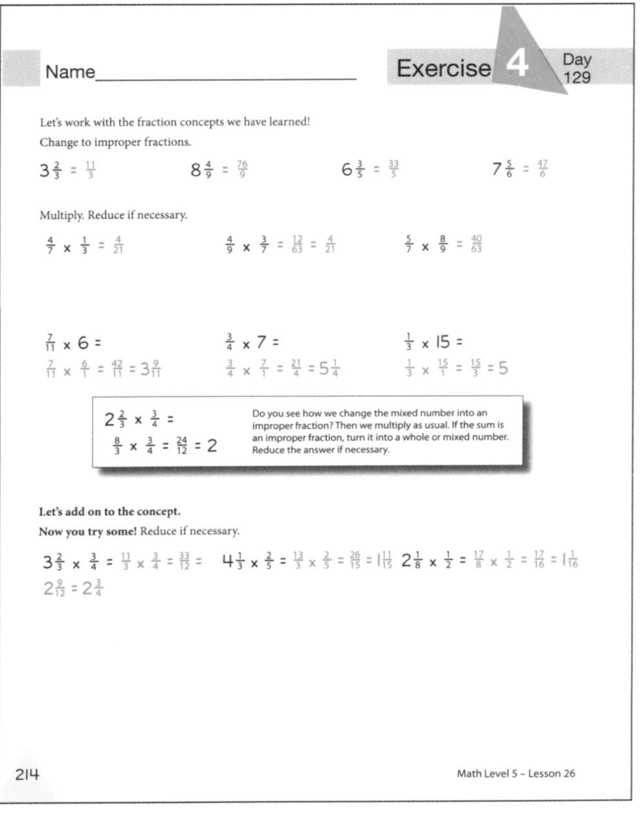

Name____________________ Exercise 4 Day 129

Let's work with the fraction concepts we have learned!

Change to improper fractions.

$3\frac{2}{3} = \frac{11}{3}$ $8\frac{4}{9} = \frac{76}{9}$ $6\frac{3}{5} = \frac{33}{5}$ $7\frac{5}{6} = \frac{47}{6}$

Multiply. Reduce if necessary.

$\frac{4}{7} \times \frac{1}{3} = \frac{4}{21}$ $\frac{4}{9} \times \frac{3}{7} = \frac{12}{63} = \frac{4}{21}$ $\frac{5}{7} \times \frac{8}{9} = \frac{40}{63}$

$\frac{7}{11} \times 6 =$ $\frac{7}{11} \times \frac{6}{1} = \frac{42}{11} = 3\frac{9}{11}$

$\frac{3}{4} \times 7 =$ $\frac{3}{4} \times \frac{7}{1} = \frac{21}{4} = 5\frac{1}{4}$

$\frac{1}{3} \times 15 =$ $\frac{1}{3} \times \frac{15}{1} = \frac{15}{3} = 5$

$2\frac{2}{3} \times \frac{3}{4} =$
$\frac{8}{3} \times \frac{3}{4} = \frac{24}{12} = 2$

Do you see how we change the mixed number into an improper fraction? Then we multiply as usual. If the sum is an improper fraction, turn it into a whole or mixed number. Reduce the answer if necessary.

Let's add on to the concept.

Now you try some! Reduce if necessary.

$3\frac{2}{3} \times \frac{3}{4} = \frac{11}{3} \times \frac{3}{4} = \frac{33}{12} = 2\frac{9}{12} = 2\frac{3}{4}$ $4\frac{1}{3} \times \frac{2}{5} = \frac{13}{3} \times \frac{2}{5} = \frac{26}{15} = 1\frac{11}{15}$ $2\frac{1}{8} \times \frac{1}{2} = \frac{17}{8} \times \frac{1}{2} = \frac{17}{16} = 1\frac{1}{16}$

214 Math Level 5 – Lesson 26

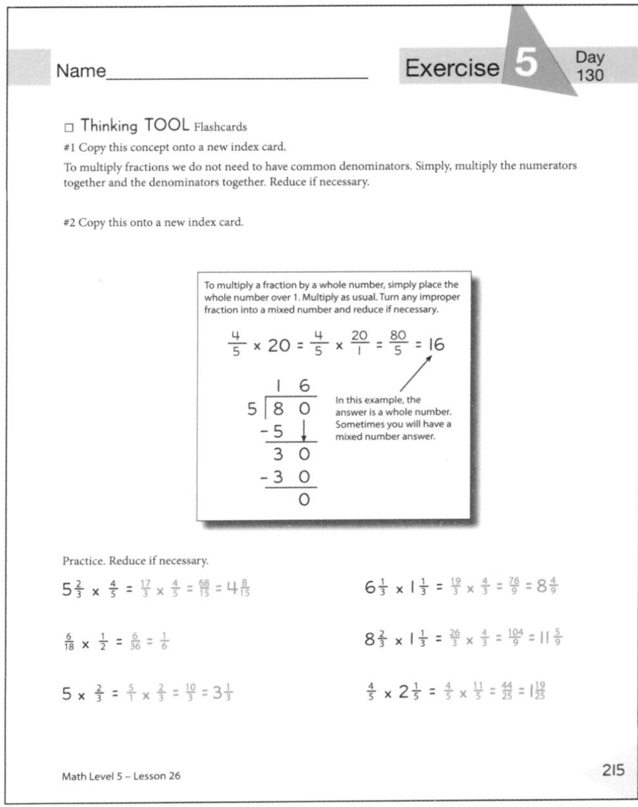

Name____________________ Exercise 5 Day 130

☐ Thinking TOOL Flashcards

#1 Copy this concept onto a new index card.

To multiply fractions we do not need to have common denominators. Simply, multiply the numerators together and the denominators together. Reduce if necessary.

#2 Copy this onto a new index card.

To multiply a fraction by a whole number, simply place the whole number over 1. Multiply as usual. Turn any improper fraction into a mixed number and reduce if necessary.

$\frac{4}{5} \times 20 = \frac{4}{5} \times \frac{20}{1} = \frac{80}{5} = 16$

$$\begin{array}{r} 16 \\ 5\overline{)80} \\ -5\downarrow \\ 30 \\ -30 \\ 0 \end{array}$$

In this example, the answer is a whole number. Sometimes you will have a mixed number answer.

Practice. Reduce if necessary.

$5\frac{2}{3} \times \frac{4}{5} = \frac{17}{3} \times \frac{4}{5} = \frac{68}{15} = 4\frac{8}{15}$ $6\frac{1}{3} \times 1\frac{1}{3} = \frac{19}{3} \times \frac{4}{3} = \frac{76}{9} = 8\frac{4}{9}$

$\frac{6}{18} \times \frac{1}{2} = \frac{6}{36} = \frac{1}{6}$ $8\frac{2}{3} \times 1\frac{1}{3} = \frac{26}{3} \times \frac{4}{3} = \frac{104}{9} = 11\frac{5}{9}$

$5 \times \frac{2}{3} = \frac{5}{1} \times \frac{2}{3} = \frac{10}{3} = 3\frac{1}{3}$ $\frac{4}{5} \times 2\frac{1}{5} = \frac{4}{5} \times \frac{11}{5} = \frac{44}{25} = 1\frac{19}{25}$

Math Level 5 – Lesson 26 215

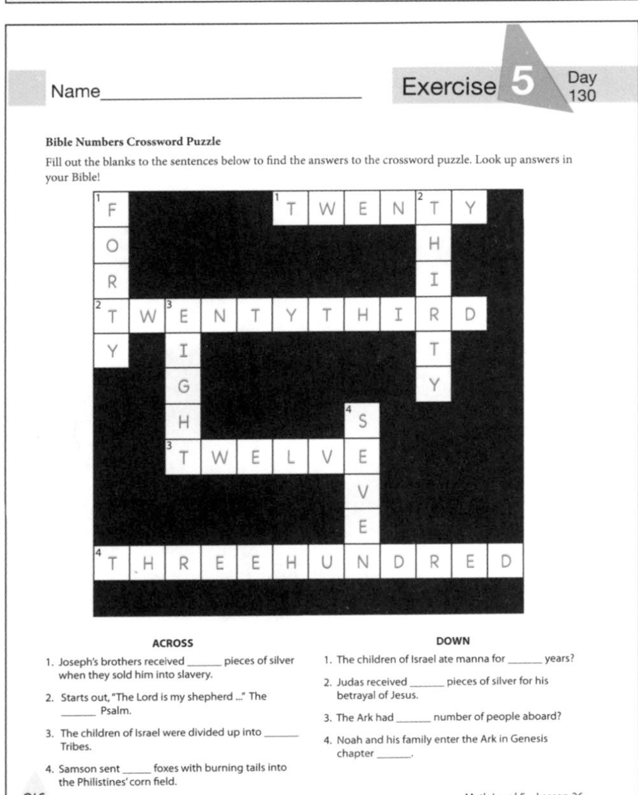

Name____________________ Exercise 5 Day 130

Bible Numbers Crossword Puzzle

Fill out the blanks to the sentences below to find the answers to the crossword puzzle. Look up answers in your Bible!

ACROSS

1. Joseph's brothers received ______ pieces of silver when they sold him into slavery.
2. Starts out, "The Lord is my shepherd ..." The ______ Psalm.
3. The children of Israel were divided up into ______ Tribes.
4. Samson sent _____ foxes with burning tails into the Philistines' corn field.

DOWN

1. The children of Israel ate manna for ______ years?
2. Judas received ______ pieces of silver for his betrayal of Jesus.
3. The Ark had ______ number of people aboard?
4. Noah and his family enter the Ark in Genesis chapter ______.

216 Math Level 5 – Lesson 26

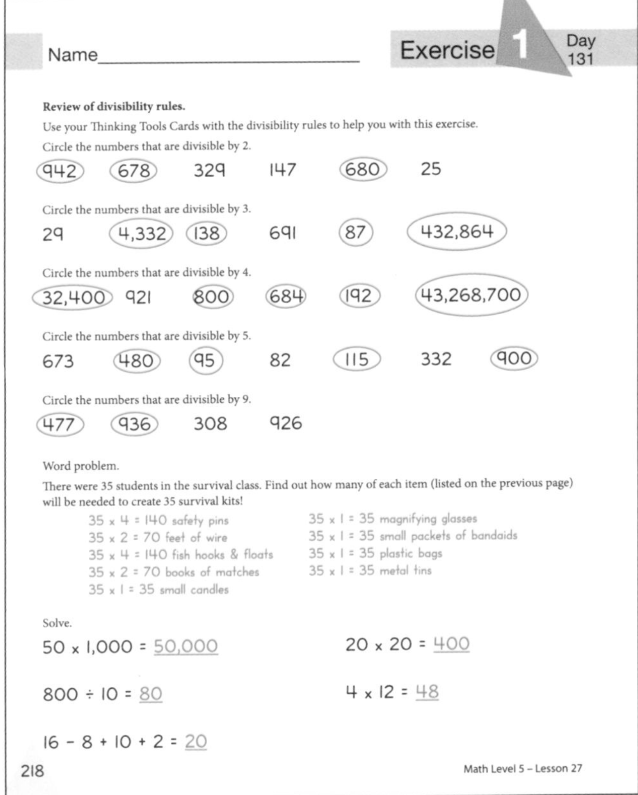

Name____________________ Exercise 1 Day 131

Review of divisibility rules.

Use your Thinking Tools Cards with the divisibility rules to help you with this exercise.

Circle the numbers that are divisible by 2.

(942) (678) 329 147 (680) 25

Circle the numbers that are divisible by 3.

29 (4,332) (138) 691 (87) (432,864)

Circle the numbers that are divisible by 4.

(32,400) 921 (800) (684) (192) (43,268,700)

Circle the numbers that are divisible by 5.

673 (480) (95) 82 (115) 332 (900)

Circle the numbers that are divisible by 9.

(477) (936) 308 926

Word problem.

There were 35 students in the survival class. Find out how many of each item (listed on the previous page) will be needed to create 35 survival kits!

35 x 4 = 140 safety pins
35 x 2 = 70 feet of wire
35 x 4 = 140 fish hooks & floats
35 x 2 = 70 books of matches
35 x 1 = 35 small candles
35 x 1 = 35 magnifying glasses
35 x 1 = 35 small packets of bandaids
35 x 1 = 35 plastic bags
35 x 1 = 35 metal tins

Solve.

50 x 1,000 = 50,000 20 x 20 = 400

800 ÷ 10 = 80 4 x 12 = 48

16 − 8 + 10 + 2 = 20

218 Math Level 5 – Lesson 27

Name______________________ **Exercise 2** Day 132

In this Lesson we will be learning about dividing fractions. Don't worry! Dividing fractions is extremely simple. In fact, you don't ever divide fractions at all! Are you confused? Study this explanation.

> To divide a whole number by a fraction, place the whole number over a 1. Flip the second number and multiply. See! You never divide fractions.
>
> $9 \div \frac{2}{3} \rightarrow \frac{9}{1} \times \frac{3}{2} = \frac{27}{2} \rightarrow 13\frac{1}{2}$
>
> Change any improper fractions to a mixed number.

Now you try it! Don't forget to reduce if necessary! The first one is done for you.

$6 \div \frac{1}{3} = \frac{6}{1} \times \frac{3}{1} = \frac{18}{1} = 18$

$5 \div \frac{2}{7} = \frac{5}{1} \times \frac{7}{2} = \frac{35}{2} = 17\frac{1}{2}$

$4 \div \frac{3}{5} = \frac{4}{1} \times \frac{5}{3} = \frac{20}{3} = 6\frac{2}{3}$

$7 \div \frac{4}{9} = \frac{7}{1} \times \frac{9}{4} = \frac{63}{4} = 15\frac{3}{4}$

Mixed Review!

Write the lowest common denominator for each. Use your LCD chart if necessary. Solve. Reduce if necessary.

$\frac{1}{5} + \frac{1}{2} + \frac{1}{3} = \frac{6}{30} + \frac{15}{30} + \frac{10}{30} = \frac{31}{30} = 1\frac{1}{30}$ LCD = 30

$\frac{1}{8} + \frac{1}{4} + \frac{1}{3} = \frac{3}{24} + \frac{6}{24} + \frac{8}{24} = \frac{17}{24}$ LCD = 24

$\frac{1}{15} + \frac{1}{30} + \frac{1}{6} = \frac{2}{30} + \frac{1}{30} + \frac{5}{30} = \frac{8}{30} = \frac{4}{15}$ LCD = 30

$\frac{1}{6} + \frac{1}{8} + \frac{1}{4} = \frac{4}{24} + \frac{3}{24} + \frac{6}{24} = \frac{13}{24}$ LCD = 24

Write true or false in the blank.

True 1,092 is divisible by 4
True 24,111 is divisible by 9
True 456 is divisible by 2
True 4,320 is divisible by 5
False 872 is divisible by 3
False 342 is divisible by 10
False 3,042 is divisible by 4

Math Level 5 – Lesson 27 219

Name______________________ **Exercise 3** Day 133

Let's add onto the concept!

We have learned that we don't actually divide fractions. We multiply them by the reciprocal (which is the "flipped" second fraction). This is true for all fraction division problems.

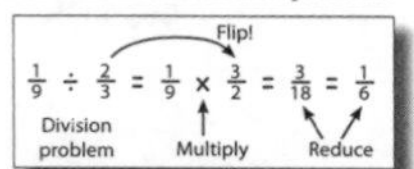

You try it! Reduce if necessary.

$\frac{1}{3} \div \frac{4}{7} = \frac{1}{3} \times \frac{7}{4} = \frac{7}{12}$

$\frac{2}{5} \div \frac{2}{3} = \frac{2}{5} \times \frac{3}{2} = \frac{6}{10} = \frac{3}{5}$

$\frac{5}{7} \div \frac{5}{9} = \frac{5}{7} \times \frac{9}{5} = \frac{45}{35} = 1\frac{10}{35} = 1\frac{2}{7}$

$\frac{6}{7} \div \frac{1}{4} = \frac{6}{7} \times \frac{4}{1} = \frac{24}{7} = 3\frac{3}{7}$

$\frac{3}{8} \div \frac{5}{6} = \frac{3}{8} \times \frac{6}{5} = \frac{18}{40} = \frac{9}{20}$

$\frac{4}{11} \div \frac{1}{5} = \frac{4}{11} \times \frac{5}{1} = \frac{20}{11} = 1\frac{9}{11}$

Review!

Put an x in the space if the number on the left of the chart is divisible by number at the top of the chart.

	2	3	4	5	9	10
432	X	X	X		X	
120	X	X	X	X		X
900	X	X	X	X	X	X
84	X	X	X			
40	X		X	X		X
639		X			X	
135		X		X	X	

220 Math Level 5 – Lesson 27

Name______________________ **Exercise 4** Day 134

Let's add onto the concept some more.

Now let's learn how to divide a mixed number by a fraction.
This is what it looks like!

> $3\frac{3}{4} \div \frac{5}{6}$ Mixed number divided by a fraction
>
> $\frac{15}{4} \div \frac{5}{6}$ Change mixed number into an improper fraction
>
> $\frac{15}{4} \times \frac{6}{5}$ Flip second fraction and multiply
>
> $\frac{90}{20} = \frac{9}{2} = 4\frac{1}{2}$ Reduce!

As you work this problem, fill in the blanks to explain what you are doing.

First, change any mixed number into an improper fraction.
Second, flip the second fraction to get its reciprocal.
Third, multiply the numerator and the denominator as usual.
Lastly, change any improper fractions into a mixed number and reduce if necessary.

You try it! Reduce if necessary.

$3\frac{1}{3} \div \frac{4}{7} = \frac{10}{3} \times \frac{7}{4} = \frac{70}{12} = 5\frac{10}{12} = 5\frac{5}{6}$

$2\frac{3}{5} \div \frac{5}{9} = \frac{13}{5} \times \frac{9}{5} = \frac{117}{25} = 4\frac{17}{25}$

$6\frac{2}{3} \div \frac{5}{9} = \frac{20}{3} \times \frac{9}{5} = \frac{180}{15} = 12$

$2\frac{4}{5} \div \frac{4}{7} = \frac{14}{5} \times \frac{7}{4} = \frac{98}{20} = 4\frac{18}{20} = 4\frac{9}{10}$

Mixed Review!

Solve and estimate.

5,011 + 5,219 = 10,230 (estimate: 5,000 + 5,000 = 10,000)

199 x 2 = 398 (estimate: 200 x 2 = 400)

901 − 699 = 202 (estimate: 900 − 700 = 200)

Math Level 5 – Lesson 27 221

Name______________________ **Exercise 1** Day 136

Multiplying decimals is simple! Study the examples below.

Multiplying decimals... We multiply as usual. Next, starting at the right, count the total number of decimal places in both factors and count off that many decimal places in the product.

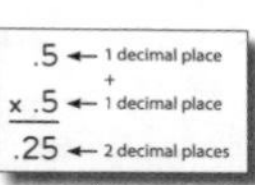

Decimal places: 6.2 (1) + x .38 (2) = 496 + 186 = 2.356 (3)

Decimal places: 1.52 (2) + x .41 (2) = 152 + 608 = .6232 (4)

Now you try it!

.9 x .2 = .18

3.45 x .3 = 1.035

5.23 x .18: 4184 + 5230 = .9414

.572 x .42: 1144 + 22880 = .24024

Round! Remember to look at the number to the right of the place you are rounding to.

Number	One Million	One Thousand	Hundred
12,456,120	12,000,000	12,456,000	12,456,100
1,347,000	1,000,000	1,347,000	1,347,000
875,351,902	875,000,000	875,352,000	875,351,900
17,892,915	18,000,000	17,893,000	17,892,900

Solve. Reduce if necessary.

$\frac{4}{9} \times \frac{6}{7} = \frac{24}{63} = \frac{8}{21}$ $8 \times \frac{1}{7} = \frac{8}{7} = 1\frac{1}{7}$ $7\frac{5}{8} \times \frac{1}{2} = \frac{61}{16} = 3\frac{13}{16}$

224 Math Level 5 – Lesson 28

Name________ Exercise 2 Day 137

When we multiply decimals, we sometimes need to add a zero to the product to make enough decimal places. Like this.

As you can see, we counted from the right the number of decimal places needed, but there were not enough places. This is where we added the zero to the left side of the product.

.12 (2) × .13 (2) = 36 + 12 = .0156 (4)

We need to add a zero to make enough decimal places.

You try it!

.23 × .16 = 138 + 230 = .0368

.41 × .17 = 287 + 410 = .0697

.33 × .16 = 198 + 330 = .0528

.36 × .21 = 36 + 720 = .0756

More work with decimals.

Circle the decimal that is more in each pair.

.003 or (.3) 6.4 or (6.45) (.93) or .9 .18 or (.194)

Change these decimals to fractions. Reduce completely.

$.50 = \frac{50}{100} = \frac{1}{2}$ $.375 = \frac{375}{1000} = \frac{3}{8}$ $.400 = \frac{400}{1000} = \frac{2}{5}$

Change these fractions to decimals and percents.

$\frac{25}{100}$ .25 25% $\frac{78}{100}$ .78 78%

$\frac{54}{100}$ .54 54% $\frac{68}{100}$ .68 68%

5.09 + 3.91 = 9.00

$8 \div \frac{5}{7} = \frac{8}{1} \times \frac{7}{5} = \frac{56}{5} = 11\frac{1}{5}$

Math Level 5 – Lesson 28 225

Name________ Exercise 3 Day 138

When we multiply money (with decimals), we use the same rules. When we find our product, however, we need to round to the hundredths place. Like this…

\$5.15 (2) × .65 (2) = 2575 + 3090 = 3.3475 (4) → \$3.35 Bigger than 5 round up!

Now you try it!

\$4.85 × .23 = 1455 + 9700 = 1.1155 → \$1.12

\$7.23 × .16 = 4338 + 7230 = 1.1568 → \$1.16

\$2.91 × .82 = 582 + 23280 = 2.3862 → \$2.39

\$5.18 × .28 = 4144 + 10360 = 1.4504 → \$1.45

Mixed practice. Work through these problems and narrate to your teacher what you are doing. Don't forget to reduce all fractions to lowest terms.

$\frac{1}{3} \div \frac{9}{11} = \frac{1}{3} \times \frac{11}{9} = \frac{11}{27}$ $\frac{1}{4} \div \frac{6}{7} = \frac{1}{4} \times \frac{7}{6} = \frac{7}{24}$ $7\frac{1}{5} \div \frac{3}{7} = \frac{36}{5} \times \frac{7}{3} = \frac{252}{15} = 16\frac{12}{15} = 16\frac{4}{5}$

$5 \div \frac{2}{5} = \frac{5}{1} \times \frac{5}{2} = \frac{25}{2} = 12\frac{1}{2}$

$6\frac{1}{5} - 3\frac{3}{10}$ → $5\frac{12}{10} - 3\frac{3}{10} = 2\frac{9}{10}$

$7\frac{1}{5} - 4\frac{4}{5}$ → $6\frac{6}{5} - 4\frac{4}{5} = 2\frac{2}{5}$

Narrate your divisibility rules to your teacher. (Let them hold your cards to check you!)

226 Math Level 5 – Lesson 28

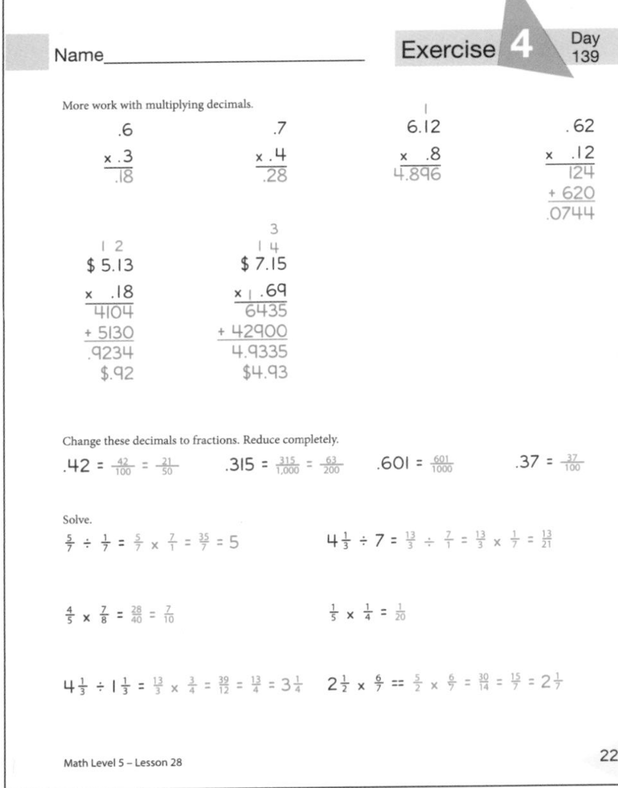

Name________ Exercise 4 Day 139

More work with multiplying decimals.

.6 × .3 = .18

.7 × .4 = .28

6.12 × .8 = 4.896

.62 × .12 = 124 + 620 = .0744

\$5.13 × .18 = 4104 + 5130 = .9234 → \$.92

\$7.15 × .69 = 6435 + 42900 = 4.9335 → \$4.93

Change these decimals to fractions. Reduce completely.

$.42 = \frac{42}{100} = \frac{21}{50}$ $.315 = \frac{315}{1,000} = \frac{63}{200}$ $.601 = \frac{601}{1000}$ $.37 = \frac{37}{100}$

Solve.

$\frac{5}{7} \div \frac{1}{7} = \frac{5}{7} \times \frac{7}{1} = \frac{35}{7} = 5$ $4\frac{1}{3} \div 7 = \frac{13}{3} \div \frac{7}{1} = \frac{13}{3} \times \frac{1}{7} = \frac{13}{21}$

$\frac{4}{5} \times \frac{7}{8} = \frac{28}{40} = \frac{7}{10}$ $\frac{1}{5} \times \frac{1}{4} = \frac{1}{20}$

$4\frac{1}{3} \div 1\frac{1}{3} = \frac{13}{3} \times \frac{3}{4} = \frac{39}{12} = \frac{13}{4} = 3\frac{1}{4}$ $2\frac{1}{2} \times \frac{6}{7} = \frac{5}{2} \times \frac{6}{7} = \frac{30}{14} = \frac{15}{7} = 2\frac{1}{7}$

Math Level 5 – Lesson 28 227

Name________ Exercise 1 Day 141

Review of Decimals, Fractions, and Percents Copywork:

In decimal place value, the place to the right of the decimal is the tenths place.

Copywork

The second place to the right of a decimal is the hundredths place.

Copywork

The third place to the right of the decimal is the thousandths place.

Copywork

Circle the digit in the tenths place.

.(2)34 782.5(6)... 782.(5)6 .(2)96 33.(4)56

Circle the digit in the hundredths place.

45.8(9)2 122.9(0)2 3.9(1)238 3.9(1)2

Circle the digit in the thousandths place.

23.56(9)1 .78(2)4 .9(1)202 .4(1)024

Turn these mixed numbers into improper fractions.

$2\frac{3}{4} = \frac{11}{4}$ $6\frac{2}{9} = \frac{56}{9}$ $1\frac{8}{11} = \frac{19}{11}$ $12\frac{1}{3} = \frac{37}{3}$

230 Math Level 5 – Lesson 29

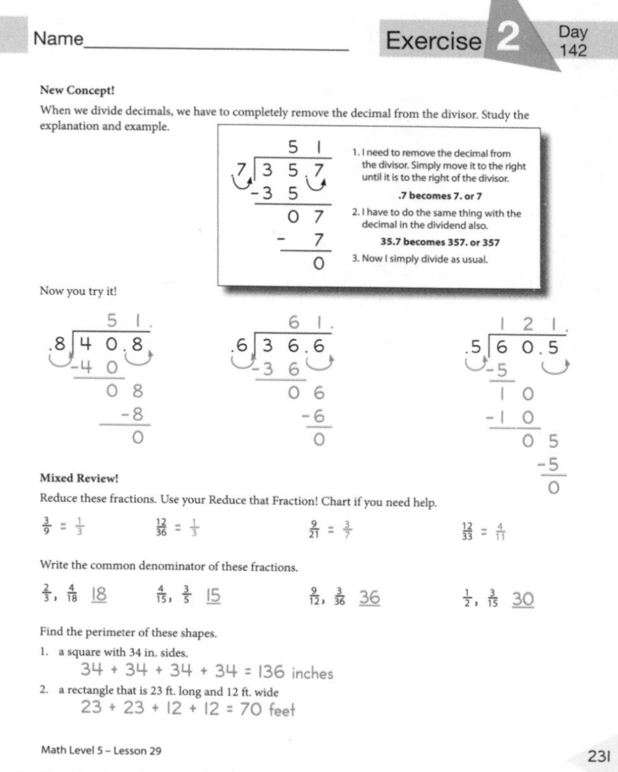

Name________________________ **Exercise 2** Day 142

New Concept!

When we divide decimals, we have to completely remove the decimal from the divisor. Study the explanation and example.

.7)35.7 = 51; −35, 07, −7, 0

1. I need to remove the decimal from the divisor. Simply move it to the right until it is to the right of the divisor.

   .7 becomes 7. or 7

2. I have to do the same thing with the decimal in the dividend also.

   35.7 becomes 357. or 357

3. Now I simply divide as usual.

Now you try it!

.8)40.8 = 51. (−40, 08, −8, 0)

.6)36.6 = 61. (−36, 06, −6, 0)

.5)60.5 = 121. (−5, 10, −10, 05, −5, 0)

Mixed Review!

Reduce these fractions. Use your Reduce that Fraction! Chart if you need help.

$\frac{3}{9} = \frac{1}{3}$ $\frac{12}{36} = \frac{1}{3}$ $\frac{9}{21} = \frac{3}{7}$ $\frac{12}{33} = \frac{4}{11}$

Write the common denominator of these fractions.

$\frac{2}{3}, \frac{4}{18}$ 18 $\frac{4}{15}, \frac{3}{5}$ 15 $\frac{9}{12}, \frac{3}{36}$ 36 $\frac{1}{2}, \frac{3}{15}$ 30

Find the perimeter of these shapes.

1. a square with 34 in. sides.
   34 + 34 + 34 + 34 = 136 inches
2. a rectangle that is 23 ft. long and 12 ft. wide
   23 + 23 + 12 + 12 = 70 feet

Math Level 5 – Lesson 29 231

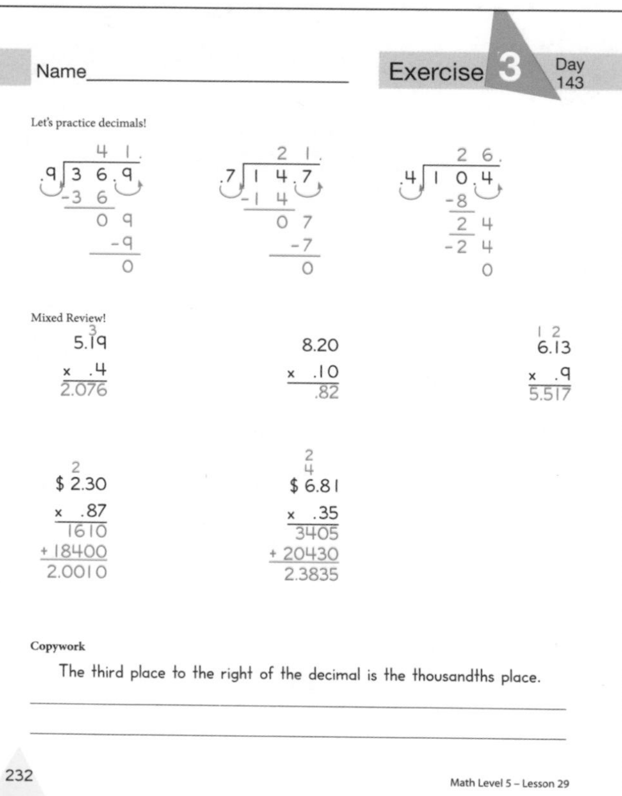

Name________________________ **Exercise 3** Day 143

Let's practice decimals!

.9)36.9 = 41. (−36, 09, −9, 0)

.7)14.7 = 21. (−14, 07, −7, 0)

.4)10.4 = 26. (−8, 24, −24, 0)

Mixed Review!

5.19 × .4 = 2.076

8.20 × .10 = .82

6.13 × .9 = 5.517

$ 2.30 × .87 = 1610 + 18400 = 2.0010

$ 6.81 × .35 = 3405 + 20430 = 2.3835

Copywork

The third place to the right of the decimal is the thousandths place.

232 Math Level 5 – Lesson 29

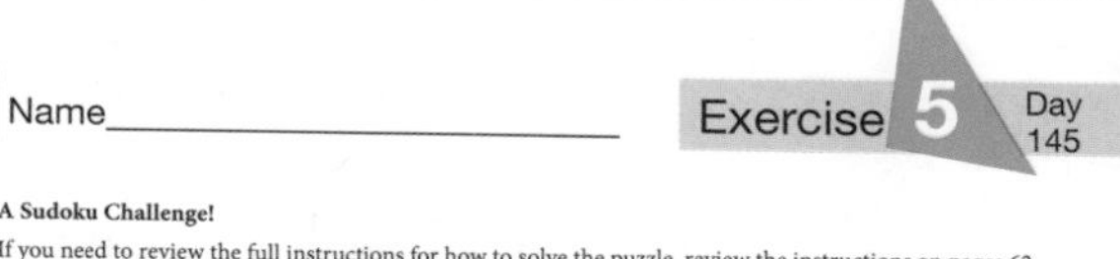

Name________________________ **Exercise 5** Day 145

A Sudoku Challenge!

If you need to review the full instructions for how to solve the puzzle, review the instructions on pages 62 and 128.

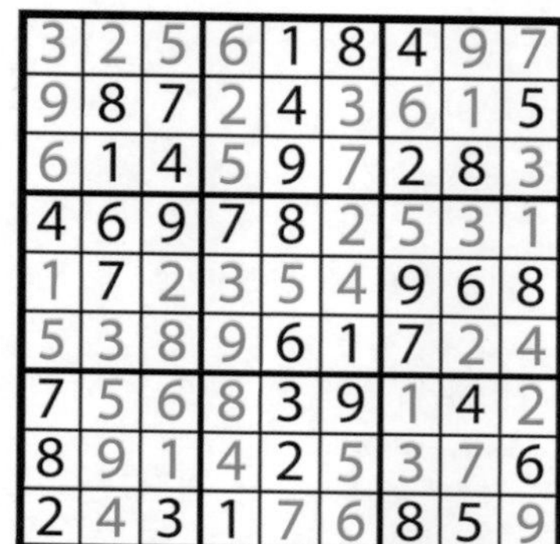

3	2	5	6	1	8	4	9	7
9	8	7	2	4	3	6	1	5
6	1	4	5	9	7	2	8	3
4	6	9	7	8	2	5	3	1
1	7	2	3	5	4	9	6	8
5	3	8	9	6	1	7	2	4
7	5	6	8	3	9	1	4	2
8	9	1	4	2	5	3	7	6
2	4	3	1	7	6	8	5	9

Just for fun: Check out some wilderness survival guides from your local library. Make a list of poisonous trees, plants, and mushrooms that you may find in your area.

234 Math Level 5 – Lesson 29

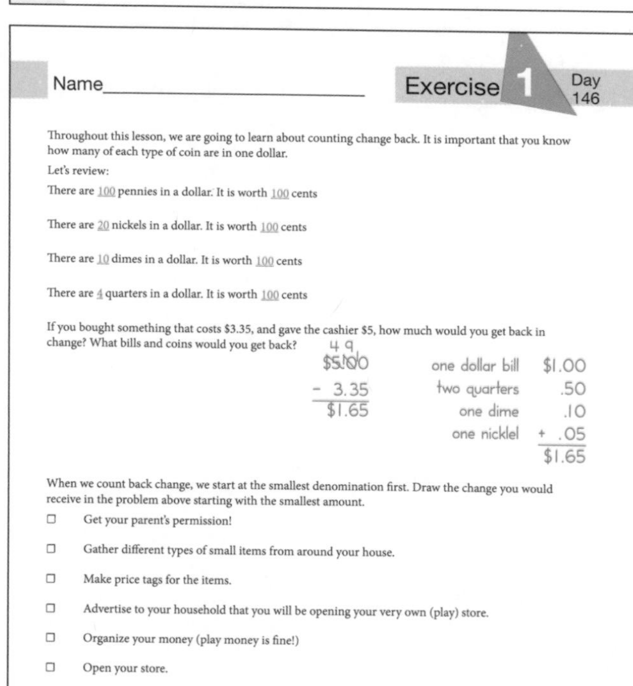

Name________________________ **Exercise 1** Day 146

Throughout this lesson, we are going to learn about counting change back. It is important that you know how many of each type of coin are in one dollar.

Let's review:

There are 100 pennies in a dollar. It is worth 100 cents

There are 20 nickels in a dollar. It is worth 100 cents

There are 10 dimes in a dollar. It is worth 100 cents

There are 4 quarters in a dollar. It is worth 100 cents

If you bought something that costs $3.35, and gave the cashier $5, how much would you get back in change? What bills and coins would you get back?

$5.00 − 3.35 = $1.65

one dollar bill	$1.00
two quarters	.50
one dime	.10
one nickel	+ .05
	$1.65

When we count back change, we start at the smallest denomination first. Draw the change you would receive in the problem above starting with the smallest amount.

- ☐ Get your parent's permission!
- ☐ Gather different types of small items from around your house.
- ☐ Make price tags for the items.
- ☐ Advertise to your household that you will be opening your very own (play) store.
- ☐ Organize your money (play money is fine!)
- ☐ Open your store.

236 Math Level 5 – Lesson 30

Name________________________ Exercise 2 Day 147

2 Word Problems.

1. Sean and Maddie took Charlie, Charlotte, Natty, Hairo, Ella, and three of their friends from survival camp, out to see a movie on Saturday night. If adult tickets cost $8.25 and children's tickets cost $5.25, how much was the total?

$5.25 × 8 = $42.00 children; $8.25 × 2 = $16.50 adults; $42.00 + 16.50 = $58.50 total

2. If Sean paid with three $20 bills, how much did he receive in change?

$60.00 − 58.50 = $1.50 in change

3. Hairo and Charlie decided to use some of their spending money to buy popcorn, which cost $8 for a large bucket. Natty and Charlotte put their money together to purchase a large box of chocolate covered raisins, which cost $3.85. How much did the children spend on popcorn and candy?

$8.00 + 3.85 = $11.85 total

4. If Charlie and Hairo paid with two $5 bills, what was their change?

$10.00 − 8.00 = $2.00 in change

5. If Charlotte and Natty paid with a $10 bill, what was their change?

$10.00 − 3.85 = $6.15 in change

6. Sean bought Maddie a chocolate bar and a small soda. The chocolate bar cost $2.75 and the soda was $3.50. Sean paid for the treat with a $5 billand two $1 bills, what was his change?

$2.75 + 3.50 = $6.25 total; $7.00 − 6.25 = $.75 or 75¢ in change

7. What was the total amount spent by the entire family, at the movie theater, on Saturday night?

$58.50 + 11.85 + 6.25 = $76.60 total

Math Level 5 – Lesson 30 237

Name________________________ Exercise 3 Day 148

TACO HUT

Item	Price
Soft Shell Taco – beef or chicken	$1.39
Hard Shell Taco – beef or chicken	$.99
Nachos	$2.29
Quesadilla – beef, cheese, or chicken	$3.50
Taco Bowl	$4.49
Fried Ice Cream	$1.59 (small) $2.89 (medium) $4.15 (large)
Iced Tea or Lemonade	$1.59 (small) $1.89 (medium) $2.15 (large)

1. Dad decided to take Mom and the five children out to the Taco Hut for dinner. He had $100 for the meal. They ordered 7 soft shell chicken tacos, 7 hard shell beef tacos, 3 nacho trays, and 7 small lemondes for dinner. How much did their total bill come to?

$1.39 × 7 = $9.73 + $.99 × 7 = $6.93 + $2.29 × 3 = $6.87 + $1.59 × 7 = $11.13 = $34.66 total

2. If Dad gives the cashier a $100 bill, how much change will he receive? What bills and coins will he get back?

$100.00 − 34.66 = $65.34 (3-$20 bills, 1-$5 dollar bill, 1-quarter, 1-nickel, 4-pennies)

3. Everyone except Ella ordered a small fried ice cream for dessert. How much did the 6 small fried ice creams come to?

$1.59 × 6 = $9.54 total

4. If Dad gives the cashier a $20 bill how much change will he receive? What bills and coins will he get back?

$20.00 − 9.54 = $10.46 (1-$10 bill, 1-quarter, 2-dimes, 1-penny)

5. How much money does Dad have left from his $100 bill?

$65.34 − 9.54 = $55.80 left

6. If Dad decided to divide the remainder of his money five ways, how much would each person receive?

55.80 ÷ 5 = 11.16

238 Math Level 5 – Lesson 30

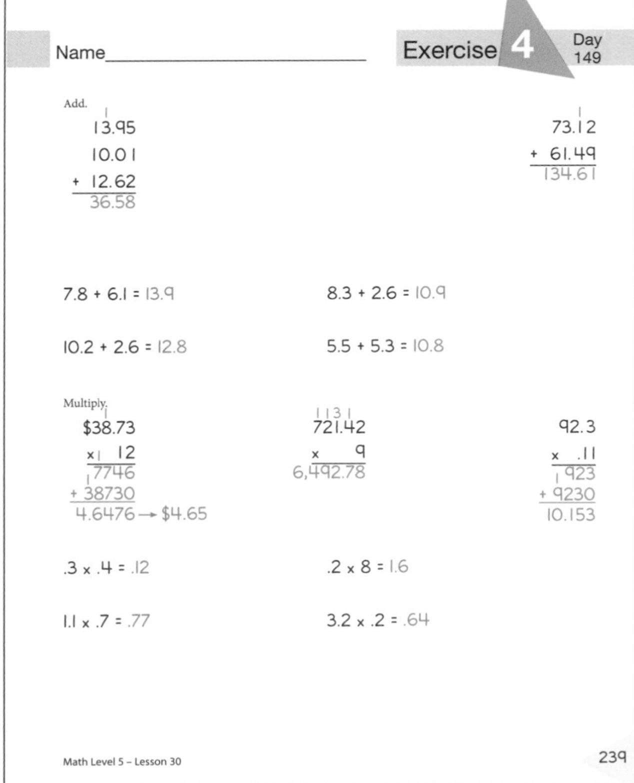
Name________________________ Exercise 4 Day 149

Add.

13.95 + 10.01 + 12.62 = 36.58

73.12 + 61.49 = 134.61

7.8 + 6.1 = 13.9 8.3 + 2.6 = 10.9

10.2 + 2.6 = 12.8 5.5 + 5.3 = 10.8

Multiply.

$38.73 × 12 = 7746 + 38730 = 4.6476 → $4.65

721.42 × 9 = 6,492.78

92.3 × .11 = 923 + 9230 = 10.153

.3 × .4 = .12 .2 × 8 = 1.6

1.1 × .7 = .77 3.2 × .2 = .64

Math Level 5 – Lesson 30 239

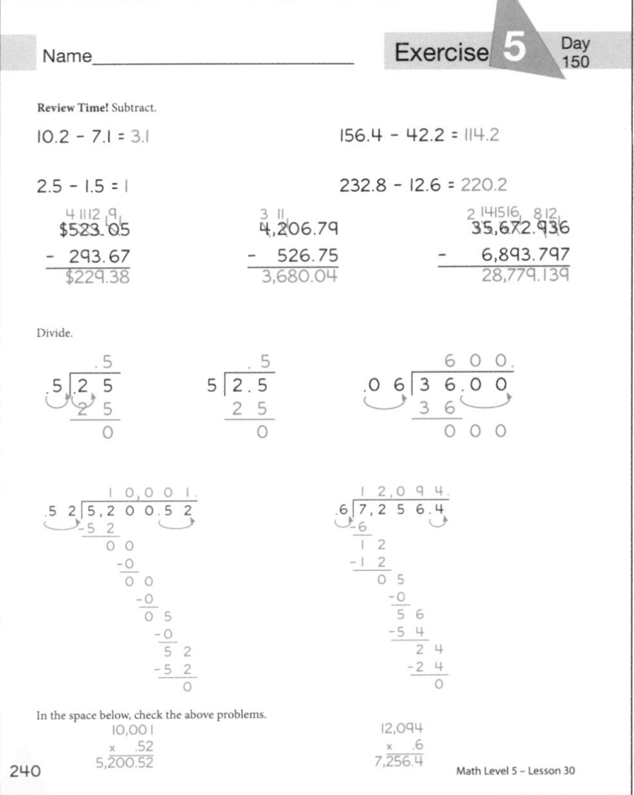
Name________________________ Exercise 5 Day 150

Review Time! Subtract.

10.2 − 7.1 = 3.1 156.4 − 42.2 = 114.2

2.5 − 1.5 = 1 232.8 − 12.6 = 220.2

$523.05 − 293.67 = $229.38

4,206.79 − 526.75 = 3,680.04

35,672.936 − 6,893.797 = 28,779.139

Divide.

2.5 ÷ .5 = 5

2.5 ÷ 5 = .5

36.00 ÷ .06 = 600.

5,200.52 ÷ .52 = 10,001.

7.2564 ÷ .6 = 12,094.

In the space below, check the above problems.

10,001 × .52 = 5,200.52

12,094 × .6 = 7,256.4

240 Math Level 5 – Lesson 30

Name____________________ **Exercise 1** Day 151

Review Time! Divide and check.

$600 \div 30 = 20$; 30 × 20: 600 − 60 = 0 0, − 0 0 = 0. Check: 20 × 30 = 600

$120 \div 40 = 3$; 120 − 120 = 0. Check: 40 × 3 = 120

$200 \div 50 = 4$; 200 − 200 = 0. Check: 50 × 4 = 200

$440 \div 20 = 22$; 44 − 40 = 4 0, 40 − 40 = 0. Check: 22 × 20 = 440

Circle the numbers that are divisible by the bolded numbers.

2: 45 (62) 103 (464) 901 (1,036)

4: (1,000) 65 (648) 23 (16) (9,100)

9: (810) 969 (333) (432) 17

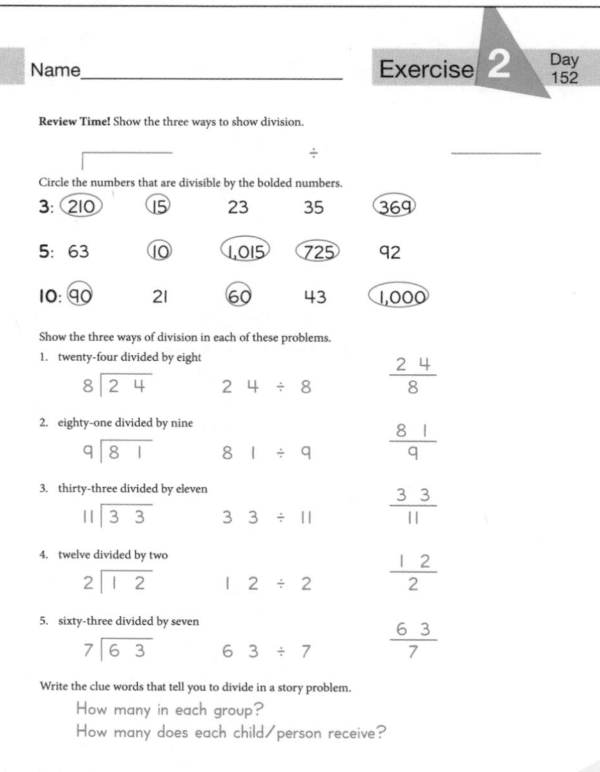

Name____________________ **Exercise 2** Day 152

Review Time! Show the three ways to show division.

Circle the numbers that are divisible by the bolded numbers.

3: (210) (15) 23 35 (369)

5: 63 (10) (1,015) (725) 92

10: (90) 21 (60) 43 (1,000)

Show the three ways of division in each of these problems.

1. twenty-four divided by eight — 8⟌24; 24 ÷ 8; $\frac{24}{8}$
2. eighty-one divided by nine — 9⟌81; 81 ÷ 9; $\frac{81}{9}$
3. thirty-three divided by eleven — 11⟌33; 33 ÷ 11; $\frac{33}{11}$
4. twelve divided by two — 2⟌12; 12 ÷ 2; $\frac{12}{2}$
5. sixty-three divided by seven — 7⟌63; 63 ÷ 7; $\frac{63}{7}$

Write the clue words that tell you to divide in a story problem.

How many in each group?
How many does each child/person receive?

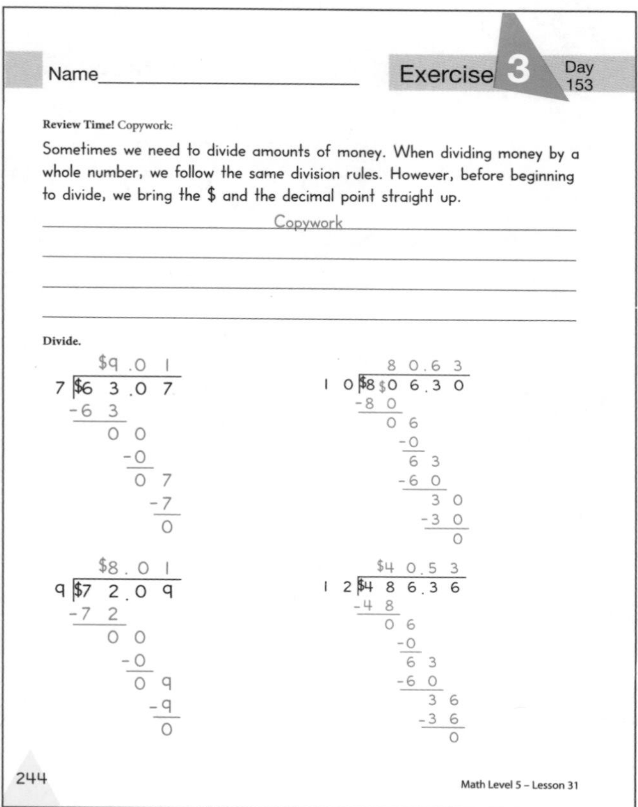

Name____________________ **Exercise 3** Day 153

Review Time! Copywork:

Sometimes we need to divide amounts of money. When dividing money by a whole number, we follow the same division rules. However, before beginning to divide, we bring the $ and the decimal point straight up.

Copywork

Divide.

7⟌$63.07 = $9.01 (−63, 0 0, −0, 0 7, −7, 0)

10⟌$806.30 = $80.63 (−80, 0 6, −0, 6 3, −6 0, 3 0, −3 0, 0)

9⟌$72.09 = $8.01 (−72, 0 0, −0, 0 9, −9, 0)

12⟌$486.36 = $40.53 (−48, 0 6, −0, 6 3, −6 0, 3 6, −3 6, 0)

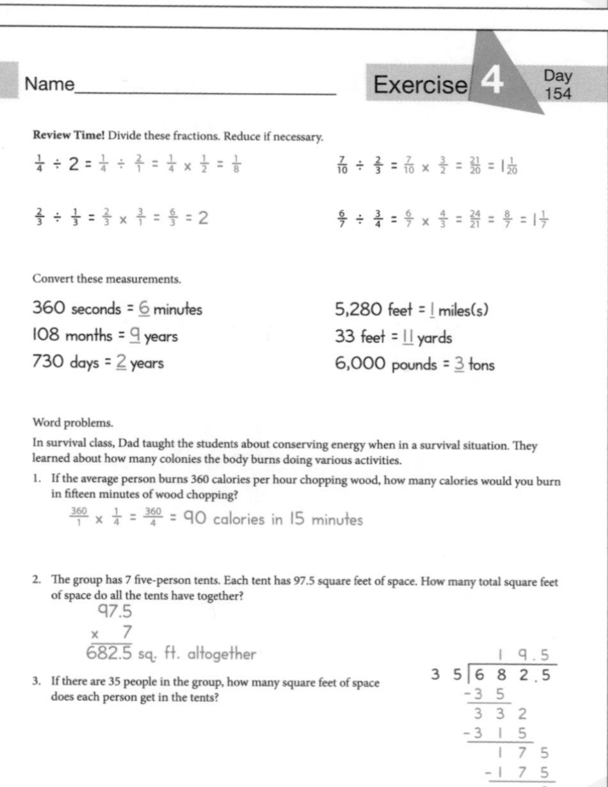

Name____________________ **Exercise 4** Day 154

Review Time! Divide these fractions. Reduce if necessary.

$\frac{1}{4} \div 2 = \frac{1}{4} \div \frac{2}{1} = \frac{1}{4} \times \frac{1}{2} = \frac{1}{8}$

$\frac{7}{10} \div \frac{2}{3} = \frac{7}{10} \times \frac{3}{2} = \frac{21}{20} = 1\frac{1}{20}$

$\frac{2}{3} \div \frac{1}{3} = \frac{2}{3} \times \frac{3}{1} = \frac{6}{3} = 2$

$\frac{6}{7} \div \frac{3}{4} = \frac{6}{7} \times \frac{4}{3} = \frac{24}{21} = \frac{8}{7} = 1\frac{1}{7}$

Convert these measurements.

360 seconds = 6 minutes
108 months = 9 years
730 days = 2 years
5,280 feet = 1 miles(s)
33 feet = 11 yards
6,000 pounds = 3 tons

Word problems.

In survival class, Dad taught the students about conserving energy when in a survival situation. They learned about how many colonies the body burns doing various activities.

1. If the average person burns 360 calories per hour chopping wood, how many calories would you burn in fifteen minutes of wood chopping?

   $\frac{360}{1} \times \frac{1}{4} = \frac{360}{4} = 90$ calories in 15 minutes

2. The group has 7 five-person tents. Each tent has 97.5 square feet of space. How many total square feet of space do all the tents have together?

   97.5 × 7 = 682.5 sq. ft. altogether

3. If there are 35 people in the group, how many square feet of space does each person get in the tents?

   35⟌682.5 = 19.5 (−35, 33 2, −31 5, 1 75, −1 75, 0)

Name______________________ **Exercise 5** Day 155

Review Time! Copywork

We can write the remainder of a division problem as a fraction. The remainder (in this problem, 1) becomes the numerator, and the divisor (in this problem, 8) becomes the denominator.

Copywork

Divide and write any remainders as fractions. Reduce if necessary.

$52 \div 9 = 5\frac{7}{9}$ (−45, remainder 7)

$79 \div 8 = 9\frac{7}{8}$ (−72, remainder 7)

$52 \div 7 = 7\frac{3}{7}$ (−49, remainder 3)

Divide and check. Narrate every step to your teacher.

$3.64 \div .4 = 9.1$ → $364 \div 4 = 91$ (−36, 04, −4, 0); check: $91 \times .4 = 36.4$

$1.68 \div .8 = 2.1$ → $168 \div 8 = 21$ (−16, 08, −8, 0); check: $21 \times .8 = 16.8$

$1.05 \div .5 = 2.1$ → $105 \div 5 = 21$ (−10, 05, −5, 0); check: $21 \times .5 = 10.5$

Name______________________ **Exercise 1** Day 156

Review Time! Copywork:

Factors are all of the different numbers that divide evenly (without a remainder) into a number. Pairs of factors are two numbers that, when multiplied together, equal this number.

Copywork

Complete the pairs of factors for these numbers.

14	20	45
1 x 14	1 x 20	1 x 45
2 x 7	2 x 10	5 x 9
7 x 2	4 x 5	9 x 5
14 x 1	5 x 4	15 x 3
	10 x 2	45 x 1
	20 x 1	

Now list the factors for each of the numbers above.

14 1, 2, 7, 14

20 1, 2, 4, 5, 10, 20

45 1, 3, 5, 9, 15, 45

☐ Write what you know about factors.

Answers will vary.

Name______________________ **Exercise 2** Day 157

Review Time! Copywork:

A common factor is a factor that two or more numbers share.

Copywork

Use your Common Factor Chart to find the common factors for the following groups of numbers. Give the LCM.

8, 16 — 8
- 8: (1) (2) (4) (8)
- 16: (1) (2) (4) (8) 16

15, 20 — 5
- 15: (1) 3, (5) 15
- 20: (1) 2, 4, (5) 10, 20

9, 21 — 3
- 9: 1, (3) 9
- 21: 1, (3) 7, 21

6, 12 — 6
- 6: (1) (2) (3) (6)
- 12: (1) (2) (3) 4, (6) 12

3, 6 — 3
- 3: (1) (2) (3)
- 6: (1) (2) (3) 6

Name______________________ **Exercise 3** Day 158

Review Time! Copywork:

The Greatest Common Factor (GCF) is the largest common factor any group of numbers have.

Copywork

Use your **Greatest Common Factor Chart** to find the greatest common factor for the following groups of numbers.

10 and 14 — 2
- 10: (1) (2) 5, 10
- 14: (1) (2) 7, 14

12, 18, and 24 — 6
- 12: (1) (2) (3) (4) (6) 12
- 18: (1) (2) (3) (6) 9, 18
- 24: (1) (2) (3) 4, (6) 8, 12, 24

36, 18, and 9 — 9
- 36: (1) (2) (3) 4, 6, (9) 12, 18, 36
- 18: (1) (2) (3) 6, (9) 18
- 9: (1) (3) (9)

35, 20, and 15 — 5
- 35: (1) (5) 7, 35
- 20: (1) 2, 4, (5) 10, 20
- 15: (1) 3, (5) 15

☐ Write what you know about greatest common factors.

Answers will vary.

Solutions Manual: Lesson 32 — Lesson 33

Name________________________ **Exercise 4** Day 159

Review Time! Use your Thinking TOOL Cards with the divisibility rules to help you with this exercise. Narrate to your teacher what you are doing. Answers will vary.

Write six numbers that are divisible by 2. (Anything ending in an even number.)

1,002 62 34 4 8 200

Write six numbers that are divisible by 3. (If sum of digits is divisible by 3.)

369 33 300 600 534 1,422

Write six numbers that are divisible by 4. (ends in "00" or last 2 numbers divisible by 4)

600 448 224 1,036 200 16

Write six numbers that are divisible by 5. (ends in 5 or 0)

35 40 500 1,000,000 60 70

Write six numbers that are divisible by 9. (Sum of digits are divisible by 9.)

900 333 432 3,600 18 45

☐ Narrate to your teacher all of the divisibility rules.

Answers will vary.

Math Level 5 – Lesson 32 251

252 Math Level 5 – Lesson 32

Name________________________ **Exercise 5** Day 160

Sudoku Time!

See if you can complete the puzzle!

2	4	6	9	5	8	1	7	3
5	9	1	2	7	3	8	6	4
7	8	3	1	4	6	2	9	5
4	6	9	5	1	2	3	8	7
1	7	5	3	8	4	6	2	9
3	2	8	6	9	7	4	5	1
6	5	4	8	3	9	7	1	2
8	1	7	4	2	5	9	3	6
9	3	2	7	6	1	5	4	8

Name________________________ **Exercise 1** Day 161

Review Time! Copywork:

When you reduce a fraction, you aren't making it smaller. A fraction, which is reduced to its lowest terms, has the smallest numbers possible in the numerator and denominator. A reduced fraction is ALWAYS equivalent to the original, when divided by the Greatest Common Factor of both numbers.

Copywork

Hands ON!

Use your "Reduce that Fraction! Chart" to reduce these fractions.

$\frac{3}{9} = \frac{1}{3}$ $\frac{8}{24} = \frac{1}{3}$ $\frac{10}{35} = \frac{2}{7}$

$\frac{9}{45} = \frac{1}{5}$ $\frac{5}{15} = \frac{1}{3}$ $\frac{36}{40} = \frac{9}{10}$

$\frac{4}{16} = \frac{1}{4}$

☐ Narrate to your teacher what you know about reducing fractions.

254 Math Level 5 – Lesson 33

Name________________________ **Exercise 2** Day 162

Review Time! New Concept for Copywork:

An improper fraction is a fraction which has a larger numerator than denominator. (Example: 7/5) A proper fraction is a fraction which has a larger denominator than numerator. (Example: 2/5)

Copywork

Let's Practice!

Circle the improper fractions and draw them on a different piece of paper.

$\frac{4}{9}$ $(\frac{7}{5})$ $\frac{2}{5}$ $(\frac{9}{3})$

$(\frac{5}{3})$ $(\frac{10}{4})$ $\frac{12}{13}$

Change the improper fractions into mixed numbers and reduce them to the lowest terms. If you need help reducing, use your Reduce that Fraction! Chart. The first one is done for you.

Example:

$\frac{10}{6}$ $10 \div 6 = 1\frac{4}{6}$ reduced to lowest terms: $1\frac{2}{3}$

Now you do these:

$\frac{10}{2} = 5$ $\frac{16}{5} = 3\frac{1}{5}$ $\frac{22}{7} = 3\frac{1}{7}$ $\frac{12}{10} = 1\frac{2}{10} = 1\frac{1}{5}$

$\frac{14}{4} = 3\frac{2}{4} = 3\frac{1}{2}$ $\frac{32}{8} = 4$ $\frac{45}{8} = 5\frac{5}{8}$ $\frac{4}{3} = 1\frac{1}{3}$

Math Level 5 – Lesson 33 255

Name____________________ **Exercise 3** Day 163

Review Time! Explain in your own words how to change an improper fraction into a mixed number.

Answers will vary.

Show your work.

$\frac{9}{4}$: $4\overline{)9}$ = $2\frac{1}{4}$; 8; 1

$\frac{22}{7}$: $7\overline{)22}$ = $3\frac{1}{7}$; −21; 1

$\frac{89}{9}$: $9\overline{)89}$ = $9\frac{8}{9}$; −81; 8

$\frac{15}{2}$: $2\overline{)15}$ = $7\frac{1}{2}$; −14; 1

Explain in your words how to change a mixed number into an improper fraction.

Answers will vary.

Show your work.

$3\frac{2}{3} = \frac{11}{3}$ — $3 \times 3 + 2 = 11$

$5\frac{1}{2} = \frac{11}{2}$ — $5 \times 2 + 1 = 11$

$10\frac{3}{5} = \frac{53}{5}$ — $10 \times 5 + 3 = 53$

$11\frac{3}{7} = \frac{80}{7}$ — $11 \times 7 + 3 = 80$

Word problem.

1. Each canteen contains $1\frac{1}{4}$ quarts of water. Write $1\frac{1}{4}$ as an improper fraction: $\frac{5}{4}$
2. How many quarts of water would it take to fill 5 canteens? $\frac{25}{4}$ or $6\frac{1}{4}$ qts. (Show your work.)

$\frac{5}{4} \times \frac{5}{1} = \frac{25}{4}$

256 Math Level 5 – Lesson 33

Name____________________ **Exercise 4** Day 164

Review Time! Change these mixed numbers into improper fractions.

$3\frac{1}{2} = \frac{7}{2}$ $1\frac{2}{3} = \frac{5}{3}$ $1\frac{1}{8} = \frac{9}{8}$ $5\frac{2}{3} = \frac{17}{3}$ $4\frac{3}{4} = \frac{19}{4}$

$5\frac{9}{10} = \frac{59}{10}$ $4\frac{3}{11} = \frac{47}{11}$ $3\frac{3}{4} = \frac{15}{4}$ $6\frac{1}{2} = \frac{13}{2}$ $5\frac{7}{8} = \frac{47}{8}$

Change these improper fractions into mixed numbers.

$\frac{17}{9} = 1\frac{8}{9}$ $\frac{14}{3} = 4\frac{2}{3}$ $\frac{23}{6} = 3\frac{5}{6}$ $\frac{82}{9} = 9\frac{1}{9}$ $\frac{16}{7} = 2\frac{2}{7}$

Word problem.

Each member of the survival group of 35 people needs to drink at least 2 canteens of water a day. If each canteen holds $1\frac{1}{4}$ quarts of water, how many quarts should each person drink per day?

$1\frac{1}{4} = \frac{5}{4}$

$\frac{5}{4} \times \frac{2}{1} = \frac{10}{4} = 2\frac{2}{4} = 2\frac{1}{2}$ qts.

How many quarts is that for the whole group?

$2\frac{1}{2} = \frac{5}{2}$

$\frac{35}{1} \times \frac{5}{2} = \frac{175}{2} = 87\frac{1}{2}$ qts.

Math Level 5 – Lesson 33 257

Name____________________ **Exercise 5** Day 165

Review Time! Reduce these fractions.

$\frac{3}{9} = \frac{1}{3}$ $\frac{7}{28} = \frac{1}{4}$ $\frac{3}{15} = \frac{1}{5}$

$\frac{9}{81} = \frac{1}{9}$ $\frac{10}{50} = \frac{1}{5}$

Change these improper fractions into mixed numbers. Reduce if needed.

$\frac{19}{4} = 4\frac{3}{4}$ $\frac{12}{8} = 1\frac{4}{8} = 1\frac{1}{2}$ $\frac{28}{9} = 3\frac{1}{9}$

$\frac{26}{5} = 5\frac{1}{5}$ $\frac{109}{8} = 13\frac{5}{8}$

Change these mixed numbers into improper fractions.

$9\frac{2}{3} = \frac{29}{3}$ $7\frac{2}{5} = \frac{37}{5}$ $5\frac{9}{10} = \frac{59}{10}$

$5\frac{2}{7} = \frac{37}{7}$ $11\frac{2}{18} = \frac{200}{18}$

258 Math Level 5 – Lesson 33

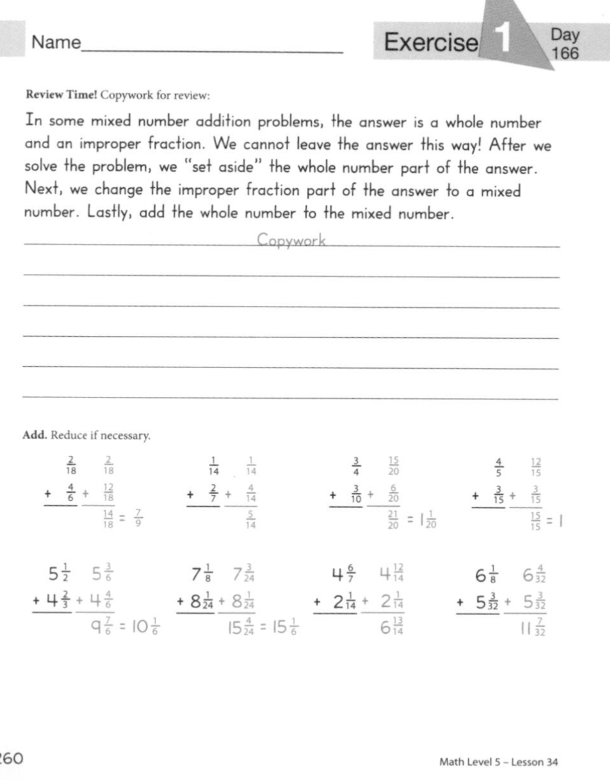

Name____________________ **Exercise 1** Day 166

Review Time! Copywork for review:

In some mixed number addition problems, the answer is a whole number and an improper fraction. We cannot leave the answer this way! After we solve the problem, we "set aside" the whole number part of the answer. Next, we change the improper fraction part of the answer to a mixed number. Lastly, add the whole number to the mixed number.

Copywork

Add. Reduce if necessary.

$\frac{2}{18} + \frac{4}{6}$ → $\frac{2}{18} + \frac{12}{18} = \frac{14}{18} = \frac{7}{9}$

$\frac{1}{14} + \frac{2}{7}$ → $\frac{1}{14} + \frac{4}{14} = \frac{5}{14}$

$\frac{3}{4} + \frac{3}{10}$ → $\frac{15}{20} + \frac{6}{20} = \frac{21}{20} = 1\frac{1}{20}$

$\frac{4}{5} + \frac{3}{15}$ → $\frac{12}{15} + \frac{3}{15} = \frac{15}{15} = 1$

$5\frac{1}{2} + 4\frac{2}{3}$ → $5\frac{3}{6} + 4\frac{4}{6} = 9\frac{7}{6} = 10\frac{1}{6}$

$7\frac{1}{8} + 8\frac{1}{24}$ → $7\frac{3}{24} + 8\frac{1}{24} = 15\frac{4}{24} = 15\frac{1}{6}$

$4\frac{6}{7} + 2\frac{1}{14}$ → $4\frac{12}{14} + 2\frac{1}{14} = 6\frac{13}{14}$

$6\frac{1}{8} + 5\frac{3}{32}$ → $6\frac{4}{32} + 5\frac{3}{32} = 11\frac{7}{32}$

260 Math Level 5 – Lesson 34

Solutions Manual: Lesson 34

Name____________________ **Exercise 2** Day 167

Review Time! Copywork:

Just as we learned in adding fractions, when we subtract fractions or mixed numbers with uncommon denominators, we need to find the least common denominator. Then we subtract as usual.

Copywork

Subtract. Reduce if necessary.

$\frac{13}{18} - \frac{4}{6} = \frac{13}{18} - \frac{12}{18} = \frac{1}{18}$

$\frac{3}{4} - \frac{2}{3} = \frac{9}{12} - \frac{8}{12} = \frac{1}{12}$

$17\frac{11}{14} - 8\frac{2}{7} = 17\frac{11}{14} - 8\frac{4}{14} = 9\frac{7}{14} = 9\frac{1}{2}$

$95\frac{9}{11} - 59\frac{3}{22} = 95\frac{18}{22} - 59\frac{3}{22} = 36\frac{15}{22}$

$93\frac{4}{5} - 42\frac{4}{10} = 93\frac{8}{10} - 42\frac{4}{10} = 51\frac{4}{10} = 51\frac{2}{5}$

$309\frac{7}{10} - 29\frac{4}{10} = 309\frac{7}{10} - 29\frac{4}{10} = 280\frac{3}{10}$

Word problem.

One student from the survival class collected dew using a tarp. He collected 3 cups of water. Another student collected moisture that dripped from bushes. She collected $1\frac{1}{8}$ cups of water. How many more cups of water did the first student collect?

$3 - 1\frac{1}{8} = 2\frac{8}{8} - 1\frac{1}{8} = 1\frac{7}{8}$ cups more

Name____________________ **Exercise 3** Day 168

Review Time! Copywork:

Sometimes we need to make a whole number into a fraction. To do this, simply use the same number in the numerator and in the denominator.

Copywork

Fill in the blank with the correct number.

$1 = \frac{4}{4}$ $1 = \frac{15}{15}$ $1 = \frac{7}{7}$

Write as mixed numbers using one "unit" as an improper fraction. The first one is done for you.

$3 = 2\frac{3}{3}$ $7 = 6\frac{7}{7}$ $4 = 3\frac{4}{4}$ $10 = 9\frac{10}{10}$ $11 = 10\frac{11}{11}$

Solve. Reduce fraction if necessary.

$4\frac{2}{3} - \frac{11}{12} = 3\frac{20}{12} - \frac{11}{12} = 3\frac{9}{12} = 3\frac{3}{4}$ ($3\frac{12}{12}$; $\frac{8}{12} + \frac{12}{12} = \frac{20}{12} = 3\frac{20}{12}$)

$6 - 5\frac{1}{3} = 5\frac{3}{3} - 5\frac{1}{3} = \frac{2}{3}$

$7\frac{1}{3} + 6\frac{2}{8} = 7\frac{8}{24} + 6\frac{6}{24} = 13\frac{14}{24} = 13\frac{7}{12}$

$4\frac{6}{17} + 3\frac{10}{51} = 4\frac{18}{51} + 3\frac{10}{51} = 7\frac{28}{51}$

$\frac{5}{8} - \frac{1}{16} = \frac{10}{16} - \frac{1}{16} = \frac{9}{16}$

$\frac{6}{7} + \frac{8}{21} = \frac{18}{21} + \frac{8}{21} = \frac{26}{21} = 1\frac{5}{21}$

$1\frac{4}{5} - \frac{1}{10} = 1\frac{8}{10} - \frac{1}{10} = 1\frac{7}{10}$

$\frac{3}{8} - \frac{1}{16} = \frac{6}{16} - \frac{1}{16} = \frac{5}{16}$

Name____________________ **Exercise 4** Day 169

Review Time! Copywork:

Sometimes we need to borrow from the minuend (the top number in a subtraction problem) by taking 1 "unit" from the whole number and rewriting it as a fraction with a common denominator.

Copywork

Solve. The first one is done for you. Reduce if necessary.

$6 - 2\frac{1}{2} = 5\frac{2}{2} - 2\frac{1}{2} = 3\frac{1}{2}$

$7 - 1\frac{1}{6} = 6\frac{6}{6} - 1\frac{1}{6} = 5\frac{5}{6}$

$5 - 1\frac{3}{4} = 4\frac{4}{4} - 1\frac{3}{4} = 3\frac{1}{4}$

$8 - \frac{3}{4} = 7\frac{4}{4} - \frac{3}{4} = 7\frac{1}{4}$

$16 - 4\frac{3}{4} = 15\frac{4}{4} - 4\frac{3}{4} = 11\frac{1}{4}$

$18 - 6\frac{7}{8} = 17\frac{8}{8} - 6\frac{7}{8} = 11\frac{1}{8}$

Word problem.

1. Look back at Exercise 2. How much water did the two students collect together?

   $3 + 1\frac{1}{8} = 4\frac{1}{8}$ cups

2. A third student collected $4\frac{1}{3}$ cups of rainwater. How many cups do the 3 students have altogether?

   $4\frac{1}{8} = \frac{3}{24}$; $+ 4\frac{1}{3} = \frac{8}{24}$; $8\frac{11}{24}$ cups of water

Name____________________ **Exercise 5** Day 170

Review Time! Solve. Reduce if necessary.

$12\frac{9}{13} + 26\frac{7}{13} = 38\frac{16}{13} = 39\frac{3}{13}$

$14\frac{1}{2} + 6\frac{2}{3}$: $\frac{1}{2} = \frac{3}{6}$, $\frac{2}{3} = \frac{4}{6}$; $20\frac{7}{6} = 21\frac{1}{6}$

$5 - \frac{4}{7} = 4\frac{7}{7} - \frac{4}{7} = 4\frac{3}{7}$

$17\frac{1}{2} - 6\frac{3}{8}$: $\frac{1}{2} = \frac{4}{8}$, $\frac{3}{8} = \frac{3}{8}$; $11\frac{1}{8}$

$9 + 1\frac{5}{6} = 10\frac{5}{6}$

$32\frac{6}{7} - 17\frac{1}{8}$: $\frac{6}{7} = \frac{48}{56}$, $\frac{1}{8} = \frac{7}{56}$; $15\frac{41}{56}$

$39\frac{6}{21} + 17\frac{1}{3}$: $\frac{6}{21} = \frac{6}{21}$, $\frac{1}{3} = \frac{7}{21}$; $56\frac{13}{21}$

$\frac{3}{4} - \frac{1}{8}$: $\frac{3}{4} = \frac{6}{8}$, $\frac{1}{8} = \frac{1}{8}$; $\frac{5}{8}$

In your own words, explain the process of subtracting fractions with borrowing.

Answers will vary.

Name__________________ **Exercise 1** Day 171

Review Time! Copywork:

To multiply fractions we do not need to have common denominators. Simply, multiply the numerators together and the denominators together. Reduce if necessary.

Copywork

Solve. Reduce if necessary.

$\frac{2}{3} \times \frac{3}{7} = \frac{6}{21} = \frac{2}{7}$ $\frac{5}{8} \times \frac{1}{3} = \frac{5}{24}$ $\frac{6}{5} \times \frac{1}{5} = \frac{6}{25}$

$\frac{3}{4} \times \frac{3}{9} = \frac{9}{36} = \frac{1}{4}$ $\frac{2}{7} \times \frac{2}{7} = \frac{4}{49}$ $\frac{6}{7} \times \frac{2}{8} = \frac{12}{56} = \frac{3}{14}$

Write what you learned about multiplying fractions.

Answers will vary.

266 Math Level 5 – Lesson 35

Name__________________ **Exercise 2** Day 172

Review Time! More Practice!

$\frac{1}{8} \times \frac{2}{5} = \frac{2}{40} = \frac{1}{20}$ $\frac{6}{4} \times \frac{1}{9} = \frac{6}{36} = \frac{1}{6}$ $\frac{3}{5} \times \frac{1}{7} = \frac{3}{35}$

$\frac{5}{6} \times \frac{1}{4} = \frac{5}{24}$ $\frac{1}{3} \times \frac{2}{3} = \frac{2}{9}$ $\frac{2}{3} \times \frac{6}{7} = \frac{12}{21} = \frac{4}{7}$

When we have a story problem that includes multiplying fractions, we watch for the clue word "OF."

Write two story problems that use multiplying fractions. Did you use the word "of" in it? Solve your story problems, or see if your teacher can solve them. Answers will vary.

1.

2.

Math Level 5 – Lesson 35 267

Name__________________ **Exercise 3** Day 173

Review Time! Copywork:

We change the mixed number into an improper fraction. Then we multiply as usual. If the sum is an improper fraction, turn it into a whole or mixed number. Reduce the answer if necessary.

Copywork

Solve. Reduce if necessary.

$3\frac{2}{3} \times \frac{3}{4} = \frac{11}{3} \times \frac{3}{4} = \frac{33}{12} = 2\frac{9}{12} = 2\frac{3}{4}$

$7\frac{1}{3} \times \frac{3}{5} = \frac{22}{3} \times \frac{3}{5} = \frac{66}{15} = 4\frac{6}{15} = 4\frac{2}{5}$

$6\frac{1}{8} \times \frac{3}{7} = \frac{49}{8} \times \frac{3}{7} = \frac{147}{56} = 2\frac{35}{56} = 2\frac{5}{8}$

$12 \times \frac{2}{5} = \frac{12}{1} \times \frac{2}{5} = \frac{24}{5} = 4\frac{4}{5}$

$6 \times \frac{3}{8} = \frac{6}{1} \times \frac{3}{8} = \frac{18}{8} = 2\frac{2}{8} = 2\frac{1}{4}$

$7 \times \frac{4}{7} = \frac{7}{1} \times \frac{4}{7} = \frac{28}{7} = 4$ $\frac{22}{3}$

Write a story problem using two mixed numbers with multiplying fractions. Solve your story problem or have your teacher solve it.

Answers will vary.

268 Math Level 5 – Lesson 35

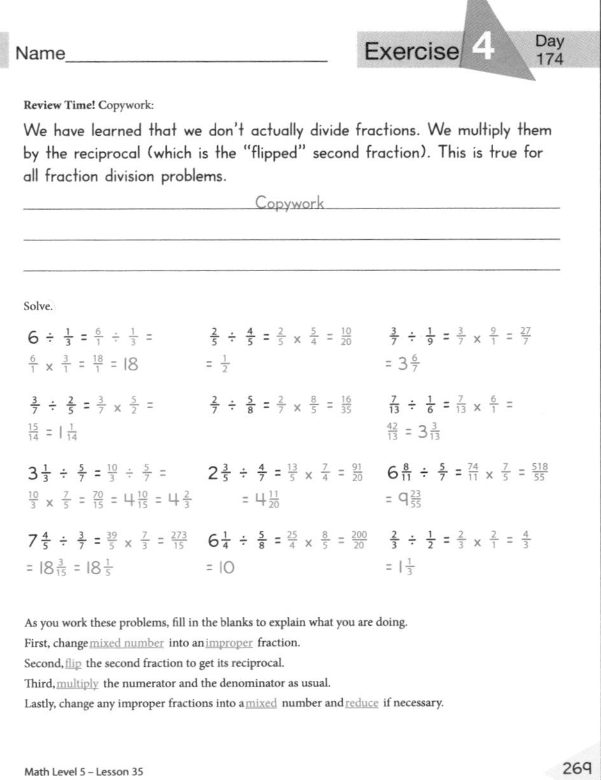

Name__________________ **Exercise 4** Day 174

Review Time! Copywork:

We have learned that we don't actually divide fractions. We multiply them by the reciprocal (which is the "flipped" second fraction). This is true for all fraction division problems.

Copywork

Solve.

$6 \div \frac{1}{3} = \frac{6}{1} \div \frac{1}{3} = \frac{6}{1} \times \frac{3}{1} = \frac{18}{1} = 18$

$\frac{2}{5} \div \frac{4}{5} = \frac{2}{5} \times \frac{5}{4} = \frac{10}{20} = \frac{1}{2}$

$\frac{3}{7} \div \frac{1}{9} = \frac{3}{7} \times \frac{9}{1} = \frac{27}{7} = 3\frac{6}{7}$

$\frac{3}{7} \div \frac{2}{5} = \frac{3}{7} \times \frac{5}{2} = \frac{15}{14} = 1\frac{1}{14}$

$\frac{2}{7} \div \frac{5}{8} = \frac{2}{7} \times \frac{8}{5} = \frac{16}{35}$

$\frac{7}{13} \div \frac{1}{6} = \frac{7}{13} \times \frac{6}{1} = \frac{42}{13} = 3\frac{3}{13}$

$3\frac{1}{3} \div \frac{5}{7} = \frac{10}{3} \div \frac{5}{7} = \frac{10}{3} \times \frac{7}{5} = \frac{70}{15} = 4\frac{10}{15} = 4\frac{2}{3}$

$2\frac{3}{5} \div \frac{4}{7} = \frac{13}{5} \times \frac{7}{4} = \frac{91}{20} = 4\frac{11}{20}$

$6\frac{8}{11} \div \frac{5}{7} = \frac{74}{11} \times \frac{7}{5} = \frac{518}{55} = 9\frac{23}{55}$

$7\frac{4}{5} \div \frac{3}{7} = \frac{39}{5} \times \frac{7}{3} = \frac{273}{15} = 18\frac{3}{15} = 18\frac{1}{5}$

$6\frac{1}{4} \div \frac{5}{8} = \frac{25}{4} \times \frac{8}{5} = \frac{200}{20} = 10$

$\frac{2}{3} \div \frac{1}{2} = \frac{2}{3} \times \frac{2}{1} = \frac{4}{3} = 1\frac{1}{3}$

As you work these problems, fill in the blanks to explain what you are doing.

First, change mixed number into an improper fraction.

Second, flip the second fraction to get its reciprocal.

Third, multiply the numerator and the denominator as usual.

Lastly, change any improper fractions into a mixed number and reduce if necessary.

Math Level 5 – Lesson 35 269

Name____________________ **Exercise 5** Day 175

Optional Math Crossword Puzzle

Solve the math problems below to find the answers to the crossword puzzle.

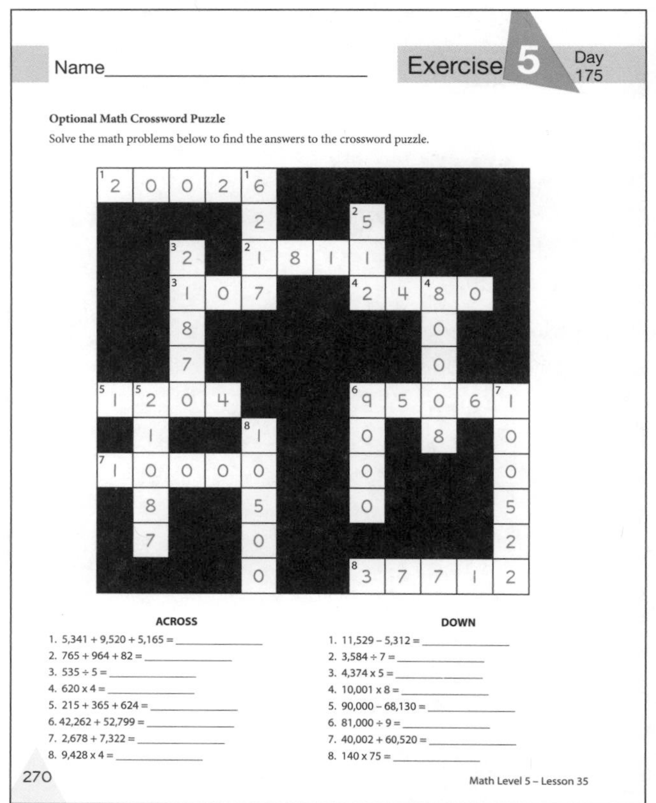

ACROSS

1. 5,341 + 9,520 + 5,165 = ______
2. 765 + 964 + 82 = ______
3. 535 ÷ 5 = ______
4. 620 x 4 = ______
5. 215 + 365 + 624 = ______
6. 42,262 + 52,799 = ______
7. 2,678 + 7,322 = ______
8. 9,428 x 4 = ______

DOWN

1. 11,529 – 5,312 = ______
2. 3,584 ÷ 7 = ______
3. 4,374 x 5 = ______
4. 10,001 x 8 = ______
5. 90,000 – 68,130 = ______
6. 81,000 ÷ 9 = ______
7. 40,002 + 60,520 = ______
8. 140 x 75 = ______

270 Math Level 5 – Lesson 35

Name____________________ **Exercise 1** Day 176

Review Time! Copywork:

Multiplying decimals...
We multiply as usual. Next, starting at the right, count the total number of decimal places in both factors and count off that many decimal places in the product.

Copywork

Solve.

.9	7.25	3.42	.642
x .4	x .3	x 1.88	x .11
.36	2.175	2736	642
		+ 27360	+ 6420
		3.0096	.07062

Write, in your own words, what you have learned about multiplying decimals.

Answers will vary.

272 Math Level 5 – Lesson 36

Name____________________ **Exercise 2** Day 177

Review Time!

When we multiply decimals, we sometimes need to add a zero to the product to make enough decimal places. Like this.
As you can see, we counted from the right the number of decimal places needed, but there were not enough places. This is where we added the zero to the left side of the product.

.12 (2)
x .13 (2)
36
+ 12
.0156 (4)

We need to add a zero to make enough decimal places.

.23	.31	.43	.25
x .15	x .17	x .16	x .21
115	217	258	25
+ 230	+ 310	+ 430	+ 500
.0345	.0527	.0688	.0525

.5	.12	17.1	14.2
x .3	x .6	x 6	x .8
.15	.072	102.6	11.36

Write what you have learned about adding zero to the product when multiplying decimals.

Answers will vary.

Math Level 5 – Lesson 36 273

Name____________________ **Exercise 3** Day 178

Review Time! Copywork:

When we multiply money (with decimals), we use the same rules. When we find our product, however, we need to round to the hundredths place.

Copywork

$ 3.85	$ 7.13	$ 2.11	$ 2.38
x .43	x .18	x .80	x 1.27
1155	5704	1.6880 = $1.69	1666
+ 15400	+ 7130		+ 4760
1.6555 = $1.66	1.2834 = $1.28		.6426 = $.64

Write what you have learned about multiplying money.

Answers will vary.

274 Math Level 5 – Lesson 36

Name________________________ **Exercise 4** Day 1

Review Time! Copywork:

When we divide decimals, we have to completely remove the decimal from the divisor.

Copywork

The third place to the right of the decimal is the thousandths place.

Copywork

Divide and check.

$.9\overline{)18.9} = 21.$; $18 - 18 = 0$, bring down 9; $9 - 9 = 0$. Check: $21 \times .9 = 18.9$

$.4\overline{)13.6} = 34.$; $13 - 12 = 1$, bring down 6; $16 - 16 = 0$. Check: $34 \times .4 = 13.6$

$.5\overline{)20.5} = 41.$; $20 - 20 = 0$, bring down 5; $5 - 5 = 0$. Check: $41 \times .5 = 20.5$

Name________________________ **Exercise 5** Day 180

The Double Sudoku Challenge!

Here is a variation on the simple Sudoku puzzles you have been completing. This is a Double Sudoku – which just means there are two Sudoku puzzles in one overlapped puzzle. We have outlined one puzzle in blue, and the other in green.

When solving this kind of Sudoku, the same rules that you have learned still apply. You just have to take into account both puzzles when finding the solutions for each. The most challenge portion of the puzzle will be the four 3 x 3 squares in the overlapped area (it is the shaded portion). Hint – use the numbers outside of the overlapped area as clues to find the missing numbers for each Sudoku!

When solved, both puzzles will be complete with no repeated numbers in the rows, columns, or 3 x 3 squares within the 9 x 9 green and blue puzzles. As always, if you are not sure about what to do, talk to your teacher and ask for help.

4	5	6	8	7	9	3	2	1			
3	8	2	1	6	5	4	7	9			
9	7	1	3	4	2	5	6	8			
5	4	3	9	8	7	2	1	6	5	3	4
2	9	8	6	3	1	7	5	4	8	2	9
6	1	7	5	2	4	9	8	3	1	7	6
1	2	4	7	9	6	8	3	5	4	1	2
7	3	5	4	1	8	6	9	2	3	5	7
8	6	9	2	5	3	1	4	7	6	9	8
			1	7	5	4	6	9	2	8	3
			8	6	2	3	7	1	9	4	5
			3	4	9	5	2	8	7	6	1